Llewellyn's

2002

Astrological Pocket Planner

Printed in the United States of America
Typography property of Llewellyn Worldwide, Ltd.

ISBN: 0-7387-0041-X

Cover design by Gavin Dayton Duffy
Designed by Susan Van Sant
Edited by K. M. Brielmaier

A special thanks to Leslie Nielsen for astrological proofreading.
Cover image of Astrologer © The Best of Art Today

Set in Eastern and Pacific Standard Times. Ephemeris and aspect data generated by ACS Publications. Re-use is prohibited.

Published by
LLEWELLYN WORLDWIDE
P.O. Box 64383 Dept. 0-7387-0041-X
St. Paul, MN 55164-0383, U.S.A.

Table of Contents

Mercury Retrograde 2002

	DATE	EST	PST			DATE	EST	PST
Mercury Retrograde	1/18	**3:52 pm**	12:52 pm	—	Mercury Direct	2/8	**12:28 pm**	9:28 pm
Mercury Retrograde	5/15	**1:51 pm**	10:51 am	—	Mercury Direct	6/8	**10:12 am**	7:12 am
Mercury Retrograde	9/14	**2:39 pm**	11:39 am	—	Mercury Direct	10/6	**2:28 pm**	11:28 am

Moon Void-of-Course 2002

Times are listed in Eastern Standard Time in this table only. All other information in the *Pocket Planner* is listed in both Eastern Standard Time and Pacific Standard Time. Refer to "Time Zone Conversions" on page 7 for changing to other time zones.

Last Aspect		Moon Enters New Sign			Last Aspect		Moon Enters New Sign			Last Aspect		Moon Enters New Sign		
Date	Time	Date	Sign	Time	Date	Time	Date	Sign	Time	Date	Time	Date	Sign	Time
JANUARY					**FEBRUARY**					**MARCH**				
2	6:16 am	2	♍	6:34 pm	1/31	6:46 am	1	♎	3:44 am	2	6:57 am	2	♏	1:51 pm
4	2:30 am	4	♎	8:23 pm	2	7:45 pm	3	♏	5:35 am	4	9:43 am	4	♐	4:55 pm
6	11:05 am	6	♏	11:41 pm	5	9:02 am	5	♐	10:21 am	6	9:31 pm	6	♑	11:48 pm
8	4:03 pm	9	♐	4:57 am	7	7:38 am	7	♑	6:08 pm	8	10:06 am	9	♒	9:56 am
11	1:49 am	11	♑	12:18 pm	10	1:50 am	10	♒	4:15 am	11	2:28 pm	11	♓	9:56 pm
13	2:24 pm	13	♒	9:41 pm	12	5:21 am	12	♓	3:53 pm	13	9:03 pm	14	♈	10:34 am
15	7:25 pm	16	♓	9:00 am	14	2:44 am	15	♈	4:26 am	16	4:08 pm	16	♉	11:01 pm
18	9:27 pm	18	♈	9:35 pm	17	2:55 pm	17	♉	4:58 pm	19	7:53 am	19	♊	10:20 am
20	8:50 pm	21	♉	9:47 am	19	6:34 pm	20	♊	3:50 am	21	1:14 pm	21	♋	7:06 pm
23	7:29 am	23	♊	7:28 pm	22	2:53 am	22	♋	11:16 am	23	5:19 am	24	♌	12:12 am
25	2:23 pm	26	♋	1:17 am	24	8:39 am	24	♌	2:36 pm	25	8:57 pm	26	♍	1:44 am
26	2:03 pm	28	♌	3:31 am	26	11:30 am	26	♍	2:47 pm	27	8:31 pm	28	♎	1:04 am
29	6:04 pm	30	♍	3:40 am	27	10:17 pm	28	♎	1:47 pm	29	7:57 pm	30	♏	12:21 am
31	6:46 am	2/1	♎	3:44 am						31	9:13 pm	4/1	♐	1:48 am

Moon Void-of-Course 2002 (cont.)

APRIL

Last Aspect Date	Time	Moon Enters New Sign Date	Sign	Time
3/31	9:13 pm	1	♐	1:48 am
3	2:13 am	3	♑	6:58 am
5	4:59 am	5	♒	4:07 pm
7	11:09 pm	8	♓	3:57 am
10	12:31 pm	10	♈	4:40 pm
13	4:52 am	13	♉	4:55 am
15	11:53 am	15	♊	3:56 pm
17	9:17 pm	18	♋	1:01 am
19	6:55 pm	20	♌	7:20 am
22	7:30 am	22	♍	10:35 am
24	9:06 am	24	♎	11:22 am
26	8:29 am	26	♏	11:15 am
28	9:25 am	28	♐	12:13 pm
30	1:10 pm	30	♑	4:03 pm

MAY

Last Aspect Date	Time	Moon Enters New Sign Date	Sign	Time
1	12:17 pm	2	♒	11:43 pm
5	7:46 am	5	♓	10:46 am
6	9:11 pm	7	♈	11:22 pm
10	8:47 am	10	♉	11:32 am
12	7:29 pm	12	♊	10:04 pm
15	4:08 am	15	♋	6:33 am
17	6:27 am	17	♌	12:52 pm
19	3:34 pm	19	♍	5:01 pm
21	11:53 am	21	♎	7:19 pm
23	6:39 pm	23	♏	8:38 pm
25	8:20 pm	25	♐	10:20 pm
28	1:40 am	28	♑	1:54 am
29	6:46 am	30	♒	8:35 am

JUNE

Last Aspect Date	Time	Moon Enters New Sign Date	Sign	Time
1	4:19 pm	1	♓	6:37 pm
3	5:58 am	4	♈	6:51 am
6	4:47 pm	6	♉	7:07 pm
9	3:14 am	9	♊	5:29 am
11	11:05 am	11	♋	1:15 pm
13	4:44 pm	13	♌	6:39 pm
15	8:17 pm	15	♍	10:23 pm
17	7:29 pm	18	♎	1:11 am
20	1:38 am	20	♏	3:42 am
22	4:27 am	22	♐	6:42 am
24	8:38 am	24	♑	11:01 am
26	2:37 am	26	♒	5:36 pm
29	12:12 am	29	♓	3:00 am

JULY

Last Aspect Date	Time	Moon Enters New Sign Date	Sign	Time
1	12:43 am	1	♈	2:49 pm
4	12:11 am	4	♉	3:16 am
6	10:57 am	6	♊	2:01 pm
8	6:37 pm	8	♋	9:36 pm
10	11:25 pm	11	♌	2:08 am
13	1:42 am	13	♍	4:41 am
15	12:08 am	15	♎	6:39 am
17	5:58 am	17	♏	9:13 am
19	9:35 am	19	♐	1:02 pm
21	2:44 pm	21	♑	6:26 pm
23	10:05 pm	24	♒	1:40 am
26	6:47 am	26	♓	11:04 am
28	9:01 pm	28	♈	10:39 pm
31	10:48 am	31	♉	11:17 am

AUGUST

Last Aspect Date	Time	Moon Enters New Sign Date	Sign	Time
2	5:58 pm	2	♊	10:46 pm
5	3:42 am	5	♋	7:02 am
5	7:02 am	7	♌	11:27 am
9	8:36 am	19	♍	1:03 pm
11	7:01 am	11	♎	1:38 pm
13	10:11 am	13	♏	3:01 pm
15	1:13 pm	15	♐	6:25 pm
17	6:39 pm	18	♑	12:15 am
19	3:13 pm	20	♒	8:16 am
22	5:29 pm	22	♓	6:11 pm
25	1:58 am	25	♈	5:48 am
27	4:18 pm	27	♉	6:32 pm
29	11:44 pm	30	♊	6:45 am

SEPTEMBER

Last Aspect Date	Time	Moon Enters New Sign Date	Sign	Time
1	11:55 am	1	♋	4:14 pm
3	3:31 pm	3	♌	9:36 pm
5	8:33 pm	5	♍	11:16 pm
7	7:54 pm	7	♎	10:57 pm
9	7:52 pm	9	♏	10:48 pm
11	5:52 pm	12	♐	12:44 am
14	2:54 am	14	♑	5:47 am
16	12:58 am	16	♒	1:54 pm
18	9:35 pm	19	♓	12:18 am
21	9:36 am	21	♈	12:11 pm
23	10:29 pm	24	♉	12:55 am
26	4:27 am	26	♊	1:26 pm
28	10:01 pm	29	♋	12:01 am
30	1:59 pm	10/1	♌	6:58 am

OCTOBER

Last Aspect Date	Time	Moon Enters New Sign Date	Sign	Time
9/30	1:59 pm	1	♌	6:58 am
3	8:16 am	3	♍	9:52 am
5	8:22 am	5	♎	9:51 am
7	7:29 am	7	♏	8:57 am
9	7:38 am	9	♐	9:21 am
11	11:08 am	11	♑	12:45 pm
13	5:42 pm	13	♒	7:51 pm
16	4:15 am	16	♓	6:07 am
18	4:17 pm	18	♈	6:13 pm
21	4:55 am	21	♉	6:57 am
23	9:14 am	23	♊	7:17 pm
26	4:01 am	26	♋	6:10 am
28	3:22 am	28	♌	2:20 pm
30	4:51 pm	30	♍	6:59 pm

NOVEMBER

Last Aspect Date	Time	Moon Enters New Sign Date	Sign	Time
1	6:19 pm	1	♎	8:28 pm
3	5:56 pm	3	♏	8:10 pm
5	11:48 am	5	♐	8:01 pm
7	7:14 pm	7	♑	9:59 pm
9	3:22 am	10	♒	3:27 am
12	9:06 am	12	♓	12:42 pm
14	8:38 pm	15	♈	12:38 am
17	9:06 am	17	♉	1:23 pm
19	8:34 pm	20	♊	1:25 am
22	7:07 am	22	♋	11:48 am
24	11:51 am	24	♌	8:00 pm
26	8:51 pm	27	♍	1:42 am
29	12:01 am	29	♎	4:54 am

DECEMBER

Last Aspect Date	Time	Moon Enters New Sign Date	Sign	Time
1	6:06 am	1	♏	6:15 am
2	11:15 pm	3	♐	6:58 am
5	2:55 am	5	♑	8:39 am
5	3:20 pm	7	♒	12:54 pm
9	1:35 pm	9	♓	8:46 pm
12	12:02 am	12	♈	7:58 am
14	12:18 pm	14	♉	8:43 pm
17	12:11 am	17	♊	8:43 am
19	2:10 pm	19	♋	6:30 pm
21	4:31 am	22	♌	1:48 am
23	11:58 pm	24	♍	7:05 am
26	2:10 am	26	♎	10:53 am
28	7:15 am	28	♏	1:41 pm
30	12:04 pm	30	♐	4:01 pm

How to Use the *Pocket Planner*

by Leslie Nielsen

This handy guide contains information that can be most valuable to you as you plan your daily activities. As you read through the first few pages, you can start to get a feel for how well-organized this guide is.

Read the Symbol Key on the next page, which is rather like astrological shorthand. The characteristics of the planets can give you direction in planning your strategies. Much like traffic signs that signal "go," "stop," or even "caution," you can determine for yourself the most propitious time to get things done.

You'll find tables that show the dates when Mercury is retrograde (℞) or direct (D). Because Mercury deals with the exchange of information, a retrograde Mercury makes miscommunication more noticeable.

There's also a section dedicated to the times when the Moon is void-of-course (v/c). These are generally poor times to conduct business because activities begun during these times usually end badly or fail to get started. If you make an appointment during a void-of-course, you might save yourself a lot of aggravation by confirming the time and date later. The Moon is only void-of-course for seven percent of the time when business is usually conducted during a normal work day (that is, 8:00 am to 5:00 pm). Sometimes, by waiting a matter of minutes or a few hours until the Moon has left the void-of-course phase, you have a much better chance to make action move more smoothly. Moon voids can also be used successfully to do routine activities or inner work, such as dream therapy or personal contemplation.

You'll find Moon phases, as well as each of the Moon's entries into a new sign. Times are expressed in Eastern Standard Time (in bold type) and Pacific Standard Time (in medium type). The New Moon time is generally best for beginning new activities, as the Moon is increasing in light and can offer the element of growth to our endeavors. When the Moon is Full, its illumination is greatest and we can see the results of our efforts. When it moves from Full stage back to the New stage, it can best be used to reflect on our projects. If necessary, we can make corrections at the New Moon.

The section of "Planetary Stations" will give you the times when the planets are changing signs or direction, thereby affording us opportunities for new starts.

The ephemeris in the back of your *Pocket Planner* can be very helpful to you. Read the particular sign and degree of planets and asteroids. As you start to work with the ephemeris, you may notice that not all planets seem to be comfortable in every sign. Think of the planets as actors, and the signs as the costumes they wear. Sometimes, costumes just itch. If you find this to be so for a certain time period, you may choose to delay your plans for a time or be more creative with the energies at hand.

As you turn to the daily pages, you'll find information about the Moon's sign, phase, and the time it changes phase. Also, you will find times and dates when the planets and asteroids change sign and go either retrograde or direct, major holidays, a three-month calendar, and room to record your appointments.

This guide is a powerful tool. Make the most of it!

Symbol Key

Planets:	☉ Sun	⚳ Ceres	♄ Saturn
	☽ Moon	⚴ Pallas	⚷ Chiron
	☿ Mercury	⚵ Juno	♅ Uranus
	♀ Venus	⚶ Vesta	♆ Neptune
	♂ Mars	♃ Jupiter	♇ Pluto
Signs:	♈ Aries	♌ Leo	♐ Sagittarius
	♉ Taurus	♍ Virgo	♑ Capricorn
	♊ Gemini	♎ Libra	♒ Aquarius
	♋ Cancer	♏ Scorpio	♓ Pisces
Aspects:	☌ Conjunction (0-8°)	⚺ Semisextile (30°)	⚹ Sextile (60°)
	□ Square (90°)	△ Trine (120°)	
	⚻ Quincunx (150°)	☍ Opposition (180°)	
Motion:	℞ Retrograde	D Direct	

World Map of Time Zones

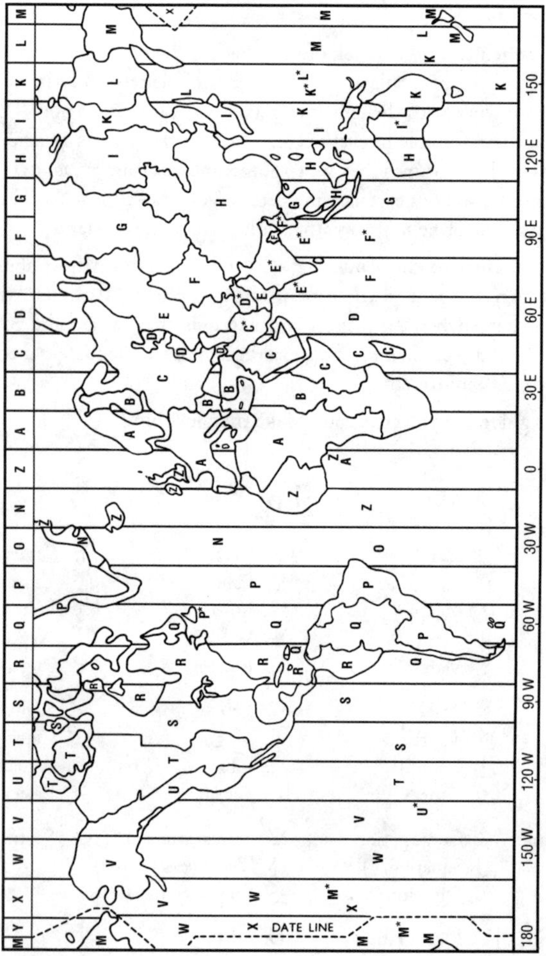

Time Zone Conversions

World Time Zones

Compared to Eastern Standard Time

( ) From Map
(S) CST/Subtract 1 hour
(R) EST (Used in calendar)
(Q) Add 1 hour
(P) Add 2 hours
(O) Add 3 hours
(N) Add 4 hours
(Z) Add 5 hours
(T) MST/Subtract 2 hours
(U) PST/Subtract 3 hours
(V) Subtract 4 hours
(W) Subtract 5 hours
(X) Subtract 6 hours
(Y) Subtract 7 hours
(A) Add 6 hours
(B) Add 7 hours
(C) Add 8 hours
(D) Add 9 hours
(E) Add 10 hours
(F) Add 11 hours
(G) Add 12 hours
(H) Add 13 hours
(I) Add 14 hours
(K) Add 15 hours
(L) Add 16 hours
(M) Add 17 hours
(C*) Add 8.5 hours
(D*) Add 9.5 hours
(E*) Add 10.5 hours
(F*) Add 11.5 hours
(I*) Add 14.5 hours
(K*) Add 15.5 hours
(L*) Add 16.5 hours
(M*) Add 18 hours
(P*) Add 2.5 hours
(V*) Subtract 4.5 hours

Planetary Stations for 2002

	2001 JAN	FEB	MAR	APR	MAY	JUN	JUL	AUG	SEP	OCT	NOV	DEC
☿	1/18–2/8				5/15–6/8				9/14–10/6			
♀										10/10–11/21		
♂												
♃	11/2–3/1											12/4–4/3
♄	9/26–2/7									10/11–2/22		
♅						6/2–11/4						
♆					5/13–10/20							
♇			3/20–8/26									
⚷				4/17–9/7								
⚳								8/13–11/23				
⚴						6/13–10/9						
⚵	12/25–03/27											
⚶	10/9–1/14											

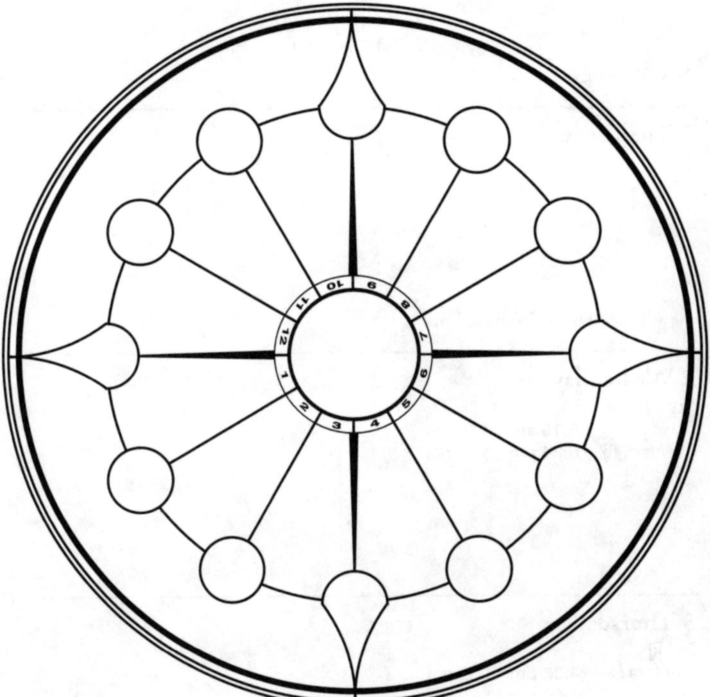
1
2
3
4
5
6
7
8
9
10
11
12

31 Monday

3rd ♋

☽ v/c	**8:43 am**	5:43 am
☽ enters ♌	**5:09 pm**	2:09 pm

New Year's Eve

1 Tuesday

3rd ♌

New Year's Day • Kwanzaa Ends

2 Wednesday

3rd ♌

☽ v/c	**6:16 am**	3:16 am
☽ enters ♍	**6:34 pm**	3:34 pm

3 Thursday

3rd ♍

☿ enters ♒	**4:38 pm**	1:38 pm
☽ v/c		11:30 pm

Eastern Standard Time in bold type
Pacific Standard Time in medium type

4 Friday

3rd ♍
☽ v/c **2:30 am**
☽ enters ♎ **8:23 pm** 5:23 pm

5 Saturday

3rd ♎
4th Quarter **10:55 pm** 7:55 pm

6 Sunday

4th ♎
☽ v/c **11:05 am** 8:05 am
☽ enters ♏ **11:41 pm** 8:41 pm

December 2001

S	M	T	W	T	F	S
						1
2	3	4	5	6	7	8
9	10	11	12	13	14	15
16	17	18	19	20	21	22
23	24	25	26	27	28	29
30	31					

January 2002

S	M	T	W	T	F	S
		1	2	3	4	5
6	7	8	9	10	11	12
13	14	15	16	17	18	19
20	21	22	23	24	25	26
27	28	29	30	31		

February 2002

S	M	T	W	T	F	S
					1	2
3	4	5	6	7	8	9
10	11	12	13	14	15	16
17	18	19	20	21	22	23
24	25	26	27	28		

Eastern Standard Time in bold type
Pacific Standard Time in medium type

7 Monday
4th ♏

8 Tuesday
4th ♏

☽ v/c **4:03 pm** 1:03 pm

9 Wednesday
4th ♏

☽ enters ♐ **4:57 am** 1:57 am

10 Thursday
4th ♐

☽ v/c 10:49 pm

Eastern Standard Time in bold type
Pacific Standard Time in medium type

11 Friday

4th ♐
☽ v/c **1:49 am**
☽ enters ♑ **12:18 pm** 9:18 am

12 Saturday

4th ♑

13 Sunday

4th ♑
New Moon **8:29 am** 5:29 am
☽ v/c **2:24 pm** 11:24 am
☽ enters ♒ **9:41 pm** 6:41 pm

December 2001

S	M	T	W	T	F	S
						1
2	3	4	5	6	7	8
9	10	11	12	13	14	15
16	17	18	19	20	21	22
23	24	25	26	27	28	29
30	31					

January 2002

S	M	T	W	T	F	S
		1	2	3	4	5
6	7	8	9	10	11	12
13	14	15	16	17	18	19
20	21	22	23	24	25	26
27	28	29	30	31		

February 2002

S	M	T	W	T	F	S
					1	2
3	4	5	6	7	8	9
10	11	12	13	14	15	16
17	18	19	20	21	22	23
24	25	26	27	28		

Eastern Standard Time in bold type
Pacific Standard Time in medium type

14 Monday

1st ♒
⚷ D **3:45 pm** 12:45 pm

15 Tuesday

1st ♒
☽ v/c **7:25 pm** 4:25 pm

16 Wednesday

1st ♒
☽ enters ♓ **9:00 am** 6:00 am

17 Thursday

1st ♓

Eastern Standard Time in bold type
Pacific Standard Time in medium type

18 Friday

1st ♓

☿ ℞	**3:52 pm**	12:52 pm
♂ enters ♈	**5:53 pm**	2:53 pm
☽ v/c	**9:27 pm**	6:27 pm
☽ enters ♈	**9:35 pm**	6:35 pm
♀ enters ♒	**10:42 pm**	7:42 pm

19 Saturday

1st ♈

☉ enters ♒		10:02 pm

Sun enters Aquarius

20 Sunday

1st ♈

☉ enters ♒	**1:02 am**	
☽ v/c	**8:50 pm**	5:50 pm

Sun enters Aquarius

December 2001

S	M	T	W	T	F	S
						1
2	3	4	5	6	7	8
9	10	11	12	13	14	15
16	17	18	19	20	21	22
23	24	25	26	27	28	29
30	31					

January 2002

S	M	T	W	T	F	S
		1	2	3	4	5
6	7	8	9	10	11	12
13	14	15	16	17	18	19
20	21	22	23	24	25	26
27	28	29	30	31		

February 2002

S	M	T	W	T	F	S
					1	2
3	4	5	6	7	8	9
10	11	12	13	14	15	16
17	18	19	20	21	22	23
24	25	26	27	28		

Eastern Standard Time in bold type
Pacific Standard Time in medium type

21 Monday

1st ♈
☽ enters ♉ **9:47 am** 6:47 am
2nd Quarter **12:47 pm** 9:47 am

Birthday of Martin Luther King, Jr. (observed)

22 Tuesday

2nd ♉

23 Wednesday

2nd ♉
☽ v/c **7:29 am** 4:29 am
☽ enters ♊ **7:28 pm** 4:28 pm

24 Thursday

2nd ♊

Eastern Standard Time in bold type
Pacific Standard Time in medium type

25 Friday

2nd ♊
☽ v/c **2:23 pm** 11:23 am
☽ enters ♋ 10:17 pm

26 Saturday

2nd ♊
☽ enters ♋ **1:17 am**
☽ v/c **2:03 pm** 11:03 am

27 Sunday

2nd ♋

December 2001

S	M	T	W	T	F	S
						1
2	3	4	5	6	7	8
9	10	11	12	13	14	15
16	17	18	19	20	21	22
23	24	25	26	27	28	29
30	31					

January 2002

S	M	T	W	T	F	S
		1	2	3	4	5
6	7	8	9	10	11	12
13	14	15	16	17	18	19
20	21	22	23	24	25	26
27	28	29	30	31		

February 2002

S	M	T	W	T	F	S
					1	2
3	4	5	6	7	8	9
10	11	12	13	14	15	16
17	18	19	20	21	22	23
24	25	26	27	28		

Eastern Standard Time in bold type
Pacific Standard Time in medium type

28 Monday

2nd ♋
☽ enters ♌ **3:31 am** 12:31 am
Full Moon **5:50 pm** 2:50 pm

29 Tuesday

3rd ♌
☽ v/c **6:04 pm** 3:04 pm

30 Wednesday

3rd ♌
☽ enters ♍ **3:40 am** 12:40 am

31 Thursday

3rd ♍
☽ v/c **6:46 am** 3:46 am

Eastern Standard Time in bold type
Pacific Standard Time in medium type

1 Friday

3rd ♍
☽ enters ♎ **3:44 am** 12:44 am

2 Saturday

3rd ♎
☽ v/c **7:45 pm** 4:45 pm

Imbolc • Groundhog Day

3 Sunday

3rd ♎
☽ enters ♏ **5:35 am** 2:35 am
☿ enters ♑ **11:19 pm** 8:19 pm

January 2002

S	M	T	W	T	F	S
		1	2	3	4	5
6	7	8	9	10	11	12
13	14	15	16	17	18	19
20	21	22	23	24	25	26
27	28	29	30	31		

February 2002

S	M	T	W	T	F	S
					1	2
3	4	5	6	7	8	9
10	11	12	13	14	15	16
17	18	19	20	21	22	23
24	25	26	27	28		

March 2002

S	M	T	W	T	F	S
					1	2
3	4	5	6	7	8	9
10	11	12	13	14	15	16
17	18	19	20	21	22	23
24	25	26	27	28	29	30
31						

Eastern Standard Time in bold type
Pacific Standard Time in medium type

4 Monday

3rd ♏

4th Quarter	**8:33 am**	5:33 am

5 Tuesday

4th ♏

☽ v/c	**9:02 am**	6:02 am
☽ enters ♐	**10:21 am**	7:21 am

6 Wednesday

4th ♐

7 Thursday

4th ♐

☽ v/c	**7:38 am**	4:38 am
☽ enters ♑	**6:08 pm**	3:08 pm
♄ D	**8:32 pm**	5:32 pm

Eastern Standard Time in bold type
Pacific Standard Time in medium type

8 Friday

4th ♑
☿ D **12:28 pm** 9:28 am
♀ enters ♒ **1:39 pm** 10:39 am

9 Saturday

4th ♑
⚵ enters ♊ **6:19 am** 3:19 am
☽ v/c 10:50 pm

10 Sunday

4th ♑
☽ v/c **1:50 am**
☽ enters ♒ **4:15 am** 1:15 am

January 2002

S	M	T	W	T	F	S
		1	2	3	4	5
6	7	8	9	10	11	12
13	14	15	16	17	18	19
20	21	22	23	24	25	26
27	28	29	30	31		

February 2002

S	M	T	W	T	F	S
					1	2
3	4	5	6	7	8	9
10	11	12	13	14	15	16
17	18	19	20	21	22	23
24	25	26	27	28		

March 2002

S	M	T	W	T	F	S
					1	2
3	4	5	6	7	8	9
10	11	12	13	14	15	16
17	18	19	20	21	22	23
24	25	26	27	28	29	30
31						

Eastern Standard Time in bold type
Pacific Standard Time in medium type

11 Monday

4th ≈
♀ enters ♓ **8:18 pm** 5:18 pm
New Moon 11:41 pm

12 Tuesday

4th ≈
New Moon **2:41 am**
☽ v/c **5:21 am** 2:21 am
☽ enters ♓ **3:53 pm** 12:53 pm

Chinese New Year (horse)

13 Wednesday

1st ♓
☿ enters ≈ **12:20 pm** 9:20 am
☽ v/c 11:44 pm

Ash Wednesday

14 Thursday

1st ♓
☽ v/c **2:44 am**

Valentine's Day

Eastern Standard Time in bold type
Pacific Standard Time in medium type

15 Friday

1st ♓
☽ enters ♈ **4:26 am** 1:26 am

16 Saturday

1st ♈

17 Sunday

1st ♈
☽ v/c **2:55 pm** 11:55 am
☽ enters ♉ **4:58 pm** 1:58 pm

January 2002

S	M	T	W	T	F	S
		1	2	3	4	5
6	7	8	9	10	11	12
13	14	15	16	17	18	19
20	21	22	23	24	25	26
27	28	29	30	31		

February 2002

S	M	T	W	T	F	S
					1	2
3	4	5	6	7	8	9
10	11	12	13	14	15	16
17	18	19	20	21	22	23
24	25	26	27	28		

March 2002

S	M	T	W	T	F	S
					1	2
3	4	5	6	7	8	9
10	11	12	13	14	15	16
17	18	19	20	21	22	23
24	25	26	27	28	29	30
31						

Eastern Standard Time in bold type
Pacific Standard Time in medium type

18 Monday

1st ♉

☉ enters ♓ **3:13 pm** 12:13 pm

Presidents' Day (observed) • Sun enters Pisces

19 Tuesday

1st ♉

☽ v/c **6:34 pm** 3:34 pm

20 Wednesday

1st ♉

☽ enters ♊ **3:50 am** 12:50 am

2nd Quarter **7:02 am** 4:02 am

21 Thursday

2nd ♊

☽ v/c 11:53 pm

Eastern Standard Time in bold type

Pacific Standard Time in medium type

22 Friday

2nd ♊

☽ v/c	**2:53 am**	
⚳ enters ♓	**5:27 am**	2:27 am
☽ enters ♋	**11:16 am**	8:16 am

23 Saturday

2nd ♋

24 Sunday

2nd ♋

☽ v/c	**8:39 am**	5:39 am
☽ enters ♌	**2:36 pm**	11:36 am

January 2002

S	M	T	W	T	F	S
		1	2	3	4	5
6	7	8	9	10	11	12
13	14	15	16	17	18	19
20	21	22	23	24	25	26
27	28	29	30	31		

February 2002

S	M	T	W	T	F	S
					1	2
3	4	5	6	7	8	9
10	11	12	13	14	15	16
17	18	19	20	21	22	23
24	25	26	27	28		

March 2002

S	M	T	W	T	F	S
					1	2
3	4	5	6	7	8	9
10	11	12	13	14	15	16
17	18	19	20	21	22	23
24	25	26	27	28	29	30
31						

25 Monday

2nd ♌

26 Tuesday

2nd ♌

☽ v/c	**11:30 am**	8:30 am
☽ enters ♍	**2:47 pm**	11:47 am

Purim

27 Wednesday

2nd ♍

Full Moon	**4:17 am**	1:17 am
☽ v/c	**10:17 pm**	7:17 pm

28 Thursday

3rd ♍

☽ enters ♎	**1:47 pm**	10:47 am

Eastern Standard Time in bold type
Pacific Standard Time in medium type

1 Friday

3rd ♎
♂ enters ♉ **10:05 am** 7:05 am
♃ D **10:15 am** 7:15 am

2 Saturday

3rd ♎
☽ v/c **6:57 am** 3:57 am
☽ enters ♏ **1:51 pm** 10:51 am

3 Sunday

3rd ♏

February 2002

S	M	T	W	T	F	S
					1	2
3	4	5	6	7	8	9
10	11	12	13	14	15	16
17	18	19	20	21	22	23
24	25	26	27	28		

March 2002

S	M	T	W	T	F	S
					1	2
3	4	5	6	7	8	9
10	11	12	13	14	15	16
17	18	19	20	21	22	23
24	25	26	27	28	29	30
31						

April 2002

S	M	T	W	T	F	S
	1	2	3	4	5	6
7	8	9	10	11	12	13
14	15	16	17	18	19	20
21	22	23	24	25	26	27
28	29	30				

Eastern Standard Time in bold type
Pacific Standard Time in medium type

4 Monday

3rd ♏

☽ v/c	**9:43 am**	6:43 am
☽ enters ♐	**4:55 pm**	1:55 pm

5 Tuesday

3rd ♐

4th Quarter	**8:25 pm**	5:25 pm

6 Wednesday

4th ♐

☽ v/c	**9:31 pm**	6:31 pm
☽ enters ♑	**11:48 pm**	8:48 pm

7 Thursday

4th ♑

♀ enters ♈	**8:42 pm**	5:42 pm

Eastern Standard Time in bold type
Pacific Standard Time in medium type

8 Friday

4th ♑
☽ v/c **10:06 am** 7:06 am

9 Saturday

4th ♑
☽ enters ♒ **9:56 am** 6:56 am

10 Sunday

4th ♒

February 2002

S	M	T	W	T	F	S
					1	2
3	4	5	6	7	8	9
10	11	12	13	14	15	16
17	18	19	20	21	22	23
24	25	26	27	28		

March 2002

S	M	T	W	T	F	S
					1	2
3	4	5	6	7	8	9
10	11	12	13	14	15	16
17	18	19	20	21	22	23
24	25	26	27	28	29	30
31						

April 2002

S	M	T	W	T	F	S
	1	2	3	4	5	6
7	8	9	10	11	12	13
14	15	16	17	18	19	20
21	22	23	24	25	26	27
28	29	30				

Eastern Standard Time in bold type
Pacific Standard Time in medium type

11 Monday

4th ≈

☽ v/c **2:28 pm** 11:28 am

☿ enters ♓ **6:34 pm** 3:34 pm

☽ enters ♓ **9:56 pm** 6:56 pm

12 Tuesday

4th ♓

13 Wednesday

4th ♓

New Moon **9:03 pm** 6:03 pm

☽ v/c **9:03 pm** 6:03 pm

14 Thursday

1st ♓

☽ enters ♈ **10:34 am** 7:34 am

Eastern Standard Time in bold type
Pacific Standard Time in medium type

15 Friday

1st ♈

Islamic New Year

16 Saturday

1st ♈

☽ v/c	**4:08 pm**	1:08 pm
☽ enters ♉	**11:01 pm**	8:01 pm

17 Sunday

1st ♉

St. Patrick's Day

February 2002

S	M	T	W	T	F	S
					1	2
3	4	5	6	7	8	9
10	11	12	13	14	15	16
17	18	19	20	21	22	23
24	25	26	27	28		

March 2002

S	M	T	W	T	F	S
					1	2
3	4	5	6	7	8	9
10	11	12	13	14	15	16
17	18	19	20	21	22	23
24	25	26	27	28	29	30
31						

April 2002

S	M	T	W	T	F	S
	1	2	3	4	5	6
7	8	9	10	11	12	13
14	15	16	17	18	19	20
21	22	23	24	25	26	27
28	29	30				

18 Monday
1st ♉

19 Tuesday
1st ♉

☽ v/c	**7:53 am**	4:53 am
☽ enters ♊	**10:20 am**	7:20 am

20 Wednesday
1st ♊

♇ ℞	**9:55 am**	6:55 am
☉ enters ♈	**2:16 pm**	11:16 am

Sun enters Aries • Spring Equinox • 2:16 pm EST/11:16 am PST
Ostara • International Astrology Day

21 Thursday
1st ♊

☽ v/c	**1:14 pm**	10:14 am
☽ enters ♋	**7:06 pm**	4:06 pm
2nd Quarter	**9:28 pm**	6:28 pm

Eastern Standard Time in bold type
Pacific Standard Time in medium type

22 Friday

2nd ♋

23 Saturday

2nd ♋

☽ v/c **5:19 am** 2:19 am

☽ enters ♌ 9:12 pm

24 Sunday

2nd ♋

☽ enters ♌ **12:12 am**

Palm Sunday

February 2002

S	M	T	W	T	F	S
					1	2
3	4	5	6	7	8	9
10	11	12	13	14	15	16
17	18	19	20	21	22	23
24	25	26	27	28		

March 2002

S	M	T	W	T	F	S
					1	2
3	4	5	6	7	8	9
10	11	12	13	14	15	16
17	18	19	20	21	22	23
24	25	26	27	28	29	30
31						

April 2002

S	M	T	W	T	F	S
	1	2	3	4	5	6
7	8	9	10	11	12	13
14	15	16	17	18	19	20
21	22	23	24	25	26	27
28	29	30				

25 Monday

2nd ♌
☽ v/c **8:57 pm** 5:57 pm
☽ enters ♍ 10:44 pm

26 Tuesday

2nd ♌
☽ enters ♍ **1:44 am**

27 Wednesday

2nd ♍
☽ v/c **8:31 pm** 5:31 pm
⚵ D **10:27 pm** 7:27 pm
☽ enters ♎ 10:04 pm

28 Thursday

2nd ♍
☽ enters ♎ **1:04 am**
Full Moon **1:25 pm** 10:25 am

Passover begins

Eastern Standard Time in bold type
Pacific Standard Time in medium type

29 Friday

3rd ♎

☿ enters ♈	**9:44 am**	6:44 am
☽ v/c	**7:57 pm**	4:57 pm
☽ enters ♏		9:21 pm

Good Friday

30 Saturday

3rd ♎

☽ enters ♏ **12:21 am**

31 Sunday

3rd ♏

☽ v/c	**9:13 pm**	6:13 pm
♀ enters ♉		10:39 pm
☽ enters ♐		10:48 pm

Easter

February 2002

S	M	T	W	T	F	S
					1	2
3	4	5	6	7	8	9
10	11	12	13	14	15	16
17	18	19	20	21	22	23
24	25	26	27	28		

March 2002

S	M	T	W	T	F	S
					1	2
3	4	5	6	7	8	9
10	11	12	13	14	15	16
17	18	19	20	21	22	23
24	25	26	27	28	29	30
31						

April 2002

S	M	T	W	T	F	S
	1	2	3	4	5	6
7	8	9	10	11	12	13
14	15	16	17	18	19	20
21	22	23	24	25	26	27
28	29	30				

1 Monday

3rd ♏
♀ enters ♉ **1:39 am**
☽ enters ♐ **1:48 am**

April Fools' Day

2 Tuesday

3rd ♐
☽ v/c 11:13 pm

3 Wednesday

3rd ♐
☽ v/c **2:13 am**
☽ enters ♑ **6:58 am** 3:58 am

Passover ends

4 Thursday

3rd ♑
4th Quarter **10:29 am** 7:29 am

Eastern Standard Time in bold type
Pacific Standard Time in medium type

5 Friday

4th ♑
☽ v/c **4:59 am** 1:59 am
☽ enters ♒ **4:07 pm** 1:07 pm

6 Saturday

4th ♒

7 Sunday

4th ♒
☽ v/c **11:09 pm** 8:09 pm

Daylight Saving Time begins at 2 am

March 2002

S	M	T	W	T	F	S
					1	2
3	4	5	6	7	8	9
10	11	12	13	14	15	16
17	18	19	20	21	22	23
24	25	26	27	28	29	30
31						

April 2002

S	M	T	W	T	F	S
	1	2	3	4	5	6
7	8	9	10	11	12	13
14	15	16	17	18	19	20
21	22	23	24	25	26	27
28	29	30				

May 2002

S	M	T	W	T	F	S
			1	2	3	4
5	6	7	8	9	10	11
12	13	14	15	16	17	18
19	20	21	22	23	24	25
26	27	28	29	30	31	

Eastern Standard Time in bold type
Pacific Standard Time in medium type

8 Monday

4th ♒
☽ enters ♓ **3:57 am** 12:57 am

9 Tuesday

4th ♓

10 Wednesday

4th ♓
☽ v/c **12:31 pm** 9:31 am
☽ enters ♈ **4:40 pm** 1:40 pm

11 Thursday

4th ♈

Eastern Standard Time in bold type
Pacific Standard Time in medium type

12 Friday

4th ♈
New Moon **2:21 pm** 11:21 am

13 Saturday

1st ♈
☽ v/c **4:52 am** 1:52 am
☽ enters ♉ **4:55 am** 1:55 am
☿ enters ♉ **5:10 am** 2:10 am
♂ enters ♊ **12:36 pm** 9:36 am

14 Sunday

1st ♉

March 2002

S	M	T	W	T	F	S
					1	2
3	4	5	6	7	8	9
10	11	12	13	14	15	16
17	18	19	20	21	22	23
24	25	26	27	28	29	30
31						

April 2002

S	M	T	W	T	F	S
	1	2	3	4	5	6
7	8	9	10	11	12	13
14	15	16	17	18	19	20
21	22	23	24	25	26	27
28	29	30				

May 2002

S	M	T	W	T	F	S
			1	2	3	4
5	6	7	8	9	10	11
12	13	14	15	16	17	18
19	20	21	22	23	24	25
26	27	28	29	30	31	

Eastern Standard Time in bold type
Pacific Standard Time in medium type

15 Monday

1st ♉

☽ v/c **11:53 am** 8:53 am

☽ enters ♊ **3:56 pm** 12:56 pm

16 Tuesday

1st ♊

⚷ ℞ 10:39 pm

17 Wednesday

1st ♊

⚷ ℞ **1:39 am**

☽ v/c **9:17 pm** 6:17 pm

☽ enters ♋ 10:01 pm

18 Thursday

1st ♊

☽ enters ♋ **1:01 am**

Eastern Standard Time in bold type
Pacific Standard Time in medium type

19 Friday

1st ♋

☽ v/c	**6:55 pm**	3:55 pm
☉ enters ♉		10:20 pm

Sun enters Taurus

20 Saturday

1st ♋

☉ enters ♉	**1:20 am**	
☽ enters ♌	**7:20 am**	4:20 am
2nd Quarter	**7:48 am**	4:48 am

Sun enters Taurus

21 Sunday

2nd ♌

March 2002

S	M	T	W	T	F	S
					1	2
3	4	5	6	7	8	9
10	11	12	13	14	15	16
17	18	19	20	21	22	23
24	25	26	27	28	29	30
31						

April 2002

S	M	T	W	T	F	S
	1	2	3	4	5	6
7	8	9	10	11	12	13
14	15	16	17	18	19	20
21	22	23	24	25	26	27
28	29	30				

May 2002

S	M	T	W	T	F	S
			1	2	3	4
5	6	7	8	9	10	11
12	13	14	15	16	17	18
19	20	21	22	23	24	25
26	27	28	29	30	31	

Eastern Standard Time in bold type
Pacific Standard Time in medium type

22 Monday

2nd ♌
☽ v/c **7:30 am** 4:30 am
☽ enters ♍ **10:35 am** 7:35 am

Earth Day

23 Tuesday

2nd ♍

24 Wednesday

2nd ♍
☽ v/c **9:06 am** 6:06 am
☽ enters ♎ **11:22 am** 8:22 am

25 Thursday

2nd ♎
♀ enters ♊ **12:57 pm** 9:57 am

Eastern Standard Time in bold type
Pacific Standard Time in medium type

26 Friday

2nd ♎

☽ v/c	**8:29 am**	5:29 am
☽ enters ♏	**11:15 am**	8:15 am
Full Moon	**10:00 pm**	7:00 pm

27 Saturday

3rd ♏

28 Sunday

3rd ♏

☽ v/c	**9:25 am**	6:25 am
☽ enters ♐	**12:13 pm**	9:13 am

March 2002

S	M	T	W	T	F	S
					1	2
3	4	5	6	7	8	9
10	11	12	13	14	15	16
17	18	19	20	21	22	23
24	25	26	27	28	29	30
31						

April 2002

S	M	T	W	T	F	S
	1	2	3	4	5	6
7	8	9	10	11	12	13
14	15	16	17	18	19	20
21	22	23	24	25	26	27
28	29	30				

May 2002

S	M	T	W	T	F	S
			1	2	3	4
5	6	7	8	9	10	11
12	13	14	15	16	17	18
19	20	21	22	23	24	25
26	27	28	29	30	31	

29 Monday

3rd ♐
☿ enters ♊ 11:15 pm

30 Tuesday

3rd ♐
☿ enters ♊ **2:15 am**
☽ v/c **1:10 pm** 10:10 am
☽ enters ♑ **4:03 pm** 1:03 pm

1 Wednesday

3rd ♑
☽ v/c **12:17 pm** 9:17 am

Beltane

2 Thursday

3rd ♑
☽ enters ♒ **11:43 pm** 8:43 pm

Eastern Standard Time in bold type
Pacific Standard Time in medium type

3 Friday

3rd ≈
4th Quarter 11:16 pm

Orthodox Good Friday

4 Saturday

3rd ≈
4th Quarter **2:16 am**

5 Sunday

4th ≈
☽ v/c **7:46 am** 4:46 am
☽ enters ♓ **10:46 am** 7:46 am

Orthodox Easter • Cinco de Mayo

April 2002

S	M	T	W	T	F	S
	1	2	3	4	5	6
7	8	9	10	11	12	13
14	15	16	17	18	19	20
21	22	23	24	25	26	27
28	29	30				

May 2002

S	M	T	W	T	F	S
			1	2	3	4
5	6	7	8	9	10	11
12	13	14	15	16	17	18
19	20	21	22	23	24	25
26	27	28	29	30	31	

June 2002

S	M	T	W	T	F	S
						1
2	3	4	5	6	7	8
9	10	11	12	13	14	15
16	17	18	19	20	21	22
23	24	25	26	27	28	29
30						

6 Monday

4th ♓
☽ v/c **9:11 pm** 6:11 pm

7 Tuesday

4th ♓
☽ enters ♈ **11:22 pm** 8:22 pm

8 Wednesday

4th ♈

9 Thursday

4th ♈

Eastern Standard Time in bold type
Pacific Standard Time in medium type

10 Friday

4th ♈

☽ v/c	**8:47 am**	5:47 am
☽ enters ♉	**11:32 am**	8:32 am

11 Saturday

4th ♉

12 Sunday

4th ♉

New Moon	**5:45 am**	2:45 am
☽ v/c	**7:29 pm**	4:29 pm
☽ enters ♊	**10:04 pm**	7:04 pm

Mother's Day

April 2002

S	M	T	W	T	F	S
	1	2	3	4	5	6
7	8	9	10	11	12	13
14	15	16	17	18	19	20
21	22	23	24	25	26	27
28	29	30				

May 2002

S	M	T	W	T	F	S
			1	2	3	4
5	6	7	8	9	10	11
12	13	14	15	16	17	18
19	20	21	22	23	24	25
26	27	28	29	30	31	

June 2002

S	M	T	W	T	F	S
						1
2	3	4	5	6	7	8
9	10	11	12	13	14	15
16	17	18	19	20	21	22
23	24	25	26	27	28	29
30						

13 Monday

1st ♊

♆ ℞	**7:10 am**	4:10 am
⚶ enters ♋		10:22 pm

14 Tuesday

1st ♊

⚶ enters ♋	**1:22 am**	
⚳ enters ♈	**8:16 am**	5:16 am

15 Wednesday

1st ♊

☽ v/c	**4:08 am**	1:08 am
☽ enters ♋	**6:33 am**	3:33 am
☿ ℞	**1:51 pm**	10:51 am

16 Thursday

1st ♋

Eastern Standard Time in bold type
Pacific Standard Time in medium type

17 Friday

1st ♋

☽ v/c	**6:27 am**	3:27 am
☽ enters ♌	**12:52 pm**	9:52 am

Shavuot

18 Saturday

1st ♌

19 Sunday

1st ♌

2nd Quarter	**2:42 pm**	11:42 am
☽ v/c	**3:34 pm**	12:34 pm
☽ enters ♍	**5:01 pm**	2:01 pm

Pentecost

April 2002

S	M	T	W	T	F	S
	1	2	3	4	5	6
7	8	9	10	11	12	13
14	15	16	17	18	19	20
21	22	23	24	25	26	27
28	29	30				

May 2002

S	M	T	W	T	F	S
			1	2	3	4
5	6	7	8	9	10	11
12	13	14	15	16	17	18
19	20	21	22	23	24	25
26	27	28	29	30	31	

June 2002

S	M	T	W	T	F	S
						1
2	3	4	5	6	7	8
9	10	11	12	13	14	15
16	17	18	19	20	21	22
23	24	25	26	27	28	29
30						

20 Monday

2nd ♍
♀ enters ♋ **8:27 am** 5:27 am
☉ enters ♊ 9:29 pm

Sun enters Gemini

21 Tuesday

2nd ♍
☉ enters ♊ **12:29 am**
☽ v/c **11:53 am** 8:53 am
☽ enters ♎ **7:19 pm** 4:19 pm

Sun enters Gemini

22 Wednesday

2nd ♎

23 Thursday

2nd ♎
☽ v/c **6:39 pm** 3:39 pm
☽ enters ♏ **8:38 pm** 5:38 pm

Eastern Standard Time in bold type
Pacific Standard Time in medium type

24 Friday

2nd ♏

25 Saturday

2nd ♏

☽ v/c	**8:20 pm**	5:20 pm
☽ enters ♐	**10:20 pm**	7:20 pm

26 Sunday

2nd ♐

Full Moon	**6:51 am**	3:51 am

Lunar Eclipse 5° ♐ 04' • 7:04 am EST/4:04 am PST

April 2002

S	M	T	W	T	F	S
	1	2	3	4	5	6
7	8	9	10	11	12	13
14	15	16	17	18	19	20
21	22	23	24	25	26	27
28	29	30				

May 2002

S	M	T	W	T	F	S
			1	2	3	4
5	6	7	8	9	10	11
12	13	14	15	16	17	18
19	20	21	22	23	24	25
26	27	28	29	30	31	

June 2002

S	M	T	W	T	F	S
						1
2	3	4	5	6	7	8
9	10	11	12	13	14	15
16	17	18	19	20	21	22
23	24	25	26	27	28	29
30						

27 Monday

3rd ♐
☽ v/c 10:40 pm
☽ enters ♑ 10:54 pm

Memorial Day (observed)

28 Tuesday

3rd ♐
☽ v/c **1:40 am**
☽ enters ♑ **1:54 am**
♂ enters ♋ **6:43 am** 3:43 am

29 Wednesday

3rd ♑
☽ v/c **6:46 am** 3:46 am

30 Thursday

3rd ♑
☽ enters ♒ **8:35 am** 5:35 am

Eastern Standard Time in bold type
Pacific Standard Time in medium type

31 Friday

3rd ♒

1 Saturday

3rd ♒

☽ v/c	**4:19 pm**	1:19 pm
☽ enters ♓	**6:37 pm**	3:37 pm

2 Sunday

3rd ♓

4th Quarter	**7:05 pm**	4:05 pm
♅ ℞	**7:11 pm**	4:11 pm

May 2002

S	M	T	W	T	F	S
			1	2	3	4
5	6	7	8	9	10	11
12	13	14	15	16	17	18
19	20	21	22	23	24	25
26	27	28	29	30	31	

June 2002

S	M	T	W	T	F	S
						1
2	3	4	5	6	7	8
9	10	11	12	13	14	15
16	17	18	19	20	21	22
23	24	25	26	27	28	29
30						

July 2002

S	M	T	W	T	F	S
	1	2	3	4	5	6
7	8	9	10	11	12	13
14	15	16	17	18	19	20
21	22	23	24	25	26	27
28	29	30	31			

Eastern Standard Time in bold type
Pacific Standard Time in medium type

3 Monday

4th ♓
☽ v/c **5:58 am** 2:58 am

4 Tuesday

4th ♓
☽ enters ♈ **6:51 am** 3:51 am

5 Wednesday

4th ♈

6 Thursday

4th ♈
☽ v/c **4:47 pm** 1:47 pm
☽ enters ♉ **7:07 pm** 4:07 pm

Eastern Standard Time in bold type
Pacific Standard Time in medium type

7 Friday
4th ♉

8 Saturday
4th ♉
☿ D **10:12 am** 7:12 am

9 Sunday
4th ♉
☽ v/c **3:14 am** 12:14 am
☽ enters ♊ **5:29 am** 2:29 am

May 2002

S	M	T	W	T	F	S
			1	2	3	4
5	6	7	8	9	10	11
12	13	14	15	16	17	18
19	20	21	22	23	24	25
26	27	28	29	30	31	

June 2002

S	M	T	W	T	F	S
						1
2	3	4	5	6	7	8
9	10	11	12	13	14	15
16	17	18	19	20	21	22
23	24	25	26	27	28	29
30						

July 2002

S	M	T	W	T	F	S
	1	2	3	4	5	6
7	8	9	10	11	12	13
14	15	16	17	18	19	20
21	22	23	24	25	26	27
28	29	30	31			

Eastern Standard Time in bold type
Pacific Standard Time in medium type

10 Monday
4th ♊
New Moon **6:46 pm** 3:46 pm

Solar Eclipse 19° ♊ 54' • 6:48 pm/EST 3:48 pm PST

11 Tuesday
1st ♊
☽ v/c **11:05 am** 8:05 am
☽ enters ♋ **1:15 pm** 10:15 am

12 Wednesday
1st ♋
⚵ enters ♍ **11:28 pm** 8:28 pm

13 Thursday
1st ♋
⚴ ℞ **12:50 pm** 9:50 am
☽ v/c **4:44 pm** 1:44 pm
☽ enters ♌ **6:39 pm** 3:39 pm

Eastern Standard Time in bold type
Pacific Standard Time in medium type

14 Friday
1st ♌
♀ enters ♌ **3:16 pm** 12:16 pm

Flag Day

15 Saturday
1st ♌
☽ v/c **8:17 pm** 7:23 pm
☽ enters ♍ **10:23 pm** 7:23 pm

16 Sunday
1st ♍

Father's Day

May 2002

S	M	T	W	T	F	S
			1	2	3	4
5	6	7	8	9	10	11
12	13	14	15	16	17	18
19	20	21	22	23	24	25
26	27	28	29	30	31	

June 2002

S	M	T	W	T	F	S
						1
2	3	4	5	6	7	8
9	10	11	12	13	14	15
16	17	18	19	20	21	22
23	24	25	26	27	28	29
30						

July 2002

S	M	T	W	T	F	S
	1	2	3	4	5	6
7	8	9	10	11	12	13
14	15	16	17	18	19	20
21	22	23	24	25	26	27
28	29	30	31			

17 Monday

1st ♍

2nd Quarter	**7:29 pm**	4:29 pm
☽ v/c	**7:29 pm**	4:29 pm
☽ enters ♎		10:11 pm

18 Tuesday

2nd ♍

☽ enters ♎ **1:11 am**

19 Wednesday

2nd ♎

☽ v/c 10:38 pm

20 Thursday

2nd ♎

☽ v/c	**1:38 am**	
☽ enters ♏	**3:42 am**	12:42 am

Eastern Standard Time in bold type
Pacific Standard Time in medium type

21 Friday

2nd ♏
☉ enters ♋ **8:24 am** 5:24 am

Sun enters Cancer • Litha • Summer Solstice • 8:24 am EST/5:24 am PST

22 Saturday

2nd ♏
☽ v/c **4:27 am** 1:27 am
☽ enters ♐ **6:42 am** 3:42 am

23 Sunday

2nd ♐

May 2002

S	M	T	W	T	F	S
			1	2	3	4
5	6	7	8	9	10	11
12	13	14	15	16	17	18
19	20	21	22	23	24	25
26	27	28	29	30	31	

June 2002

S	M	T	W	T	F	S
						1
2	3	4	5	6	7	8
9	10	11	12	13	14	15
16	17	18	19	20	21	22
23	24	25	26	27	28	29
30						

July 2002

S	M	T	W	T	F	S
	1	2	3	4	5	6
7	8	9	10	11	12	13
14	15	16	17	18	19	20
21	22	23	24	25	26	27
28	29	30	31			

Eastern Standard Time in bold type
Pacific Standard Time in medium type

24 Monday

2nd ♐

☽ v/c	**8:38 am**	5:38 am
☽ enters ♑	**11:01 am**	8:01 am
Full Moon	**4:42 pm**	1:42 pm

Lunar Eclipse 3° ♑ 11' • 4:28 pm EST/1:28 pm PST

25 Tuesday

3rd ♑

☽ v/c		11:37 pm

26 Wednesday

3rd ♑

☽ v/c	**2:37 am**	
☽ enters ≈	**5:36 pm**	2:36 pm

27 Thursday

3rd ≈

Eastern Standard Time in bold type
Pacific Standard Time in medium type

28 Friday

3rd ♒
☽ v/c 9:12 pm

29 Saturday

3rd ♒
☽ v/c **12:12 am**
☽ enters ♓ **3:00 am** 12:00 am

30 Sunday

3rd ♓
☽ v/c 9:43 pm

May 2002

S	M	T	W	T	F	S
			1	2	3	4
5	6	7	8	9	10	11
12	13	14	15	16	17	18
19	20	21	22	23	24	25
26	27	28	29	30	31	

June 2002

S	M	T	W	T	F	S
						1
2	3	4	5	6	7	8
9	10	11	12	13	14	15
16	17	18	19	20	21	22
23	24	25	26	27	28	29
30						

July 2002

S	M	T	W	T	F	S
	1	2	3	4	5	6
7	8	9	10	11	12	13
14	15	16	17	18	19	20
21	22	23	24	25	26	27
28	29	30	31			

1 Monday

3rd ♓
☽ v/c **12:43 am**
☽ enters ♈ **2:49 pm** 11:49 am

2 Tuesday

3rd ♈
4th Quarter **12:19 pm** 9:19 am

3 Wednesday

4th ♈
☽ v/c 9:11 pm

4 Thursday

4th ♈
☽ v/c **12:11 am**
☽ enters ♉ **3:16 am** 12:16 am

Independence Day

Eastern Standard Time in bold type
Pacific Standard Time in medium type

5 Friday

4th ♉

6 Saturday

4th ♉

☽ v/c **10:57 am** 7:57 am

☽ enters ♊ **2:01 pm** 11:01 am

7 Sunday

4th ♊

☿ enters ♋ **5:35 am** 2:35 am

June 2002

S	M	T	W	T	F	S
						1
2	3	4	5	6	7	8
9	10	11	12	13	14	15
16	17	18	19	20	21	22
23	24	25	26	27	28	29
30						

July 2002

S	M	T	W	T	F	S
	1	2	3	4	5	6
7	8	9	10	11	12	13
14	15	16	17	18	19	20
21	22	23	24	25	26	27
28	29	30	31			

August 2002

S	M	T	W	T	F	S
				1	2	3
4	5	6	7	8	9	10
11	12	13	14	15	16	17
18	19	20	21	22	23	24
25	26	27	28	29	30	31

Eastern Standard Time in bold type
Pacific Standard Time in medium type

8 Monday

4th ♊
☽ v/c **6:37 pm** 3:37 pm
☽ enters ♋ **9:36 pm** 6:36 pm

9 Tuesday

4th ♋

10 Wednesday

4th ♋
New Moon **5:26 am** 2:26 am
♀ enters ♍ **4:09 pm** 1:09 pm
☽ v/c **11:25 pm** 8:25 pm
☽ enters ♌ 11:08 pm

11 Thursday

1st ♋
☽ enters ♌ **2:08 am**

Eastern Standard Time in bold type
Pacific Standard Time in medium type

12 Friday

1st ♌
☽ v/c 10:42 pm

13 Saturday

1st ♌
☽ v/c **1:42 am**
☽ enters ♍ **4:41 am** 1:41 am
♂ enters ♌ **10:23 am** 7:23 am

14 Sunday

1st ♍
☽ v/c 9:08 pm

June 2002

S	M	T	W	T	F	S
						1
2	3	4	5	6	7	8
9	10	11	12	13	14	15
16	17	18	19	20	21	22
23	24	25	26	27	28	29
30						

July 2002

S	M	T	W	T	F	S
	1	2	3	4	5	6
7	8	9	10	11	12	13
14	15	16	17	18	19	20
21	22	23	24	25	26	27
28	29	30	31			

August 2002

S	M	T	W	T	F	S
				1	2	3
4	5	6	7	8	9	10
11	12	13	14	15	16	17
18	19	20	21	22	23	24
25	26	27	28	29	30	31

Eastern Standard Time in bold type
Pacific Standard Time in medium type

15 Monday

1st ♍
☽ v/c **12:08 am**
☽ enters ♎ **6:39 am** 3:39 am

16 Tuesday

1st ♎
2nd Quarter **11:47 pm** 8:47 pm

17 Wednesday

2nd ♎
☽ v/c **5:58 am** 2:58 am
☽ enters ♏ **9:13 am** 6:13 am

18 Thursday

2nd ♏

Eastern Standard Time in bold type
Pacific Standard Time in medium type

19 Friday

2nd ♏

☽ v/c	**9:35 am**	6:35 am
☽ enters ♐	**1:02 pm**	10:02 am

20 Saturday

2nd ♐

21 Sunday

2nd ♐

☽ v/c	**2:44 pm**	11:44 am
☿ enters ♌	**5:41 pm**	2:41 am
☽ enters ♑	**6:26 pm**	3:26 pm

June 2002

S	M	T	W	T	F	S
						1
2	3	4	5	6	7	8
9	10	11	12	13	14	15
16	17	18	19	20	21	22
23	24	25	26	27	28	29
30						

July 2002

S	M	T	W	T	F	S
	1	2	3	4	5	6
7	8	9	10	11	12	13
14	15	16	17	18	19	20
21	22	23	24	25	26	27
28	29	30	31			

August 2002

S	M	T	W	T	F	S
				1	2	3
4	5	6	7	8	9	10
11	12	13	14	15	16	17
18	19	20	21	22	23	24
25	26	27	28	29	30	31

Eastern Standard Time in bold type
Pacific Standard Time in medium type

22 Monday

2nd ♑
⚶ enters ♌ **10:26 am** 7:26 am
☉ enters ♌ **7:15 pm** 4:15 pm

Sun enters Leo

23 Tuesday

2nd ♑
☽ v/c **10:05 pm** 7:05 pm
☽ enters ♒ 10:40 pm

24 Wednesday

2nd ♑
☽ enters ♒ **1:40 am**
Full Moon **4:07 am** 1:07 am

25 Thursday

3rd ♒

Eastern Standard Time in bold type
Pacific Standard Time in medium type

5 Monday

4th ♊
☽ v/c **3:42 am** 12:42 am
☽ enters ♋ **7:02 am** 4:02 am

6 Tuesday

4th ♋
☿ enters ♍ **4:51 am** 1:51 am

7 Wednesday

4th ♋
♀ enters ♎ **4:09 am** 1:09 am
☽ enters ♌ **11:27 am** 8:27 am

8 Thursday

4th ♌
New Moon **2:15 pm** 11:15 am

Eastern Standard Time in bold type
Pacific Standard Time in medium type

26 Friday

3rd ≈
☽ v/c **6:47 am** 3:47 am
☽ enters ♓ **11:04 am** 8:04 am

27 Saturday

3rd ♓

28 Sunday

3rd ♓
☽ v/c **9:01 pm** 6:01 pm
☽ enters ♈ **10:39 pm** 7:39 pm

June 2002

S	M	T	W	T	F	S
						1
2	3	4	5	6	7	8
9	10	11	12	13	14	15
16	17	18	19	20	21	22
23	24	25	26	27	28	29
30						

July 2002

S	M	T	W	T	F	S
	1	2	3	4	5	6
7	8	9	10	11	12	13
14	15	16	17	18	19	20
21	22	23	24	25	26	27
28	29	30	31			

August 2002

S	M	T	W	T	F	S
				1	2	3
4	5	6	7	8	9	10
11	12	13	14	15	16	17
18	19	20	21	22	23	24
25	26	27	28	29	30	31

Eastern Standard Time in bold type
Pacific Standard Time in medium type

29 Monday

3rd ♈

30 Tuesday

3rd ♈

31 Wednesday

3rd ♈

☽ v/c	**10:48 am**	7:48 am
☽ enters ♉	**11:17 am**	8:17 am

1 Thursday

3rd ♉

4th Quarter	**5:22 am**	2:22 am
♃ enters ♌	**12:20 pm**	9:20 am

Lammas

Eastern Standard Time in bold type
Pacific Standard Time in medium type

2 Friday

4th ♉

☽ v/c	**5:58 pm**	2:58 pm
☽ enters ♊	**10:46 pm**	7:46 pm

3 Saturday

4th ♊

4 Sunday

4th ♊

July 2002

S	M	T	W	T	F	S
	1	2	3	4	5	6
7	8	9	10	11	12	13
14	15	16	17	18	19	20
21	22	23	24	25	26	27
28	29	30	31			

August 2002

S	M	T	W	T	F	S
				1	2	3
4	5	6	7	8	9	10
11	12	13	14	15	16	17
18	19	20	21	22	23	24
25	26	27	28	29	30	31

September 2002

S	M	T	W	T	F	S
1	2	3	4	5	6	7
8	9	10	11	12	13	14
15	16	17	18	19	20	21
22	23	24	25	26	27	28
29	30					

Eastern Standard Time in bold type
Pacific Standard Time in medium type

9 Friday

1st ♌

☽ v/c **8:36 am** 5:36 am

☽ enters ♍ **1:03 pm** 10:03 am

10 Saturday

1st ♍

11 Sunday

1st ♍

☽ v/c **7:01 am** 4:01 am

☽ enters ♎ **1:38 pm** 10:38 am

July 2002

S	M	T	W	T	F	S
	1	2	3	4	5	6
7	8	9	10	11	12	13
14	15	16	17	18	19	20
21	22	23	24	25	26	27
28	29	30	31			

August 2002

S	M	T	W	T	F	S
				1	2	3
4	5	6	7	8	9	10
11	12	13	14	15	16	17
18	19	20	21	22	23	24
25	26	27	28	29	30	31

September 2002

S	M	T	W	T	F	S
1	2	3	4	5	6	7
8	9	10	11	12	13	14
15	16	17	18	19	20	21
22	23	24	25	26	27	28
29	30					

12 Monday
1st ♎

13 Tuesday
1st ♎

⚳ ℞	**9:59 am**	6:59 am
☽ v/c	**10:11 am**	7:11 am
☽ enters ♏	**3:01 pm**	12:01 pm

14 Wednesday
1st ♏

15 Thursday
1st ♏

2nd Quarter	**5:12 am**	2:12 am
☽ v/c	**1:13 pm**	10:13 am
☽ enters ♐	**6:25 pm**	3:25 pm

Eastern Standard Time in bold type
Pacific Standard Time in medium type

16 Friday

2nd ♐

17 Saturday

2nd ♐

☽ v/c	**6:39 pm**	3:39 pm
☽ enters ♑		9:15 pm

18 Sunday

2nd ♐

☽ enters ♑ **12:15 am**

July 2002

S	M	T	W	T	F	S
	1	2	3	4	5	6
7	8	9	10	11	12	13
14	15	16	17	18	19	20
21	22	23	24	25	26	27
28	29	30	31			

August 2002

S	M	T	W	T	F	S
				1	2	3
4	5	6	7	8	9	10
11	12	13	14	15	16	17
18	19	20	21	22	23	24
25	26	27	28	29	30	31

September 2002

S	M	T	W	T	F	S
1	2	3	4	5	6	7
8	9	10	11	12	13	14
15	16	17	18	19	20	21
22	23	24	25	26	27	28
29	30					

Eastern Standard Time in bold type
Pacific Standard Time in medium type

19 Monday

2nd ♑
☽ v/c **3:13 pm** 12:13 pm

20 Tuesday

2nd ♑
☽ enters ♒ **8:16 am** 5:16 am

21 Wednesday

2nd ♒

22 Thursday

2nd ♒
Full Moon **5:29 pm** 2:29 pm
☽ v/c **5:29 pm** 2:29 pm
☽ enters ♓ **6:11 pm** 3:11 pm
☉ enters ♍ 11:17 pm

Sun enters Virgo

Eastern Standard Time in bold type
Pacific Standard Time in medium type

23 Friday

3rd ♓︎
☉ enters ♍︎ **2:17 am**

Sun enters Virgo

24 Saturday

3rd ♓︎
☽ v/c 10:58 pm

25 Sunday

3rd ♓︎
☽ v/c **1:58 am**
☽ enters ♈︎ **5:48 am** 2:48 am

July 2002

S	M	T	W	T	F	S
	1	2	3	4	5	6
7	8	9	10	11	12	13
14	15	16	17	18	19	20
21	22	23	24	25	26	27
28	29	30	31			

August 2002

S	M	T	W	T	F	S
				1	2	3
4	5	6	7	8	9	10
11	12	13	14	15	16	17
18	19	20	21	22	23	24
25	26	27	28	29	30	31

September 2002

S	M	T	W	T	F	S
1	2	3	4	5	6	7
8	9	10	11	12	13	14
15	16	17	18	19	20	21
22	23	24	25	26	27	28
29	30					

Eastern Standard Time in bold type
Pacific Standard Time in medium type

26 Monday

3rd ♈
♇ D **6:01 am** 3:01 am
☿ enters ♎ **4:10 pm** 1:10 pm

27 Tuesday

3rd ♈
☽ v/c **4:18 pm** 1:18 pm
☽ enters ♉ **6:32 pm** 3:32 pm

28 Wednesday

3rd ♉

29 Thursday

3rd ♉
♂ enters ♍ **9:38 am** 6:38 am
☽ v/c **11:44 pm** 8:44 pm

Eastern Standard Time in bold type
Pacific Standard Time in medium type

30 Friday

3rd ♉
☽ enters ♊ **6:45 am** 3:45 am
4th Quarter **9:31 pm** 6:31 pm

31 Saturday

4th ♊

1 Sunday

4th ♊
☽ v/c **11:55 am** 8:55 am
☽ enters ♋ **4:14 pm** 1:14 pm

July 2002

S	M	T	W	T	F	S
	1	2	3	4	5	6
7	8	9	10	11	12	13
14	15	16	17	18	19	20
21	22	23	24	25	26	27
28	29	30	31			

August 2002

S	M	T	W	T	F	S
				1	2	3
4	5	6	7	8	9	10
11	12	13	14	15	16	17
18	19	20	21	22	23	24
25	26	27	28	29	30	31

September 2002

S	M	T	W	T	F	S
1	2	3	4	5	6	7
8	9	10	11	12	13	14
15	16	17	18	19	20	21
22	23	24	25	26	27	28
29	30					

2 Monday

4th ♋

Labor Day

3 Tuesday

4th ♋

☽ v/c	**3:31 pm**	12:31 pm
☽ enters ♌	**9:36 pm**	6:36 pm

4 Wednesday

4th ♌

5 Thursday

4th ♌

⚵ enters ♎	**2:15 pm**	11:15 am
☽ v/c	**8:33 pm**	5:33 pm
☽ enters ♍	**11:16 pm**	8:16 pm

Eastern Standard Time in bold type
Pacific Standard Time in medium type

6 Friday

4th ♍

New Moon **10:10 pm** 7:10 pm

7 Saturday

1st ♍

⚷ D **8:21 am** 5:21 am

☽ v/c **7:54 pm** 4:54 pm

♀ enters ♏ **10:05 pm** 7:05 pm

☽ enters ♎ **10:57 pm** 7:57 pm

Rosh Hashanah

8 Sunday

1st ♎

August 2002

S	M	T	W	T	F	S
				1	2	3
4	5	6	7	8	9	10
11	12	13	14	15	16	17
18	19	20	21	22	23	24
25	26	27	28	29	30	31

September 2002

S	M	T	W	T	F	S
1	2	3	4	5	6	7
8	9	10	11	12	13	14
15	16	17	18	19	20	21
22	23	24	25	26	27	28
29	30					

October 2002

S	M	T	W	T	F	S
		1	2	3	4	5
6	7	8	9	10	11	12
13	14	15	16	17	18	19
20	21	22	23	24	25	26
27	28	29	30	31		

9 Monday

1st ♎
☽ v/c **7:52 pm** 4:52 pm
☽ enters ♏ **10:48 pm** 7:48 pm

10 Tuesday

1st ♏

11 Wednesday

1st ♏
☽ v/c **5:52 pm** 2:52 pm
☽ enters ♐ 9:44 pm

12 Thursday

1st ♏
☽ enters ♐ **12:44 am**

Eastern Standard Time in bold type
Pacific Standard Time in medium type

13 Friday

1st ♐
2nd Quarter **1:08 pm** 10:08 am
☽ v/c 11:54 pm

14 Saturday

2nd ♐
☽ v/c **2:54 am**
☽ enters ♑ **5:47 am** 2:47 am
☿ ℞ **2:39 pm** 11:39 am

15 Sunday

2nd ♑
☽ v/c 9:58 pm

August 2002

S	M	T	W	T	F	S
				1	2	3
4	5	6	7	8	9	10
11	12	13	14	15	16	17
18	19	20	21	22	23	24
25	26	27	28	29	30	31

September 2002

S	M	T	W	T	F	S
1	2	3	4	5	6	7
8	9	10	11	12	13	14
15	16	17	18	19	20	21
22	23	24	25	26	27	28
29	30					

October 2002

S	M	T	W	T	F	S
		1	2	3	4	5
6	7	8	9	10	11	12
13	14	15	16	17	18	19
20	21	22	23	24	25	26
27	28	29	30	31		

16 Monday

2nd ♑
☽ v/c **12:58 am**
☽ enters ♒ **1:54 pm** 10:54 am

Yom Kippur

17 Tuesday

2nd ♒

18 Wednesday

2nd ♒
☽ v/c **9:35 pm** 6:35 pm
☽ enters ♓ 9:18 pm

19 Thursday

2nd ♒
☽ enters ♓ **12:18 am**

Eastern Standard Time in bold type
Pacific Standard Time in medium type

20 Friday

2nd ♓

21 Saturday

2nd ♓

Full Moon	**8:59 am**	5:59 am
☽ v/c	**9:36 am**	6:36 am
☽ enters ♈	**12:11 pm**	9:11 am

Sukkot begins

22 Sunday

3rd ♈

☉ enters ♎	**11:55 pm**	8:55 pm

Sun enters Libra • Mabon • Fall Equinox • 11:55 pm EST/8:55 pm PST

August 2002

S	M	T	W	T	F	S
				1	2	3
4	5	6	7	8	9	10
11	12	13	14	15	16	17
18	19	20	21	22	23	24
25	26	27	28	29	30	31

September 2002

S	M	T	W	T	F	S
1	2	3	4	5	6	7
8	9	10	11	12	13	14
15	16	17	18	19	20	21
22	23	24	25	26	27	28
29	30					

October 2002

S	M	T	W	T	F	S
		1	2	3	4	5
6	7	8	9	10	11	12
13	14	15	16	17	18	19
20	21	22	23	24	25	26
27	28	29	30	31		

23 Monday
3rd ♈
☽ v/c **10:29 pm** 7:29 pm
☽ enters ♉ 9:55 pm

24 Tuesday
3rd ♈
☽ enters ♉ **12:55 am**

25 Wednesday
3rd ♉

26 Thursday
3rd ♉
☽ v/c **4:27 am** 1:27 am
☽ enters ♊ **1:26 pm** 10:26 am

Eastern Standard Time in bold type
Pacific Standard Time in medium type

27 Friday

3rd ♊
⚶ enters ♍ **8:20 am** 5:20 am

Sukkot ends

28 Saturday

3rd ♊
☽ v/c **10:01 pm** 7:01 pm
☽ enters ♋ 9:01 pm

29 Sunday

3rd ♊
☽ enters ♋ **12:01 am**
4th Quarter **12:03 pm** 9:03 am

August 2002

S	M	T	W	T	F	S
				1	2	3
4	5	6	7	8	9	10
11	12	13	14	15	16	17
18	19	20	21	22	23	24
25	26	27	28	29	30	31

September 2002

S	M	T	W	T	F	S
1	2	3	4	5	6	7
8	9	10	11	12	13	14
15	16	17	18	19	20	21
22	23	24	25	26	27	28
29	30					

October 2002

S	M	T	W	T	F	S
		1	2	3	4	5
6	7	8	9	10	11	12
13	14	15	16	17	18	19
20	21	22	23	24	25	26
27	28	29	30	31		

30 Monday

4th ♋

☽ v/c **1:59 pm** 10:59 am

1 Tuesday

4th ♋

☽ enters ♌ **6:58 am** 3:58 am

2 Wednesday

4th ♌

☿ enters ♍ **4:26 am** 1:26 am

3 Thursday

4th ♌

☽ v/c **8:16 am** 5:16 am

☽ enters ♍ **9:52 am** 6:52 am

4 Friday
4th ♍

5 Saturday
4th ♍

☽ v/c	**8:22 am**	5:22 am
☽ enters ♎	**9:51 am**	6:51 am

6 Sunday
4th ♎

New Moon	**6:18 am**	3:18 am
☿ D	**2:28 pm**	11:28 am

September 2002

S	M	T	W	T	F	S
1	2	3	4	5	6	7
8	9	10	11	12	13	14
15	16	17	18	19	20	21
22	23	24	25	26	27	28
29	30					

October 2002

S	M	T	W	T	F	S
		1	2	3	4	5
6	7	8	9	10	11	12
13	14	15	16	17	18	19
20	21	22	23	24	25	26
27	28	29	30	31		

November 2002

S	M	T	W	T	F	S
					1	2
3	4	5	6	7	8	9
10	11	12	13	14	15	16
17	18	19	20	21	22	23
24	25	26	27	28	29	30

Eastern Standard Time in bold type
Pacific Standard Time in medium type

7 Monday

1st ♎

☽ v/c	**7:29 am**	4:29 am
☽ enters ♏	**8:57 am**	5:57 am

8 Tuesday

1st ♏

⚳ D		9:56 pm

9 Wednesday

1st ♏

⚳ D	**12:56 am**	
☽ v/c	**7:38 am**	4:38 am
☽ enters ♐	**9:21 am**	6:21 am

10 Thursday

1st ♐

♀ ℞	**1:35 pm**	10:35 am
☿ enters ♎		9:56 pm

Eastern Standard Time in bold type
Pacific Standard Time in medium type

11 Friday

1st ♐
☿ enters ♎ **12:56 am**
♄ ℞ **8:01 am** 5:01 am
☽ v/c **11:08 am** 8:08 am
☽ enters ♑ **12:45 pm** 9:45 am

12 Saturday

1st ♑
2nd Quarter 9:33 pm

13 Sunday

1st ♑
2nd Quarter **12:33 am**
☽ v/c **5:42 pm** 2:42 pm
☽ enters ♒ **7:51 pm** 4:51 pm

September 2002

S	M	T	W	T	F	S
1	2	3	4	5	6	7
8	9	10	11	12	13	14
15	16	17	18	19	20	21
22	23	24	25	26	27	28
29	30					

October 2002

S	M	T	W	T	F	S
		1	2	3	4	5
6	7	8	9	10	11	12
13	14	15	16	17	18	19
20	21	22	23	24	25	26
27	28	29	30	31		

November 2002

S	M	T	W	T	F	S
					1	2
3	4	5	6	7	8	9
10	11	12	13	14	15	16
17	18	19	20	21	22	23
24	25	26	27	28	29	30

14 Monday

2nd ≈

Columbus Day (observed)

15 Tuesday

2nd ≈

♂ enters ♎ **12:38 pm** 9:38 am

16 Wednesday

2nd ≈

☽ v/c **4:15 am** 1:15 am

☽ enters ♓ **6:07 am** 3:07 am

17 Thursday

2nd ♓

Eastern Standard Time in bold type

Pacific Standard Time in medium type

18 Friday

2nd ♓

☽ v/c	**4:17 pm**	1:17 pm
☽ enters ♈	**6:13 pm**	3:13 pm

19 Saturday

2nd ♈

20 Sunday

2nd ♈

♆ D	**8:53 am**	5:53 am
Full Moon		11:20 pm

September 2002

S	M	T	W	T	F	S
1	2	3	4	5	6	7
8	9	10	11	12	13	14
15	16	17	18	19	20	21
22	23	24	25	26	27	28
29	30					

October 2002

S	M	T	W	T	F	S
		1	2	3	4	5
6	7	8	9	10	11	12
13	14	15	16	17	18	19
20	21	22	23	24	25	26
27	28	29	30	31		

November 2002

S	M	T	W	T	F	S
					1	2
3	4	5	6	7	8	9
10	11	12	13	14	15	16
17	18	19	20	21	22	23
24	25	26	27	28	29	30

21 Monday

2nd ♈

Full Moon	**2:20 am**	
☽ v/c	**4:55 am**	1:55 am
☽ enters ♉	**6:57 am**	3:57 am

22 Tuesday

3rd ♉

23 Wednesday

3rd ♉

☽ v/c	**9:14 pm**	6:14 pm
☉ enters ♏	**9:18 am**	6:18 am
☽ enters ♊	**7:17 pm**	4:17 pm

Sun enters Scorpio

24 Thursday

3rd ♊

Eastern Standard Time in bold type
Pacific Standard Time in medium type

25 Friday
3rd ♊

26 Saturday
3rd ♊

☽ v/c	**4:01 am**	1:01 am
☽ enters ♋	**6:10 am**	3:10 am

27 Sunday
3rd ♋

Daylight Saving Time ends at 2 am

September 2002

S	M	T	W	T	F	S
1	2	3	4	5	6	7
8	9	10	11	12	13	14
15	16	17	18	19	20	21
22	23	24	25	26	27	28
29	30					

October 2002

S	M	T	W	T	F	S
		1	2	3	4	5
6	7	8	9	10	11	12
13	14	15	16	17	18	19
20	21	22	23	24	25	26
27	28	29	30	31		

November 2002

S	M	T	W	T	F	S
					1	2
3	4	5	6	7	8	9
10	11	12	13	14	15	16
17	18	19	20	21	22	23
24	25	26	27	28	29	30

28 Monday

3rd ♋

☽ v/c	**3:22 am**	12:22 am
☽ enters ♌	**2:20 pm**	11:20 am
4th Quarter		9:28 pm

29 Tuesday

3rd ♌

4th Quarter **12:28 am**

30 Wednesday

4th ♌

☽ v/c	**4:51 pm**	1:51 pm
☽ enters ♍	**6:59 pm**	3:59 pm

31 Thursday

4th ♍

☿ enters ♏	**5:43 pm**	2:43 pm

Halloween/Samhain

Eastern Standard Time in bold type
Pacific Standard Time in medium type

1 Friday

4th ♍

☽ v/c	**6:19 pm**	3:19 pm
☽ enters ♎	**8:28 pm**	5:28 pm

All Saints' Day

2 Saturday

4th ♎

3 Sunday

4th ♎

☽ v/c	**5:56 pm**	2:56 pm
☽ enters ♏	**8:10 pm**	5:10 pm
♅ D		10:27 pm

October 2002

S	M	T	W	T	F	S
		1	2	3	4	5
6	7	8	9	10	11	12
13	14	15	16	17	18	19
20	21	22	23	24	25	26
27	28	29	30	31		

November 2002

S	M	T	W	T	F	S
					1	2
3	4	5	6	7	8	9
10	11	12	13	14	15	16
17	18	19	20	21	22	23
24	25	26	27	28	29	30

December 2002

S	M	T	W	T	F	S
1	2	3	4	5	6	7
8	9	10	11	12	13	14
15	16	17	18	19	20	21
22	23	24	25	26	27	28
29	30	31				

4 Monday

4th ♏

♅ D	**1:27 am**	
New Moon	**3:34 pm**	12:34 pm

5 Tuesday

1st ♏

☽ v/c	**11:48 am**	8:48 am
☽ enters ♐	**8:01 pm**	5:01 pm

Election Day (general)

6 Wednesday

1st ♐

Ramadan beings

7 Thursday

1st ♐

☽ v/c	**7:14 pm**	4:14 pm
☽ enters ♑	**9:59 pm**	6:59 pm

Eastern Standard Time in bold type
Pacific Standard Time in medium type

8 Friday
1st ♑

9 Saturday
1st ♑
☽ v/c **3:22 am** 12:22 am

10 Sunday
1st ♑
☽ enters ♒ **3:27 am** 12:27 am

October 2002

S	M	T	W	T	F	S
		1	2	3	4	5
6	7	8	9	10	11	12
13	14	15	16	17	18	19
20	21	22	23	24	25	26
27	28	29	30	31		

November 2002

S	M	T	W	T	F	S
					1	2
3	4	5	6	7	8	9
10	11	12	13	14	15	16
17	18	19	20	21	22	23
24	25	26	27	28	29	30

December 2002

S	M	T	W	T	F	S
1	2	3	4	5	6	7
8	9	10	11	12	13	14
15	16	17	18	19	20	21
22	23	24	25	26	27	28
29	30	31				

11 Monday

1st ≈

2nd Quarter **3:52 pm** 12:52 pm

Veterans Day

12 Tuesday

2nd ≈

☽ v/c **9:06 am** 6:06 am

☽ enters ♓ **12:42 pm** 9:42 am

13 Wednesday

2nd ♓

14 Thursday

2nd ♓

☽ v/c **8:38 pm** 5:38 pm

☽ enters ♈ 9:38 pm

Eastern Standard Time in bold type
Pacific Standard Time in medium type

15 Friday
2nd ♓
☽ enters ♈ **12:38 am**

16 Saturday
2nd ♈

17 Sunday
2nd ♈
☽ v/c **9:06 am** 6:06 am
☽ enters ♉ **1:23 pm** 10:23 am

October 2002

S	M	T	W	T	F	S
		1	2	3	4	5
6	7	8	9	10	11	12
13	14	15	16	17	18	19
20	21	22	23	24	25	26
27	28	29	30	31		

November 2002

S	M	T	W	T	F	S
					1	2
3	4	5	6	7	8	9
10	11	12	13	14	15	16
17	18	19	20	21	22	23
24	25	26	27	28	29	30

December 2002

S	M	T	W	T	F	S
1	2	3	4	5	6	7
8	9	10	11	12	13	14
15	16	17	18	19	20	21
22	23	24	25	26	27	28
29	30	31				

Eastern Standard Time in bold type
Pacific Standard Time in medium type

18 Monday

2nd ♉

19 Tuesday

2nd ♉

☿ enters ♐	**6:29 am**	3:29 am
Full Moon	**8:34 pm**	5:34 pm
☽ v/c	**8:34 pm**	5:34 pm
☽ enters ♊		10:25 pm

Lunar Eclipse 27° ♉ 33' • 8:46 pm EST/5:46 pm PST

20 Wednesday

3rd ♉

☽ enters ♊	**1:25 am**	
♀ D		11:12 pm

21 Thursday

3rd ♊

♀ D	**2:12 am**	

Eastern Standard Time in bold type
Pacific Standard Time in medium type

22 Friday

3rd ♊

☉ enters ♐	**6:54 am**	3:54 am
☽ v/c	**7:07 am**	4:07 am
☽ enters ♋	**11:48 am**	8:48 am

Sun enters Sagittarius

23 Saturday

3rd ♋

24 Sunday

3rd ♋

☽ v/c	**11:51 am**	8:51 am
☽ enters ♌	**8:00 pm**	5:00 pm

October 2002

S	M	T	W	T	F	S
		1	2	3	4	5
6	7	8	9	10	11	12
13	14	15	16	17	18	19
20	21	22	23	24	25	26
27	28	29	30	31		

November 2002

S	M	T	W	T	F	S
					1	2
3	4	5	6	7	8	9
10	11	12	13	14	15	16
17	18	19	20	21	22	23
24	25	26	27	28	29	30

December 2002

S	M	T	W	T	F	S
1	2	3	4	5	6	7
8	9	10	11	12	13	14
15	16	17	18	19	20	21
22	23	24	25	26	27	28
29	30	31				

Eastern Standard Time in bold type
Pacific Standard Time in medium type

25 Monday

3rd ♌

26 Tuesday

3rd ♌

☽ v/c **8:51 pm** 5:51 pm

☽ enters ♍ 10:42 pm

27 Wednesday

3rd ♌

☽ enters ♍ **1:42 am**

4th Quarter **10:46 am** 7:46 am

⚵ enters ♏ **3:09 pm** 12:09 pm

28 Thursday

4th ♍

☽ v/c 9:01 pm

Thanksgiving Day

Eastern Standard Time in bold type
Pacific Standard Time in medium type

29 Friday

4th ♍
☽ v/c **12:01 am**
☽ enters ♎ **4:54 am** 1:54 am

30 Saturday

4th ♎

Hanukkah begins

1 Sunday

4th ♎
☽ v/c **6:06 am** 3:06 am
☽ enters ♏ **6:15 am** 3:15 am
♂ enters ♏ **9:26 am** 6:26 am

October 2002

S	M	T	W	T	F	S
		1	2	3	4	5
6	7	8	9	10	11	12
13	14	15	16	17	18	19
20	21	22	23	24	25	26
27	28	29	30	31		

November 2002

S	M	T	W	T	F	S
					1	2
3	4	5	6	7	8	9
10	11	12	13	14	15	16
17	18	19	20	21	22	23
24	25	26	27	28	29	30

December 2002

S	M	T	W	T	F	S
1	2	3	4	5	6	7
8	9	10	11	12	13	14
15	16	17	18	19	20	21
22	23	24	25	26	27	28
29	30	31				

Eastern Standard Time in bold type
Pacific Standard Time in medium type

2 Monday

4th ♏

☽ v/c	**11:15 pm**	8:15 pm

3 Tuesday

4th ♏

☽ enters ♐	**6:58 am**	3:58 am
New Moon		11:34 pm

Solar Eclipse 11° ♐ 58' • 11:38 pm PST

4 Wednesday

4th ♐

New Moon	**2:34 am**	
♃ ℞	**7:22 am**	4:22 am
☽ v/c		11:55 pm

Solar Eclipse 11° ♐ 58' • 2:38 am EST

5 Thursday

1st ♐

☽ v/c	**2:55 am**	
☽ enters ♑	**8:39 am**	5:39 am
☽ v/c	**3:20 pm**	12:20 pm

Eastern Standard Time in bold type
Pacific Standard Time in medium type

6 Friday

1st ♑

7 Saturday

1st ♑
☽ enters ♒ **12:54 pm** 9:54 am

Hanukkah ends

8 Sunday

1st ♒
☿ enters ♑ **3:21 pm** 12:21 pm

Ramadan ends

November 2002

S	M	T	W	T	F	S
					1	2
3	4	5	6	7	8	9
10	11	12	13	14	15	16
17	18	19	20	21	22	23
24	25	26	27	28	29	30

December 2002

S	M	T	W	T	F	S
1	2	3	4	5	6	7
8	9	10	11	12	13	14
15	16	17	18	19	20	21
22	23	24	25	26	27	28
29	30	31				

January 2003

S	M	T	W	T	F	S
			1	2	3	4
5	6	7	8	9	10	11
12	13	14	15	16	17	18
19	20	21	22	23	24	25
26	27	28	29	30	31	

Eastern Standard Time in bold type
Pacific Standard Time in medium type

9 Monday

1st ♒
☽ v/c **1:35 pm** 10:35 am
☽ enters ♓ **8:46 pm** 5:46 pm

10 Tuesday

1st ♓
⚶ enters ♎ **9:52 am** 6:52 am

11 Wednesday

1st ♓
2nd Quarter **10:49 am** 7:49 am
☽ v/c 9:02 pm

12 Thursday

2nd ♓
☽ v/c **12:02 am**
☽ enters ♈ **7:58 am** 4:58 am

Eastern Standard Time in bold type
Pacific Standard Time in medium type

13 Friday

2nd ♈

14 Saturday

2nd ♈

☽ v/c	**12:18 pm**	9:18 am
☽ enters ♉	**8:43 pm**	5:43 pm

15 Sunday

2nd ♉

November 2002

S	M	T	W	T	F	S
					1	2
3	4	5	6	7	8	9
10	11	12	13	14	15	16
17	18	19	20	21	22	23
24	25	26	27	28	29	30

December 2002

S	M	T	W	T	F	S
1	2	3	4	5	6	7
8	9	10	11	12	13	14
15	16	17	18	19	20	21
22	23	24	25	26	27	28
29	30	31				

January 2003

S	M	T	W	T	F	S
			1	2	3	4
5	6	7	8	9	10	11
12	13	14	15	16	17	18
19	20	21	22	23	24	25
26	27	28	29	30	31	

16 Monday

2nd ♉
☽ v/c 9:11 pm

17 Tuesday

2nd ♉
☽ v/c **12:11 am**
☽ enters ♊ **8:43 am** 5:43 am

18 Wednesday

2nd ♊

19 Thursday

2nd ♊
Full Moon **2:10 pm** 11:10 am
☽ v/c **2:10 pm** 11:10 am
☽ enters ♋ **6:30 pm** 3:30 pm

Eastern Standard Time in bold type
Pacific Standard Time in medium type

20 Friday

3rd ♋

21 Saturday

3rd ♋

☽ v/c	**4:31 am**	1:31 am
☉ enters ♑	**8:14 pm**	5:14 pm
☽ enters ♌		10:48 pm

Sun enters Capricorn • Winter Solstice • Yule • 8:14 pm EST/5:14 pm PST

22 Sunday

3rd ♋

☽ enters ♌ **1:48 am**

November 2002

S	M	T	W	T	F	S
					1	2
3	4	5	6	7	8	9
10	11	12	13	14	15	16
17	18	19	20	21	22	23
24	25	26	27	28	29	30

December 2002

S	M	T	W	T	F	S
1	2	3	4	5	6	7
8	9	10	11	12	13	14
15	16	17	18	19	20	21
22	23	24	25	26	27	28
29	30	31				

January 2003

S	M	T	W	T	F	S
			1	2	3	4
5	6	7	8	9	10	11
12	13	14	15	16	17	18
19	20	21	22	23	24	25
26	27	28	29	30	31	

23 Monday

3rd ♌
☽ v/c **11:58 pm** 8:58 pm

24 Tuesday

3rd ♌
☽ enters ♍ **7:05 am** 4:05 am

Christmas Eve

25 Wednesday

3rd ♍
☽ v/c 11:10 pm

Christmas Day

26 Thursday

3rd ♍
☽ v/c **2:10 am**
☽ enters ♎ **10:53 am** 7:53 am
4th Quarter **7:31 pm** 4:31 pm

Kwanzaa begins

Eastern Standard Time in bold type
Pacific Standard Time in medium type

27 Friday

4th ♎

28 Saturday

4th ♎

☽ v/c	**7:15 am**	4:15 am
☽ enters ♏	**1:41 pm**	10:41 am

29 Sunday

4th ♏

30 Monday

4th ♏

☽ v/c	**12:04 pm**	9:04 am
☽ enters ♐	**4:01 pm**	1:01 pm

31 Tuesday

4th ♐

New Year's Eve

Eastern Standard Time in bold type
Pacific Standard Time in medium type

January 2003

	6 Monday	13 Monday	20 Monday	27 Monday
	7 Tuesday	14 Tuesday	21 Tuesday	28 Tuesday
1 Wednesday	8 Wednesday	15 Wednesday	22 Wednesday	29 Wednesday
2 Thursday	9 Thursday	16 Thursday	23 Thursday	30 Thursday
3 Friday	10 Friday	17 Friday	24 Friday	31 Friday
4 Saturday	11 Saturday	18 Saturday	25 Saturday	
5 Sunday	12 Sunday	19 Sunday	26 Sunday	

February 2003

	3 Monday	10 Monday	17 Monday	24 Monday
	4 Tuesday	11 Tuesday	18 Tuesday	25 Tuesday
	5 Wednesday	12 Wednesday	19 Wednesday	26 Wednesday
	6 Thursday	13 Thursday	20 Thursday	27 Thursday
	7 Friday	14 Friday	21 Friday	28 Friday
1 Saturday	8 Saturday	15 Saturday	22 Saturday	
2 Sunday	9 Sunday	16 Sunday	23 Sunday	

March 2003

	3 Monday	10 Monday	17 Monday	24 Monday / 31 Monday
	4 Tuesday	11 Tuesday	18 Tuesday	25 Tuesday
	5 Wednesday	12 Wednesday	19 Wednesday	26 Wednesday
	6 Thursday	13 Thursday	20 Thursday	27 Thursday
	7 Friday	14 Friday	21 Friday	28 Friday
1 Saturday	8 Saturday	15 Saturday	22 Saturday	29 Saturday
2 Sunday	9 Sunday	16 Sunday	23 Sunday	30 Sunday

April 2003

	7 Monday	14 Monday	21 Monday	28 Monday
1 Tuesday	8 Tuesday	15 Tuesday	22 Tuesday	29 Tuesday
2 Wednesday	9 Wednesday	16 Wednesday	23 Wednesday	30 Wednesday
3 Thursday	10 Thursday	17 Thursday	24 Thursday	
4 Friday	11 Friday	18 Friday	25 Friday	
5 Saturday	12 Saturday	19 Saturday	26 Saturday	
6 Sunday	13 Sunday	20 Sunday	27 Sunday	

May 2003

	5 Monday	12 Monday	19 Monday	26 Monday
	6 Tuesday	13 Tuesday	20 Tuesday	27 Tuesday
	7 Wednesday	14 Wednesday	21 Wednesday	28 Wednesday
1 Thursday	8 Thursday	15 Thursday	22 Thursday	29 Thursday
2 Friday	9 Friday	16 Friday	23 Friday	30 Friday
3 Saturday	10 Saturday	17 Saturday	24 Saturday	31 Saturday
4 Sunday	11 Sunday	18 Sunday	25 Sunday	

June 2003

	2 Monday	9 Monday	16 Monday	23 Monday / 30 Monday
	3 Tuesday	10 Tuesday	17 Tuesday	24 Tuesday
	4 Wednesday	11 Wednesday	18 Wednesday	25 Wednesday
	5 Thursday	12 Thursday	19 Thursday	26 Thursday
	6 Friday	13 Friday	20 Friday	27 Friday
	7 Saturday	14 Saturday	21 Saturday	28 Saturday
1 Sunday	8 Sunday	15 Sunday	22 Sunday	29 Sunday

July 2003

	7 Monday	14 Monday	21 Monday	28 Monday
1 Tuesday	8 Tuesday	15 Tuesday	22 Tuesday	29 Tuesday
2 Wednesday	9 Wednesday	16 Wednesday	23 Wednesday	30 Wednesday
3 Thursday	10 Thursday	17 Thursday	24 Thursday	31 Thursday
4 Friday	11 Friday	18 Friday	25 Friday	
5 Saturday	12 Saturday	19 Saturday	26 Saturday	
6 Sunday	13 Sunday	20 Sunday	27 Sunday	

August 2003

	4 Monday	11 Monday	18 Monday	25 Monday
	5 Tuesday	12 Tuesday	19 Tuesday	26 Tuesday
	6 Wednesday	13 Wednesday	20 Wednesday	27 Wednesday
	7 Thursday	14 Thursday	21 Thursday	28 Thursday
1 Friday	8 Friday	15 Friday	22 Friday	29 Friday
2 Saturday	9 Saturday	16 Saturday	23 Saturday	30 Saturday
3 Sunday	10 Sunday	17 Sunday	24 Sunday	31 Sunday

September 2003

1 Monday	8 Monday	15 Monday	22 Monday	29 Monday
2 Tuesday	9 Tuesday	16 Tuesday	23 Tuesday	30 Tuesday
3 Wednesday	10 Wednesday	17 Wednesday	24 Wednesday	
4 Thursday	11 Thursday	18 Thursday	25 Thursday	
5 Friday	12 Friday	19 Friday	26 Friday	
6 Saturday	13 Saturday	20 Saturday	27 Saturday	
7 Sunday	14 Sunday	21 Sunday	28 Sunday	

October 2003

	6 Monday	13 Monday	20 Monday	27 Monday
	7 Tuesday	14 Tuesday	21 Tuesday	28 Tuesday
1 Wednesday	8 Wednesday	15 Wednesday	22 Wednesday	29 Wednesday
2 Thursday	9 Thursday	16 Thursday	23 Thursday	30 Thursday
3 Friday	10 Friday	17 Friday	24 Friday	31 Friday
4 Saturday	11 Saturday	18 Saturday	25 Saturday	
5 Sunday	12 Sunday	19 Sunday	26 Sunday	

November 2003

	3 Monday	10 Monday	17 Monday	24 Monday
	4 Tuesday	11 Tuesday	18 Tuesday	25 Tuesday
	5 Wednesday	12 Wednesday	19 Wednesday	26 Wednesday
	6 Thursday	13 Thursday	20 Thursday	27 Thursday
	7 Friday	14 Friday	21 Friday	28 Friday
1 Saturday	8 Saturday	15 Saturday	22 Saturday	29 Saturday
2 Sunday	9 Sunday	16 Sunday	23 Sunday	30 Sunday

December 2003

1 Monday	8 Monday	15 Monday	22 Monday	29 Monday
2 Tuesday	9 Tuesday	16 Tuesday	23 Tuesday	30 Tuesday
3 Wednesday	10 Wednesday	17 Wednesday	24 Wednesday	31 Wednesday
4 Thursday	11 Thursday	18 Thursday	25 Thursday	
5 Friday	12 Friday	19 Friday	26 Friday	
6 Saturday	13 Saturday	20 Saturday	27 Saturday	
7 Sunday	14 Sunday	21 Sunday	28 Sunday	

JANUARY 2002

1 TUESDAY
♀ ⚺ ♆ **12:33 am**
☉ ☍ ♃ **12:53 am**
☽ ☍ ♆ **5:29 am** 2:29 am
☽ ⚻ ♀ **5:56 am** 2:56 am
☽ ⚹ ♄ **8:29 am** 5:29 am
☽ ☍ ⚳ **9:26 am** 6:26 am
☽ ⚺ ♃ **10:37 am** 7:37 am
☽ ⚻ ☉ **11:27 am** 8:27 am
☽ ⚻ ♀ **7:11 pm** 4:11 pm
☽ △ ♇ **7:40 pm** 4:40 pm
☽ ⚻ ♂ **10:22 pm** 7:22 pm

2 WEDNESDAY
☽ ☍ ♅ **6:16 am** 3:16 am
♀ ⚻ ♄ **10:17 am** 7:17 am
☿ △ ⚶ **2:00 pm** 11:00 am
♇ ⚺ ♀ **2:57 pm** 11:57 am
☽ □ ⚶ **3:49 pm** 12:49 pm
☽ ⚻ ☿ **4:02 pm** 1:02 pm
☽ ☌ ⚵ **6:13 pm** 3:13 pm
♃ ⚻ ⚳ **7:29 pm** 4:29 pm
☽ △ ⚷ **10:31 pm** 7:31 pm

3 THURSDAY
☽ ⚻ ♆ **6:59 am** 3:59 am
♀ ☍ ♃ **7:22 am** 4:22 am
☽ □ ♄ **9:41 am** 6:41 am
☽ ⚹ ♃ **11:34 am** 8:34 am
☽ △ ♀ **12:01 pm** 9:01 am
☽ ⚻ ⚳ **12:09 pm** 9:09 am
☿ ⚻ ⚵ **12:15 pm** 9:15 am
♀ ⚺ ⚳ **2:18 pm** 11:18 am
☽ △ ☉ **4:36 pm** 1:36 pm
☽ □ ♇ **9:15 pm** 6:15 pm
☽ △ ♀ **10:00 pm** 7:00 pm
☽ ☍ ♂ 11:30 pm

4 FRIDAY
☽ ☍ ♂ **2:30 am**
☽ ⚻ ♅ **8:02 am** 5:02 am
☽ △ ⚶ **5:18 pm** 2:18 pm
☽ ⚺ ⚵ **7:45 pm** 4:45 pm
☽ △ ☿ **11:35 pm** 8:35 pm
☽ □ ⚷ 9:48 pm

5 SATURDAY
☽ □ ⚷ **12:48 am**
☽ △ ♆ **9:14 am** 6:14 am
☽ △ ♄ **11:39 am** 8:39 am
☿ ⚺ ⚷ **12:23 pm** 9:23 am
☽ □ ♃ **1:20 pm** 10:20 am
☽ △ ⚳ **3:47 pm** 12:47 pm
☽ □ ♀ **7:11 pm** 4:11 pm
☽ □ ☉ **10:55 pm** 7:55 pm
☽ ⚹ ♇ **11:54 pm** 8:54 pm
☽ □ ♀ 10:58 pm

6 SUNDAY
☽ □ ♀ **1:58 am**
☽ ⚻ ♂ **7:59 am** 4:59 am
☽ △ ♅ **11:05 am** 8:05 am
☉ ⚺ ♇ **12:54 pm** 9:54 am
☽ ⚻ ⚶ **8:14 pm** 5:14 pm
☽ ⚹ ⚵ **10:41 pm** 7:41 pm

7 MONDAY
☽ ⚹ ⚷ **4:39 am** 1:39 am
☽ □ ☿ **8:52 am** 5:52 am
☽ □ ♆ **1:08 pm** 10:08 am
☽ ⚻ ♄ **3:18 pm** 12:18 pm
☽ △ ♃ **4:45 pm** 1:45 pm
☽ □ ⚳ **9:19 pm** 6:19 pm
♀ ⚺ ♇ 10:08 pm

8 TUESDAY
♀ ⚺ ♇ **1:08 am**
☽ ⚺ ♇ **4:22 am** 1:22 am
☽ ⚹ ♀ **4:41 am** 1:41 am
☽ ⚹ ☉ **7:29 am** 4:29 am
☽ ⚹ ♀ **7:55 am** 4:55 am
☽ △ ♂ **3:41 pm** 12:41 pm
☽ □ ♅ **4:03 pm** 1:03 pm
☉ ☌ ♀ **4:30 pm** 1:30 pm
♂ ⚺ ♅ **10:56 pm** 7:56 pm
☽ ☍ ⚶ 10:10 pm

9 WEDNESDAY
☽ ☍ ⚶ **1:10 am**
☽ □ ⚵ **3:28 am** 12:28 am
☿ ☌ ♆ **6:56 am** 3:56 am
☽ ⚺ ⚷ **10:33 am** 7:33 am
☽ ⚹ ♆ **7:05 pm** 4:05 pm
☽ ⚹ ☿ **8:17 pm** 5:17 pm
☽ ☍ ♄ **8:59 pm** 5:59 pm
☽ ⚻ ♃ **10:09 pm** 7:09 pm

10 THURSDAY
☿ △ ♄ **3:36 am** 12:36 am
☽ ⚹ ⚳ **5:04 am** 2:04 am
♀ ☌ ♀ **5:05 am** 2:05 am
☽ ☌ ♇ **10:54 am** 7:54 am
☿ ⚻ ♃ **3:19 pm** 12:19 pm
☽ ⚺ ♀ **4:07 pm** 1:07 pm
☽ ⚺ ♀ **4:57 pm** 1:57 pm
☽ ⚺ ☉ **6:40 pm** 3:40 pm
☽ ⚹ ♅ **11:07 pm** 8:07 pm
☽ □ ♂ 10:49 pm

11 FRIDAY
☽ □ ♂ **1:49 am**
☽ ⚻ ⚶ **8:14 am** 5:14 am
☽ △ ⚵ **10:11 am** 7:11 am
☽ ☌ ⚷ **6:34 pm** 3:34 pm

12 SATURDAY
☽ ⚺ ♆ **3:07 am** 12:07 am
☽ ⚻ ♄ **4:42 am** 1:42 am
☽ ☍ ♃ **5:34 am** 2:34 am
☽ ⚺ ☿ **9:29 am** 6:29 am
☽ ⚺ ⚳ **3:05 pm** 12:05 pm
☽ ⚺ ♇ **7:31 pm** 4:31 pm
☽ ☌ ♀ 11:34 pm

13 SUNDAY
☽ ☌ ♀ **2:34 am**
☉ ⚺ ♅ **5:47 am** 2:47 am
☽ ☌ ♀ **8:00 am** 5:00 am
☽ ⚺ ♅ **8:16 am** 5:16 am
☽ ☌ ☉ **8:29 am** 5:29 am
♀ ⚺ ♅ **10:41 am** 7:41 am
☽ ⚹ ♂ **2:24 pm** 11:24 am
☽ △ ⚶ **5:24 pm** 2:24 pm
☽ ⚻ ⚵ **6:49 pm** 3:49 pm

14 MONDAY
☽ ⚺ ⚷ **4:40 am** 1:40 am
☉ ☌ ♀ **6:32 am** 3:32 am
☽ ☌ ♆ **1:13 pm** 10:13 am
☽ △ ♄ **2:27 pm** 11:27 am
☽ ⚻ ♃ **2:58 pm** 11:58 am
☽ ☌ ☿ **11:43 pm** 8:43 pm

15 TUESDAY
☽ ☌ ⚳ **3:20 am** 12:20 am
☽ ⚹ ♇ **6:09 am** 3:09 am
☽ ⚺ ♀ **3:11 pm** 12:11 pm
♂ ⚹ ⚶ **5:15 pm** 2:15 pm
☽ ☌ ♅ **7:25 pm** 4:25 pm
☽ ⚺ ☉ 9:50 pm
☽ ⚺ ♀ 10:46 pm

16 WEDNESDAY
☽ ⚺ ☉ **12:50 am**
☽ ⚺ ♀ **1:46 am**
♂ ⚻ ⚵ **4:11 am** 1:11 am
☽ □ ⚶ **4:35 am** 1:35 am
☽ ☍ ⚵ **5:14 am** 2:14 am
☽ ⚺ ♂ **5:19 am** 2:19 am
☽ ⚹ ⚷ **4:42 pm** 1:42 pm
☽ ⚺ ♆ 10:09 pm
☽ □ ♄ 11:02 pm
☽ △ ♃ 11:09 pm

17 THURSDAY
☽ ⚺ ♆ **1:09 am**
☽ □ ♄ **2:02 am**
☽ △ ♃ **2:09 am**
♀ △ ⚶ **4:56 am** 1:56 am
♀ ⚻ ⚵ **7:05 am** 4:05 am
☽ ⚺ ☿ **1:57 pm** 10:57 am
☽ ⚺ ⚳ **5:26 pm** 2:26 pm
☽ □ ♇ **6:28 pm** 3:28 pm
♃ ⚺ ♄ **7:33 pm** 4:33 pm
⚵ □ ⚶ **7:58 pm** 4:58 pm
☉ ⚻ ⚵ **9:29 pm** 6:29 pm
☉ △ ⚶ **9:48 pm** 6:48 pm

18 FRIDAY
☽ ⚹ ♀ **5:31 am** 2:31 am
☽ ⚺ ♅ **8:06 am** 5:06 am
☽ ⚻ ⚵ **4:51 pm** 1:51 pm
☽ ⚹ ⚶ **5:13 pm** 2:13 pm
☽ ⚹ ☉ **7:00 pm** 4:00 pm
☽ ⚹ ♀ **9:27 pm** 6:27 pm
☽ ☌ ♂ **9:49 pm** 6:49 pm

19 SATURDAY
♇ ⚹ ⚳ **3:16 am** 12:16 am
♀ ⚹ ♂ **5:20 am** 2:20 am
☽ □ ⚷ **5:52 am** 2:52 am
☽ ⚹ ♆ **2:01 pm** 11:01 am
☽ □ ♃ **2:14 pm** 11:14 am
☽ ⚹ ♄ **2:31 pm** 11:31 am
☽ ⚹ ☿ 11:26 pm

20 SUNDAY
☽ ⚹ ☿ **2:26 am**
♃ ⚻ ♆ **5:58 am** 2:58 am
☽ △ ♇ **7:15 am** 4:15 am
☽ ⚹ ⚳ **8:07 am** 5:07 am
☽ □ ♀ **7:59 pm** 4:59 pm
☽ ⚹ ♅ **8:50 pm** 5:50 pm

21 MONDAY
☽ △ ⚵ **4:10 am** 1:10 am
☽ ⚺ ⚶ **5:43 am** 2:43 am
☽ □ ☉ **12:47 pm** 9:47 am
☽ ⚺ ♂ **1:51 pm** 10:51 am
☽ □ ♀ **4:35 pm** 1:35 pm
☽ △ ⚷ **6:20 pm** 3:20 pm
☽ ⚹ ♃ 10:23 pm
☽ □ ♆ 10:56 pm
☽ ⚺ ♄ 11:04 pm

22 TUESDAY
☽ ⚹ ♃ **1:23 am**
☽ □ ♆ **1:56 am**
☽ ⚺ ♄ **2:04 am**
♅ ⚺ ♀ **3:37 am** 12:37 am
♀ ⚺ ⚷ **10:56 am** 7:56 am
☽ □ ☿ **11:22 am** 8:22 am
☽ ⚻ ♇ **6:26 pm** 3:26 pm
☽ □ ⚳ **9:00 pm** 6:00 pm

23 WEDNESDAY
♄ △ ♆ **3:19 am** 12:19 am
☉ ⚹ ♂ **7:25 am** 4:25 am
☽ □ ♅ **7:29 am** 4:29 am
☽ △ ♀ **8:12 am** 5:12 am
☽ □ ⚵ **1:13 pm** 10:13 am
☽ ☌ ⚶ **3:53 pm** 12:53 pm
☽ ⚹ ♂ 11:42 pm

24 THURSDAY
☽ ⚹ ♂ **2:42 am**
☽ △ ☉ **3:10 am** 12:10 am
☽ ⚻ ⚷ **3:56 am** 12:56 am
☽ △ ♀ **7:57 am** 4:57 am
☽ ⚺ ♃ **9:38 am** 6:38 am
☽ ☌ ♄ **10:37 am** 7:37 am
☽ △ ♆ **10:47 am** 7:47 am
☉ ⚺ ⚷ **2:03 pm** 11:03 am
☽ △ ☿ **3:52 pm** 12:52 pm
♀ ⚻ ♃ 9:15 pm
☽ ☍ ♇ 11:08 pm

25 FRIDAY
♀ ⚻ ♃ **12:15 am**
☽ ☍ ♇ **2:08 am**
♂ □ ⚷ **4:09 am** 1:09 am
☽ △ ⚳ **6:03 am** 3:03 am
♀ △ ♄ **11:17 am** 8:17 am
♀ ☌ ♆ **2:16 pm** 11:16 am
☽ △ ♅ **2:23 pm** 11:23 am
☽ ⚻ ♀ **4:22 pm** 1:22 pm
☽ ⚹ ⚵ **6:37 pm** 3:37 pm
☽ ⚺ ⚶ **10:14 pm** 7:14 pm

26 SATURDAY
☿ ☌ ♀ **7:17 am** 4:17 am
☽ ☍ ⚷ **9:31 am** 6:31 am
☽ □ ♂ **10:55 am** 7:55 am
☽ ⚻ ☉ **12:35 pm** 9:35 am
☽ ☌ ♃ **2:03 pm** 11:03 am
☽ ⚺ ♄ **3:16 pm** 12:16 pm
☽ ⚻ ♆ **3:39 pm** 12:39 pm
☽ ⚻ ☿ **4:19 pm** 1:19 pm
☽ ⚻ ♀ **6:03 pm** 3:03 pm
☿ ☌ ♆ **11:39 pm** 8:39 pm

27 SUNDAY
☿ △ ♄ **4:26 am** 1:26 am
☽ ⚻ ♇ **5:55 am** 2:55 am
☉ ⚻ ♃ **7:17 am** 4:17 am
☽ ⚻ ⚳ **10:54 am** 7:54 am
☉ ☌ ☿ **1:55 pm** 10:55 am
☽ ⚻ ♅ **5:28 pm** 2:28 pm
♀ ⚻ ⚵ **7:52 pm** 4:52 pm
☿ ⚻ ♃ **8:18 pm** 5:18 pm
☽ ⚺ ⚵ **8:26 pm** 5:26 pm
☽ ☍ ♀ **8:28 pm** 5:28 pm
☽ ⚹ ⚶ 9:56 pm
☉ △ ♄ 10:12 pm

28 MONDAY
☽ ⚹ ⚶ **12:56 am**
☉ △ ♄ **1:12 am**
☿ ⚹ ♂ **4:52 am** 1:52 am
☉ ☌ ♆ **8:45 am** 5:45 am
☽ ⚻ ⚷ **11:37 am** 8:37 am
☽ ☍ ☿ **1:54 pm** 10:54 am
☽ △ ♂ **3:10 pm** 12:10 pm
☽ ⚺ ♃ **3:16 pm** 12:16 pm
☽ ⚹ ♄ **4:41 pm** 1:41 pm
♂ □ ♃ **4:58 pm** 1:58 pm
☽ ☍ ♆ **5:15 pm** 2:15 pm
☽ ☍ ☉ **5:50 pm** 2:50 pm
☽ ☍ ♀ **11:55 pm** 8:55 pm

29 TUESDAY
☽ △ ♇ **6:50 am** 3:50 am
☽ ☍ ⚳ **12:50 pm** 9:50 am
☿ ⚺ ⚷ **3:02 pm** 12:02 pm
☽ ☍ ♅ **6:04 pm** 3:04 pm
☽ ☌ ⚵ **8:00 pm** 5:00 pm
♂ ⚹ ♄ **9:35 pm** 6:35 pm
☽ ⚻ ♀ **10:01 pm** 7:01 pm
☽ □ ⚶ 10:28 pm

30 WEDNESDAY
☽ □ ⚶ **1:28 am**
☽ ⚻ ☿ **10:16 am** 7:16 am
☽ △ ⚷ **11:55 am** 8:55 am
♂ ⚹ ♆ **11:59 am** 8:59 am
☽ ⚹ ♃ **2:55 pm** 11:55 am
☽ □ ♄ **4:33 pm** 1:33 pm
☽ ⚻ ♆ **5:17 pm** 2:17 pm
☽ ⚻ ♂ **5:32 pm** 2:32 pm
☽ ⚻ ☉ **9:13 pm** 6:13 pm

31 THURSDAY
☽ ⚻ ♀ **4:10 am** 1:10 am
☽ □ ♇ **6:46 am** 3:46 am
☽ ⚻ ⚳ **2:01 pm** 11:01 am
☽ ⚻ ♅ **6:10 pm** 3:10 pm
☽ ⚺ ⚵ **7:10 pm** 4:10 pm
☽ △ ♀ **11:13 pm** 8:13 pm
☽ △ ⚶ 10:52 pm

Eastern Standard Time in bold type
Pacific Standard Time in medium type

JANUARY 2002

☽ Last Aspect				☽ Ingress			
day	EST / hr:mn / PST		asp	sign	day	EST / hr:mn / PST	
2	**6:16 am**	3:16 am	☍ ♅	♍	2	**6:34 pm**	3:34 pm
3		11:30 pm	☍ ♂	♎	4	**8:23 pm**	5:23 pm
4	**2:30 am**		☍ ♂	♎	4	**8:23 pm**	5:23 pm
6	**11:05 am**	8:05 am	△ ♅	♏	6	**11:41 pm**	8:41 pm
8	**4:03 pm**	1:03 pm	□ ♅	♐	9	**4:57 am**	1:57 am
10		10:49 pm	□ ♂	♑	11	**12:18 pm**	9:18 am
11	**1:49 am**		□ ♂	♑	11	**12:18 pm**	9:18 am
13	**2:24 pm**	11:24 am	⚹ ♂	♒	13	**9:41 pm**	6:41 pm
15	**7:25 pm**	4:25 pm	☌ ♅	♓	16	**9:00 am**	6:00 am
18	**9:27 pm**	6:27 pm	⚹ ♀	♈	18	**9:35 pm**	6:35 pm

☽ Last Aspect				☽ Ingress			
day	EST / hr:mn / PST		asp	sign	day	EST / hr:mn / PST	
20	**8:50 pm**	5:50 pm	⚹ ♅	♉	21	**9:47 am**	6:47 am
23	**7:29 am**	4:29 am	□ ♅	♊	23	**7:28 pm**	4:28 pm
25	**2:23 pm**	11:23 am	△ ♅	♋	25		10:17 pm
25	**2:23 pm**	11:23 am	△ ♅	♋	26	**1:17 am**	
26	**2:03 pm**	11:03 am	☌ ♃	♌	28	**3:31 am**	12:31 am
29	**6:04 pm**	3:04 pm	☍ ♅	♍	30	**3:40 am**	12:40 am
31	**6:46 am**	3:46 am	□ ♇	♎	2/1	**3:44 am**	12:44 am

☽ Phases & Eclipses			
phase	day	EST / hr:mn / PST	
4th Quarter	5	**10:55 pm**	7:55 pm
New Moon	13	**8:29 am**	5:29 am
2nd Quarter	21	**12:47 pm**	9:47 am
Full Moon	28	**5:50 pm**	2:50 pm

Planet Ingress				
		day	EST / hr:mn / PST	
☿	♒	3	**4:38 pm**	1:38 pm
♂	♈	18	**5:53 pm**	2:53 pm
♀	♒	18	**10:42 pm**	7:42 pm
☉	♒	19		10:02 pm
☉	♒	20	**1:02 am**	

Planetary Motion				
		day	EST / hr:mn / PST	
⚵	D	14	**3:45 pm**	12:45 pm
☿	℞	18	**3:52 pm**	12:52 pm

DATE		SID.TIME	SUN	MOON	NODE	MERCURY	VENUS	MARS	JUPITER	SATURN	URANUS	NEPTUNE	PLUTO	CERES	PALLAS	JUNO	VESTA	CHIRON
1	T	6:41:53	10 ♑ 23 01	1 ♌ 07	27 ♊ ℞ 10	25 ♑ 35	7 ♑ 10	16 ♓ 53	10 ♋ ℞ 40	9 ♊ ℞ 19	22 ♒ 28	7 ♒ 27	16 ♐ 02	9 ♒ 38	15 ♑ 24	29 ♌ ℞ 54	28 ♉ ℞ 30	2 ♑ 10
2	W	6:45:50	11 24 10	15 40	27 08	27 07	8 25	17 37	10 32	9 16	22 30	7 29	16 04	10 00	15 47	29 51	28 24	2 16
3	Th	6:49:46	12 25 18	0 ♍ 16	27 06	28 39	9 41	18 21	10 24	9 12	22 33	7 31	16 06	10 23	16 10	29 47	28 19	2 23
4	F	6:53:43	13 26 26	14 47	27 04	0 ♒ 09	10 56	19 05	10 16	9 08	22 36	7 33	16 09	10 46	16 33	29 42	28 14	2 29
5	Sa	6:57:39	14 27 35	29 10	27 03	1 37	12 12	19 48	10 08	9 05	22 39	7 35	16 11	11 09	16 56	29 37	28 09	2 36
6	Su	7:01:36	15 28 44	13 ♎ 21	27 D 02	3 04	13 27	20 32	9 59	9 01	22 42	7 37	16 13	11 31	17 19	29 32	28 05	2 42
7	M	7:05:32	16 29 53	27 18	27 03	4 28	14 43	21 16	9 51	8 58	22 45	7 39	16 15	11 54	17 42	29 26	28 01	2 48
8	T	7:09:29	17 31 02	11 ♏ 01	27 04	5 49	15 58	22 00	9 43	8 55	22 48	7 42	16 17	12 17	18 05	29 20	27 58	2 55
9	W	7:13:26	18 32 12	24 29	27 05	7 07	17 14	22 44	9 35	8 51	22 51	7 44	16 19	12 40	18 28	29 13	27 55	3 01
10	Th	7:17:22	19 33 21	7 ♐ 43	27 07	8 22	18 29	23 28	9 28	8 48	22 54	7 46	16 21	13 03	18 51	29 06	27 53	3 07
11	F	7:21:19	20 34 31	20 44	27 ℞ 08	9 31	19 45	24 12	9 20	8 45	22 57	7 48	16 23	13 26	19 14	28 58	27 51	3 13
12	Sa	7:25:15	21 35 40	3 ♑ 33	27 08	10 36	21 00	24 56	9 12	8 42	23 00	7 50	16 25	13 49	19 37	28 49	27 49	3 20
13	Su	7:29:12	22 36 49	16 11	27 06	11 34	22 16	25 39	9 04	8 39	23 03	7 52	16 27	14 12	20 00	28 41	27 48	3 26
14	M	7:33:08	23 37 58	28 37	27 04	12 25	23 31	26 23	8 57	8 37	23 06	7 55	16 29	14 35	20 23	28 31	27 D 47	3 32
15	T	7:37:05	24 39 07	10 ♒ 53	27 00	13 09	24 47	27 07	8 49	8 34	23 09	7 57	16 31	14 58	20 46	28 22	27 47	3 38
16	W	7:41:02	25 40 14	23 00	26 54	13 44	26 02	27 51	8 41	8 31	23 12	7 59	16 33	15 21	21 09	28 11	27 48	3 44
17	Th	7:44:58	26 41 22	4 ♓ 59	26 49	14 10	27 17	28 35	8 34	8 29	23 16	8 01	16 35	15 44	21 31	28 01	27 48	3 51
18	F	7:48:55	27 42 28	16 52	26 43	14 ℞ 25	28 33	29 18	8 27	8 27	23 19	8 04	16 36	16 08	21 54	27 50	27 49	3 57
19	Sa	7:52:51	28 43 34	28 44	26 39	14 29	29 48	0 ♈ 02	8 20	8 24	23 22	8 06	16 38	16 31	22 17	27 39	27 51	4 03
20	Su	7:56:48	29 44 39	10 ♈ 36	26 35	14 22	1 ♒ 04	0 46	8 12	8 22	23 25	8 08	16 40	16 54	22 39	27 27	27 53	4 09
21	M	8:00:44	0 ♒ 45 43	22 33	26 D 33	14 03	2 19	1 29	8 05	8 20	23 28	8 10	16 42	17 17	23 02	27 15	27 55	4 15
22	T	8:04:41	1 46 46	4 ♉ 41	26 33	13 32	3 35	2 13	7 59	8 18	23 32	8 13	16 44	17 41	23 25	27 02	27 58	4 21
23	W	8:08:37	2 47 48	17 03	26 34	12 51	4 50	2 57	7 52	8 16	23 35	8 15	16 45	18 04	23 47	26 49	28 02	4 27
24	Th	8:12:34	3 48 49	29 45	26 36	11 59	6 05	3 40	7 45	8 15	23 38	8 17	16 47	18 27	24 10	26 36	28 05	4 33
25	F	8:16:31	4 49 50	12 ♊ 51	26 37	10 59	7 21	4 24	7 39	8 13	23 42	8 20	16 49	18 51	24 32	26 23	28 09	4 38
26	Sa	8:20:27	5 50 49	26 23	26 ℞ 38	9 51	8 36	5 08	7 32	8 12	23 45	8 22	16 51	19 14	24 55	26 09	28 14	4 44
27	Su	8:24:24	6 51 47	10 ♋ 22	26 37	8 39	9 52	5 51	7 26	8 10	23 48	8 24	16 52	19 38	25 17	25 55	28 19	4 50
28	M	8:28:20	7 52 44	24 48	26 34	7 24	11 07	6 35	7 20	8 09	23 52	8 26	16 54	20 01	25 40	25 41	28 24	4 56
29	T	8:32:17	8 53 41	9 ♌ 34	26 30	6 08	12 22	7 18	7 14	8 08	23 55	8 29	16 56	20 25	26 02	25 27	28 30	5 02
30	W	8:36:13	9 54 36	24 34	26 23	4 54	13 38	8 02	7 08	8 07	23 58	8 31	16 57	20 48	26 24	25 12	28 36	5 07
31	Th	8:40:10	10 55 30	9 ♍ 38	26 16	3 44	14 53	8 45	7 03	8 06	24 02	8 33	16 59	21 11	26 47	24 57	28 42	5 13

EPHEMERIS CALCULATED FOR 12 MIDNIGHT GREENWICH MEAN TIME. ALL OTHER DATA AND FACING ASPECTARIAN PAGE IN **EASTERN STANDARD TIME (BOLD)** AND PACIFIC STANDARD TIME (REGULAR).

FEBRUARY 2002

1 FRIDAY

☽△⚶	**1:52 am**	
☽△☿	**7:13 am**	4:13 am
♀⚹♇	**11:55 am**	8:55 am
☽□⚷	**12:29 pm**	9:29 am
☽□♃	**2:57 pm**	11:57 am
☽△♄	**4:54 pm**	1:54 pm
☽△♆	**5:49 pm**	2:49 pm
☽☍♂	**8:29 pm**	5:29 pm
☽△☉		10:24 pm

2 SATURDAY

☽△☉	**1:24 am**	
☽⚹♇	**7:44 am**	4:44 am
☽△♀	**9:36 am**	6:36 am
☽△⚳	**4:35 pm**	1:35 pm
♅☍⚵	**6:14 pm**	3:14 pm
☽⚹⚵	**7:43 pm**	4:43 pm
☽△♅	**7:45 pm**	4:45 pm
☽□⚴		11:10 pm

3 SUNDAY

☽□⚴	**2:10 am**	
☽⚻⚶	**4:03 am**	1:03 am
☽□☿	**6:23 am**	3:23 am
☽⚹⚷	**3:08 pm**	12:08 pm
☽△♃	**5:06 pm**	2:06 pm
☽⚻♄	**7:26 pm**	4:26 pm
☽□♆	**8:34 pm**	5:34 pm
☽⚻♂		11:04 pm

4 MONDAY

☽⚻♂	**2:04 am**	
☽□☉	**8:33 am**	5:33 am
☽⚺♇	**11:16 am**	8:16 am
☽□♀	**6:25 pm**	3:25 pm
☽□⚳	**10:07 pm**	7:07 pm
☽□⚵	**10:53 pm**	7:53 pm
☽□♅		9:08 pm

5 TUESDAY

☽□♅	**12:08 am**	
☿△⚶	**3:34 am**	12:34 am
☽⚹⚴	**8:13 am**	5:13 am
☽⚹☿	**9:02 am**	6:02 am
☽☍⚶	**9:17 am**	6:17 am
⚳☍⚵	**2:21 pm**	11:21 am
☽⚺⚷	**8:51 pm**	5:51 pm
☉⚹♇	**9:45 pm**	6:45 pm
☽⚻♃	**10:15 pm**	7:15 pm
☿☌♀	**11:10 pm**	8:10 pm
☽☍♄		10:01 pm
☽⚹♆		11:25 pm

6 WEDNESDAY

☽☍♄	**1:01 am**	
☽⚹♆	**2:25 am**	
♀☍⚵	**10:56 am**	7:56 am
☽△♂	**11:16 am**	8:16 am
☽☌♇	**5:54 pm**	2:54 pm
☽⚹☉	**7:35 pm**	4:35 pm
♀☌⚳		11:32 pm

7 THURSDAY

♀☌⚳	**2:32 am**	
☽△⚵	**4:58 am**	1:58 am
☽⚹⚳	**7:01 am**	4:01 am
☽⚹♀	**7:21 am**	4:21 am
☽⚹♅	**7:38 am**	4:38 am
♀☌♅	**10:23 am**	7:23 am
☽⚺☿	**3:38 pm**	12:38 pm
☽⚺⚴	**5:34 pm**	2:34 pm
☽⚻⚶	**5:41 pm**	2:41 pm
⚴△⚶		9:28 pm

8 FRIDAY

⚴△⚶	**12:28 am**	
☽☌⚷	**5:33 am**	2:33 am
☽☍♃	**6:18 am**	3:18 am
♅☌⚳	**6:34 am**	3:34 am
☽⚻♄	**9:30 am**	6:30 am
☽⚺♆	**11:08 am**	8:08 am
☽□♂	**11:43 pm**	8:43 pm

9 SATURDAY

☽⚺♇	**3:13 am**	12:13 am
☽⚺☉	**10:00 am**	7:00 am
☽⚻⚵	**1:25 pm**	10:25 am
☽⚺♅	**5:39 pm**	2:39 pm
☽⚺⚳	**6:39 pm**	3:39 pm
☽⚺♀	**11:40 pm**	8:40 pm
☽☌☿		10:50 pm

10 SUNDAY

☽☌☿	**1:50 am**	
☽△⚶	**4:33 am**	1:33 am
☽☌⚴	**5:26 am**	2:26 am
☽⚺⚷	**4:26 pm**	1:26 pm
☽⚻♃	**4:28 pm**	1:28 pm
♃☍⚷	**7:33 pm**	4:33 pm
☉☍⚵	**7:39 pm**	4:39 pm
☽△♄	**8:06 pm**	5:06 pm
☽☌♆	**9:57 pm**	6:57 pm
☿⚺♀		10:12 pm

11 MONDAY

☿⚺♀	**1:12 am**	
♂△♇	**1:34 pm**	10:34 am
☽⚹♇	**2:23 pm**	11:23 am
☽⚹♂	**2:26 pm**	11:26 am
☽☍⚵	**11:28 pm**	8:28 pm
☽☌☉		11:41 pm

12 TUESDAY

☽☌☉	**2:41 am**	
☽☌♅	**5:21 am**	2:21 am
♀□⚶	**6:09 am**	3:09 am
☽☌⚳	**8:05 am**	5:05 am
☽⚺☿	**3:02 pm**	12:02 pm
☽□⚶	**5:05 pm**	2:05 pm
☽☌♀	**6:10 pm**	3:10 pm
☽⚺⚴	**6:56 pm**	3:56 pm

13 WEDNESDAY

☽△♃	**4:03 am**	1:03 am
♀⚺⚴	**4:10 am**	1:10 am
☽⚹⚷	**4:43 am**	1:43 am
☽□♄	**8:05 am**	5:05 am
☽⚺♆	**10:06 am**	7:06 am
☉☌♅	**12:06 pm**	9:06 am
☽□♇		11:44 pm

14 THURSDAY

☽□♇	**2:44 am**	
☽⚺♂	**6:33 am**	3:33 am
☽⚻⚵	**10:33 am**	7:33 am
☽⚺♅	**6:05 pm**	3:05 pm
☽⚺☉	**8:43 pm**	5:43 pm
☽⚺⚳	**10:38 pm**	7:38 pm

15 FRIDAY

☽⚹☿	**6:31 am**	3:31 am
☽⚹⚶	**6:37 am**	3:37 am
☿△⚶	**9:03 am**	6:03 am
☽⚹⚴	**9:24 am**	6:24 am
☽⚺♀	**1:54 pm**	10:54 am
☽□♃	**4:27 pm**	1:27 pm
☽□⚷	**5:47 pm**	2:47 pm
☽⚹♄	**8:49 pm**	5:49 pm
☽⚹♆	**10:58 pm**	7:58 pm

16 SATURDAY

☉☌⚳	**8:16 am**	5:16 am
♂△⚵	**8:34 am**	5:34 am
♀△♃	**1:18 pm**	10:18 am
☽△♇	**3:31 pm**	12:31 pm
☽△⚵	**9:59 pm**	6:59 pm
☽☌♂	**11:08 pm**	8:08 pm

17 SUNDAY

♀⚹⚷	**4:57 am**	1:57 am
☽⚹♅	**7:01 am**	4:01 am
☽⚹⚳	**1:17 pm**	10:17 am
☽⚹☉	**2:55 pm**	11:55 am
☽⚺⚶	**8:09 pm**	5:09 pm
☽□☿	**11:01 pm**	8:01 pm
☽□⚴	**11:43 pm**	8:43 pm

18 MONDAY

☽⚹♃	**4:36 am**	1:36 am
☽△⚷	**6:31 am**	3:31 am
♀□♄	**8:14 am**	5:14 am
☽⚺♄	**9:11 am**	6:11 am
☽⚹♀	**9:17 am**	6:17 am
☽□♆	**11:23 am**	8:23 am
☿☌⚴	**3:21 pm**	12:21 pm

19 TUESDAY

☽⚻♇	**3:25 am**	12:25 am
♀⚺♆	**6:09 am**	3:09 am
☽□⚵	**8:26 am**	5:26 am
☽⚺♂	**2:22 pm**	11:22 am
☽□♅	**6:34 pm**	3:34 pm
☽□⚳		11:14 pm

20 WEDNESDAY

☽□⚳	**2:14 am**	
☽□☉	**7:02 am**	4:02 am
☽☌⚶	**7:54 am**	4:54 am
☽△⚴	**11:57 am**	8:57 am
☽△☿	**2:06 pm**	11:06 am
☽⚺♃	**2:46 pm**	11:46 am
☽⚻⚷	**5:05 pm**	2:05 pm
☽☌♄	**7:22 pm**	4:22 pm
☉□⚶	**8:37 pm**	5:37 pm
☽△♆	**9:31 pm**	6:31 pm
☿⚻♃	**10:34 pm**	7:34 pm
☽□♀		10:39 pm

21 THURSDAY

☽□♀	**1:39 am**	
☽☍♇	**12:32 pm**	9:32 am
☽⚹⚵	**4:10 pm**	1:10 pm
☽⚹♂		10:55 pm
☽△♅		11:53 pm

22 FRIDAY

☽⚹♂	**1:55 am**	
☽△♅	**2:53 am**	
☿⚺⚷	**6:38 am**	3:38 am
☽△⚳	**11:26 am**	8:26 am
☽⚺⚶	**3:58 pm**	12:58 pm
☽△☉	**6:39 pm**	3:39 pm
☽⚻⚴	**8:15 pm**	5:15 pm
☽☌♃	**9:19 pm**	6:19 pm
♂⚹♅	**9:28 pm**	6:28 pm
☽☍⚷	**11:51 pm**	8:51 pm
☽⚻☿		10:11 pm
☽⚺♄		10:47 pm

23 SATURDAY

☽⚻☿	**1:11 am**	
☽⚺♄	**1:47 am**	
☽⚻♆	**3:48 am**	12:48 am
☿△♄	**8:52 am**	5:52 am
☽△♀	**12:47 pm**	9:47 am
☽⚻♇	**5:37 pm**	2:37 pm
☽⚺⚵	**8:06 pm**	5:06 pm
☉⚺⚴		11:55 pm

24 SUNDAY

☉⚺⚴	**2:55 am**	
☉△♃	**6:15 am**	3:15 am
☽⚻♅	**7:03 am**	4:03 am
☽□♂	**8:39 am**	5:39 am
☿☌♆	**10:59 am**	7:59 am
♃⚻⚴	**12:21 pm**	9:21 am
☽⚻⚳	**4:11 pm**	1:11 pm
☽⚹⚶	**7:47 pm**	4:47 pm
☽⚺♃	**11:53 pm**	8:53 pm
☽☍⚴		9:10 pm
☽⚻☉		10:11 pm
☽⚻⚷		11:33 pm

25 MONDAY

☽☍⚴	**12:10 am**	
☽⚻☉	**1:11 am**	
☽⚻⚷	**2:33 am**	
☽⚹♄	**4:12 am**	1:12 am
☽☍♆	**6:06 am**	3:06 am
☽☍☿	**7:39 am**	4:39 am
☽⚻⚴	**6:53 pm**	3:53 pm
☽△♇	**6:57 pm**	3:57 pm
♀□♇	**7:46 pm**	4:46 pm
☽☌⚵	**8:35 pm**	5:35 pm
☉⚹⚷	**10:32 pm**	7:32 pm

26 TUESDAY

☽☍♅	**7:47 am**	4:47 am
☽△♂	**11:30 am**	8:30 am
♀⚻⚵	**12:37 pm**	9:37 am
☽☍⚳	**5:34 pm**	2:34 pm
☽□⚶	**8:31 pm**	5:31 pm
☉□♄	**10:54 pm**	7:54 pm
☽⚹♃	**11:38 pm**	8:38 pm
☽⚻⚴		10:03 pm
☽△⚷		11:27 pm

27 WEDNESDAY

☽⚻⚴	**1:03 am**	
☽△⚷	**2:27 am**	
☽□♄	**3:56 am**	12:56 am
☽☍☉	**4:17 am**	1:17 am
☽⚻♆	**5:47 am**	2:47 am
☽⚻☿	**11:10 am**	8:10 am
☽□♇	**6:13 pm**	3:13 pm
☽⚺⚵	**7:09 pm**	4:09 pm
☽☍♀	**10:17 pm**	7:17 pm

28 THURSDAY

☉⚺♆	**3:56 am**	12:56 am
☽⚻♅	**6:59 am**	3:59 am
☽⚻♂	**12:47 pm**	9:47 am
☽⚻⚳	**5:48 pm**	2:48 pm
☽△⚶	**8:18 pm**	5:18 pm
☽□♃	**10:39 pm**	7:39 pm
☽△⚴		10:10 pm
☽□⚷		10:43 pm

Eastern Standard Time in bold type
Pacific Standard Time in medium type

FEBRUARY 2002

☽ Last Aspect day	EST / hr:mn / PST		asp	☽ Ingress sign	day	EST / hr:mn / PST	
1/31	**6:46 am**	3:46 am	□ ♇	♎	1	**3:44 am**	12:44 am
2	**7:45 pm**	4:45 pm	△ ♅	♏	3	**5:35 am**	2:35 am
5	**9:02 am**	6:02 am	⚹ ☿	♐	5	**10:21 am**	7:21 am
7	**7:38 am**	4:38 am	⚹ ♅	♑	7	**6:08 pm**	3:08 pm
9		10:50 pm	☌ ☿	♒	10	**4:15 am**	1:15 am
10	**1:50 am**		☌ ☿	♒	10	**4:15 am**	1:15 am
12	**5:21 am**	2:21 am	☌ ♅	♓	12	**3:53 pm**	12:53 pm
13		11:44 pm	□ ♇	♈	15	**4:26 am**	1:26 am
14	**2:44 am**		□ ♇	♈	15	**4:26 am**	1:26 am
17	**2:55 pm**	11:55 am	⚹ ☉	♉	17	**4:58 pm**	1:58 pm
19	**6:34 pm**	3:34 pm	□ ♅	♊	20	**3:50 am**	12:50 am
21		11:53 pm	△ ♅	♋	22	**11:16 am**	8:16 am
22	**2:53 am**		△ ♅	♋	22	**11:16 am**	8:16 am
24	**8:39 am**	5:39 am	□ ♂	♌	24	**2:36 pm**	11:36 am
26	**11:30 am**	8:30 am	△ ♂	♍	26	**2:47 pm**	11:47 am
27	**10:17 pm**	7:17 pm	☍ ♀	♎	28	**1:47 pm**	10:47 am

☽ Phases & Eclipses phase	day	EST / hr:mn / PST	
4th Quarter	4	**8:33 am**	5:33 am
New Moon	11		11:41 pm
New Moon	12	**2:41 am**	
2nd Quarter	20	**7:02 am**	4:02 am
Full Moon	27	**4:17 am**	1:17 am

Planet Ingress		day	EST / hr:mn / PST	
☿	♑	3	**11:19 pm**	8:19 pm
⚴	♒	8	**1:39 pm**	10:39 am
⚶	♊	9	**6:19 am**	3:19 am
♀	♓	11	**8:18 pm**	5:18 pm
☿	♒	13	**12:20 pm**	9:20 am
☉	♓	18	**3:13 pm**	12:13 pm
⚳	♓	22	**5:27 am**	2:27 am

Planetary Motion		day	EST / hr:mn / PST	
♄	D	7	**8:32 pm**	5:32 pm
☿	D	8	**12:28 pm**	9:28 am

DATE		SID.TIME	SUN	MOON	NODE	MERCURY	VENUS	MARS	JUPITER	SATURN	URANUS	NEPTUNE	PLUTO	CERES	PALLAS	JUNO	VESTA	CHIRON
1	F	8:44:06	11 ♒ 56 24	24 ♍ 36	26 ♊ ℞ 09	2 ♒ ℞ 39	16 ♒ 08	9 ♈ 29	6 ♋ ℞ 57	8 ♊ ℞ 05	24 ♒ 05	8 ♒ 35	17 ♐ 00	21 ♒ 35	27 ♑ 09	24 ♌ ℞ 42	28 ♉ 49	5 ♑ 18
2	Sa	8:48:03	12 57 16	9 ♎ 21	26 03	1 40	17 23	10 12	6 52	8 04	24 09	8 38	17 02	21 58	27 31	24 27	28 56	5 24
3	Su	8:52:00	13 58 08	23 46	26 00	0 50	18 39	10 55	6 47	8 03	24 12	8 40	17 03	22 22	27 53	24 12	29 03	5 29
4	M	8:55:56	14 58 59	7 ♏ 48	25 D 58	0 07	19 54	11 39	6 42	8 03	24 16	8 42	17 05	22 45	28 15	23 56	29 11	5 35
5	T	8:59:53	15 59 49	21 27	25 58	29 ♑ 32	21 09	12 22	6 37	8 02	24 19	8 45	17 06	23 09	28 37	23 41	29 19	5 40
6	W	9:03:49	17 00 39	4 ♐ 45	25 58	29 07	22 25	13 05	6 32	8 02	24 22	8 47	17 07	23 33	28 59	23 25	29 28	5 46
7	Th	9:07:46	18 01 27	17 44	26 ℞ 00	28 49	23 40	13 49	6 28	8 02	24 26	8 49	17 09	23 56	29 21	23 09	29 37	5 51
8	F	9:11:42	19 02 15	0 ♑ 27	26 00	28 D 40	24 55	14 32	6 24	8 D 02	24 29	8 51	17 10	24 20	29 43	22 54	29 46	5 56
9	Sa	9:15:39	20 03 01	12 57	25 58	28 38	26 10	15 15	6 19	8 02	24 33	8 54	17 11	24 43	0 ♒ 05	22 38	29 55	6 01
10	Su	9:19:35	21 03 47	25 17	25 54	28 44	27 26	15 58	6 15	8 02	24 36	8 56	17 13	25 07	0 27	22 22	0 ♊ 05	6 06
11	M	9:23:32	22 04 31	7 ♒ 29	25 47	28 56	28 41	16 42	6 12	8 02	24 40	8 58	17 14	25 30	0 48	22 07	0 15	6 12
12	T	9:27:29	23 05 14	19 34	25 38	29 15	29 56	17 25	6 08	8 03	24 43	9 00	17 15	25 54	1 10	21 51	0 26	6 17
13	W	9:31:25	24 05 55	1 ♓ 33	25 27	29 39	1 ♓ 11	18 08	6 05	8 03	24 47	9 03	17 16	26 18	1 32	21 36	0 37	6 22
14	Th	9:35:22	25 06 36	13 28	25 15	0 ♒ 09	2 26	18 51	6 02	8 04	24 50	9 05	17 18	26 41	1 53	21 20	0 48	6 26
15	F	9:39:18	26 07 14	25 21	25 03	0 44	3 41	19 34	5 59	8 05	24 54	9 07	17 19	27 05	2 15	21 05	0 59	6 31
16	Sa	9:43:15	27 07 51	7 ♈ 12	24 52	1 23	4 57	20 17	5 56	8 05	24 57	9 09	17 20	27 28	2 36	20 50	1 11	6 36
17	Su	9:47:11	28 08 26	19 04	24 43	2 06	6 12	21 00	5 53	8 06	25 01	9 11	17 21	27 52	2 57	20 35	1 23	6 41
18	M	9:51:08	29 09 00	1 ♉ 01	24 36	2 54	7 27	21 43	5 51	8 07	25 04	9 13	17 22	28 15	3 19	20 20	1 35	6 46
19	T	9:55:04	0 ♓ 09 32	13 06	24 32	3 45	8 42	22 26	5 49	8 09	25 08	9 16	17 23	28 39	3 40	20 06	1 48	6 50
20	W	9:59:01	1 10 02	25 24	24 D 31	4 39	9 57	23 09	5 47	8 10	25 11	9 18	17 24	29 03	4 01	19 51	2 01	6 55
21	Th	10:02:57	2 10 30	8 ♊ 00	24 31	5 36	11 12	23 52	5 45	8 11	25 14	9 20	17 25	29 26	4 22	19 37	2 14	6 59
22	F	10:06:54	3 10 56	20 58	24 ℞ 31	6 36	12 27	24 34	5 43	8 13	25 18	9 22	17 26	29 50	4 43	19 23	2 27	7 04
23	Sa	10:10:51	4 11 21	4 ♋ 22	24 31	7 38	13 42	25 17	5 42	8 15	25 21	9 24	17 27	0 ♓ 13	5 04	19 10	2 41	7 08
24	Su	10:14:47	5 11 44	18 17	24 29	8 43	14 57	26 00	5 41	8 16	25 25	9 26	17 27	0 37	5 25	18 56	2 55	7 12
25	M	10:18:44	6 12 04	2 ♌ 40	24 24	9 50	16 12	26 43	5 40	8 18	25 28	9 28	17 28	1 00	5 46	18 43	3 09	7 17
26	T	10:22:40	7 12 23	17 31	24 17	11 00	17 27	27 25	5 39	8 20	25 32	9 30	17 29	1 24	6 06	18 31	3 23	7 21
27	W	10:26:37	8 12 40	2 ♍ 41	24 07	12 11	18 42	28 08	5 38	8 22	25 35	9 33	17 30	1 47	6 27	18 18	3 38	7 25
28	Th	10:30:33	9 12 55	18 01	23 56	13 24	19 56	28 51	5 38	8 24	25 38	9 35	17 31	2 11	6 47	18 06	3 53	7 29

EPHEMERIS CALCULATED FOR 12 MIDNIGHT GREENWICH MEAN TIME. ALL OTHER DATA AND FACING ASPECTARIAN PAGE IN **EASTERN STANDARD TIME (BOLD)** AND PACIFIC STANDARD TIME (REGULAR).

MARCH 2002

1 FRIDAY

☽ △ ♀	**1:10 am**	
☽ □ ⚷	**1:43 am**	
☽ △ ♄	**3:08 am**	12:08 am
☽ △ ♆	**4:59 am**	1:59 am
☽ ⚻ ☉	**6:42 am**	3:42 am
☽ △ ☿	**2:40 pm**	11:40 am
☽ ⚹ ♇	**5:36 pm**	2:36 pm
☽ ⚹ ⚵	**5:56 pm**	2:56 pm
☽ ⚻ ♀		11:07 pm

2 SATURDAY

☽ ⚻ ♀	**2:07 am**	
☽ △ ♅	**6:57 am**	3:57 am
⚷ ⚺ ♀	**7:14 am**	4:14 am
☽ ☍ ♂	**3:16 pm**	12:16 pm
♇ △ ⚵	**7:10 pm**	4:10 pm
☽ △ ⚳	**7:24 pm**	4:24 pm
☽ ⚻ ⚶	**9:34 pm**	6:34 pm
☽ △ ♃	**11:10 pm**	8:10 pm
☿ ☍ ⚵	**11:59 pm**	8:59 pm
☿ ⚹ ♇		9:40 pm
☽ ⚹ ⚷		11:37 pm
☽ □ ♀		11:59 pm

3 SUNDAY

☿ ⚹ ♇	**12:40 am**	
☽ ⚹ ⚷	**2:37 am**	
☽ □ ♀	**2:59 am**	
☽ ⚻ ♄	**4:01 am**	1:01 am
☽ □ ♆	**5:57 am**	2:57 am
☽ △ ☉	**11:23 am**	8:23 am
☽ □ ⚵	**6:58 pm**	3:58 pm
☽ ⚺ ♇	**7:17 pm**	4:17 pm
☽ □ ☿	**9:13 pm**	6:13 pm

4 MONDAY

☽ △ ♀	**9:19 am**	6:19 am
☽ □ ♅	**9:43 am**	6:43 am
♀ ⚺ ♅	**1:52 pm**	10:52 am
☽ ⚻ ♂	**9:15 pm**	6:15 pm
☽ □ ⚳		9:24 pm
☽ ☍ ⚶		11:14 pm
☽ ⚻ ♃		11:57 pm

5 TUESDAY

☽ □ ⚳	**12:24 am**	
☽ ☍ ⚶	**2:14 am**	
☽ ⚻ ♃	**2:57 am**	
♄ △ ♀	**5:49 am**	2:49 am
☽ ⚺ ⚷	**6:52 am**	3:52 am
☽ ☍ ♄	**8:19 am**	5:19 am
☽ ⚹ ♀	**8:22 am**	5:22 am
☽ ⚹ ♆	**10:21 am**	7:21 am
☽ □ ☉	**8:25 pm**	5:25 pm
☽ △ ⚵	**11:33 pm**	8:33 pm
☽ ☌ ♇		9:36 pm

6 WEDNESDAY

☽ ☌ ♇	**12:36 am**	
☽ ⚹ ☿	**9:00 am**	6:00 am
♃ ⚺ ⚶	**3:00 pm**	12:00 pm
☽ ⚹ ♅	**4:19 pm**	1:19 pm
☽ □ ♀	**9:31 pm**	6:31 pm

7 THURSDAY

☽ △ ♂	**7:43 am**	4:43 am
☉ ⚻ ⚵	**8:27 am**	5:27 am
☽ ⚹ ⚳	**9:35 am**	6:35 am
☽ ☍ ♃	**10:36 am**	7:36 am
☽ ⚻ ⚶	**11:00 am**	8:00 am
☽ ☌ ⚷	**2:58 pm**	11:58 am
☽ ⚻ ♄	**4:28 pm**	1:28 pm
☽ ⚺ ♀	**5:51 pm**	2:51 pm
☽ ⚺ ♆	**6:34 pm**	3:34 pm

8 FRIDAY

☉ □ ♇	**3:29 am**	12:29 am
☽ ⚻ ⚵	**7:45 am**	4:45 am
☽ ⚺ ♇	**9:34 am**	6:34 am
☽ ⚹ ☉	**10:06 am**	7:06 am
♃ △ ⚳	**8:09 pm**	5:09 pm
♆ ☌ ♀		9:02 pm
☽ ⚺ ☿		11:02 pm
☽ ⚺ ♅		11:21 pm

9 SATURDAY

♆ ☌ ♀	**12:02 am**	
☽ ⚺ ☿	**2:02 am**	
☽ ⚺ ♅	**2:21 am**	
☿ ☌ ♅	**4:52 am**	1:52 am
♂ ⚹ ♃	**12:46 pm**	9:46 am
☽ ⚹ ♀	**2:12 pm**	11:12 am
☽ ⚻ ♃	**9:19 pm**	6:19 pm
☽ □ ♂	**9:50 pm**	6:50 pm
☽ ⚺ ⚳	**10:06 pm**	7:06 pm
☽ △ ⚶	**11:02 pm**	8:02 pm
☽ ⚺ ⚷		11:01 pm

10 SUNDAY

☽ ⚺ ⚷	**2:01 am**	
☽ △ ♄	**3:34 am**	12:34 am
☽ ☌ ♆	**5:38 am**	2:38 am
☽ ☌ ♀	**6:23 am**	3:23 am
♂ ⚹ ⚳	**7:56 am**	4:56 am
☽ ☍ ⚵	**6:27 pm**	3:27 pm
☽ ⚹ ♇	**9:01 pm**	6:01 pm
☽ ⚺ ☉		11:57 pm

11 MONDAY

☽ ⚺ ☉	**2:57 am**	
♂ ⚺ ⚶	**7:57 am**	4:57 am
☽ ☌ ♅	**2:28 pm**	11:28 am
☽ ☌ ☿	**10:26 pm**	7:26 pm

12 TUESDAY

☽ ⚺ ♀	**9:18 am**	6:18 am
☽ △ ♃	**9:41 am**	6:41 am
☽ ☌ ⚳	**12:21 pm**	9:21 am
☽ □ ⚶	**12:46 pm**	9:46 am
♀ □ ♃	**1:05 pm**	10:05 am
☽ ⚹ ♂	**1:50 pm**	10:50 am
☽ ⚹ ⚷	**2:33 pm**	11:33 am
☽ □ ♄	**4:09 pm**	1:09 pm
☽ ⚺ ♆	**6:07 pm**	3:07 pm
☽ ⚺ ♀	**8:25 pm**	5:25 pm

13 WEDNESDAY

♂ △ ⚷	**3:04 am**	12:04 am
☽ ⚻ ⚵	**6:19 am**	3:19 am
☽ □ ♇	**9:31 am**	6:31 am
☽ ☌ ☉	**9:03 pm**	6:03 pm
♀ ⚺ ⚳		11:20 pm

14 THURSDAY

♀ ⚺ ⚳	**2:20 am**	
☽ ⚺ ♅	**3:21 am**	12:21 am
♀ ⚹ ⚶	**3:48 am**	12:48 am
♂ ⚺ ♄	**8:40 am**	5:40 am
♀ □ ⚷	**1:28 pm**	10:28 am
⚳ □ ⚶	**6:14 pm**	3:14 pm
☽ ⚺ ☿	**8:11 pm**	5:11 pm
☽ □ ♃	**10:32 pm**	7:32 pm
☽ ⚹ ⚶		11:59 pm

15 FRIDAY

☽ ⚹ ⚶	**2:59 am**	
☽ ⚺ ⚳	**3:03 am**	12:03 am
☽ □ ⚷	**3:28 am**	12:28 am
☽ ☌ ♀	**5:02 am**	2:02 am
☽ ⚹ ♄	**5:07 am**	2:07 am
♀ ⚹ ♄	**5:53 am**	2:53 am
☽ ⚺ ♂	**6:17 am**	3:17 am
☽ ⚹ ♆	**6:55 am**	3:55 am
☽ ⚹ ♀	**10:44 am**	7:44 am
☿ △ ♃	**2:13 pm**	11:13 am
♂ □ ♆	**5:23 pm**	2:23 pm
⚷ ⚹ ⚳	**5:30 pm**	2:30 pm
☽ △ ⚵	**6:27 pm**	3:27 pm
☽ △ ♇	**10:09 pm**	7:09 pm
♀ ⚹ ♆	**11:26 pm**	8:26 pm
⚷ ⚻ ⚶		10:06 pm

16 SATURDAY

⚷ ⚻ ⚶	**1:06 am**	
♀ ⚺ ♂	**6:57 am**	3:57 am
☽ ⚺ ☉	**3:06 pm**	12:06 pm
☽ ⚹ ♅	**4:08 pm**	1:08 pm

17 SUNDAY

☿ ⚹ ⚷	**3:25 am**	12:25 am
☉ ⚺ ♅	**3:56 am**	12:56 am
☿ □ ⚶	**8:37 am**	5:37 am
☽ ⚹ ♃	**11:06 am**	8:06 am
☿ ☌ ⚳	**12:41 pm**	9:41 am
☽ △ ⚷	**3:56 pm**	12:56 pm
☿ □ ♄	**4:29 pm**	1:29 pm
☽ ⚺ ⚶	**4:48 pm**	1:48 pm
☽ ⚹ ⚳	**5:18 pm**	2:18 pm
☽ ⚺ ♄	**5:40 pm**	2:40 pm
☽ ⚹ ☿	**5:51 pm**	2:51 pm
☽ □ ♆	**7:15 pm**	4:15 pm
☽ ☌ ♂	**10:12 pm**	7:12 pm
☽ ⚺ ♀		9:09 pm
☽ □ ♀		9:29 pm

18 MONDAY

☽ ⚺ ♀	**12:09 am**	
☽ □ ♀	**12:29 am**	
☿ ⚺ ♆	**4:20 am**	1:20 am
♀ ⚹ ♀	**4:23 am**	1:23 am
☽ □ ⚵	**6:04 am**	3:04 am
♄ □ ⚳	**7:24 am**	4:24 am
☽ ⚻ ♇	**10:05 am**	7:05 am

19 TUESDAY

☽ □ ♅	**3:53 am**	12:53 am
☽ ⚹ ☉	**7:53 am**	4:53 am
♄ ☌ ⚶	**11:17 am**	8:17 am
☿ ⚹ ♂	**9:12 pm**	6:12 pm
☽ ⚺ ♃	**10:17 pm**	7:17 pm
☽ ⚻ ⚷		11:53 pm

20 WEDNESDAY

☽ ⚻ ⚷	**2:53 am**	
☿ ⚺ ♀	**3:35 am**	12:35 am
☽ ☌ ♄	**4:40 am**	1:40 am
☽ ☌ ⚶	**5:01 am**	2:01 am
☽ □ ⚳	**5:51 am**	2:51 am
☽ △ ♆	**6:00 am**	3:00 am
♀ △ ⚵	**7:27 am**	4:27 am
♆ ⚺ ⚳	**11:29 am**	8:29 am
☽ ⚺ ♂	**12:08 pm**	9:08 am
☽ △ ♀	**12:23 pm**	9:23 am
☽ □ ☿	**1:29 pm**	10:29 am
☽ ⚹ ⚵	**3:58 pm**	12:58 pm
☽ ⚹ ♀	**4:56 pm**	1:56 pm
♂ □ ♀	**7:50 pm**	4:50 pm
☽ ☍ ♇	**8:05 pm**	5:05 pm

21 THURSDAY

☿ ⚻ ⚵	**7:25 am**	4:25 am
☽ △ ♅	**1:14 pm**	10:14 am
☽ □ ☉	**9:28 pm**	6:28 pm
♆ △ ⚶	**11:19 pm**	8:19 pm
♀ △ ♇		10:22 pm

22 FRIDAY

♀ △ ♇	**1:22 am**	
☽ ☌ ♃	**6:37 am**	3:37 am
☽ ☍ ⚷	**10:51 am**	7:51 am
☽ ⚺ ♄	**12:40 pm**	9:40 am
☽ ⚻ ♆	**1:43 pm**	10:43 am
☽ ⚺ ⚶	**2:03 pm**	11:03 am
☿ □ ♇	**2:11 pm**	11:11 am
☽ △ ⚳	**3:06 pm**	12:06 pm
☽ ⚻ ♀	**8:51 pm**	5:51 pm
☽ ⚹ ♂	**10:21 pm**	7:21 pm
☽ ⚺ ⚵	**10:45 pm**	7:45 pm
☽ ⚻ ♇		11:47 pm

23 SATURDAY

☽ ⚻ ♇	**2:47 am**	
☽ △ ☿	**4:38 am**	1:38 am
☽ □ ♀	**5:19 am**	2:19 am
♂ □ ⚵	**5:57 am**	2:57 am
☽ ⚻ ♅	**6:57 pm**	3:57 pm
☿ ⚺ ♀	**8:52 pm**	5:52 pm

24 SUNDAY

☽ △ ☉	**6:24 am**	3:24 am
☽ ⚺ ♃	**11:10 am**	8:10 am
☽ ⚻ ⚷	**2:58 pm**	11:58 am
☽ ⚹ ♄	**4:48 pm**	1:48 pm
☽ ☍ ♆	**5:37 pm**	2:37 pm
☽ ⚹ ⚶	**7:01 pm**	4:01 pm
☽ ⚻ ⚳	**8:12 pm**	5:12 pm
☽ ☍ ♀		10:15 pm
☽ ☌ ⚵		10:49 pm

25 MONDAY

☽ ☍ ♀	**1:15 am**	
☽ ☌ ⚵	**1:49 am**	
☽ □ ♂	**4:06 am**	1:06 am
☽ △ ♇	**5:40 am**	2:40 am
☽ △ ♀	**12:41 pm**	9:41 am
☽ ⚻ ☿	**2:23 pm**	11:23 am
☽ ☍ ♅	**8:57 pm**	5:57 pm

26 TUESDAY

♀ ☍ ⚵	**4:09 am**	1:09 am
☽ ⚻ ☉	**11:01 am**	8:01 am
☽ ⚹ ♃	**12:18 pm**	9:18 am
♂ ⚻ ♇	**12:49 pm**	9:49 am
☽ △ ⚷	**3:46 pm**	12:46 pm
☽ □ ♄	**5:39 pm**	2:39 pm
☽ ⚻ ♆	**6:15 pm**	3:15 pm
☽ □ ⚶	**8:35 pm**	5:35 pm
☽ ☍ ⚳	**9:52 pm**	6:52 pm
☽ ⚺ ⚵		10:57 pm
☽ ⚻ ♀		11:24 pm

27 WEDNESDAY

☽ ⚺ ⚵	**1:57 am**	
☽ ⚻ ♀	**2:24 am**	
☽ □ ♇	**5:39 am**	2:39 am
☽ △ ♂	**6:28 am**	3:28 am
☉ □ ♃	**8:24 am**	5:24 am
☽ ⚻ ♀	**4:37 pm**	1:37 pm
☽ ☍ ☿	**8:31 pm**	5:31 pm
☽ ⚻ ♅	**8:33 pm**	5:33 pm
☿ ⚺ ♅	**8:51 pm**	5:51 pm

28 THURSDAY

☽ □ ♃	**11:41 am**	8:41 am
☽ ☍ ☉	**1:25 pm**	10:25 am
☽ □ ⚷	**2:57 pm**	11:57 am
☽ △ ♄	**4:58 pm**	1:58 pm
☽ △ ♆	**5:23 pm**	2:23 pm
☽ △ ⚶	**8:41 pm**	5:41 pm
☽ ⚻ ⚳	**10:07 pm**	7:07 pm
☽ ⚹ ⚵		9:59 pm
☽ △ ♀		11:21 pm

29 FRIDAY

☽ ⚹ ⚵	**12:59 am**	
☽ △ ♀	**2:21 am**	
☽ ⚹ ♇	**4:41 am**	1:41 am
☽ ⚻ ♂	**7:45 am**	4:45 am
☉ □ ⚷	**1:49 pm**	10:49 am
♀ ⚹ ♅	**7:24 pm**	4:24 pm
☽ △ ♅	**7:54 pm**	4:54 pm
☽ ☍ ♀	**7:57 pm**	4:57 pm
☽ ⚻ ☿		11:29 pm

30 SATURDAY

☽ ⚻ ☿	**2:29 am**	
☽ △ ♃	**11:34 am**	8:34 am
☽ ⚹ ⚷	**2:45 pm**	11:45 am
☽ ⚻ ☉	**4:29 pm**	1:29 pm
☽ ⚻ ♄	**5:02 pm**	2:02 pm
☽ □ ♆	**5:16 pm**	2:16 pm
☽ ⚻ ⚶	**9:46 pm**	6:46 pm
☽ △ ⚳	**11:23 pm**	8:23 pm
☽ □ ⚵		10:10 pm
☉ ⚹ ♄		10:22 pm

31 SUNDAY

☽ □ ⚵	**1:10 am**	
☉ ⚹ ♄	**1:22 am**	
☽ □ ♀	**3:32 am**	12:32 am
☉ ⚹ ♆	**4:19 am**	1:19 am
☽ ⚺ ♇	**4:58 am**	1:58 am
☽ ☍ ♂	**10:39 am**	7:39 am
☽ □ ♅	**9:13 pm**	6:13 pm
☽ ⚻ ♀		10:49 pm

Eastern Standard Time in bold type
Pacific Standard Time in medium type

MARCH 2002

☽ Last Aspect day	EST / hr:mn / PST	asp	☽ Ingress sign day	EST / hr:mn / PST
2	**6:57 am** 3:57 am	△ ♅	♏ 2	**1:51 pm** 10:51 am
4	**9:43 am** 6:43 am	□ ♅	♐ 4	**4:55 pm** 1:55 pm
6	**9:31 pm** 6:31 pm	□ ♀	♑ 6	**11:48 pm** 8:48 pm
8	**10:06 am** 7:06 am	⚹ ☉	♒ 9	**9:56 am** 6:56 am
11	**2:28 pm** 11:28 am	☌ ♅	♓ 11	**9:56 pm** 6:56 pm
13	**9:03 pm** 6:03 pm	☌ ☉	♈ 14	**10:34 am** 7:34 am
16	**4:08 pm** 1:08 pm	⚹ ♅	♉ 16	**11:01 pm** 8:01 pm
19	**7:53 am** 4:53 am	⚹ ☉	♊ 19	**10:20 am** 7:20 am
21	**1:14 pm** 10:14 am	△ ♅	♋ 21	**7:06 pm** 4:06 pm
23	**5:19 am** 2:19 am	□ ♀	♌ 23	9:12 pm
23	**5:19 am** 2:19 am	□ ♀	♌ 24	**12:12 am**
25	**8:57 pm** 5:57 pm	☍ ♅	♍ 25	10:44 pm
25	**8:57 pm** 5:57 pm	☍ ♅	♍ 26	**1:44 am**
27	**8:31 pm** 5:31 pm	☍ ☿	♎ 27	10:04 pm
27	**8:31 pm** 5:31 pm	☍ ☿	♎ 28	**1:04 am**
29	**7:57 pm** 4:57 pm	☍ ♀	♏ 29	9:21 pm
29	**7:57 pm** 4:57 pm	☍ ♀	♏ 30	**12:21 am**
31	**9:13 pm** 6:13 pm	□ ♅	♐ 31	10:48 pm
31	**9:13 pm** 6:13 pm	□ ♅	♐ 4/1	**1:48 am**

☽ Phases & Eclipses phase	day	EST / hr:mn / PST
4th Quarter	5	**8:25 pm** 5:25 pm
New Moon	13	**9:03 pm** 6:03 pm
2nd Quarter	21	**9:28 pm** 6:28 pm
Full Moon	28	**1:25 pm** 10:25 am

Planet Ingress	day	EST / hr:mn / PST
♂ ♉	1	**10:05 am** 7:05 am
♀ ♈	7	**8:42 pm** 5:42 pm
☿ ♓	11	**6:34 pm** 3:34 pm
☉ ♈	20	**2:16 pm** 11:16 am
☿ ♈	29	**9:44 am** 6:44 am
♀ ♉	31	10:39 pm
♀ ♉	4/1	**1:39 am**

Planetary Motion	day	EST / hr:mn / PST
♃ D	1	**10:15 am** 7:15 am
♇ ℞	20	**9:55 am** 6:55 am
⚵ D	27	**10:27 pm** 7:27 pm

DATE		SID.TIME	SUN	MOON	NODE	MERCURY	VENUS	MARS	JUPITER	SATURN	URANUS	NEPTUNE	PLUTO	CERES	PALLAS	JUNO	VESTA	CHIRON
1	F	10:34:30	10 ♓ 13 09	3 ♎ 19	23 ♊ ℞ 45	14 ♒ 39	21 ♓ 11	29 ♈ 33	5 ♋ D 37	8 ♊ 27	25 ♒ 42	9 ♒ 37	17 ♐ 31	2 ♓ 34	7 ♒ 08	17 ♌ ℞ 55	4 ♊ 08	7 ♑ 33
2	Sa	10:38:26	11 13 20	18 24	23 36	15 56	22 26	0 ♉ 16	5 37	8 29	25 45	9 39	17 32	2 58	7 28	17 43	4 23	7 37
3	Su	10:42:23	12 13 31	3 ♏ 07	23 28	17 14	23 41	0 58	5 38	8 31	25 49	9 41	17 32	3 21	7 49	17 33	4 38	7 40
4	M	10:46:20	13 13 39	17 23	23 24	18 34	24 56	1 41	5 38	8 34	25 52	9 43	17 33	3 45	8 09	17 22	4 54	7 44
5	T	10:50:16	14 13 47	1 ♐ 11	23 22	19 55	26 11	2 23	5 39	8 37	25 55	9 45	17 34	4 08	8 29	17 12	5 10	7 48
6	W	10:54:13	15 13 52	14 31	23 21	21 18	27 25	3 06	5 39	8 39	25 59	9 47	17 34	4 32	8 49	17 02	5 26	7 51
7	Th	10:58:9	16 13 57	27 27	23 21	22 42	28 40	3 48	5 40	8 42	26 02	9 48	17 35	4 55	9 09	16 53	5 43	7 55
8	F	11:02:06	17 13 59	10 ♑ 04	23 21	24 07	29 55	4 30	5 41	8 45	26 05	9 50	17 35	5 18	9 29	16 44	5 59	7 58
9	Sa	11:06:02	18 14 00	22 25	23 18	25 34	1 ♈ 09	5 13	5 43	8 48	26 09	9 52	17 35	5 42	9 49	16 35	6 16	8 02
10	Su	11:09:59	19 14 00	4 ♒ 34	23 12	27 02	2 24	5 55	5 44	8 52	26 12	9 54	17 36	6 05	10 08	16 27	6 33	8 05
11	M	11:13:55	20 13 57	16 36	23 04	28 31	3 39	6 37	5 46	8 55	26 15	9 56	17 36	6 28	10 28	16 19	6 50	8 08
12	T	11:17:52	21 13 53	28 32	22 53	0 ♓ 02	4 53	7 19	5 48	8 58	26 18	9 58	17 36	6 52	10 47	16 12	7 08	8 12
13	W	11:21:49	22 13 47	10 ♓ 26	22 39	1 33	6 08	8 01	5 50	9 02	26 21	10 00	17 37	7 15	11 07	16 05	7 25	8 15
14	Th	11:25:45	23 13 39	22 18	22 24	3 06	7 22	8 44	5 52	9 05	26 25	10 01	17 37	7 38	11 26	15 59	7 43	8 18
15	F	11:29:42	24 13 29	4 ♈ 10	22 09	4 41	8 37	9 26	5 55	9 09	26 28	10 03	17 37	8 01	11 45	15 53	8 01	8 20
16	Sa	11:33:38	25 13 17	16 04	21 55	6 16	9 52	10 08	5 58	9 13	26 31	10 05	17 37	8 25	12 04	15 47	8 19	8 23
17	Su	11:37:35	26 13 03	28 00	21 44	7 53	11 06	10 50	6 00	9 17	26 34	10 07	17 38	8 48	12 23	15 42	8 38	8 26
18	M	11:41:31	27 12 46	10 ♉ 01	21 35	9 31	12 20	11 32	6 04	9 21	26 37	10 08	17 38	9 11	12 42	15 38	8 56	8 29
19	T	11:45:28	28 12 28	22 09	21 30	11 10	13 35	12 14	6 07	9 25	26 40	10 10	17 38	9 34	13 01	15 33	9 15	8 31
20	W	11:49:24	29 12 08	4 ♊ 29	21 27	12 50	14 49	12 56	6 10	9 29	26 43	10 12	17 ℞ 38	9 57	13 20	15 30	9 34	8 34
21	Th	11:53:21	0 ♈ 11 45	17 03	21 D 26	14 32	16 04	13 37	6 14	9 33	26 46	10 13	17 38	10 20	13 38	15 26	9 53	8 36
22	F	11:57:18	1 11 20	29 57	21 ℞ 26	16 15	17 18	14 19	6 18	9 38	26 49	10 15	17 38	10 43	13 57	15 23	10 12	8 39
23	Sa	12:01:14	2 10 53	13 ♋ 14	21 26	17 59	18 32	15 01	6 22	9 42	26 52	10 17	17 38	11 06	14 15	15 21	10 31	8 41
24	Su	12:05:11	3 10 23	26 57	21 24	19 44	19 47	15 43	6 26	9 46	26 55	10 18	17 38	11 29	14 33	15 19	10 51	8 43
25	M	12:09:07	4 09 51	11 ♌ 10	21 20	21 31	21 01	16 25	6 30	9 51	26 58	10 20	17 37	11 52	14 51	15 18	11 10	8 45
26	T	12:13:04	5 09 17	25 49	21 13	23 19	22 15	17 06	6 34	9 56	27 01	10 21	17 37	12 15	15 09	15 16	11 30	8 47
27	W	12:17:00	6 08 41	10 ♍ 51	21 04	25 08	23 29	17 48	6 39	10 00	27 04	10 23	17 37	12 38	15 27	15 16	11 50	8 49
28	Th	12:20:57	7 08 02	26 08	20 53	26 59	24 43	18 29	6 44	10 05	27 07	10 24	17 37	13 00	15 45	15 D 15	12 10	8 51
29	F	12:24:53	8 07 21	11 ♎ 27	20 43	28 51	25 57	19 11	6 49	10 10	27 10	10 26	17 37	13 23	16 02	15 16	12 30	8 53
30	Sa	12:28:50	9 06 38	26 39	20 33	0 ♈ 44	27 11	19 52	6 54	10 15	27 13	10 27	17 36	13 46	16 20	15 16	12 50	8 54
31	Su	12:32:47	10 05 53	11 ♏ 32	20 26	2 38	28 25	20 34	6 59	10 20	27 15	10 28	17 36	14 09	16 37	15 17	13 11	8 56

EPHEMERIS CALCULATED FOR 12 MIDNIGHT GREENWICH MEAN TIME. ALL OTHER DATA AND FACING ASPECTARIAN PAGE IN **EASTERN STANDARD TIME (BOLD)** AND PACIFIC STANDARD TIME (REGULAR).

APRIL 2002

1 MONDAY
☽⚻♀ **1:49 am**
☽△☿ **12:02 pm** 9:02 am
☽⚻♃ **2:07 pm** 11:07 am
☽⚺⚷ **5:17 pm** 2:17 pm
☽☍♄ **7:58 pm** 4:58 pm
☽⚹♆ **7:58 pm** 4:58 pm
♄△♆ **9:37 pm** 6:37 pm
☽△☉ **10:59 pm** 7:59 pm
☽☍⚴ 11:03 pm

2 TUESDAY
☽☍⚴ **2:03 am**
☿□♃ **3:18 am** 12:18 am
☽□⚳ **3:56 am** 12:56 am
☽△⚵ **4:30 am** 1:30 am
☽⚹♀ **8:02 am** 5:02 am
☽☌♇ **8:28 am** 5:28 am
☽⚻♂ **5:27 pm** 2:27 pm
☿□⚷ 10:03 pm
☽⚹♅ 11:13 pm
⚳⚻⚵ 11:22 pm

3 WEDNESDAY
☿□⚷ **1:03 am**
☽⚹♅ **2:13 am**
⚳⚻⚵ **2:22 am**
♇⚹♀ **3:36 am** 12:36 am
☽△♀ **12:34 pm** 9:34 am
☿⚹♆ **7:45 pm** 4:45 pm
☽☍♃ **8:41 pm** 5:41 pm
☿⚹♄ **9:22 pm** 6:22 pm
☽☌⚷ **11:46 pm** 8:46 pm
☽⚺♆ 11:41 pm
☽⚻♄ 11:58 pm

4 THURSDAY
☽⚺♆ **2:41 am**
☽⚻♄ **2:58 am**
☽□☿ **3:58 am** 12:58 am
☽□☉ **10:29 am** 7:29 am
☽⚻⚴ **10:42 am** 7:42 am
☽⚻⚵ **11:57 am** 8:57 am
☽⚹⚳ **12:52 pm** 9:52 am
☉⚹⚴ **2:46 pm** 11:46 am
☽⚺♇ **4:00 pm** 1:00 pm
☽⚺♀ **4:51 pm** 1:51 pm

5 FRIDAY
☽△♂ **4:59 am** 1:59 am
☉△⚵ **6:18 am** 3:18 am
☽⚺♅ **11:14 am** 8:14 am

6 SATURDAY
☽□♀ **4:32 am** 1:32 am
☿⚹⚴ **5:16 am** 2:16 am
☿△⚵ **6:48 am** 3:48 am
☽⚻♃ **7:09 am** 4:09 am
☉⚺⚳ **9:59 am** 6:59 am
☽⚺⚷ **10:00 am** 7:00 am
☽☌♆ **1:04 pm** 10:04 am
☽△♄ **1:43 pm** 10:43 am
⚵⚹⚴ **3:37 pm** 12:37 pm
☿⚺⚳ **9:25 pm** 6:25 pm
☽☍⚵ **11:00 pm** 8:00 pm
☽△⚴ **11:11 pm** 8:11 pm
☽⚺⚳ 10:33 pm
☽⚹☿ 11:15 pm
☽⚹☉ 11:25 pm
☽⚹♇ 11:54 pm

7 SUNDAY
☽⚺⚳ **1:33 am**
☽⚹☿ **2:15 am**
☽⚹☉ **2:25 am**
☽⚹♇ **2:54 am**
☉☌☿ **3:55 am** 12:55 am
☽☌♀ **5:13 am** 2:13 am
☿△♇ **6:00 am** 3:00 am
☉△♇ **8:16 am** 5:16 am
♀⚹♃ **8:38 am** 5:38 am
☽□♂ **8:06 pm** 5:06 pm
☿⚹⚳ **9:33 pm** 6:33 pm
☽☌♅ **11:09 pm** 8:09 pm

8 MONDAY
♀△⚷ **10:58 am** 7:58 am
☽△♃ **7:57 pm** 4:57 pm
♇□⚳ **7:59 pm** 4:59 pm
☽⚹⚷ **10:22 pm** 7:22 pm
☽⚹♀ **11:40 pm** 8:40 pm
☉⚹♀ 9:20 pm
☽⚺♆ 10:32 pm
☽□♄ 11:35 pm

9 TUESDAY
☉⚹♀ **12:20 am**
☽⚺♆ **1:32 am**
☽□♄ **2:35 am**
☽⚻⚵ **11:54 am** 8:54 am
☽□⚴ **1:36 pm** 10:36 am
☽□♇ **3:25 pm** 12:25 pm
☽☌⚳ **4:03 pm** 1:03 pm
♀□♆ **5:51 pm** 2:51 pm
☽⚺♀ **7:12 pm** 4:12 pm
☽⚺☉ **8:27 pm** 5:27 pm

10 WEDNESDAY
☽⚺☿ **3:42 am** 12:42 am
♂□♅ **4:04 am** 1:04 am
♀⚺♄ **5:56 am** 2:56 am
☽⚺♅ **12:04 pm** 9:04 am
☽⚹♂ **12:31 pm** 9:31 am

11 THURSDAY
☽□♃ **9:14 am** 6:14 am
☽□⚷ **11:06 am** 8:06 am
☽⚹♆ **2:17 pm** 11:17 am
☽⚹♄ **3:44 pm** 12:44 pm
☽⚺♀ **7:18 pm** 4:18 pm
♇☍⚴ **10:51 pm** 7:51 pm
☽△⚵ 9:57 pm

12 FRIDAY
☽△⚵ **12:57 am**
☿⚹♅ **3:46 am** 12:46 am
☽△♇ **3:54 am** 12:54 am
☽⚹⚴ **4:04 am** 1:04 am
☽⚺⚳ **6:32 am** 3:32 am
☽⚹♀ **9:04 am** 6:04 am
☽☌☉ **2:21 pm** 11:21 am
☽⚹♅ 9:34 pm
☿⚺♂ 10:34 pm

13 SATURDAY
☽⚹♅ **12:34 am**
☿⚺♂ **1:34 am**
☽⚺♂ **4:28 am** 1:28 am
☽☌☿ **4:52 am** 1:52 am
☽⚹♃ **9:49 pm** 6:49 pm
☽△⚷ **11:04 pm** 8:04 pm
☽□♆ 11:14 pm

14 SUNDAY
☽□♆ **2:14 am**
☽⚺♄ **4:05 am** 1:05 am
♀□⚵ **6:47 am** 3:47 am
☽□⚵ **1:08 pm** 10:08 am
☽☌♀ **1:46 pm** 10:46 am
☽⚻♇ **3:27 pm** 12:27 pm
☽⚺⚴ **5:32 pm** 2:32 pm
☽⚹⚳ **7:55 pm** 4:55 pm
☽□♀ **9:50 pm** 6:50 pm

15 MONDAY
♀⚻♇ **6:21 am** 3:21 am
☽⚺☉ **6:52 am** 3:52 am
☽□♅ **11:53 am** 8:53 am
☽☌♂ **6:56 pm** 3:56 pm

16 TUESDAY
☽⚺☿ **3:42 am** 12:42 am
☽⚺♃ **8:59 am** 5:59 am
☽⚻⚷ **9:35 am** 6:35 am
☽△♆ **12:44 pm** 9:44 am
☽☌♄ **2:56 pm** 11:56 am
♀⚺⚴ **6:00 pm** 3:00 pm
☽⚹⚵ **11:45 pm** 8:45 pm
☽☍♇ 10:23 pm

17 WEDNESDAY
☽☍♇ **1:23 am**
☽☌⚴ **5:12 am** 2:12 am
☽⚺♀ **6:02 am** 3:02 am
☽□⚳ **7:27 am** 4:27 am
☽△♀ **8:45 am** 5:45 am
☿⚹♃ **2:12 pm** 11:12 am
☿△⚷ **4:05 pm** 1:05 pm
☽⚹☉ **9:03 pm** 6:03 pm
☽△♅ **9:17 pm** 6:17 pm
☉⚹♅ 9:15 pm
♀⚹⚳ 11:27 pm

18 THURSDAY
☉⚹♅ **12:15 am**
♀⚹⚳ **2:27 am**
☽⚺♂ **7:03 am** 4:03 am
☿□♆ **12:13 pm** 9:13 am
♀□♀ **4:31 pm** 1:31 pm
☽☌♃ **5:54 pm** 2:54 pm
☽☍⚷ **5:54 pm** 2:54 pm
♃☍⚷ **5:55 pm** 2:55 pm
☽⚻♆ **8:58 pm** 5:58 pm
☽⚹☿ **10:29 pm** 7:29 pm
☽⚺♄ **11:27 pm** 8:27 pm

19 FRIDAY
☿⚺♄ **5:23 am** 2:23 am
☽⚺⚵ **7:57 am** 4:57 am
☽⚻♇ **8:53 am** 5:53 am
☽⚺⚴ **2:11 pm** 11:11 am
☽△⚳ **4:15 pm** 1:15 pm
☽⚻♀ **4:57 pm** 1:57 pm
☽⚹♀ **6:55 pm** 3:55 pm

20 SATURDAY
☽⚻♅ **3:57 am** 12:57 am
☽□☉ **7:48 am** 4:48 am
☽⚹♂ **3:51 pm** 12:51 pm
☽⚻⚷ **11:16 pm** 8:16 pm
☽⚺♃ **11:49 pm** 8:49 pm
☽☍♆ 11:13 pm

21 SUNDAY
☽☍♆ **2:13 am**
☽⚹♄ **4:56 am** 1:56 am
☽□☿ **11:54 am** 8:54 am
☽☌⚵ **1:03 pm** 10:03 am
☽△♇ **1:20 pm** 10:20 am
☽⚹⚴ **7:50 pm** 4:50 pm
☿□⚵ **9:31 pm** 6:31 pm
☽⚻⚳ **9:41 pm** 6:41 pm
☽☍♀ **9:52 pm** 6:52 pm
☿⚻♇ **10:57 pm** 7:57 pm

22 MONDAY
☽□♀ **3:42 am** 12:42 am
☽☍♅ **7:30 am** 4:30 am
♇△⚵ **1:03 pm** 10:03 am
☽△☉ **2:43 pm** 11:43 am
⚳⚺♀ **5:43 pm** 2:43 pm
☽□♂ **9:05 pm** 6:05 pm
☽△⚷ 10:37 pm
☽⚹♃ 11:39 pm

23 TUESDAY
☽△⚷ **1:37 am**
☽⚹♃ **2:39 am**
☽⚻♆ **4:28 am** 1:28 am
☽□♄ **7:23 am** 4:23 am
☽□♇ **2:58 pm** 11:58 am
☽⚺⚵ **3:16 pm** 12:16 pm
☽△☿ **8:23 pm** 5:23 pm
☽□⚴ **10:31 pm** 7:31 pm
☽⚻♀ **11:55 pm** 8:55 pm
☽☍⚳ 9:12 pm
♀□♅ 10:32 pm

24 WEDNESDAY
☽☍⚳ **12:12 am**
♀□♅ **1:32 am**
☽⚻♅ **8:30 am** 5:30 am
☽△♀ **9:06 am** 6:06 am
☽⚻☉ **6:44 pm** 3:44 pm
☿⚺⚴ **8:26 pm** 5:26 pm
☽△♂ **11:49 pm** 8:49 pm
☽□⚷ 10:54 pm

25 THURSDAY
☽□⚷ **1:54 am**
☽□♃ **3:26 am** 12:26 am
☽△♆ **4:45 am** 1:45 am
☽△♄ **7:56 am** 4:56 am
☿□♀ **8:39 am** 5:39 am
☽⚹♇ **2:57 pm** 11:57 am
☿⚹⚳ **3:17 pm** 12:17 pm
☽⚹⚵ **3:50 pm** 12:50 pm
☽△⚴ **11:43 pm** 8:43 pm
☽△♀ 9:34 pm
☽⚻⚳ 10:17 pm
☽⚻☿ 11:11 pm

26 FRIDAY
☽△♀ **12:34 am**
☽⚻⚳ **1:17 am**
☽⚻☿ **2:11 am**
☽△♅ **8:29 am** 5:29 am
☽⚻♀ **1:14 pm** 10:14 am
♂⚻⚷ **9:32 pm** 6:32 pm
☽☍☉ **10:00 pm** 7:00 pm
☽⚹⚷ 10:52 pm
☽⚻♂ 11:04 pm

27 SATURDAY
☽⚹⚷ **1:52 am**
☽⚻♂ **2:04 am**
☽△♃ **3:57 am** 12:57 am
☽□♆ **4:50 am** 1:50 am
☽⚻♄ **8:24 am** 5:24 am
☽⚺♇ **3:09 pm** 12:09 pm
☽□⚵ **4:41 pm** 1:41 pm
☽⚻⚴ 10:35 pm
☽□♀ 10:51 pm

28 SUNDAY
☽⚻⚴ **1:35 am**
☽□♀ **1:51 am**
☽△⚳ **3:03 am** 12:03 am
☽☍☿ **8:19 am** 5:19 am
☽□♅ **9:25 am** 6:25 am
☽☍♀ **6:50 pm** 3:50 pm
☿□♅ **8:03 pm** 5:03 pm
♀△⚴ **10:57 pm** 7:57 pm

29 MONDAY
☽⚻☉ **3:07 am** 12:07 am
☽⚺⚷ **3:28 am** 12:28 am
☽☍♂ **6:15 am** 3:15 am
☽⚻♃ **6:16 am** 3:16 am
☽⚹♆ **6:41 am** 3:41 am
♂⚺♃ **6:53 am** 3:53 am
☉△⚷ **8:10 am** 5:10 am
☽☍♄ **10:50 am** 7:50 am
♂△♆ **3:26 pm** 12:26 pm
☽☌♇ **5:30 pm** 2:30 pm
☽△⚵ **7:53 pm** 4:53 pm

30 TUESDAY
☽⚹♀ **5:45 am** 2:45 am
☽☍⚴ **6:11 am** 3:11 am
☽□⚳ **7:36 am** 4:36 am
☽⚹♅ **1:10 pm** 10:10 am
☽⚻☿ **5:27 pm** 2:27 pm
♃⚻♆ **8:43 pm** 5:43 pm

Eastern Standard Time in bold type
Pacific Standard Time in medium type

APRIL 2002

☽ Last Aspect day	EST / hr:mn / PST	asp	☽ Ingress sign day	EST / hr:mn / PST
3/31	**9:13 pm** 6:13 pm	□ ♅	♐ 3/31	10:48 pm
3/31	**9:13 pm** 6:13 pm	□ ♅	♐ 1	**1:48 am**
2	11:13 pm	⚹ ♅	♑ 3	**6:58 am** 3:58 am
3	**2:13 am**	⚹ ♅	♑ 3	**6:58 am** 3:58 am
5	**4:59 am** 1:59 am	△ ♂	♒ 5	**4:07 pm** 1:07 pm
7	**11:09 pm** 8:09 pm	☌ ♅	♓ 8	**3:57 am** 12:57 am
10	**12:31 pm** 9:31 am	⚹ ♂	♈ 10	**4:40 pm** 1:40 pm
13	**4:52 am** 1:52 am	☌ ☿	♉ 13	**4:55 am** 1:55 am
15	**11:53 am** 8:53 am	□ ♅	♊ 15	**3:56 pm** 12:56 pm
17	**9:17 pm** 6:17 pm	△ ♅	♋ 17	10:01 pm
17	**9:17 pm** 6:17 pm	△ ♅	♋ 18	**1:01 am**
19	**6:55 pm** 3:55 pm	⚹ ♀	♌ 20	**7:20 am** 4:20 am
22	**7:30 am** 4:30 am	☍ ♅	♍ 22	**10:35 am** 7:35 am
24	**9:06 am** 6:06 am	△ ♀	♎ 24	**11:22 am** 8:22 am
26	**8:29 am** 5:29 am	△ ♅	♏ 26	**11:15 am** 8:15 am
28	**9:25 am** 6:25 am	□ ♅	♐ 28	**12:13 pm** 9:13 am
30	**1:10 pm** 10:10 am	⚹ ♅	♑ 30	**4:03 pm** 1:03 pm

☽ Phases & Eclipses phase	day	EST / hr:mn / PST
4th Quarter	4	**10:29 am** 7:29 am
New Moon	12	**2:21 pm** 11:21 am
2nd Quarter	20	**7:48 am** 4:48 am
Full Moon	26	**10:00 pm** 7:00 pm

Planet Ingress	day	EST / hr:mn / PST
♀ ♉	3/31	10:39 pm
♀ ♉	1	**1:39 am**
☿ ♉	13	**5:10 am** 2:10 am
♂ ♊	13	**12:36 pm** 9:36 am
☉ ♉	19	10:20 pm
☉ ♉	20	**1:20 am**
♀ ♊	25	**12:57 pm** 9:57 am
☿ ♊	29	11:15 pm
☿ ♊	30	**2:15 am**

Planetary Motion	day	EST / hr:mn / PST
⚷ ℞	16	10:39 pm
⚷ ℞	17	**1:39 am**

DATE		SID.TIME	SUN	MOON	NODE	MERCURY	VENUS	MARS	JUPITER	SATURN	URANUS	NEPTUNE	PLUTO	CERES	PALLAS	JUNO	VESTA	CHIRON
1	M	12:36:43	11 ♈ 05 07	25 ♏ 59	20 ♊ ℞ 21	4 ♈ 34	29 ♈ 39	21 ♉ 15	7 ♋ 05	10 ♊ 25	27 ♒ 18	10 ♒ 30	17 ♐ ℞ 36	14 ♓ 31	16 ♒ 55	15 ♌ 19	13 ♊ 31	8 ♑ 57
2	T	12:40:40	12 04 18	9 ♐ 58	20 D 19	6 32	0 ♉ 53	21 57	7 11	10 31	27 21	10 31	17 35	14 54	17 12	15 20	13 52	8 59
3	W	12:44:36	13 03 28	23 27	20 19	8 30	2 07	22 38	7 16	10 36	27 24	10 32	17 35	15 16	17 29	15 22	14 13	9 00
4	Th	12:48:33	14 02 36	6 ♑ 29	20 ℞ 19	10 30	3 21	23 20	7 22	10 41	27 26	10 34	17 34	15 39	17 45	15 25	14 34	9 01
5	F	12:52:29	15 01 43	19 08	20 19	12 31	4 35	24 01	7 28	10 47	27 29	10 35	17 34	16 01	18 02	15 28	14 55	9 02
6	Sa	12:56:26	16 00 47	1 ♒ 28	20 18	14 33	5 49	24 42	7 35	10 52	27 31	10 36	17 33	16 24	18 19	15 31	15 16	9 03
7	Su	13:00:22	16 59 50	13 35	20 15	16 36	7 03	25 23	7 41	10 58	27 34	10 37	17 33	16 46	18 35	15 35	15 38	9 04
8	M	13:04:19	17 58 51	25 34	20 09	18 40	8 17	26 04	7 48	11 03	27 36	10 38	17 32	17 08	18 51	15 39	15 59	9 05
9	T	13:08:16	18 57 50	7 ♓ 26	20 00	20 44	9 30	26 46	7 54	11 09	27 39	10 39	17 32	17 31	19 07	15 44	16 21	9 06
10	W	13:12:12	19 56 48	19 17	19 50	22 50	10 44	27 27	8 01	11 15	27 41	10 41	17 31	17 53	19 23	15 49	16 42	9 07
11	Th	13:16:09	20 55 43	1 ♈ 09	19 39	24 55	11 58	28 08	8 08	11 21	27 44	10 42	17 30	18 15	19 39	15 54	17 04	9 07
12	F	13:20:05	21 54 36	13 03	19 27	27 01	13 11	28 49	8 15	11 27	27 46	10 43	17 30	18 37	19 55	15 59	17 26	9 08
13	Sa	13:24:02	22 53 28	25 02	19 17	29 07	14 25	29 30	8 23	11 33	27 48	10 44	17 29	18 59	20 10	16 05	17 48	9 08
14	Su	13:27:58	23 52 17	7 ♉ 05	19 08	1 ♉ 12	15 39	0 ♊ 11	8 30	11 39	27 51	10 45	17 28	19 21	20 26	16 11	18 10	9 08
15	M	13:31:55	24 51 05	19 16	19 01	3 17	16 52	0 52	8 38	11 45	27 53	10 46	17 27	19 43	20 41	16 18	18 32	9 09
16	T	13:35:51	25 49 50	1 ♊ 35	18 58	5 20	18 06	1 33	8 45	11 51	27 55	10 46	17 26	20 05	20 56	16 25	18 55	9 09
17	W	13:39:48	26 48 34	14 04	18 D 56	7 23	19 19	2 14	8 53	11 57	27 57	10 47	17 26	20 27	21 11	16 32	19 17	9 ℞ 09
18	Th	13:43:44	27 47 15	26 47	18 56	9 23	20 33	2 55	9 01	12 04	28 00	10 48	17 25	20 49	21 25	16 40	19 40	9 09
19	F	13:47:41	28 45 54	9 ♋ 45	18 57	11 22	21 46	3 35	9 09	12 10	28 02	10 49	17 24	21 10	21 40	16 48	20 02	9 09
20	Sa	13:51:38	29 44 31	23 02	18 ℞ 58	13 19	22 59	4 16	9 17	12 16	28 04	10 50	17 23	21 32	21 54	16 56	20 25	9 09
21	Su	13:55:34	0 ♉ 43 06	6 ♌ 40	18 58	15 12	24 13	4 57	9 26	12 23	28 06	10 51	17 22	21 53	22 08	17 05	20 48	9 08
22	M	13:59:31	1 41 38	20 42	18 56	17 03	25 26	5 38	9 34	12 29	28 08	10 51	17 21	22 15	22 22	17 13	21 10	9 08
23	T	14:03:27	2 40 08	5 ♍ 06	18 53	18 51	26 39	6 18	9 43	12 36	28 10	10 52	17 20	22 36	22 36	17 23	21 33	9 08
24	W	14:07:24	3 38 36	19 49	18 48	20 35	27 52	6 59	9 52	12 43	28 12	10 53	17 19	22 58	22 50	17 32	21 56	9 07
25	Th	14:11:20	4 37 02	4 ♎ 47	18 41	22 15	29 05	7 39	10 00	12 49	28 13	10 53	17 18	23 19	23 03	17 42	22 20	9 06
26	F	14:15:17	5 35 26	19 50	18 35	23 52	0 ♊ 18	8 20	10 09	12 56	28 15	10 54	17 17	23 40	23 16	17 52	22 43	9 06
27	Sa	14:19:13	6 33 48	4 ♏ 49	18 29	25 24	1 31	9 00	10 18	13 03	28 17	10 54	17 16	24 01	23 29	18 02	23 06	9 05
28	Su	14:23:10	7 32 08	19 36	18 24	26 53	2 44	9 41	10 27	13 10	28 19	10 55	17 15	24 23	23 42	18 13	23 30	9 04
29	M	14:27:07	8 30 26	4 ♐ 03	18 22	28 17	3 57	10 21	10 37	13 16	28 20	10 55	17 14	24 44	23 55	18 23	23 53	9 03
30	T	14:31:03	9 28 43	18 04	18 D 21	29 37	5 10	11 02	10 46	13 23	28 22	10 56	17 12	25 05	24 07	18 34	24 17	9 02

EPHEMERIS CALCULATED FOR 12 MIDNIGHT GREENWICH MEAN TIME. ALL OTHER DATA AND FACING ASPECTARIAN PAGE IN **EASTERN STANDARD TIME (BOLD)** AND PACIFIC STANDARD TIME (REGULAR).

MAY 2002

1 WEDNESDAY
☽ ⚻ ♀ **4:26 am** 1:26 am
☉ □ ♆ **7:10 am** 4:10 am
☽ ☌ ⚷ **8:20 am** 5:20 am
☉ ⚹ ♃ **9:09 am** 6:09 am
☽ ⚺ ♆ **11:54 am** 8:54 am
☽ ☍ ♃ **12:05 pm** 9:05 am
☽ △ ☉ **12:17 pm** 9:17 am
☽ ⚻ ♂ **2:18 pm** 11:18 am
☽ ⚻ ♄ **4:49 pm** 1:49 pm
☽ ⚺ ♇ **11:25 pm** 8:25 pm
☽ ⚻ ⚵ 11:54 pm

2 THURSDAY
☽ ⚻ ⚵ **2:54 am**
☽ ⚺ ⚴ **1:34 pm** 10:34 am
☽ ⚻ ⚶ **2:55 pm** 11:55 am
☽ ⚹ ⚳ **4:13 pm** 1:13 pm
☽ ⚺ ♅ **8:45 pm** 5:45 pm
♀ ⚻ ⚷ **10:03 pm** 7:03 pm

3 FRIDAY
☽ △ ☿ **6:46 am** 3:46 am
☽ ⚺ ⚷ **5:03 pm** 2:03 pm
☽ △ ♀ **7:10 pm** 4:10 pm
☽ ☌ ♆ **8:58 pm** 5:58 pm
☽ ⚻ ♃ **9:54 pm** 6:54 pm
♂ ☌ ♄ 9:58 pm
☽ □ ☉ 11:16 pm
☽ △ ♄ 11:44 pm
☽ △ ♂ 11:50 pm

4 SATURDAY
♂ ☌ ♄ **12:58 am**
☽ □ ☉ **2:16 am**
☽ △ ♄ **2:44 am**
☽ △ ♂ **2:50 am**
☉ ⚺ ♄ **9:00 am** 6:00 am
☽ ⚹ ♇ **9:05 am** 6:05 am
♀ △ ♆ **1:29 pm** 10:29 am
☽ ☍ ⚵ **1:50 pm** 10:50 am
☉ ⚺ ♂ **11:52 pm** 8:52 pm
☽ ☌ ⚴ 10:04 pm
♀ ⚺ ♃ 11:47 pm

5 SUNDAY
☽ ☌ ⚴ **1:04 am**
♀ ⚺ ♃ **2:47 am**
☽ △ ⚶ **3:33 am** 12:33 am
☽ ⚺ ⚳ **4:38 am** 1:38 am
☽ ☌ ♅ **7:46 am** 4:46 am
☽ □ ☿ **11:03 pm** 8:03 pm

6 MONDAY
☽ ⚹ ⚷ **4:39 am** 1:39 am
☽ ⚺ ♆ **8:52 am** 5:52 am
☽ △ ♃ **10:39 am** 7:39 am
☽ □ ♀ **1:46 pm** 10:46 am
☽ □ ♄ **3:23 pm** 12:23 pm
☽ □ ♂ **6:27 pm** 3:27 pm
☽ ⚹ ☉ **7:37 pm** 4:37 pm
☽ □ ♇ **9:11 pm** 6:11 pm

7 TUESDAY
☽ ⚻ ⚵ **3:14 am** 12:14 am
♀ ☌ ♄ **7:11 am** 4:11 am
☉ ⚻ ♇ **2:16 pm** 11:16 am
☽ ⚺ ⚴ **2:31 pm** 11:31 am
☽ □ ⚶ **6:12 pm** 3:12 pm
☽ ☌ ⚳ **6:58 pm** 3:58 pm
☽ ⚺ ♅ **8:28 pm** 5:28 pm

8 WEDNESDAY
☽ ⚹ ☿ **3:29 pm** 12:29 pm
☽ □ ⚷ **5:10 pm** 2:10 pm
♂ ☍ ♇ **5:14 pm** 2:14 pm
☽ ⚹ ♆ **9:31 pm** 6:31 pm
☽ □ ♃ 9:10 pm

9 THURSDAY
☽ □ ♃ **12:10 am**
☽ ⚹ ♄ **4:36 am** 1:36 am
☽ ⚹ ♀ **9:12 am** 6:12 am
☽ △ ♇ **9:37 am** 6:37 am
☽ ⚹ ♂ **10:37 am** 7:37 am
♀ ☍ ♇ **1:17 pm** 10:17 am
☽ ⚺ ☉ **1:31 pm** 10:31 am
☽ △ ⚵ **4:51 pm** 1:51 pm

10 FRIDAY
♅ ⚺ ⚳ **3:15 am** 12:15 am
☽ ⚹ ⚴ **3:43 am** 12:43 am
☿ ⚻ ⚷ **4:11 am** 1:11 am
☽ ⚹ ⚶ **8:33 am** 5:33 am
☽ ⚹ ♅ **8:47 am** 5:47 am
☽ ⚺ ⚳ **8:56 am** 5:56 am
♀ ☌ ♂ **2:56 pm** 11:56 am
♅ △ ⚶ **3:56 pm** 12:56 pm

11 SATURDAY
☽ △ ⚷ **4:47 am** 1:47 am
☽ ⚺ ☿ **5:42 am** 2:42 am
☽ □ ♆ **9:11 am** 6:11 am
☽ ⚹ ♃ **12:37 pm** 9:37 am
☽ ⚺ ♄ **4:40 pm** 1:40 pm
☉ □ ⚵ **6:48 pm** 3:48 pm
☽ ⚻ ♇ **8:50 pm** 5:50 pm
☽ ⚺ ♂ 10:19 pm
☽ ⚺ ♀ 11:58 pm

12 SUNDAY
☽ ⚺ ♂ **1:19 am**
☽ ⚺ ♀ **2:58 am**
☽ □ ⚵ **5:05 am** 2:05 am
☽ ☌ ☉ **5:45 am** 2:45 am
☽ □ ⚴ **3:17 pm** 12:17 pm
☽ □ ♅ **7:29 pm** 4:29 pm
⚳ □ ⚶ **9:03 pm** 6:03 pm
☽ ⚹ ⚳ **9:09 pm** 6:09 pm
☽ ⚺ ⚶ **9:09 pm** 6:09 pm

13 MONDAY
♀ ⚹ ⚵ **5:27 am** 2:27 am
☽ ⚻ ⚷ **2:35 pm** 11:35 am
☽ ☌ ☿ **4:50 pm** 1:50 pm
☽ △ ♆ **6:59 pm** 3:59 pm
☽ ⚺ ♃ **11:07 pm** 8:07 pm
☽ ☌ ♄ 11:47 pm

14 TUESDAY
☽ ☌ ♄ **2:47 am**
☽ ☍ ♇ **6:08 am** 3:08 am
☽ ☌ ♂ **1:41 pm** 10:41 am
☽ ⚹ ⚵ **3:16 pm** 12:16 pm
☽ ☌ ♀ **6:04 pm** 3:04 pm
☽ ⚺ ☉ **7:28 pm** 4:28 pm
☽ △ ⚴ 9:42 pm

15 WEDNESDAY
☽ △ ⚴ **12:42 am**
☽ △ ♅ **4:08 am** 1:08 am
☽ □ ⚳ **7:08 am** 4:08 am
☽ ☌ ⚶ **7:30 am** 4:30 am
☽ ☍ ⚷ **10:17 pm** 7:17 pm
☽ ⚺ ☿ 9:52 pm
☽ ⚻ ♆ 11:41 pm

16 THURSDAY
☽ ⚺ ☿ **12:52 am**
☽ ⚻ ♆ **2:41 am**
☽ ☌ ♃ **7:26 am** 4:26 am
☽ ⚺ ♄ **10:43 am** 7:43 am
♂ ⚹ ⚵ **1:12 pm** 10:12 am
☽ ⚻ ♇ **1:18 pm** 10:18 am
☽ ⚺ ⚵ **11:13 pm** 8:13 pm
☽ ⚺ ♂ **11:33 pm** 8:33 pm

17 FRIDAY
☽ ⚺ ♀ **6:16 am** 3:16 am
☽ ⚹ ☉ **6:27 am** 3:27 am
☽ ⚻ ⚴ **7:49 am** 4:49 am
☽ ⚻ ♅ **10:36 am** 7:36 am
☽ △ ⚳ **2:45 pm** 11:45 am
☽ ⚺ ⚶ **3:29 pm** 12:29 pm
☉ ⚺ ♀ **3:30 pm** 12:30 pm
♀ △ ⚴ 10:43 pm

18 SATURDAY
♀ △ ⚴ **1:43 am**
☽ ⚻ ⚷ **3:49 am** 12:49 am
☉ □ ⚴ **4:40 am** 1:40 am
☽ ⚹ ☿ **5:58 am** 2:58 am
☽ ☍ ♆ **8:11 am** 5:11 am
☽ ⚺ ♃ **1:29 pm** 10:29 am
☽ ⚹ ♄ **4:23 pm** 1:23 pm
☽ △ ♇ **6:17 pm** 3:17 pm

19 SUNDAY
☽ ☌ ⚵ **4:52 am** 1:52 am
☽ ⚹ ♂ **6:51 am** 3:51 am
♀ △ ♅ **7:26 am** 4:26 am
☽ ☍ ⚴ **12:40 pm** 9:40 am
☽ □ ☉ **2:42 pm** 11:42 am
☽ ☍ ♅ **2:53 pm** 11:53 am
☽ ⚹ ♀ **3:34 pm** 12:34 pm
☉ □ ♅ **5:25 pm** 2:25 pm
☽ ⚻ ⚳ **8:02 pm** 5:02 pm
☽ ⚹ ⚶ **9:05 pm** 6:05 pm

20 MONDAY
☽ △ ⚷ **7:14 am** 4:14 am
☽ □ ☿ **8:29 am** 5:29 am
☽ ⚻ ♆ **11:35 am** 8:35 am
☽ ⚹ ♃ **5:22 pm** 2:22 pm
☽ □ ♄ **7:57 pm** 4:57 pm
☽ □ ♇ **9:14 pm** 6:14 pm

21 TUESDAY
☽ ⚺ ⚵ **8:28 am** 5:28 am
☽ □ ♂ **11:53 am** 8:53 am
☽ ⚻ ⚴ **3:32 pm** 12:32 pm
☽ ⚻ ♅ **5:17 pm** 2:17 pm
☽ △ ☉ **8:39 pm** 5:39 pm
☽ □ ♀ **10:27 pm** 7:27 pm
☽ ☍ ⚳ **11:21 pm** 8:21 pm
☽ □ ⚶ 9:45 pm

22 WEDNESDAY
☽ □ ⚶ **12:45 am**
☽ □ ⚷ **9:00 am** 6:00 am
☽ △ ☿ **9:02 am** 6:02 am
☿ ⚻ ⚷ **10:17 am** 7:17 am
♀ □ ⚳ **1:04 pm** 10:04 am
☽ △ ♆ **1:23 pm** 10:23 am
☽ □ ♃ **7:43 pm** 4:43 pm
☽ △ ♄ **10:01 pm** 7:01 pm
☽ ⚹ ♇ **10:46 pm** 7:46 pm

23 THURSDAY
☽ ⚹ ⚵ **10:49 am** 7:49 am
☽ △ ♂ **3:37 pm** 12:37 pm
♀ ☌ ⚶ **4:09 pm** 1:09 pm
☽ △ ⚴ **5:17 pm** 2:17 pm
☽ △ ♅ **6:39 pm** 3:39 pm
☽ ⚻ ☉ 10:26 pm
☽ ⚻ ⚳ 10:44 pm

24 FRIDAY
☽ ⚻ ☉ **1:26 am**
☽ ⚻ ⚳ **1:44 am**
☽ △ ⚶ **3:30 am** 12:30 am
☽ △ ♀ **4:09 am** 1:09 am
☉ ⚹ ⚳ **7:56 am** 4:56 am
☽ ⚻ ☿ **8:42 am** 5:42 am
☽ ⚹ ⚷ **10:07 am** 7:07 am
☽ □ ♆ **2:39 pm** 11:39 am
☽ △ ♃ **9:42 pm** 6:42 pm
☽ ⚻ ♄ **11:47 pm** 8:47 pm
☽ ⚺ ♇ 9:01 pm

25 SATURDAY
☽ ⚺ ♇ **12:01 am**
♂ △ ⚴ **10:53 am** 7:53 am
☽ □ ⚵ **1:16 pm** 10:16 am
☽ □ ⚴ **7:16 pm** 4:16 pm
☽ ⚻ ♂ **7:36 pm** 4:36 pm
☿ ⚺ ♀ **7:44 pm** 4:44 pm
☽ □ ♅ **8:20 pm** 5:20 pm
♄ ☍ ♇ **9:44 pm** 6:44 pm

26 SUNDAY
☽ △ ⚳ **4:39 am** 1:39 am
☽ ☍ ☉ **6:51 am** 3:51 am
☽ ⚻ ⚶ **6:52 am** 3:52 am
☉ ⚺ ⚶ **7:22 am** 4:22 am
☽ ☍ ☿ **8:51 am** 5:51 am
☽ ⚻ ♀ **10:38 am** 7:38 am
♂ △ ♅ **11:30 am** 8:30 am
☽ ⚺ ⚷ **12:00 pm** 9:00 am
☽ ⚹ ♆ **4:50 pm** 1:50 pm
☽ ⚻ ♃ 9:52 pm
☉ ☌ ☿ 11:09 pm
♀ ☍ ⚷ 11:20 pm
☽ ☌ ♇ 11:29 pm
☽ ☍ ♄ 11:48 pm

27 MONDAY
☽ ⚻ ♃ **12:52 am**
☉ ☌ ☿ **2:09 am**
♀ ☍ ⚷ **2:20 am**
☽ ☌ ♇ **2:29 am**
☽ ☍ ♄ **2:48 am**
☿ ⚺ ⚶ **12:25 pm** 9:25 am
☽ △ ⚵ **5:27 pm** 2:27 pm
☽ ⚹ ⚴ **11:02 pm** 8:02 pm
☽ ⚹ ♅ **11:50 pm** 8:50 pm
☽ ☍ ♂ 10:40 pm

28 TUESDAY
☽ ☍ ♂ **1:40 am**
☽ □ ⚳ **9:46 am** 6:46 am
☽ ⚻ ☿ **10:53 am** 7:53 am
☽ ☍ ⚶ **12:35 pm** 9:35 am
☽ ⚻ ☉ **2:53 pm** 11:53 am
☽ ☌ ⚷ **4:07 pm** 1:07 pm
☽ ☍ ♀ **7:59 pm** 4:59 pm
☽ ⚺ ♆ **9:24 pm** 6:24 pm

29 WEDNESDAY
☿ ⚹ ⚳ **4:13 am** 1:13 am
☽ ☍ ♃ **6:46 am** 3:46 am
☉ ⚻ ⚷ **7:15 am** 4:15 am
☽ ⚺ ♇ **7:34 am** 4:34 am
☽ ⚻ ♄ **8:32 am** 5:32 am
♀ ⚻ ♆ **11:38 am** 8:38 am
☽ ⚻ ⚵ 9:47 pm

30 THURSDAY
☽ ⚻ ⚵ **12:47 am**
☽ ⚺ ⚴ **5:53 am** 2:53 am
☽ ⚺ ♅ **6:23 am** 3:23 am
☽ ⚻ ♂ **11:18 am** 8:18 am
☽ △ ☿ **3:53 pm** 12:53 pm
☽ ⚹ ⚳ **6:17 pm** 3:17 pm
☽ ⚻ ⚶ **9:53 pm** 6:53 pm
☽ ⚺ ⚷ **11:29 pm** 8:29 pm

31 FRIDAY
☽ △ ☉ **3:00 am** 12:00 am
♃ ⚻ ♇ **5:05 am** 2:05 am
☽ ☌ ♆ **5:18 am** 2:18 am
☽ ⚻ ♀ **9:44 am** 6:44 am
☽ ⚹ ♇ **4:01 pm** 1:01 pm
☽ ⚻ ♃ **4:13 pm** 1:13 pm
☽ △ ♄ **5:46 pm** 2:46 pm

Eastern Standard Time in bold type
Pacific Standard Time in medium type

MAY 2002

☽ Last Aspect				☽ Ingress			
day	EST / hr:mn / PST		asp	sign	day	EST / hr:mn / PST	
1	**12:17 pm**	9:17 am	△☉	♒	2	**11:43 pm**	8:43 pm
5	**7:46 am**	4:46 am	☌♅	♓	5	**10:46 am**	7:46 am
6	**9:11 pm**	6:11 pm	□♇	♈	7	**11:22 pm**	8:22 pm
10	**8:47 am**	5:47 am	⚹♅	♉	10	**11:32 am**	8:32 am
12	**7:29 pm**	4:29 pm	□♅	♊	12	**10:04 pm**	7:04 pm
15	**4:08 am**	1:08 am	△♅	♋	15	**6:33 am**	3:33 am
17	**6:27 am**	3:27 am	⚹☉	♌	17	**12:52 pm**	9:52 am
19	**3:34 pm**	12:34 pm	⚹♀	♍	19	**5:01 pm**	2:01 pm
21	**11:53 am**	8:53 am	□♂	♎	21	**7:19 pm**	4:19 pm
23	**6:39 pm**	3:39 pm	△♅	♏	23	**8:38 pm**	5:38 pm
25	**8:20 pm**	5:20 pm	□♅	♐	25	**10:20 pm**	7:20 pm
27		10:40 pm	☍♂	♑	27		10:54 pm
28	**1:40 am**		☍♂	♑	28	**1:54 am**	
29	**6:46 am**	3:46 am	☍♃	♒	30	**8:35 am**	5:35 am

☽ Phases & Eclipses			
phase	day	EST / hr:mn / PST	
4th Quarter	3		11:16 pm
4th Quarter	4	**2:16 am**	
New Moon	12	**5:45 am**	2:45 am
2nd Quarter	19	**2:42 pm**	11:42 am
Full Moon	26	**6:51 am**	3:51 am
●	26	5° ♐ 04'	

Planet Ingress			
	day	EST / hr:mn / PST	
⚶ ♋	13		10:22 pm
⚶ ♋	14	**1:22 am**	
⚳ ♈	14	**8:16 am**	5:16 am
♀ ♋	20	**8:27 am**	5:27 am
☉ ♊	20		9:29 pm
☉ ♊	21	**12:29 am**	
♂ ♋	28	**6:43 am**	3:43 am

Planetary Motion			
	day	EST / hr:mn / PST	
♆ ℞	13	**7:10 am**	4:10 am
☿ ℞	15	**1:51 pm**	10:51 am

DATE		SID.TIME	SUN	MOON	NODE	MERCURY	VENUS	MARS	JUPITER	SATURN	URANUS	NEPTUNE	PLUTO	CERES	PALLAS	JUNO	VESTA	CHIRON
1	W	14:35:00	10 ♉ 26 59	1 ♑ 39	18 ♊ 22	0 ♊ 52	6 ♊ 23	11 ♊ 42	10 ♋ 56	13 ♊ 30	28 ♒ 24	10 ♒ 56	17 ♐ ℞ 11	25 ♓ 25	24 ♒ 19	18 ♌ 46	24 ♊ 40	9 ♑ ℞ 01
2	Th	14:38:56	11 25 12	14 47	18 23	2 03	7 36	12 23	11 05	13 37	28 25	10 57	17 10	25 46	24 32	18 57	25 04	9 00
3	F	14:42:53	12 23 24	27 32	18 25	3 09	8 49	13 03	11 15	13 44	28 27	10 57	17 09	26 07	24 43	19 09	25 28	8 58
4	Sa	14:46:49	13 21 35	9 ♒ 57	18 ℞ 25	4 10	10 02	13 43	11 25	13 51	28 28	10 57	17 08	26 28	24 55	19 21	25 51	8 57
5	Su	14:50:46	14 19 44	22 07	18 25	5 07	11 14	14 23	11 35	13 58	28 30	10 58	17 06	26 48	25 06	19 33	26 15	8 55
6	M	14:54:42	15 17 52	4 ♓ 06	18 23	5 58	12 27	15 04	11 45	14 06	28 31	10 58	17 05	27 09	25 18	19 46	26 39	8 54
7	T	14:58:39	16 15 59	15 59	18 20	6 45	13 40	15 44	11 55	14 13	28 32	10 58	17 04	27 29	25 29	19 59	27 03	8 52
8	W	15:02:36	17 14 03	27 50	18 16	7 27	14 52	16 24	12 05	14 20	28 34	10 58	17 02	27 49	25 39	20 12	27 27	8 51
9	Th	15:06:32	18 12 07	9 ♈ 44	18 11	8 04	16 05	17 04	12 15	14 27	28 35	10 59	17 01	28 09	25 50	20 25	27 52	8 49
10	F	15:10:29	19 10 09	21 41	18 06	8 35	17 17	17 44	12 26	14 35	28 36	10 59	17 00	28 30	26 00	20 38	28 16	8 47
11	Sa	15:14:25	20 08 09	3 ♉ 46	18 01	9 02	18 30	18 24	12 36	14 42	28 37	10 59	16 58	28 50	26 10	20 52	28 40	8 45
12	Su	15:18:22	21 06 08	16 00	17 57	9 24	19 42	19 04	12 47	14 49	28 38	10 59	16 57	29 10	26 20	21 06	29 05	8 43
13	M	15:22:18	22 04 06	28 24	17 55	9 40	20 54	19 44	12 57	14 57	28 39	10 ℞ 59	16 55	29 29	26 29	21 20	29 29	8 41
14	T	15:26:15	23 02 02	10 ♊ 59	17 D 53	9 51	22 07	20 24	13 08	15 04	28 40	10 59	16 54	29 49	26 39	21 34	29 53	8 39
15	W	15:30:11	23 59 57	23 46	17 53	9 ℞ 58	23 19	21 04	13 19	15 12	28 41	10 59	16 53	0 ♈ 09	26 48	21 49	0 ♋ 18	8 37
16	Th	15:34:08	24 57 49	6 ♋ 46	17 54	9 59	24 31	21 44	13 30	15 19	28 42	10 59	16 51	0 28	26 57	22 03	0 43	8 34
17	F	15:38:05	25 55 41	20 00	17 55	9 56	25 43	22 24	13 41	15 26	28 43	10 59	16 50	0 48	27 05	22 18	1 07	8 32
18	Sa	15:42:01	26 53 30	3 ♌ 28	17 57	9 48	26 56	23 04	13 52	15 34	28 44	10 59	16 48	1 07	27 14	22 33	1 32	8 30
19	Su	15:45:58	27 51 18	17 11	17 ℞ 58	9 35	28 08	23 44	14 03	15 42	28 45	10 58	16 47	1 26	27 22	22 48	1 57	8 27
20	M	15:49:54	28 49 04	1 ♍ 10	17 58	9 19	29 20	24 23	14 14	15 49	28 45	10 58	16 45	1 45	27 29	23 04	2 22	8 25
21	T	15:53:51	29 46 49	15 23	17 58	8 58	0 ♋ 32	25 03	14 26	15 57	28 46	10 58	16 44	2 05	27 37	23 19	2 47	8 22
22	W	15:57:47	0 ♊ 44 31	29 49	17 56	8 34	1 44	25 43	14 37	16 04	28 47	10 58	16 42	2 23	27 44	23 35	3 12	8 19
23	Th	16:01:44	1 42 12	14 ♎ 23	17 54	8 07	2 55	26 23	14 48	16 12	28 47	10 57	16 41	2 42	27 51	23 51	3 37	8 16
24	F	16:05:40	2 39 52	29 00	17 52	7 38	4 07	27 02	15 00	16 20	28 48	10 57	16 39	3 01	27 58	24 07	4 02	8 14
25	Sa	16:09:37	3 37 30	13 ♏ 35	17 51	7 07	5 19	27 42	15 12	16 27	28 48	10 57	16 38	3 19	28 04	24 23	4 27	8 11
26	Su	16:13:34	4 35 07	28 01	17 49	6 34	6 31	28 22	15 23	16 35	28 49	10 56	16 36	3 38	28 10	24 39	4 52	8 08
27	M	16:17:30	5 32 43	12 ♐ 12	17 D 49	6 00	7 42	29 01	15 35	16 43	28 49	10 56	16 34	3 56	28 16	24 56	5 17	8 05
28	T	16:21:27	6 30 17	26 05	17 49	5 26	8 54	29 41	15 47	16 50	28 49	10 55	16 33	4 15	28 22	25 12	5 42	8 02
29	W	16:25:23	7 27 51	9 ♑ 35	17 50	4 52	10 05	0 ♋ 20	15 59	16 58	28 50	10 55	16 31	4 33	28 27	25 29	6 08	7 59
30	Th	16:29:20	8 25 23	22 44	17 50	4 19	11 17	1 00	16 10	17 06	28 50	10 55	16 30	4 51	28 32	25 46	6 33	7 56
31	F	16:33:16	9 22 55	5 ♒ 31	17 51	3 48	12 28	1 39	16 22	17 14	28 50	10 54	16 28	5 08	28 36	26 03	6 58	7 52

EPHEMERIS CALCULATED FOR 12 MIDNIGHT GREENWICH MEAN TIME. ALL OTHER DATA AND FACING ASPECTARIAN PAGE IN **EASTERN STANDARD TIME (BOLD)** AND PACIFIC STANDARD TIME (REGULAR).

JUNE 2002

1 SATURDAY
☉△♆ **8:37 am** 5:37 am
☽☍⚵ **11:47 am** 8:47 am
☽☌♀ **4:08 pm** 1:08 pm
☽☌♅ **4:19 pm** 1:19 pm
⚷☍⚶ **4:24 pm** 1:24 pm
☿⊻♂ **4:40 pm** 1:40 pm
☽□☿ 9:07 pm
☽△♂ 9:50 pm

2 SUNDAY
☽□☿ **12:07 am**
☽△♂ **12:50 am**
☽⊻⚳ **6:17 am** 3:17 am
☽⚹⚷ **10:01 am** 7:01 am
☽△⚶ **10:45 am** 7:45 am
☽⊻♆ **4:18 pm** 1:18 pm
☽□☉ **7:05 pm** 4:05 pm
♀⊼♇ 11:08 pm

3 MONDAY
♀⊼♇ **2:08 am**
☽□♇ **3:22 am** 12:22 am
☽△♀ **3:30 am** 12:30 am
☽△♃ **4:44 am** 1:44 am
♅☌♀ **5:24 am** 2:24 am
☽□♄ **5:58 am** 2:58 am
♀☌♃ **6:12 pm** 3:12 pm
☽⊼⚵ 10:23 pm

4 TUESDAY
☽⊼⚵ **1:23 am**
☽⊻♅ **4:30 am** 1:30 am
☽⊻♀ **4:37 am** 1:37 am
♀⊻♄ **7:03 am** 4:03 am
☽⚹☿ **10:44 am** 7:44 am
☽□♂ **4:42 pm** 1:42 pm
☽☌⚳ **8:13 pm** 5:13 pm
☽□⚷ **10:11 pm** 7:11 pm
☽□⚶ 10:27 pm

5 WEDNESDAY
☽□⚶ **1:27 am**
☽⚹♆ **4:45 am** 1:45 am
☽⚹☉ **12:54 pm** 9:54 am
☽△♇ **3:46 pm** 12:46 pm
☽□♃ **6:19 pm** 3:19 pm
☽⚹♄ **7:09 pm** 4:09 pm
☽□♀ **10:41 pm** 7:41 pm

6 THURSDAY
☽△⚵ **3:15 pm** 12:15 pm
☽⚹♅ **4:47 pm** 1:47 pm
☽⚹♀ **5:08 pm** 2:08 pm
☽⊻☿ **9:58 pm** 6:58 pm
☉☍♇ **11:44 pm** 8:44 pm

7 FRIDAY
☽⚹♂ **8:10 am** 5:10 am
☽⊻⚳ **9:36 am** 6:36 am
☽△⚷ **9:49 am** 6:49 am
☽⚹⚶ **3:27 pm** 12:27 pm
☽□♆ **4:26 pm** 1:26 pm
⚷□⚳ **5:39 pm** 2:39 pm

8 SATURDAY
☽⊼♇ **3:02 am** 12:02 am
☽⊻☉ **5:23 am** 2:23 am
☽⚹♃ **6:38 am** 3:38 am
☽⊻♄ **7:04 am** 4:04 am
♂☍⚷ **12:31 pm** 9:31 am
☽⚹♀ **4:03 pm** 1:03 pm
♆⊼⚶ **6:24 pm** 3:24 pm
☉⊻♃ 10:43 pm

9 SUNDAY
☉⊻♃ **1:43 am**
☽□⚵ **3:13 am** 12:13 am
☽□♅ **3:14 am** 12:14 am
♅☍⚵ **3:41 am** 12:41 am
☽□♀ **3:44 am** 12:44 am
♂□⚳ **5:19 am** 2:19 am
☉☌♄ **6:24 am** 3:24 am
☽☌☿ **8:07 am** 5:07 am
☽⊼⚷ **7:18 pm** 4:18 pm
☽⚹⚳ **8:38 pm** 5:38 pm
☽⊻♂ **9:07 pm** 6:07 pm
♀☍⚵ 10:45 pm
☽△♆ 10:49 pm
☽⊻⚶ 11:57 pm

10 MONDAY
♀☍⚵ **1:45 am**
☽△♆ **1:49 am**
☽⊻⚶ **2:57 am**
☽☍♇ **11:53 am** 8:53 am
☽⊻♃ **4:23 pm** 1:23 pm
☽☌♄ **4:26 pm** 1:26 pm
☽☌☉ **6:46 pm** 3:46 pm
♃⊻♄ 11:36 pm

11 TUESDAY
♃⊻♄ **2:36 am**
☽⊻♀ **6:00 am** 3:00 am
☽△♅ **11:05 am** 8:05 am
☽△♀ **11:39 am** 8:39 am
☽⚹⚵ **12:25 pm** 9:25 am
☽⊻☿ **4:26 pm** 1:26 pm
☽☍⚷ 11:11 pm

12 WEDNESDAY
☽☍⚷ **2:11 am**
☽□⚳ **4:51 am** 1:51 am
☽☌♂ **7:00 am** 4:00 am
☽⊼♆ **8:37 am** 5:37 am
☽☌⚶ **11:34 am** 8:34 am
☽⊼♇ **6:12 pm** 3:12 pm
☽⊻♄ **11:12 pm** 8:12 pm
☽☌♃ **11:28 pm** 8:28 pm

13 THURSDAY
☽⊻☉ **5:00 am** 2:00 am
♀⊼♅ **2:29 pm** 11:29 am
♂⊼♆ **3:29 pm** 12:29 pm
☽⊼♅ **4:32 pm** 1:32 pm
☽☌♀ **4:44 pm** 1:44 pm
☽⊼♀ **5:09 pm** 2:09 pm
☽⊻⚵ **7:06 pm** 4:06 pm
♀⊼♀ **9:34 pm** 6:34 pm
☽⚹☿ **11:02 pm** 8:02 pm

14 FRIDAY
☽⊼⚷ **6:54 am** 3:54 am
☽△⚳ **10:44 am** 7:44 am
☽☍♆ **1:17 pm** 10:17 am
☽⊻♂ **2:23 pm** 11:23 am
☽⊻⚶ **5:53 pm** 2:53 pm
☽△♇ **10:31 pm** 7:31 pm

15 SATURDAY
☽⚹♄ **3:57 am** 12:57 am
☽⊻♃ **4:31 am** 1:31 am
♀⊻⚵ **5:51 am** 2:51 am
☽⚹☉ **12:55 pm** 9:55 am
☽☍♅ **8:17 pm** 5:17 pm
☽☍♀ **8:53 pm** 5:53 pm
☽☌⚵ 9:01 pm
☽⊻♀ 10:13 pm

16 SUNDAY
☽☌⚵ **12:01 am**
☽⊻♀ **1:13 am**
☽□☿ **4:32 am** 1:32 am
☽△⚷ **10:07 am** 7:07 am
☽⊼⚳ **3:03 pm** 12:03 pm
☽⊼♆ **4:32 pm** 1:32 pm
☽⚹♂ **8:09 pm** 5:09 pm
☽⚹⚶ **10:44 pm** 7:44 pm
☽□♇ 10:34 pm

17 MONDAY
☽□♇ **1:34 am**
☽□♄ **7:28 am** 4:28 am
☽⚹♃ **8:20 am** 5:20 am
☽□☉ **7:29 pm** 4:29 pm
☽⊼♅ **11:04 pm** 8:04 pm
☽⊼♀ **11:37 pm** 8:37 pm

18 TUESDAY
☽⊻⚵ **3:57 am** 12:57 am
☽⚹♀ **8:30 am** 5:30 am
☽△☿ **9:42 am** 6:42 am
☽□⚷ **12:34 pm** 9:34 am
☽☍⚳ **6:35 pm** 3:35 pm
☽△♆ **7:06 pm** 4:06 pm
☽□♂ 10:10 pm
☽□⚶ 11:54 pm

19 WEDNESDAY
☽□♂ **1:10 am**
☽□⚶ **2:54 am**
☽⚹♇ **4:02 am** 1:02 am
☽△♄ **10:28 am** 7:28 am
☽□♃ **11:39 am** 8:39 am
♆⚹⚳ **9:47 pm** 6:47 pm
☉△♅ 9:08 pm
☽△♅ 10:32 pm
☽△☉ 10:38 pm
☽△♀ 11:02 pm

20 THURSDAY
☉△♅ **12:08 am**
☽△♅ **1:32 am**
☽△☉ **1:38 am**
☽△♀ **2:02 am**
☿⚹♀ **3:52 am** 12:52 am
☉△♀ **7:16 am** 4:16 am
☽⚹⚵ **7:39 am** 4:39 am
♀⊼⚷ **7:42 am** 4:42 am
☿⊼⚷ **8:58 am** 5:58 am
♇⊼⚶ **2:11 pm** 11:11 am
☽⚹⚷ **2:54 pm** 11:54 am
☽⊼☿ **3:19 pm** 12:19 pm
☽□♀ **3:34 pm** 12:34 pm
☽□♆ **9:38 pm** 6:38 pm
☽⊼⚳ **10:05 pm** 7:05 pm

21 FRIDAY
☽△♂ **6:15 am** 3:15 am
☽⊻♇ **6:37 am** 3:37 am
☽△⚶ **7:10 am** 4:10 am
☽⊼♄ **1:41 pm** 10:41 am
♂⊼♇ **1:59 pm** 10:59 am
☽△♃ **3:12 pm** 12:12 pm

22 SATURDAY
☽□♅ **4:27 am** 1:27 am
☽□♀ **4:50 am** 1:50 am
☽⊼☉ **8:20 am** 5:20 am
☽□⚵ **11:56 am** 8:56 am
☽⊻⚷ **5:52 pm** 2:52 pm
☽☍☿ **10:20 pm** 7:20 pm
☽△♀ **11:29 pm** 8:29 pm
☽⚹♆ 9:55 pm
☽△⚳ 11:21 pm

23 SUNDAY
☽⚹♆ **12:55 am**
☽△⚳ **2:21 am**
☽☌♇ **10:06 am** 7:06 am
☽⊼♂ **12:23 pm** 9:23 am
☽⊼⚶ **12:28 pm** 9:28 am
♀☍♆ **4:21 pm** 1:21 pm
♂☌⚶ **5:52 pm** 2:52 pm
☽☍♄ **5:57 pm** 2:57 pm
☽⊼♃ **7:52 pm** 4:52 pm

24 MONDAY
☿△♆ **6:59 am** 3:59 am
☽⚹♅ **8:38 am** 5:38 am
☽⚹♀ **8:52 am** 5:52 am
☽☍☉ **4:42 pm** 1:42 pm
♀△⚳ **5:37 pm** 2:37 pm
☽△⚵ **5:46 pm** 2:46 pm
☽☌⚷ **10:21 pm** 7:21 pm

25 TUESDAY
☽⊻♆ **5:51 am** 2:51 am
☽⊼☿ **8:04 am** 5:04 am
☽□⚳ **8:22 am** 5:22 am
☽⊼♀ **9:30 am** 6:30 am
☿⚹⚳ **12:13 pm** 9:13 am
☉⚹⚵ **2:57 pm** 11:57 am
☽⊻♇ **3:25 pm** 12:25 pm
☽☍⚶ **7:49 pm** 4:49 pm
☽☍♂ **8:40 pm** 5:40 pm
☽⊼♄ 9:15 pm
☽☍♃ 11:37 pm

26 WEDNESDAY
☽⊼♄ **12:15 am**
☽☍♃ **2:37 am**
☽⊻♅ **3:01 pm** 12:01 pm
☽⊻♀ **3:03 pm** 12:03 pm
♅☌♀ **10:37 pm** 7:37 pm
☽⊼⚵ 11:09 pm

27 THURSDAY
☽⊼⚵ **2:09 am**
☽⊼☉ **4:00 am** 1:00 am
☽⊻⚷ **5:13 am** 2:13 am
☽☌♆ **1:18 pm** 10:18 am
☽⚹⚳ **5:03 pm** 2:03 pm
☉☍⚷ **7:23 pm** 4:23 pm
☽△☿ **9:57 pm** 6:57 pm
☽☍♀ **10:53 pm** 7:53 pm
☽⚹♇ **11:20 pm** 8:20 pm

28 FRIDAY
♀△♇ **3:50 am** 12:50 am
☽⊼⚶ **6:09 am** 3:09 am
☽⊼♂ **8:04 am** 5:04 am
☽△♄ **9:20 am** 6:20 am
☿☍♇ **10:39 am** 7:39 am
☽⊼♃ **12:16 pm** 9:16 am
☽☌♀ **11:56 pm** 8:56 pm
☽☌♅ 9:12 pm

29 SATURDAY
☽☌♅ **12:12 am**
☽☍⚵ **1:37 pm** 10:37 am
♂⊻♄ **2:01 pm** 11:01 am
☽⚹⚷ **2:54 pm** 11:54 am
☿⚹♀ **5:16 pm** 2:16 pm
☽△☉ **6:52 pm** 3:52 pm
☽⊻♆ **11:34 pm** 8:34 pm

30 SUNDAY
☽⊻⚳ **4:40 am** 1:40 am
☽□♇ **10:02 am** 7:02 am
☽⊼♀ **3:54 pm** 12:54 pm
☽□☿ **4:37 pm** 1:37 pm
☽△⚶ **7:30 pm** 4:30 pm
☽□♄ **9:11 pm** 6:11 pm
☽△♂ **10:37 pm** 7:37 pm
☽△♃ 9:43 pm

Eastern Standard Time in bold type
Pacific Standard Time in medium type

JUNE 2002

☽ Last Aspect day	EST	hr:mn / PST	asp	☽ Ingress sign	day	EST	hr:mn / PST
1	**4:19 pm**	1:19 pm	☌ ♅	♓	1	**6:37 pm**	3:37 pm
3	**5:58 am**	2:58 am	□ ♄	♈	4	**6:51 am**	3:51 am
6	**4:47 pm**	1:47 pm	⚹ ♅	♉	6	**7:07 pm**	4:07 pm
9	**3:14 am**	12:14 am	□ ♅	♊	9	**5:29 am**	2:29 am
11	**11:05 am**	8:05 am	△ ♅	♋	11	**1:15 pm**	10:15 am
13	**4:44 pm**	1:44 pm	☌ ♀	♌	13	**6:39 pm**	3:39 pm
15	**8:17 pm**	5:17 pm	☍ ♅	♍	15	**10:23 pm**	7:23 pm
17	**7:29 pm**	4:29 pm	□ ☉	♎	17		10:11 pm
17	**7:29 pm**	4:29 pm	□ ☉	♎	18	**1:11 am**	
19		10:38 pm	△ ☉	♏	20	**3:42 am**	12:42 am
20	**1:38 am**		△ ☉	♏	20	**3:42 am**	12:42 am
22	**4:27 am**	1:27 am	□ ♅	♐	22	**6:42 am**	3:42 am
24	**8:38 am**	5:38 am	⚹ ♅	♑	24	**11:01 am**	8:01 am
25		11:37 pm	☍ ♃	♒	26	**5:36 pm**	2:36 pm
26	**2:37 am**		☍ ♃	♒	26	**5:36 pm**	2:36 pm
28		9:12 pm	☌ ♅	♓	29	**3:00 am**	12:00 am
29	**12:12 am**		☌ ♅	♓	29	**3:00 am**	12:00 am
30		9:43 pm	△ ♃	♈	7/1	**2:49 pm**	11:49 am
7/1	**12:43 am**		△ ♃	♈	7/1	**2:49 pm**	11:49 am

☽ Phases & Eclipses phase	day	EST	hr:mn / PST
4th Quarter	2	**7:05 pm**	4:05 pm
New Moon	10	**6:46 pm**	3:46 pm
●	10	19° ♊ 54'	
2nd Quarter	17	**7:29 pm**	4:29 pm
Full Moon	24	**4:42 pm**	1:42 pm
○●	24	3° ♑ 11'	

Planet Ingress	day	EST	hr:mn / PST
⚵ ♍	12	**11:28 pm**	8:28 pm
♀ ♌	14	**3:16 pm**	12:16 pm
☉ ♋	21	**8:24 am**	5:24 am

Planetary Motion	day	EST	hr:mn / PST
♅ ℞	2	**7:11 pm**	4:11 pm
☿ D	8	**10:12 am**	7:12 am
♀ ℞	13	**12:50 pm**	9:50 am

DATE		SID.TIME	SUN	MOON	NODE	MERCURY	VENUS	MARS	JUPITER	SATURN	URANUS	NEPTUNE	PLUTO	CERES	PALLAS	JUNO	VESTA	CHIRON
1	Sa	16:37:13	10 ♊ 20 26	17 ♒ 59	17 ♊ 52	3 ♊ ℞ 19	13 ♋ 39	2 ♋ 19	16 ♋ 34	17 ♊ 21	28 ♒ 50	10 ♒ ℞ 53	16 ♐ ℞ 27	5 ♈ 26	28 ♒ 41	26 ♌ 20	7 ♋ 24	7 ♑ ℞ 49
2	Su	16:41:10	11 17 55	0 ♓ 12	17 52	2 52	14 51	2 58	16 47	17 29	28 50	10 53	16 25	5 44	28 45	26 38	7 49	7 46
3	M	16:45:06	12 15 25	12 13	17 ℞ 52	2 28	16 02	3 37	16 59	17 37	28 ℞ 50	10 52	16 23	6 01	28 49	26 55	8 15	7 43
4	T	16:49:03	13 12 53	24 08	17 52	2 07	17 13	4 17	17 11	17 45	28 50	10 52	16 22	6 19	28 52	27 13	8 40	7 39
5	W	16:52:59	14 10 20	6 ♈ 01	17 52	1 50	18 24	4 56	17 23	17 52	28 50	10 51	16 20	6 36	28 55	27 30	9 06	7 36
6	Th	16:56:56	15 07 47	17 56	17 52	1 36	19 35	5 36	17 35	18 00	28 50	10 50	16 18	6 53	28 58	27 48	9 31	7 32
7	F	17:00:52	16 05 14	29 57	17 51	1 27	20 46	6 15	17 48	18 08	28 50	10 49	16 17	7 10	29 00	28 06	9 57	7 29
8	Sa	17:04:49	17 02 39	12 ♉ 08	17 D 51	1 D 22	21 57	6 54	18 00	18 16	28 50	10 49	16 15	7 26	29 02	28 24	10 23	7 25
9	Su	17:08:45	18 00 04	24 31	17 51	1 22	23 08	7 33	18 13	18 24	28 49	10 48	16 14	7 43	29 04	28 43	10 48	7 22
10	M	17:12:42	18 57 28	7 ♊ 09	17 ℞ 51	1 25	24 18	8 13	18 25	18 31	28 49	10 47	16 12	8 00	29 06	29 01	11 14	7 18
11	T	17:16:39	19 54 52	20 02	17 51	1 34	25 29	8 52	18 38	18 39	28 49	10 46	16 10	8 16	29 07	29 19	11 40	7 15
12	W	17:20:35	20 52 15	3 ♋ 10	17 51	1 47	26 40	9 31	18 50	18 47	28 48	10 45	16 09	8 32	29 08	29 38	12 06	7 11
13	Th	17:24:32	21 49 37	16 34	17 51	2 04	27 50	10 10	19 03	18 55	28 48	10 44	16 07	8 48	29 ℞ 08	29 57	12 32	7 07
14	F	17:28:28	22 46 58	0 ♌ 12	17 51	2 26	29 01	10 49	19 16	19 03	28 47	10 43	16 06	9 04	29 08	0 ♍ 15	12 58	7 03
15	Sa	17:32:25	23 44 18	14 01	17 50	2 53	0 ♌ 11	11 28	19 28	19 10	28 47	10 42	16 04	9 20	29 08	0 34	13 24	7 00
16	Su	17:36:21	24 41 38	28 01	17 49	3 23	1 21	12 07	19 41	19 18	28 46	10 41	16 02	9 35	29 07	0 53	13 50	6 56
17	M	17:40:18	25 38 56	12 ♍ 08	17 49	3 58	2 31	12 47	19 54	19 26	28 45	10 40	16 01	9 50	29 06	1 12	14 16	6 52
18	T	17:44:14	26 36 14	26 20	17 D 49	4 38	3 42	13 26	20 07	19 34	28 45	10 39	15 59	10 06	29 05	1 31	14 42	6 48
19	W	17:48:11	27 33 30	10 ♎ 35	17 49	5 21	4 52	14 05	20 20	19 41	28 44	10 38	15 58	10 21	29 03	1 51	15 08	6 44
20	Th	17:52:08	28 30 46	24 50	17 49	6 09	6 02	14 44	20 33	19 49	28 43	10 37	15 56	10 35	29 01	2 10	15 34	6 41
21	F	17:56:04	29 28 01	9 ♏ 03	17 50	7 00	7 11	15 23	20 45	19 57	28 42	10 36	15 55	10 50	28 59	2 29	16 00	6 37
22	Sa	18:00:01	0 ♋ 25 16	23 10	17 51	7 56	8 21	16 02	20 58	20 05	28 42	10 35	15 53	11 05	28 56	2 49	16 26	6 33
23	Su	18:03:57	1 22 30	7 ♐ 09	17 ℞ 52	8 56	9 31	16 40	21 11	20 12	28 41	10 34	15 52	11 19	28 53	3 09	16 53	6 29
24	M	18:07:54	2 19 43	20 56	17 52	9 59	10 41	17 19	21 24	20 20	28 40	10 33	15 50	11 33	28 50	3 28	17 19	6 25
25	T	18:11:50	3 16 56	4 ♑ 29	17 52	11 06	11 50	17 58	21 38	20 28	28 39	10 32	15 48	11 47	28 46	3 48	17 45	6 21
26	W	18:15:47	4 14 09	17 45	17 50	12 17	12 59	18 37	21 51	20 35	28 38	10 30	15 47	12 01	28 42	4 08	18 11	6 17
27	Th	18:19:43	5 11 22	0 ♒ 45	17 48	13 32	14 09	19 16	22 04	20 43	28 37	10 29	15 45	12 14	28 37	4 28	18 38	6 13
28	F	18:23:40	6 08 34	13 28	17 46	14 50	15 18	19 55	22 17	20 51	28 35	10 28	15 44	12 27	28 32	4 48	19 04	6 10
29	Sa	18:27:37	7 05 46	25 54	17 43	16 12	16 27	20 34	22 30	20 58	28 34	10 27	15 43	12 41	28 27	5 08	19 30	6 06
30	Su	18:31:33	8 02 58	8 ♓ 07	17 40	17 37	17 36	21 12	22 43	21 06	28 33	10 25	15 41	12 54	28 21	5 28	19 57	6 02

EPHEMERIS CALCULATED FOR 12 MIDNIGHT GREENWICH MEAN TIME. ALL OTHER DATA AND FACING ASPECTARIAN PAGE IN **EASTERN STANDARD TIME (BOLD)** AND PACIFIC STANDARD TIME (REGULAR).

JULY 2002

1 MONDAY
☽ △ ♃ **12:43 am**
⚷ △ ⚵ **4:30 am** 1:30 am
☽ ⚺ ♀ **11:10 am** 8:10 am
☽ ⚺ ♅ **11:49 am** 8:49 am
☿ ⚺ ⚶ **10:47 pm** 7:47 pm
☽ □ ⚷ 11:41 pm

2 TUESDAY
☽ □ ⚷ **2:41 am**
☽ ⚻ ⚵ **3:28 am** 12:28 am
☉ ⚻ ♆ **5:20 am** 2:20 am
☿ ☌ ♄ **6:34 am** 3:34 am
☽ ⚹ ♆ **11:45 am** 8:45 am
☽ □ ☉ **12:19 pm** 9:19 am
☽ ☌ ⚳ **6:06 pm** 3:06 pm
☽ △ ♇ **10:21 pm** 7:21 pm
♀ ⚺ ⚶ 11:42 pm

3 WEDNESDAY
♀ ⚺ ⚶ **2:42 am**
♀ ⚹ ♄ **5:14 am** 2:14 am
♂ ☌ ♃ **8:24 am** 5:24 am
☽ □ ⚶ **10:19 am** 7:19 am
☽ ⚹ ♄ **10:20 am** 7:20 am
☽ △ ♀ **10:49 am** 7:49 am
♄ ⚺ ⚶ **10:51 am** 7:51 am
☿ ⚺ ♃ **2:06 pm** 11:06 am
☽ □ ♃ **2:22 pm** 11:22 am
☽ ⚹ ☿ **2:24 pm** 11:24 am
☽ □ ♂ **2:35 pm** 11:35 am
☿ ⚺ ♂ **4:27 pm** 1:27 pm
☽ ⚹ ♀ **11:04 pm** 8:04 pm
☽ ⚹ ♅ 9:11 pm

4 THURSDAY
☽ ⚹ ♅ **12:11 am**
☽ △ ⚷ **2:39 pm** 11:39 am
☽ △ ⚵ **5:29 pm** 2:29 pm
☽ □ ♆ **11:44 pm** 8:44 pm

5 FRIDAY
☽ ⚹ ☉ **5:31 am** 2:31 am
☽ ⚺ ⚳ **7:03 am** 4:03 am
♀ ⚺ ♃ **8:01 am** 5:01 am
☽ ⚻ ♇ **10:03 am** 7:03 am
☽ ⚺ ♄ **10:22 pm** 7:22 pm
☿ △ ♀ **10:42 pm** 7:42 pm
☽ ⚹ ⚶ **11:57 pm** 8:57 pm
☽ ⚹ ♃ 11:43 pm

6 SATURDAY
☽ ⚹ ♃ **2:43 am**
☽ □ ♀ **4:14 am** 1:14 am
☽ ⚹ ♂ **5:06 am** 2:06 am
☉ □ ⚳ **5:40 am** 2:40 am
☿ △ ♅ **8:42 am** 5:42 am
☽ □ ♀ **9:24 am** 6:24 am
☽ □ ♅ **10:57 am** 7:57 am
☽ ⚺ ☿ **11:20 am** 8:20 am
☽ ⚻ ⚷ 9:34 pm
♀ ⚺ ♂ 9:55 pm

7 SUNDAY
☽ ⚻ ⚷ **12:34 am**
♀ ⚺ ♂ **12:55 am**
☽ □ ⚵ **5:10 am** 2:10 am
☽ △ ♆ **9:23 am** 6:23 am
☉ ⚻ ♇ **2:35 pm** 11:35 am
☽ ⚹ ⚳ **5:15 pm** 2:15 pm
☽ ☍ ♇ **7:09 pm** 4:09 pm
☽ ⚺ ☉ **7:31 pm** 4:31 pm

8 MONDAY
♀ ☍ ♀ **7:14 am** 4:14 am
☽ ☌ ♄ **7:24 am** 4:24 am
☽ ⚺ ⚶ **10:19 am** 7:19 am
☽ ⚺ ♃ **11:56 am** 8:56 am
☽ ⚺ ♂ **4:05 pm** 1:05 pm
☽ △ ♀ **4:40 pm** 1:40 pm
☽ ⚹ ♀ **5:40 pm** 2:40 pm
☽ △ ♅ **6:37 pm** 3:37 pm
♂ ⚻ ♀ 10:59 pm

9 TUESDAY
♂ ⚻ ♀ **1:59 am**
☽ ☌ ☿ **4:14 am** 1:14 am
♀ ☍ ♅ **4:38 am** 1:38 am
☽ ☍ ⚷ **7:18 am** 4:18 am
☽ ⚹ ⚵ **1:18 pm** 10:18 am
☽ ⚻ ♆ **3:45 pm** 12:45 pm
☽ □ ⚳ **12:00 pm** 9:00 pm
☿ ☍ ⚷ 9:39 pm
☽ ⚻ ♇ 9:59 pm

10 WEDNESDAY
☿ ☍ ⚷ **12:39 am**
☽ ⚻ ♇ **12:59 am**
☽ ☌ ☉ **5:26 am** 2:26 am
☽ ⚺ ♄ **1:07 pm** 10:07 am
☽ ☌ ⚶ **5:10 pm** 2:10 pm
☽ ☌ ♃ **5:48 pm** 2:48 pm
♂ ⚻ ♅ **6:23 pm** 3:23 pm
☽ ⚻ ♀ **8:51 pm** 5:51 pm
☽ ⚻ ♅ **11:11 pm** 8:11 pm
☽ ☌ ♂ **11:25 pm** 8:25 pm
☽ ⚺ ♀ 12:00 pm

11 THURSDAY
☽ ⚺ ♀ **3:00 am**
☽ ⚻ ⚷ **11:08 am** 8:08 am
☽ ⚺ ☿ **5:02 pm** 2:02 pm
☽ ⚺ ⚵ **6:25 pm** 3:25 pm
☽ ☍ ♆ **7:22 pm** 4:22 pm

12 FRIDAY
☽ △ ⚳ **3:59 am** 12:59 am
☽ △ ♇ **4:14 am** 1:14 am
☿ ⚹ ⚵ **4:19 am** 1:19 am
♃ ☌ ⚶ **8:43 am** 5:43 am
☿ ⚻ ♆ **9:00 am** 6:00 am
☽ ⚺ ☉ **12:16 pm** 9:16 am
☽ ⚹ ♄ **4:28 pm** 1:28 pm
☽ ⚺ ♃ **9:22 pm** 6:22 pm
☽ ⚺ ⚶ **9:35 pm** 6:35 pm
☽ ☍ ♀ **10:57 pm** 7:57 pm
♇ △ ⚳ **11:40 pm** 8:40 pm
☽ ☍ ♅ 10:42 pm

13 SATURDAY
☽ ☍ ♅ **1:42 am**
☽ ⚺ ♂ **4:25 am** 1:25 am
♆ ⚻ ⚵ **6:21 am** 3:21 am
☽ ☌ ♀ **9:49 am** 6:49 am
☽ △ ⚷ **1:16 pm** 10:16 am
☽ ⚻ ♆ **9:29 pm** 6:29 pm
☽ ☌ ⚵ **9:53 pm** 6:53 pm

14 SUNDAY
☽ ⚹ ☿ **3:43 am** 12:43 am
♀ ⚻ ⚶ **5:57 am** 2:57 am
☽ □ ♇ **6:15 am** 3:15 am
☽ ⚻ ⚳ **6:39 am** 3:39 am
☽ ⚹ ☉ **5:49 pm** 2:49 pm
☽ □ ♄ **6:53 pm** 3:53 pm
☿ ⚻ ♇ **8:56 pm** 5:56 pm
☽ ⚹ ♃ 9:08 pm
☽ ⚻ ♀ 9:19 pm
☿ □ ⚳ 10:03 pm
☽ ⚹ ⚶ 10:09 pm

15 MONDAY
☽ ⚹ ♃ **12:08 am**
☽ ⚻ ♀ **12:19 am**
☿ □ ⚳ **1:03 am**
☽ ⚹ ⚶ **1:09 am**
☽ ⚻ ♅ **3:35 am** 12:35 am
♀ △ ⚷ **4:10 am** 1:10 am
♃ ⚻ ♀ **6:43 am** 3:43 am
☽ ⚹ ♂ **8:44 am** 5:44 am
☉ ⚺ ♄ **11:55 am** 8:55 am
☽ □ ⚷ **3:04 pm** 12:04 pm
☽ ⚺ ♀ **4:02 pm** 1:02 pm
☽ △ ♆ **11:27 pm** 8:27 pm
☽ ⚺ ⚵ 10:13 pm

16 TUESDAY
☽ ⚺ ⚵ **1:13 am**
☽ ⚹ ♇ **8:21 am** 5:21 am
☽ ☍ ⚳ **9:21 am** 6:21 am
☽ □ ☿ **2:38 pm** 11:38 am
☽ △ ♄ **9:39 pm** 6:39 pm
☽ □ ☉ **11:47 pm** 8:47 pm
☽ △ ♀ 11:06 pm

17 WEDNESDAY
☽ △ ♀ **2:06 am**
☽ □ ♃ **3:23 am** 12:23 am
☽ □ ⚶ **5:15 am** 2:15 am
☽ △ ♅ **5:58 am** 2:58 am
☽ □ ♂ **1:45 pm** 10:45 am
☽ ⚹ ⚷ **5:35 pm** 2:35 pm
☽ ⚹ ♀ **11:11 pm** 8:11 pm
☽ □ ♆ 11:17 pm
♅ ⚻ ⚶ 11:36 pm

18 THURSDAY
☽ □ ♆ **2:17 am**
♅ ⚻ ⚶ **2:36 am**
☉ ⚻ ♀ **4:38 am** 1:38 am
☽ ⚹ ⚵ **5:31 am** 2:31 am
☽ ⚺ ♇ **11:25 am** 8:25 am
☽ ⚻ ⚳ **1:03 pm** 10:03 am
☿ ⚺ ♄ **3:23 pm** 12:23 pm
☽ ⚻ ♄ 10:35 pm

19 FRIDAY
☽ ⚻ ♄ **1:35 am**
☽ △ ☿ **3:22 am** 12:22 am
☽ □ ♀ **4:59 am** 1:59 am
☽ △ ☉ **7:11 am** 4:11 am
☽ △ ♃ **7:54 am** 4:54 am
☽ □ ♅ **9:35 am** 6:35 am
☽ △ ⚶ **10:42 am** 7:42 am
☿ ⚻ ♀ **1:01 pm** 10:01 am
♀ ⚻ ♆ **1:26 pm** 10:26 am
☽ △ ♂ **8:16 pm** 5:16 pm
☉ ☌ ♃ **8:19 pm** 5:19 pm
☽ ⚺ ⚷ **9:26 pm** 6:26 pm

20 SATURDAY
☽ ⚹ ♆ **6:30 am** 3:30 am
☽ □ ♀ **8:04 am** 5:04 am
☽ □ ⚵ **11:21 am** 8:21 am
☿ ☌ ♃ **11:24 am** 8:24 am
☽ ☌ ♇ **3:57 pm** 12:57 pm
☉ ⚻ ♅ **4:34 pm** 1:34 pm
☽ △ ⚳ **6:13 pm** 3:13 pm
☿ ⚻ ♅ **6:51 pm** 3:51 pm
♂ ⚻ ⚷ **7:14 pm** 4:14 pm
☉ ☌ ☿ **8:47 pm** 5:47 pm

21 SUNDAY
☽ ☍ ♄ **7:05 am** 4:05 am
☽ ⚹ ♀ **9:18 am** 6:18 am
☿ ☌ ⚶ **1:12 pm** 10:12 am
☽ ⚻ ♃ **2:02 pm** 11:02 am
☽ ⚹ ♅ **2:44 pm** 11:44 am
☽ ⚻ ☉ **4:30 pm** 1:30 pm
☽ ⚻ ⚶ **5:52 pm** 2:52 pm
☽ ⚻ ☿ **6:34 pm** 3:34 pm
☽ ☌ ⚷ 11:52 pm

22 MONDAY
☽ ☌ ⚷ **2:52 am**
☽ ⚻ ♂ **4:38 am** 1:38 am
☽ ⚺ ♆ **12:22 pm** 9:22 am
♀ ☌ ⚵ **6:17 pm** 3:17 pm
☽ △ ⚵ **7:00 pm** 4:00 pm
☽ △ ♀ **7:03 pm** 4:03 pm
☽ ⚺ ♇ **10:10 pm** 7:10 pm
☽ □ ⚳ 10:07 pm
♃ ⚻ ♅ 11:18 pm

23 TUESDAY
☽ □ ⚳ **1:07 am**
♃ ⚻ ♅ **2:18 am**
☉ ☌ ⚶ **3:01 am** 12:01 am
☽ ⚻ ♄ **2:23 pm** 11:23 am
☽ ⚺ ♀ **3:18 pm** 12:18 pm
☽ ⚺ ♅ **9:41 pm** 6:41 pm
☿ ⚻ ⚷ **9:50 pm** 6:50 pm
☽ ☍ ♃ **10:05 pm** 7:05 pm

24 WEDNESDAY
☽ ☍ ⚶ **3:05 am** 12:05 am
☽ ☍ ☉ **4:07 am** 1:07 am
♀ □ ♇ **7:41 am** 4:41 am
☽ ⚺ ⚷ **10:11 am** 7:11 am
☽ ☍ ☿ **12:39 pm** 9:39 am
☽ ☍ ♂ **3:12 pm** 12:12 pm
☽ ☌ ♆ **8:10 pm** 5:10 pm
♄ △ ♀ 10:48 pm

25 THURSDAY
♄ △ ♀ **1:48 am**
☽ ⚻ ⚵ **4:50 am** 1:50 am
☽ ⚹ ♇ **6:24 am** 3:24 am
☽ ⚻ ♀ **8:36 am** 5:36 am
☽ ⚹ ⚳ **10:02 am** 7:02 am
☿ ☌ ♂ **10:20 am** 7:20 am
☽ ☌ ♀ **11:16 pm** 8:16 pm
☽ △ ♄ **11:52 pm** 8:52 pm
♀ ⚻ ⚳ 11:46 pm

26 FRIDAY
♀ ⚻ ⚳ **2:46 am**
☽ ☌ ♅ **6:47 am** 3:47 am
☽ ⚻ ♃ **8:24 am** 5:24 am
☿ ☍ ♆ **10:39 am** 7:39 am
☽ ⚻ ⚶ **2:44 pm** 11:44 am
☽ ⚻ ☉ **6:29 pm** 3:29 pm
☽ ⚹ ⚷ **7:42 pm** 4:42 pm

27 SATURDAY
☽ ⚻ ♂ **4:23 am** 1:23 am
☽ ⚺ ♆ **6:12 am** 3:12 am
♇ □ ⚵ **9:01 am** 6:01 am
☉ ⚻ ⚷ **9:12 am** 6:12 am
☽ ⚻ ☿ **10:07 am** 7:07 am
☽ □ ♇ **4:53 pm** 1:53 pm
☽ ☍ ⚵ **5:08 pm** 2:08 pm
☽ ⚺ ⚳ **9:13 pm** 6:13 pm
☽ ☍ ♀ 10:03 pm

28 SUNDAY
☽ ☍ ♀ **1:03 am**
☽ ⚺ ♀ **9:19 am** 6:19 am
☽ □ ♄ **11:37 am** 8:37 am
♂ ☍ ♆ **1:31 pm** 10:31 am
☽ ⚺ ♅ **6:02 pm** 3:02 pm
☽ △ ♃ **9:01 pm** 6:01 pm

29 MONDAY
☿ △ ♇ **3:12 am** 12:12 am
☽ △ ⚶ **4:45 am** 1:45 am
☽ □ ⚷ **7:16 am** 4:16 am
☽ △ ☉ **11:30 am** 8:30 am
☿ ⚺ ⚵ **1:13 pm** 10:13 am
☽ ⚹ ♆ **6:09 pm** 3:09 pm
☽ △ ♂ **7:51 pm** 4:51 pm

30 TUESDAY
☽ △ ♇ **5:08 am** 2:08 am
☽ ⚻ ⚵ **7:22 am** 4:22 am
☿ △ ⚳ **9:10 am** 6:10 am
☽ ☌ ⚳ **10:04 am** 7:04 am
☽ △ ☿ **10:14 am** 7:14 am
☽ ⚻ ♀ **7:33 pm** 4:33 pm
☽ ⚹ ♀ **8:40 pm** 5:40 pm
☽ ⚹ ♄ 9:45 pm

31 WEDNESDAY
☽ ⚹ ♄ **12:45 am**
♀ ⚻ ♀ **5:50 am** 2:50 am
☽ ⚹ ♅ **6:28 am** 3:28 am
☽ □ ♃ **10:48 am** 7:48 am
⚷ ⚻ ⚶ **5:20 pm** 2:20 pm
☽ △ ⚷ **7:39 pm** 4:39 pm
☽ □ ⚶ **7:45 pm** 4:45 pm

Eastern Standard Time in bold type
Pacific Standard Time in medium type

JULY 2002

☽ Last Aspect day	EST / hr:mn / PST	asp	☽ Ingress sign day	EST / hr:mn / PST
6/30	9:43 pm	△ ♃	♈ 1	**2:49 pm** 11:49 am
1	**12:43 am**	△ ♃	♈ 1	**2:49 pm** 11:49 am
3	9:11 pm	⚹ ♅	♉ 4	**3:16 am** 12:16 am
4	**12:11 am**	⚹ ♅	♉ 4	**3:16 am** 12:16 am
6	**10:57 am** 7:57 am	□ ♅	♊ 6	**2:01 pm** 11:01 am
8	**6:37 pm** 3:37 pm	△ ♅	♋ 8	**9:36 pm** 6:36 pm
10	**11:25 pm** 8:25 pm	☌ ♂	♌ 10	11:08 pm
10	**11:25 pm** 8:25 pm	☌ ♂	♌ 11	**2:08 am**
12	10:42 pm	☍ ♅	♍ 13	**4:41 am** 1:41 am
13	**1:42 am**	☍ ♅	♍ 13	**4:41 am** 1:41 am
14	9:08 pm	⚹ ♃	♎ 15	**6:39 am** 3:39 am
15	**12:08 am**	⚹ ♃	♎ 15	**6:39 am** 3:39 am
17	**5:58 am** 2:58 am	△ ♅	♏ 17	**9:13 am** 6:13 am
19	**9:35 am** 6:35 am	□ ♅	♐ 19	**1:02 pm** 10:02 am
21	**2:44 pm** 11:44 am	⚹ ♅	♑ 21	**6:26 pm** 3:26 pm
23	**10:05 pm** 7:05 pm	☍ ♃	♒ 23	10:40 pm
23	**10:05 pm** 7:05 pm	☍ ♃	♒ 24	**1:40 am**
26	**6:47 am** 3:47 am	☌ ♅	♓ 26	**11:04 am** 8:04 am
28	**9:01 pm** 6:01 pm	△ ♃	♈ 28	**10:39 pm** 7:39 pm
31	**10:48 am** 7:48 am	□ ♃	♉ 31	**11:17 am** 8:17 am

☽ Phases & Eclipses phase	day	EST / hr:mn / PST
4th Quarter	2	**12:19 pm** 9:19 am
New Moon	10	**5:26 am** 2:26 am
2nd Quarter	16	**11:47 pm** 8:47 pm
Full Moon	24	**4:07 am** 1:07 am

Planet Ingress	day	EST / hr:mn / PST
☿ ♋	7	**5:35 am** 2:35 am
♀ ♍	10	**4:09 pm** 1:09 pm
♂ ♌	13	**10:23 am** 7:23 am
☿ ♌	21	**5:41 pm** 2:41 pm
⚵ ♌	22	**10:26 am** 7:26 am
☉ ♌	22	**7:15 pm** 4:15 pm

Planetary Motion	day	EST / hr:mn / PST

DATE		SID.TIME	SUN	MOON	NODE	MERCURY	VENUS	MARS	JUPITER	SATURN	URANUS	NEPTUNE	PLUTO	CERES	PALLAS	JUNO	VESTA	CHIRON
1	M	18:35:30	9 ♋ 00 11	20 ♓ 09	17 ♊ ℞ 38	19 ♊ 06	18 ♌ 45	21 ♋ 51	22 ♋ 56	21 ♊ 13	28 ♒ ℞ 32	10 ♒ ℞ 24	15 ♐ ℞ 40	13 ♈ 06	28 ♒ ℞ 15	5 ♍ 48	20 ♋ 23	5 ♑ ℞ 58
2	T	18:39:26	9 57 23	2 ♈ 04	17 D 37	20 39	19 54	22 30	23 10	21 21	28 30	10 23	15 38	13 19	28 09	6 09	20 50	5 54
3	W	18:43:23	10 54 35	13 57	17 37	22 15	21 03	23 09	23 23	21 29	28 29	10 21	15 37	13 31	28 02	6 29	21 16	5 50
4	Th	18:47:19	11 51 48	25 52	17 38	23 54	22 11	23 47	23 36	21 36	28 28	10 20	15 35	13 43	27 55	6 49	21 43	5 46
5	F	18:51:16	12 49 01	7 ♉ 54	17 39	25 37	23 20	24 26	23 49	21 44	28 26	10 19	15 34	13 55	27 48	7 10	22 09	5 42
6	Sa	18:55:12	13 46 14	20 08	17 41	27 22	24 28	25 05	24 03	21 51	28 25	10 17	15 33	14 07	27 40	7 30	22 36	5 38
7	Su	18:59:09	14 43 28	2 ♊ 37	17 42	29 11	25 36	25 43	24 16	21 58	28 23	10 16	15 31	14 18	27 32	7 51	23 02	5 35
8	M	19:03:06	15 40 41	15 25	17 ℞ 43	1 ♋ 03	26 44	26 22	24 29	22 06	28 22	10 14	15 30	14 29	27 23	8 12	23 29	5 31
9	T	19:07:02	16 37 55	28 33	17 42	2 57	27 52	27 01	24 43	22 13	28 20	10 13	15 29	14 40	27 15	8 33	23 55	5 27
10	W	19:10:59	17 35 10	12 ♋ 02	17 40	4 54	29 00	27 39	24 56	22 21	28 19	10 11	15 27	14 51	27 06	8 53	24 22	5 23
11	Th	19:14:55	18 32 24	25 51	17 37	6 54	0 ♍ 08	28 18	25 09	22 28	28 17	10 10	15 26	15 01	26 56	9 14	24 49	5 20
12	F	19:18:52	19 29 39	9 ♌ 55	17 33	8 56	1 16	28 57	25 23	22 35	28 15	10 08	15 25	15 11	26 46	9 35	25 15	5 16
13	Sa	19:22:48	20 26 53	24 12	17 28	10 59	2 23	29 35	25 36	22 42	28 14	10 07	15 23	15 21	26 36	9 56	25 42	5 12
14	Su	19:26:45	21 24 08	8 ♍ 36	17 24	13 04	3 31	0 ♌ 14	25 50	22 50	28 12	10 05	15 22	15 31	26 26	10 17	26 09	5 08
15	M	19:30:42	22 21 23	23 01	17 20	15 11	4 38	0 52	26 03	22 57	28 10	10 04	15 21	15 40	26 15	10 38	26 35	5 05
16	T	19:34:38	23 18 37	7 ♎ 23	17 17	17 18	5 45	1 31	26 16	23 04	28 08	10 02	15 20	15 50	26 04	11 00	27 02	5 01
17	W	19:38:35	24 15 52	21 38	17 D 16	19 26	6 52	2 09	26 30	23 11	28 07	10 01	15 19	15 59	25 52	11 21	27 29	4 58
18	Th	19:42:31	25 13 07	5 ♏ 44	17 17	21 35	7 59	2 48	26 43	23 18	28 05	9 59	15 18	16 07	25 41	11 42	27 56	4 54
19	F	19:46:28	26 10 22	19 39	17 18	23 43	9 05	3 26	26 57	23 25	28 03	9 58	15 16	16 16	25 29	12 03	28 22	4 51
20	Sa	19:50:24	27 07 37	3 ♐ 24	17 19	25 52	10 12	4 05	27 10	23 32	28 01	9 56	15 15	16 24	25 17	12 25	28 49	4 47
21	Su	19:54:21	28 04 53	16 57	17 ℞ 20	28 00	11 18	4 43	27 23	23 39	27 59	9 54	15 14	16 31	25 04	12 46	29 16	4 44
22	M	19:58:17	29 02 08	0 ♑ 19	17 19	0 ♌ 07	12 24	5 22	27 37	23 46	27 57	9 53	15 13	16 39	24 51	13 07	29 43	4 40
23	T	20:02:14	29 59 25	13 29	17 16	2 13	13 30	6 00	27 50	23 53	27 55	9 51	15 12	16 46	24 39	13 29	0 ♌ 10	4 37
24	W	20:06:11	0 ♌ 56 41	26 26	17 12	4 19	14 36	6 39	28 04	23 59	27 53	9 50	15 11	16 53	24 25	13 50	0 36	4 34
25	Th	20:10:07	1 53 58	9 ♒ 11	17 05	6 23	15 42	7 17	28 17	24 06	27 51	9 48	15 10	17 00	24 12	14 12	1 03	4 31
26	F	20:14:04	2 51 16	21 43	16 58	8 26	16 47	7 56	28 30	24 13	27 49	9 46	15 09	17 06	23 58	14 34	1 30	4 27
27	Sa	20:18:00	3 48 35	4 ♓ 03	16 49	10 27	17 52	8 34	28 44	24 19	27 47	9 45	15 08	17 12	23 44	14 55	1 57	4 24
28	Su	20:21:57	4 45 54	16 12	16 41	12 28	18 57	9 12	28 57	24 26	27 44	9 43	15 07	17 18	23 30	15 17	2 24	4 21
29	M	20:25:53	5 43 14	28 11	16 34	14 26	20 02	9 51	29 10	24 33	27 42	9 42	15 07	17 23	23 16	15 39	2 51	4 18
30	T	20:29:50	6 40 35	10 ♈ 05	16 29	16 23	21 07	10 29	29 24	24 39	27 40	9 40	15 06	17 29	23 01	16 00	3 18	4 15
31	W	20:33:46	7 37 58	21 56	16 25	18 19	22 11	11 07	29 37	24 46	27 38	9 38	15 05	17 33	22 47	16 22	3 45	4 12

EPHEMERIS CALCULATED FOR 12 MIDNIGHT GREENWICH MEAN TIME. ALL OTHER DATA AND FACING ASPECTARIAN PAGE IN **EASTERN STANDARD TIME (BOLD)** AND PACIFIC STANDARD TIME (REGULAR).

AUGUST 2002

1 THURSDAY

☽ □ ☉	**5:22 am**	2:22 am
☽ □ ♆	**6:34 am**	3:34 am
☽ □ ♂	**11:46 am**	8:46 am
☽ ⚻ ♇	**5:26 pm**	2:26 pm
☉ ☍ ♆	**7:57 pm**	4:57 pm
☿ ☍ ⚴	**9:24 pm**	6:24 pm
☽ △ ⚵	**9:34 pm**	6:34 pm
☽ ⚺ ⚳	**10:42 pm**	7:42 pm

2 FRIDAY

☽ □ ⚴	**7:28 am**	4:28 am
☽ □ ☿	**9:30 am**	6:30 am
♀ □ ♄	**11:10 am**	8:10 am
☽ ⚺ ♄	**1:08 pm**	10:08 am
☽ △ ♀	**1:18 pm**	10:18 am
☽ □ ♅	**5:58 pm**	2:58 pm
☽ ✶ ♃	**11:24 pm**	8:24 pm

3 SATURDAY

☽ ⚻ ⚷	**6:35 am**	3:35 am
☽ ✶ ⚶	**9:06 am**	6:06 am
☿ ✶ ♄	**11:11 am**	8:11 am
☽ △ ♆	**5:04 pm**	2:04 pm
⚳ ⚻ ⚵	**6:56 pm**	3:56 pm
☽ ✶ ☉	**8:52 pm**	5:52 pm
☽ ✶ ♂		10:13 pm

4 SUNDAY

☽ ✶ ♂	**1:13 am**	
☽ ☍ ♇	**3:26 am**	12:26 am
☽ ✶ ⚳	**8:44 am**	5:44 am
☽ □ ⚵	**9:04 am**	6:04 am
☽ △ ⚴	**3:37 pm**	12:37 pm
♀ ⚻ ♅	**5:45 pm**	2:45 pm
☿ ☍ ♅	**5:59 pm**	2:59 pm
☿ ⚺ ♀	**6:20 pm**	3:20 pm
☽ ☌ ♄	**10:28 pm**	7:28 pm
☽ △ ♅		11:22 pm

5 MONDAY

☽ △ ♅	**2:22 am**	
☽ □ ♀	**3:09 am**	12:09 am
☽ ✶ ☿	**3:42 am**	12:42 am
☽ ⚺ ♃	**8:34 am**	5:34 am
☽ ☍ ⚷	**2:08 pm**	11:08 am
☽ ⚺ ⚶	**6:35 pm**	3:35 pm
♂ △ ♇	**8:58 pm**	5:58 pm
☽ ⚻ ♆	**11:58 pm**	8:58 pm

6 TUESDAY

☽ ⚺ ☉	**7:44 am**	4:44 am
☽ ⚻ ♇	**9:42 am**	6:42 am
☽ ⚺ ♂	**10:19 am**	7:19 am
☽ □ ⚳	**2:50 pm**	11:50 am
☽ ✶ ⚵	**4:26 pm**	1:26 pm
☽ ⚻ ⚴	**8:06 pm**	5:06 pm
☿ ⚺ ♃	**9:20 pm**	6:20 pm

7 WEDNESDAY

☽ ⚺ ♄	**3:51 am**	12:51 am
☽ ⚻ ♅	**6:57 am**	3:57 am
☉ △ ♇	**11:29 am**	8:29 am
☽ ✶ ♀	**12:02 pm**	9:02 am
☽ ☌ ♃	**1:43 pm**	10:43 am
☽ ⚺ ☿	**3:39 pm**	12:39 pm
☽ ⚻ ⚷	**5:57 pm**	2:57 pm
☽ ☌ ⚶	**11:56 pm**	8:56 pm

8 THURSDAY

☽ ☍ ♆	**3:14 am**	12:14 am
☿ △ ⚷	**10:38 am**	7:38 am
☽ △ ♇	**12:28 pm**	9:28 am
☽ ☌ ☉	**2:15 pm**	11:15 am
☽ ☌ ♂	**3:26 pm**	12:26 pm
♀ ✶ ♃	**4:41 pm**	1:41 pm
☽ △ ⚳	**5:30 pm**	2:30 pm
☽ ⚺ ⚵	**8:12 pm**	5:12 pm
☽ ☍ ⚴	**9:30 pm**	6:30 pm

9 FRIDAY

☽ ✶ ♄	**6:06 am**	3:06 am
☽ ☍ ♅	**8:36 am**	5:36 am
☽ ⚺ ♃	**3:58 pm**	12:58 pm
☽ ⚺ ♀	**5:21 pm**	2:21 pm
☽ △ ⚷	**7:11 pm**	4:11 pm
☽ ☌ ☿	**11:23 pm**	8:23 pm
☽ ⚺ ⚶		11:39 pm

10 SATURDAY

☽ ⚺ ⚶	**2:39 am**	
⚴ ⚻ ⚵	**3:09 am**	12:09 am
☽ ⚻ ♆	**4:13 am**	1:13 am
☽ □ ♇	**1:17 pm**	10:17 am
♂ △ ⚳	**4:14 pm**	1:14 pm
☉ △ ⚳	**4:36 pm**	1:36 pm
☉ ☌ ♂	**5:17 pm**	2:17 pm
☽ ⚻ ⚳	**6:19 pm**	3:19 pm
☽ ⚺ ♂	**6:25 pm**	3:25 pm
☽ ⚺ ☉	**6:26 pm**	3:26 pm
♀ □ ⚷	**6:46 pm**	3:46 pm
☽ ⚻ ⚴	**9:22 pm**	6:22 pm
☽ ☌ ⚵	**10:09 pm**	7:09 pm

11 SUNDAY

☽ □ ♄	**7:01 am**	4:01 am
☽ ⚻ ♅	**9:04 am**	6:04 am
☿ ⚺ ⚶	**3:36 pm**	12:36 pm
☽ ✶ ♃	**5:17 pm**	2:17 pm
☿ ⚻ ♆	**7:11 pm**	4:11 pm
☽ □ ⚷	**7:39 pm**	4:39 pm
☽ ☌ ♀	**9:34 pm**	6:34 pm

12 MONDAY

♆ ☍ ⚶	**3:47 am**	12:47 am
☽ △ ♆	**4:47 am**	1:47 am
☽ ✶ ⚶	**4:49 am**	1:49 am
☽ ⚺ ☿	**5:58 am**	2:58 am
☉ ☍ ⚴	**6:37 am**	3:37 am
☽ ✶ ♇	**2:03 pm**	11:03 am
☽ ☍ ⚳	**7:13 pm**	4:13 pm
♂ ☍ ⚴	**8:02 pm**	5:02 pm
☽ △ ⚴	**9:26 pm**	6:26 pm
☽ ✶ ♂	**9:32 pm**	6:32 pm
☽ ✶ ☉	**10:46 pm**	7:46 pm
☽ ⚺ ⚵		9:23 pm

13 TUESDAY

☽ ⚺ ⚵	**12:23 am**	
☽ △ ♄	**8:32 am**	5:32 am
☽ △ ♅	**10:11 am**	7:11 am
☽ □ ♃	**7:32 pm**	4:32 pm
☽ ✶ ⚷	**9:07 pm**	6:07 pm

14 WEDNESDAY

☽ ⚺ ♀	**3:03 am**	12:03 am
☽ □ ♆	**6:36 am**	3:36 am
☽ □ ⚶	**8:23 am**	5:23 am
☉ ⚺ ⚵	**1:23 pm**	10:23 am
☽ ✶ ☿	**2:06 pm**	11:06 am
☽ ⚺ ♇	**4:18 pm**	1:18 pm
☽ ⚻ ⚳	**9:43 pm**	6:43 pm
☽ □ ⚴	**11:07 pm**	8:07 pm
☽ □ ♂		11:34 pm

15 THURSDAY

☽ □ ♂	**2:34 am**	
☽ ✶ ⚵	**4:31 am**	1:31 am
☽ □ ☉	**5:12 am**	2:12 am
☿ □ ♇	**10:31 am**	7:31 am
☽ ⚻ ♄	**11:59 am**	8:59 am
☽ □ ♅	**1:13 pm**	10:13 am
☽ △ ♃		9:00 pm
☽ ⚺ ⚷		9:41 pm

16 FRIDAY

☽ △ ♃	**12:00 am**	
☽ ⚺ ⚷	**12:41 am**	
♀ △ ♆	**4:01 am**	1:01 am
☽ ✶ ♆	**10:40 am**	7:40 am
☽ ✶ ♀	**11:12 am**	8:12 am
☽ △ ⚶	**2:26 pm**	11:26 am
☽ ☌ ♇	**8:54 pm**	5:54 pm
☽ □ ☿		10:12 pm
☽ △ ⚳		11:32 pm

17 SATURDAY

☽ □ ☿	**1:12 am**	
☽ △ ⚳	**2:32 am**	
☽ ✶ ⚴	**3:04 am**	12:04 am
☽ △ ♂	**10:22 am**	7:22 am
☽ □ ⚵	**11:14 am**	8:14 am
☿ ⚻ ⚳	**1:24 pm**	10:24 am
♃ ⚻ ⚷	**2:27 pm**	11:27 am
☽ △ ☉	**2:37 pm**	11:37 am
☿ ⚻ ⚴	**4:05 pm**	1:05 pm
☽ ☍ ♄	**5:53 pm**	2:53 pm
☽ ✶ ♅	**6:39 pm**	3:39 pm

18 SUNDAY

☽ ☌ ⚷	**6:41 am**	3:41 am
☽ ⚻ ♃	**6:59 am**	3:59 am
⚳ ✶ ⚴	**9:29 am**	6:29 am
☽ ⚺ ♆	**5:06 pm**	2:06 pm
☽ □ ♀	**10:18 pm**	7:18 pm
☽ ⚻ ⚶	**11:06 pm**	8:06 pm

19 MONDAY

☽ ⚺ ♇	**3:51 am**	12:51 am
♂ ⚺ ⚵	**4:55 am**	1:55 am
☽ ⚺ ⚴	**9:12 am**	6:12 am
☽ □ ⚳	**9:36 am**	6:36 am
☽ △ ☿	**3:13 pm**	12:13 pm
☉ ✶ ♄	**3:35 pm**	12:35 pm
♀ ✶ ⚶	**5:13 pm**	2:13 pm
☉ ☍ ♅	**7:54 pm**	4:54 pm
☽ △ ⚵	**8:27 pm**	5:27 pm
☽ ⚻ ♂	**8:47 pm**	5:47 pm
☽ ⚻ ♄		11:03 pm
☽ ⚺ ♅		11:17 pm
☽ ⚻ ☉		11:50 pm

20 TUESDAY

☽ ⚻ ♄	**2:03 am**	
☽ ⚺ ♅	**2:17 am**	
☽ ⚻ ☉	**2:50 am**	
☽ ⚺ ⚷	**2:49 pm**	11:49 am
☽ ☍ ♃	**4:14 pm**	1:14 pm
☽ ☌ ♆		10:36 pm
♄ △ ♅		11:18 pm

21 WEDNESDAY

☽ ☌ ♆	**1:36 am**	
♄ △ ♅	**2:18 am**	
☽ ☍ ⚶	**10:04 am**	7:04 am
☽ △ ♀	**11:55 am**	8:55 am
☽ ✶ ♇	**12:49 pm**	9:49 am
☽ ☌ ⚴	**5:14 pm**	2:14 pm
☽ ✶ ⚳	**6:35 pm**	3:35 pm
♀ ✶ ♇	**11:35 pm**	8:35 pm

22 THURSDAY

☽ ⚻ ☿	**7:36 am**	4:36 am
☽ ⚻ ⚵	**7:46 am**	4:46 am
☽ ☍ ♂	**9:28 am**	6:28 am
☿ ☌ ⚵	**9:34 am**	6:34 am
☽ ☌ ♅	**11:49 am**	8:49 am
☽ △ ♄	**12:09 pm**	9:09 am
☽ ☍ ☉	**5:29 pm**	2:29 pm
☽ ✶ ⚷		9:49 pm

23 FRIDAY

☽ ✶ ⚷	**12:49 am**	
☽ ⚻ ♃	**3:25 am**	12:25 am
☽ ⚺ ♆	**11:55 am**	8:55 am
☿ ⚺ ♂	**4:48 pm**	1:48 pm
♀ △ ⚴	**8:03 pm**	5:03 pm
☿ ⚻ ♅	**10:52 pm**	7:52 pm
☽ ⚻ ⚶	**11:02 pm**	8:02 pm
☽ □ ♇	**11:36 pm**	8:36 pm
☽ ⚺ ⚴		11:59 pm

24 SATURDAY

☽ ⚺ ⚴	**2:59 am**	
☽ ⚻ ♀	**3:44 am**	12:44 am
♂ ☍ ♅	**4:29 am**	1:29 am
☽ ⚺ ⚳	**5:15 am**	2:15 am
☿ □ ♄	**5:58 am**	2:58 am
♇ △ ⚶	**2:08 pm**	11:08 am
♂ ✶ ♄	**8:40 pm**	5:40 pm
☽ ☍ ⚵	**9:00 pm**	6:00 pm
♀ ☍ ⚳	**10:01 pm**	7:01 pm
☽ ⚺ ♅	**11:04 pm**	8:04 pm
☽ □ ♄		9:01 pm
☽ ⚻ ♂		9:10 pm
☽ ☍ ☿		10:58 pm

25 SUNDAY

☽ □ ♄	**12:01 am**	
☽ ⚻ ♂	**12:10 am**	
☽ ☍ ☿	**1:58 am**	
☽ ⚻ ☉	**10:19 am**	7:19 am
☽ □ ⚷	**12:31 pm**	9:31 am
☽ △ ♃	**4:20 pm**	1:20 pm
☽ ✶ ♆	**11:51 pm**	8:51 pm

26 MONDAY

☽ △ ♇	**11:54 am**	8:54 am
☉ △ ⚷	**12:54 pm**	9:54 am
☽ △ ⚶	**1:42 pm**	10:42 am
☽ ✶ ⚴	**2:10 pm**	11:10 am
☽ ☌ ⚳	**5:17 pm**	2:17 pm
☽ ☍ ♀	**9:18 pm**	6:18 pm
⚴ ☍ ⚶	**9:59 pm**	6:59 pm

27 TUESDAY

♅ ⚻ ⚵	**9:10 am**	6:10 am
☽ ✶ ♅	**11:32 am**	8:32 am
☽ ⚻ ⚵	**11:37 am**	8:37 am
☽ ✶ ♄	**1:05 pm**	10:05 am
☽ △ ♂	**4:18 pm**	1:18 pm
☽ ⚻ ☿	**9:22 pm**	6:22 pm
☽ △ ⚷		10:12 pm

28 WEDNESDAY

☽ △ ⚷	**1:12 am**	
☽ △ ☉	**4:29 am**	1:29 am
☽ □ ♃	**6:13 am**	3:13 am
☽ □ ♆	**12:32 pm**	9:32 am
☽ ⚻ ♇		9:39 pm
☽ □ ⚴		10:46 pm

29 THURSDAY

☽ ⚻ ♇	**12:39 am**	
☽ □ ⚴	**1:46 am**	
☽ □ ⚶	**4:49 am**	1:49 am
☽ ⚺ ⚳	**5:33 am**	2:33 am
☉ ⚺ ♃	**7:11 am**	4:11 am
☿ □ ⚷	**2:22 pm**	11:22 am
☽ ⚻ ♀	**2:57 pm**	11:57 am
⚳ △ ⚶	**9:01 pm**	6:01 pm
♄ □ ⚵	**9:15 pm**	6:15 pm
☽ □ ♅	**11:44 pm**	8:44 pm
☽ ⚺ ♄		10:49 pm
☽ △ ⚵		10:56 pm

30 FRIDAY

☽ ⚺ ♄	**1:49 am**	
☽ △ ⚵	**1:56 am**	
☽ □ ♂	**7:55 am**	4:55 am
☽ ⚻ ⚷	**1:11 pm**	10:11 am
☽ △ ☿	**3:20 pm**	12:20 pm
☽ ✶ ♃	**7:07 pm**	4:07 pm
☽ □ ☉	**9:31 pm**	6:31 pm
☽ △ ♆		9:03 pm

31 SATURDAY

☽ △ ♆	**12:03 am**	
☽ ☍ ♇	**11:47 am**	8:47 am
☽ △ ⚴	**11:49 am**	8:49 am
♇ ✶ ⚴	**1:57 pm**	10:57 am
☽ ✶ ⚳	**3:58 pm**	12:58 pm
☽ ✶ ⚶	**5:56 pm**	2:56 pm

Eastern Standard Time in bold type
Pacific Standard Time in medium type

AUGUST 2002

☽ Last Aspect				☽ Ingress		
day	EST / hr:mn / PST		asp	sign day	EST / hr:mn / PST	
2	**5:58 pm**	2:58 pm	□♅	♊ 2	**10:46 pm**	7:46 pm
5	**3:42 am**	12:42 am	⚹☿	♋ 5	**7:02 am**	4:02 am
5	**7:02 am**	4:02 am	★	♌ 7	**11:27 am**	8:27 am
9	**8:36 am**	5:36 am	☍♅	♍ 9	**1:03 pm**	10:03 am
11	**7:01 am**	4:01 am	□♄	♎ 11	**1:38 pm**	10:38 am
13	**10:11 am**	7:11 am	△♅	♏ 13	**3:01 pm**	12:01 pm
15	**1:13 pm**	10:13 am	□♅	♐ 15	**6:25 pm**	3:25 pm
17	**6:39 pm**	3:39 pm	⚹♅	♑ 17		9:15 pm
17	**6:39 pm**	3:39 pm	⚹♅	♑ 18	**12:15 am**	
19	**3:13 pm**	12:13 pm	△☿	♒ 20	**8:16 am**	5:16 am
22	**5:29 pm**	2:29 pm	☍☉	♓ 22	**6:11 pm**	3:11 pm
24		10:58 pm	☍☿	♈ 25	**5:48 am**	2:48 am
25	**1:58 am**		☍☿	♈ 25	**5:48 am**	2:48 am
27	**4:18 pm**	1:18 pm	△♂	♉ 27	**6:32 pm**	3:32 pm
29	**11:44 pm**	8:44 pm	□♅	♊ 30	**6:45 am**	3:45 am

★ The moon never makes an aspect while in the sign of Cancer, and thus never goes void-of-course before entering the sign of Leo.

☽ Phases & Eclipses			
phase	day	EST / hr:mn / PST	
4th Quarter	1	**5:22 am**	2:22 am
New Moon	8	**2:15 pm**	11:15 am
2nd Quarter	15	**5:12 am**	2:12 am
Full Moon	22	**5:29 pm**	2:29 pm
4th Quarter	30	**9:31 pm**	6:31 pm

Planet Ingress			
	day	EST / hr:mn / PST	
♃ ♌	1	**12:20 pm**	9:20 am
☿ ♍	6	**4:51 am**	1:51 am
♀ ♎	7	**4:09 am**	1:09 am
☉ ♍	22		11:17 pm
☉ ♍	23	**2:17 am**	
☿ ♎	26	**4:10 pm**	1:10 pm
♂ ♍	29	**9:38 am**	6:38 am

Planetary Motion			
	day	EST / hr:mn / PST	
⚳ ℞	13	**9:59 am**	6:59 am
♇ D	26	**6:01 am**	3:01 am

DATE		SID.TIME	SUN	MOON	NODE	MERCURY	VENUS	MARS	JUPITER	SATURN	URANUS	NEPTUNE	PLUTO	CERES	PALLAS	JUNO	VESTA	CHIRON
1	Th	20:37:43	8 ♌ 35 21	3 ♉ 50	16 ♊ D 24	20 ♌ 12	23 ♍ 15	11 ♌ 46	29 ♋ 50	24 ♊ 52	27 ♒ ℞ 36	9 ♒ ℞ 37	15 ♐ ℞ 04	17 ♈ 38	22 ♒ ℞ 32	16 ♍ 44	4 ♌ 12	4 ♑ ℞ 09
2	F	20:41:40	9 32 45	15 51	16 24	22 05	24 19	12 24	0 ♌ 04	24 58	27 34	9 35	15 03	17 42	22 17	17 06	4 38	4 07
3	Sa	20:45:36	10 30 11	28 03	16 25	23 55	25 23	13 02	0 17	25 05	27 31	9 33	15 03	17 46	22 02	17 28	5 05	4 04
4	Su	20:49:33	11 27 37	10 ♊ 33	16 ℞ 25	25 44	26 27	13 41	0 30	25 11	27 29	9 32	15 02	17 49	21 47	17 50	5 32	4 01
5	M	20:53:29	12 25 05	23 24	16 25	27 31	27 30	14 19	0 43	25 17	27 27	9 30	15 01	17 53	21 32	18 11	5 59	3 59
6	T	20:57:26	13 22 35	6 ♋ 40	16 24	29 17	28 33	14 57	0 57	25 23	27 24	9 29	15 01	17 56	21 16	18 33	6 26	3 56
7	W	21:01:22	14 20 05	20 22	16 20	1 ♍ 01	29 36	15 36	1 10	25 29	27 22	9 27	15 00	17 58	21 01	18 55	6 53	3 54
8	Th	21:05:19	15 17 36	4 ♌ 29	16 13	2 44	0 ♎ 39	16 14	1 23	25 35	27 20	9 25	14 59	18 00	20 46	19 18	7 20	3 51
9	F	21:09:15	16 15 09	18 57	16 05	4 25	1 41	16 52	1 36	25 41	27 18	9 24	14 59	18 02	20 30	19 40	7 47	3 49
10	Sa	21:13:12	17 12 42	3 ♍ 40	15 56	6 04	2 43	17 31	1 49	25 47	27 15	9 22	14 58	18 03	20 14	20 02	8 14	3 47
11	Su	21:17:09	18 10 17	18 30	15 47	7 42	3 45	18 09	2 03	25 53	27 13	9 20	14 58	18 05	19 59	20 24	8 41	3 44
12	M	21:21:05	19 07 52	3 ♎ 18	15 39	9 18	4 46	18 47	2 16	25 58	27 10	9 19	14 57	18 05	19 43	20 46	9 08	3 42
13	T	21:25:02	20 05 29	17 58	15 33	10 53	5 48	19 25	2 29	26 04	27 08	9 17	14 57	18 ℞ 06	19 28	21 08	9 35	3 40
14	W	21:28:58	21 03 06	2 ♏ 23	15 29	12 26	6 49	20 04	2 42	26 10	27 06	9 16	14 57	18 06	19 12	21 30	10 02	3 38
15	Th	21:32:55	22 00 44	16 30	15 D 28	13 58	7 49	20 42	2 55	26 15	27 03	9 14	14 56	18 05	18 57	21 52	10 29	3 36
16	F	21:36:51	22 58 23	0 ♐ 20	15 28	15 28	8 49	21 20	3 08	26 21	27 01	9 12	14 56	18 05	18 41	22 15	10 56	3 34
17	Sa	21:40:48	23 56 03	13 52	15 ℞ 28	16 56	9 49	21 58	3 21	26 26	26 59	9 11	14 55	18 04	18 26	22 37	11 23	3 32
18	Su	21:44:44	24 53 45	27 08	15 28	18 23	10 49	22 37	3 34	26 31	26 56	9 09	14 55	18 02	18 11	22 59	11 50	3 31
19	M	21:48:41	25 51 27	10 ♑ 10	15 25	19 48	11 48	23 15	3 46	26 37	26 54	9 08	14 55	18 01	17 55	23 21	12 17	3 29
20	T	21:52:38	26 49 10	22 59	15 21	21 12	12 47	23 53	3 59	26 42	26 51	9 06	14 55	17 59	17 40	23 44	12 45	3 28
21	W	21:56:34	27 46 55	5 ♒ 38	15 13	22 34	13 45	24 31	4 12	26 47	26 49	9 05	14 55	17 56	17 25	24 06	13 12	3 26
22	Th	22:00:31	28 44 41	18 06	15 02	23 54	14 43	25 09	4 25	26 52	26 47	9 03	14 54	17 53	17 10	24 28	13 39	3 25
23	F	22:04:27	29 42 28	0 ♓ 25	14 50	25 13	15 41	25 48	4 37	26 57	26 44	9 02	14 54	17 50	16 56	24 51	14 06	3 23
24	Sa	22:08:24	0 ♍ 40 16	12 35	14 37	26 29	16 38	26 26	4 50	27 02	26 42	9 00	14 54	17 46	16 41	25 13	14 33	3 22
25	Su	22:12:20	1 38 06	24 37	14 24	27 44	17 35	27 04	5 03	27 06	26 39	8 59	14 54	17 42	16 27	25 35	15 00	3 21
26	M	22:16:17	2 35 58	6 ♈ 33	14 13	28 57	18 31	27 42	5 15	27 11	26 37	8 57	14 D 54	17 38	16 13	25 58	15 27	3 20
27	T	22:20:13	3 33 51	18 24	14 03	0 ♎ 08	19 27	28 20	5 28	27 16	26 35	8 56	14 54	17 33	15 59	26 20	15 54	3 19
28	W	22:24:10	4 31 46	0 ♉ 14	13 56	1 17	20 22	28 59	5 40	27 20	26 32	8 54	14 54	17 28	15 45	26 42	16 21	3 18
29	Th	22:28:06	5 29 42	12 06	13 52	2 24	21 17	29 37	5 53	27 25	26 30	8 53	14 54	17 23	15 31	27 05	16 48	3 17
30	F	22:32:03	6 27 41	24 04	13 50	3 29	22 11	0 ♍ 15	6 05	27 29	26 28	8 52	14 54	17 17	15 18	27 27	17 15	3 16
31	Sa	22:36:00	7 25 41	6 ♊ 14	13 50	4 31	23 05	0 53	6 18	27 33	26 25	8 50	14 54	17 11	15 05	27 50	17 42	3 16

EPHEMERIS CALCULATED FOR 12 MIDNIGHT GREENWICH MEAN TIME. ALL OTHER DATA AND FACING ASPECTARIAN PAGE IN **EASTERN STANDARD TIME (BOLD)** AND PACIFIC STANDARD TIME (REGULAR).

SEPTEMBER 2002

1 SUNDAY
☉ ⚻ ♆ **5:08 am** 2:08 am
☽ △ ♀ **5:44 am** 2:44 am
☽ △ ♅ **9:28 am** 6:28 am
☽ ☌ ♄ **11:55 am** 8:55 am
☽ □ ⚵ **1:26 pm** 10:26 am
☽ ⚹ ♂ **8:17 pm** 5:17 pm
☽ ☍ ⚷ **10:13 pm** 7:13 pm
☿ ⚹ ♃ 11:53 pm

2 MONDAY
☿ ⚹ ♃ **2:53 am**
☽ ⚺ ♃ **4:41 am** 1:41 am
☽ □ ☿ **4:47 am** 1:47 am
☽ ⚻ ♆ **8:18 am** 5:18 am
☽ ⚹ ☉ **10:29 am** 7:29 am
☽ ⚻ ♀ **6:28 pm** 3:28 pm
☽ ⚻ ♇ **7:18 pm** 4:18 pm
☽ □ ⚳ **10:42 pm** 7:42 pm
☽ ⚺ ⚶ 11:51 pm

3 TUESDAY
☽ ⚺ ⚶ **2:51 am**
♀ △ ♅ **10:40 am** 7:40 am
♂ △ ⚷ **11:31 am** 8:31 am
☽ ⚻ ♅ **3:12 pm** 12:12 pm
☽ □ ♀ **3:31 pm** 12:31 pm
☽ ⚺ ♄ **5:52 pm** 2:52 pm
☽ ⚹ ⚵ **8:30 pm** 5:30 pm

4 WEDNESDAY
☽ ⚻ ⚷ **3:06 am** 12:06 am
☽ ⚺ ♂ **3:51 am** 12:51 am
☽ ☌ ♃ **9:52 am** 6:52 am
☿ △ ♆ **9:53 am** 6:53 am
☽ ☍ ♆ **12:23 pm** 9:23 am
☽ ⚹ ☿ **12:32 pm** 9:32 am
☽ ⚺ ☉ **6:14 pm** 3:14 pm
☽ ☍ ♀ **9:12 pm** 6:12 pm
☽ △ ♇ **10:42 pm** 7:42 pm
☽ △ ⚳ 10:23 pm

5 THURSDAY
☽ △ ⚳ **1:23 am**
☽ ☌ ⚶ **7:19 am** 4:19 am
♀ △ ♄ **9:26 am** 6:26 am
☽ ☍ ♅ **5:07 pm** 2:07 pm
☽ ⚹ ♄ **7:58 pm** 4:58 pm
☽ ⚹ ♀ **8:33 pm** 5:33 pm
☽ ⚺ ⚵ **11:30 pm** 8:30 pm

6 FRIDAY
☽ △ ⚷ **4:27 am** 1:27 am
☽ ☌ ♂ **7:20 am** 4:20 am
☉ ⚻ ♀ **7:43 am** 4:43 am
☽ ⚺ ♃ **11:31 am** 8:31 am
☽ ⚻ ♆ **1:11 pm** 10:11 am
☽ ⚺ ☿ **3:53 pm** 12:53 pm
☽ ⚻ ♀ **9:05 pm** 6:05 pm
☽ ☌ ☉ **10:10 pm** 7:10 pm
☽ □ ♇ **11:07 pm** 8:07 pm
☽ ⚻ ⚳ 10:14 pm

7 SATURDAY
☽ ⚻ ⚳ **1:14 am**
☽ ⚺ ⚶ **8:52 am** 5:52 am
☉ □ ♇ **1:05 pm** 10:05 am
☽ ⚻ ♅ **4:49 pm** 1:49 pm
☽ □ ♄ **7:54 pm** 4:54 pm
☽ ⚺ ♀ **11:00 pm** 8:00 pm
☽ ☌ ⚵ 9:23 pm

8 SUNDAY
☽ ☌ ⚵ **12:23 am**
☽ □ ⚷ **4:02 am** 1:02 am
☽ ⚺ ♂ **8:59 am** 5:59 am
☽ ⚹ ♃ **11:40 am** 8:40 am
☽ △ ♆ **12:38 pm** 9:38 am
☉ ⚻ ⚳ **4:01 pm** 1:01 pm
☽ ☌ ☿ **5:20 pm** 2:20 pm
☽ △ ♀ **8:01 pm** 5:01 pm
☽ ⚹ ♇ **10:39 pm** 7:39 pm
☽ ☍ ⚳ 9:17 pm
☽ ⚺ ☉ 9:57 pm

9 MONDAY
☽ ☍ ⚳ **12:17 am**
☽ ⚺ ☉ **12:57 am**
☽ ⚹ ⚶ **9:56 am** 6:56 am
☽ △ ♅ **4:25 pm** 1:25 pm
☽ △ ♄ **7:52 pm** 4:52 pm
♀ ⚺ ⚵ 9:13 pm
☽ ⚺ ⚵ 10:31 pm
☽ ☌ ♀ 10:34 pm

10 TUESDAY
♀ ⚺ ⚵ **12:13 am**
☽ ⚺ ⚵ **1:31 am**
☽ ☌ ♀ **1:34 am**
☽ ⚹ ⚷ **4:03 am** 1:03 am
☽ ⚹ ♂ **11:20 am** 8:20 am
☽ □ ♃ **12:35 pm** 9:35 am
☽ □ ♆ **12:51 pm** 9:51 am
☽ ⚺ ☿ **7:20 pm** 4:20 pm
☽ □ ♀ **8:02 pm** 5:02 pm
☽ ⚺ ♇ **11:22 pm** 8:22 pm
☽ ⚻ ⚳ 9:31 pm

11 WEDNESDAY
☽ ⚻ ⚳ **12:31 am**
☽ ⚹ ☉ **5:17 am** 2:17 am
♃ ☍ ♆ **7:06 am** 4:06 am
☽ □ ⚶ **12:46 pm** 9:46 am
☿ △ ♀ **4:44 pm** 1:44 pm
☽ □ ♅ **5:52 pm** 2:52 pm
♂ ⚻ ♆ **9:18 pm** 6:18 pm
☽ ⚻ ♄ **9:50 pm** 6:50 pm
♀ ⚹ ⚷ 11:02 pm

12 THURSDAY
♀ ⚹ ⚷ **2:02 am**
♂ ⚺ ♃ **4:07 am** 1:07 am
☽ ⚹ ⚵ **5:00 am** 2:00 am
☽ ⚺ ⚷ **6:18 am** 3:18 am
☽ ⚺ ♀ **6:33 am** 3:33 am
☽ ⚹ ♆ **3:33 pm** 12:33 pm
☽ △ ♃ **4:04 pm** 1:04 pm
☽ □ ♂ **4:28 pm** 1:28 pm
☽ ⚹ ♀ **10:40 pm** 7:40 pm
☽ ⚹ ☿ **11:31 pm** 8:31 pm
☽ ☌ ♇ 11:50 pm

13 FRIDAY
☽ ☌ ♇ **2:50 am**
☽ △ ⚳ **3:22 am** 12:22 am
☽ □ ☉ **1:08 pm** 10:08 am
☽ △ ⚶ **6:52 pm** 3:52 pm
☽ ⚹ ♅ **10:20 pm** 7:20 pm
☽ ☍ ♄ 11:54 pm

14 SATURDAY
☽ ☍ ♄ **2:54 am**
⚷ □ ⚵ **6:53 am** 3:53 am
☽ ☌ ⚷ **11:45 am** 8:45 am
☽ □ ⚵ **11:53 am** 8:53 am
☽ ⚹ ♀ **3:07 pm** 12:07 pm
♇ △ ⚳ **5:49 pm** 2:49 pm
☽ ⚺ ♆ **9:27 pm** 6:27 pm
☽ ⚻ ♃ **10:53 pm** 7:53 pm
☽ △ ♂ 10:18 pm

15 SUNDAY
☽ △ ♂ **1:18 am**
☽ ⚺ ♀ **4:28 am** 1:28 am
☽ □ ☿ **6:11 am** 3:11 am
☽ □ ⚳ **9:18 am** 6:18 am
☽ ⚺ ♇ **9:32 am** 6:32 am
☽ △ ☉ 9:58 pm

16 MONDAY
☽ △ ☉ **12:58 am**
☽ ⚻ ⚶ **4:27 am** 1:27 am
☽ ⚺ ♅ **5:55 am** 2:55 am
☽ ⚻ ♄ **11:05 am** 8:05 am
☽ ⚺ ⚷ **8:12 pm** 5:12 pm
☽ △ ⚵ **10:03 pm** 7:03 pm
☽ □ ♀ 11:59 pm

17 TUESDAY
☽ □ ♀ **2:59 am**
☽ ☌ ♆ **6:14 am** 3:14 am
♂ ⚻ ♀ **6:58 am** 3:58 am
☽ ☍ ♃ **8:40 am** 5:40 am
☽ ☌ ♀ **1:01 pm** 10:01 am
☽ ⚻ ♂ **1:24 pm** 10:24 am
☽ △ ☿ **2:30 pm** 11:30 am
☽ ⚹ ⚳ **5:47 pm** 2:47 pm
☽ ⚹ ♇ **6:57 pm** 3:57 pm
♅ ☍ ⚶ **7:23 pm** 4:23 pm

18 WEDNESDAY
☿ ⚺ ♂ **3:21 am** 12:21 am
☉ ⚻ ♅ **3:14 pm** 12:14 pm
☽ ☌ ♅ **3:54 pm** 12:54 pm
☽ ⚻ ☉ **3:57 pm** 12:57 pm
☽ ☍ ⚶ **4:44 pm** 1:44 pm
☽ △ ♄ **9:35 pm** 6:35 pm

19 THURSDAY
☽ ⚹ ⚷ **6:52 am** 3:52 am
☉ ⚺ ⚶ **9:07 am** 6:07 am
☽ ⚻ ⚵ **10:34 am** 7:34 am
♀ □ ♆ **4:19 pm** 1:19 pm
☽ ⚺ ♆ **5:02 pm** 2:02 pm
☽ △ ♀ **5:04 pm** 2:04 pm
☿ △ ♀ **8:24 pm** 5:24 pm
☽ ⚻ ♃ **8:32 pm** 5:32 pm
☽ ⚻ ☿ **11:23 pm** 8:23 pm
☽ ⚺ ♀ **11:30 pm** 8:30 pm

20 FRIDAY
☽ ☍ ♂ **3:47 am** 12:47 am
☽ ⚺ ⚳ **4:01 am** 1:01 am
☽ □ ♇ **6:14 am** 3:14 am
♂ ⚻ ⚳ **7:06 am** 4:06 am

21 SATURDAY
☽ ⚺ ♅ **3:27 am** 12:27 am
☽ ⚻ ⚶ **6:46 am** 3:46 am
☽ ☍ ☉ **8:59 am** 5:59 am
☽ □ ♄ **9:36 am** 6:36 am
☿ ⚹ ♃ **1:44 pm** 10:44 am
☉ □ ♄ **4:47 pm** 1:47 pm
☽ □ ⚷ **6:58 pm** 3:58 pm
☽ ☍ ⚵ 9:35 pm

22 SUNDAY
☽ ☍ ⚵ **12:35 am**
♂ □ ♇ **3:12 am** 12:12 am
☽ ⚹ ♆ **5:09 am** 2:09 am
☿ ⚺ ♀ **6:00 am** 3:00 am
☽ ☍ ☿ **8:08 am** 5:08 am
☽ ⚻ ♀ **8:24 am** 5:24 am
☽ △ ♃ **9:43 am** 6:43 am
☽ ⚹ ♀ **11:16 am** 8:16 am
☽ ☌ ⚳ **3:20 pm** 12:20 pm
☽ △ ♇ **6:42 pm** 3:42 pm
☽ ⚻ ♂ **7:34 pm** 4:34 pm

23 MONDAY
☽ ⚹ ♅ **3:56 pm** 12:56 pm
☽ △ ⚶ **9:49 pm** 6:49 pm
☽ ⚹ ♄ **10:29 pm** 7:29 pm
☿ △ ♆ **10:45 pm** 7:45 pm
♀ □ ♃ 11:53 pm

24 TUESDAY
♀ □ ♃ **2:53 am**
☽ ⚻ ☉ **3:10 am** 12:10 am
☽ △ ⚷ **7:52 am** 4:52 am
♀ □ ♀ **3:14 pm** 12:14 pm
☽ ⚻ ⚵ **3:22 pm** 12:22 pm
☽ ⚻ ☿ **4:23 pm** 1:23 pm
♄ ⚹ ⚶ **4:55 pm** 1:55 pm
☽ □ ♆ **5:53 pm** 2:53 pm
☽ □ ♃ **11:28 pm** 8:28 pm
☽ □ ♀ **11:38 pm** 8:38 pm
☽ ☍ ♀ 9:04 pm
☿ ☌ ⚵ 9:35 pm

25 WEDNESDAY
☽ ☍ ♀ **12:04 am**
☿ ☌ ⚵ **12:35 am**
☽ ⚺ ⚳ **3:04 am** 12:04 am
♃ ☍ ♀ **7:20 am** 4:20 am
☽ ⚻ ♇ **7:36 am** 4:36 am
☽ △ ♂ **11:49 am** 8:49 am

26 THURSDAY
☽ □ ♅ **4:27 am** 1:27 am
☽ ⚺ ♄ **11:12 am** 8:12 am
☽ □ ⚶ **12:43 pm** 9:43 am
☉ □ ⚷ **1:17 pm** 10:17 am
☽ ⚻ ⚷ **8:24 pm** 5:24 pm
☽ △ ☉ **9:00 pm** 6:00 pm
☽ △ ☿ **11:38 pm** 8:38 pm

27 FRIDAY
♀ ⚻ ⚳ **4:48 am** 1:48 am
☽ △ ⚵ **5:31 am** 2:31 am
☽ △ ♆ **6:00 am** 3:00 am
☽ △ ♀ **11:18 am** 8:18 am
☽ ⚹ ♃ **12:22 pm** 9:22 am
☉ ☌ ☿ **1:31 pm** 10:31 am
☽ ⚹ ⚳ **1:57 pm** 10:57 am
☽ ⚻ ♀ **2:28 pm** 11:28 am
☽ ☍ ♇ **7:28 pm** 4:28 pm
♆ △ ⚵ **8:57 pm** 5:57 pm
☽ □ ♂ 11:42 pm

28 SATURDAY
☽ □ ♂ **2:42 am**
☿ □ ⚷ **10:01 am** 7:01 am
☽ △ ♅ **3:19 pm** 12:19 pm
☽ ☌ ♄ **10:01 pm** 7:01 pm
☽ ⚹ ⚶ 10:28 pm

29 SUNDAY
☽ ⚹ ⚶ **1:28 am**
☽ □ ☿ **5:07 am** 2:07 am
☽ ☍ ⚷ **6:46 am** 3:46 am
☽ □ ☉ **12:03 pm** 9:03 am
♃ △ ⚳ **2:27 pm** 11:27 am
☽ ⚻ ♆ **3:40 pm** 12:40 pm
☽ □ ⚵ **4:58 pm** 1:58 pm
☽ ⚻ ♀ **8:26 pm** 5:26 pm
☽ □ ⚳ **10:13 pm** 7:13 pm
☽ ⚺ ♃ **10:28 pm** 7:28 pm
☽ △ ♀ 10:28 pm

30 MONDAY
☽ △ ♀ **1:28 am**
☽ ⚻ ♇ **4:27 am** 1:27 am
☿ ⚺ ⚶ **12:22 pm** 9:22 am
☽ ⚹ ♂ **1:59 pm** 10:59 am
☽ ⚻ ♅ **10:46 pm** 7:46 pm

Eastern Standard Time in bold type
Pacific Standard Time in medium type

SEPTEMBER 2002

☽ Last Aspect day	EST / hr:mn / PST		asp	☽ Ingress sign day	EST / hr:mn / PST	
1	**11:55 am**	8:55 am	☌ ♄	♋ 1	**4:14 pm**	1:14 pm
3	**3:31 pm**	12:31 pm	□ ♀	♌ 3	**9:36 pm**	6:36 pm
5	**8:33 pm**	5:33 pm	✶ ♀	♍ 5	**11:16 pm**	8:16 pm
7	**7:54 pm**	4:54 pm	□ ♄	♎ 7	**10:57 pm**	7:57 pm
9	**7:52 pm**	4:52 pm	△ ♄	♏ 9	**10:48 pm**	7:48 pm
11	**5:52 pm**	2:52 pm	□ ♅	♐ 11		9:44 pm
11	**5:52 pm**	2:52 pm	□ ♅	♐ 12	**12:44 am**	
13		11:54 pm	☍ ♄	♑ 14	**5:47 am**	2:47 am
14	**2:54 am**		☍ ♄	♑ 14	**5:47 am**	2:47 am
15		9:58 pm	△ ☉	♒ 16	**1:54 pm**	10:54 am

☽ Last Aspect day	EST / hr:mn / PST		asp	☽ Ingress sign day	EST / hr:mn / PST	
16	**12:58 am**		△ ☉	♒ 16	**1:54 pm**	10:54 am
18	**9:35 pm**	6:35 pm	△ ♄	♓ 18		9:18 pm
18	**9:35 pm**	6:35 pm	△ ♄	♓ 19	**12:18 am**	
21	**9:36 am**	6:36 am	□ ♄	♈ 21	**12:11 pm**	9:11 am
23	**10:29 pm**	7:29 pm	✶ ♄	♉ 23		9:55 pm
23	**10:29 pm**	7:29 pm	✶ ♄	♉ 24	**12:55 am**	
26	**4:27 am**	1:27 am	□ ♅	♊ 26	**1:26 pm**	10:26 am
28	**10:01 pm**	7:01 pm	☌ ♄	♋ 28		9:01 pm
28	**10:01 pm**	7:01 pm	☌ ♄	♋ 29	**12:01 am**	
30	**1:59 pm**	10:59 am	✶ ♂	♌ 10/1	**6:58 am**	3:58 am

☽ Phases & Eclipses phase	day	EST / hr:mn / PST	
New Moon	6	**10:10 pm**	7:10 pm
2nd Quarter	13	**1:08 pm**	10:08 am
Full Moon	21	**8:59 am**	5:59 am
4th Quarter	29	**12:03 pm**	9:03 am

Planet Ingress	day	EST / hr:mn / PST	
⚵ ♎	5	**2:15 pm**	11:15 am
♀ ♏	7	**10:05 pm**	7:05 pm
☉ ♎	22	**11:55 pm**	8:55 pm
⚶ ♍	27	**8:20 am**	5:20 am

Planetary Motion	day	EST / hr:mn / PST	
⚷ D	7	**8:21 am**	5:21 am
☿ ℞	14	**2:39 pm**	11:39 am

DATE		SID.TIME	SUN	MOON	NODE	MERCURY	VENUS	MARS	JUPITER	SATURN	URANUS	NEPTUNE	PLUTO	CERES	PALLAS	JUNO	VESTA	CHIRON
1	Su	22:39:56	8 ♍ 23 44	18 ♊ 41	13 ♊ ℞ 50	5 ♎ 31	23 ♎ 58	1 ♍ 31	6 ♌ 30	27 ♊ 37	26 ♒ ℞ 23	8 ♒ ℞ 49	14 ♐ 55	17 ♈ ℞ 05	14 ♒ ℞ 52	28 ♍ 12	18 ♌ 09	3 ♑ ℞ 15
2	M	22:43:53	9 21 48	1 ♋ 30	13 49	6 28	24 51	2 09	6 42	27 42	26 21	8 47	14 55	16 58	14 39	28 35	18 35	3 15
3	T	22:47:49	10 19 54	14 45	13 46	7 22	25 43	2 48	6 54	27 46	26 18	8 46	14 55	16 51	14 27	28 57	19 02	3 14
4	W	22:51:46	11 18 02	28 29	13 41	8 14	26 35	3 26	7 06	27 50	26 16	8 45	14 55	16 43	14 15	29 20	19 29	3 14
5	Th	22:55:42	12 16 12	12 ♌ 42	13 34	9 02	27 25	4 04	7 19	27 53	26 14	8 44	14 56	16 35	14 03	29 42	19 56	3 14
6	F	22:59:39	13 14 24	27 21	13 24	9 47	28 16	4 42	7 31	27 57	26 12	8 42	14 56	16 27	13 51	0 ♎ 04	20 23	3 13
7	Sa	23:03:35	14 12 38	12 ♍ 20	13 13	10 28	29 05	5 20	7 43	28 01	26 09	8 41	14 56	16 19	13 40	0 27	20 50	3 D 13
8	Su	23:07:32	15 10 53	27 30	13 02	11 05	29 54	5 59	7 54	28 04	26 07	8 40	14 57	16 10	13 29	0 49	21 17	3 13
9	M	23:11:29	16 09 10	12 ♎ 40	12 52	11 39	0 ♏ 42	6 37	8 06	28 08	26 05	8 39	14 57	16 01	13 18	1 12	21 44	3 13
10	T	23:15:25	17 07 29	27 39	12 44	12 08	1 29	7 15	8 18	28 11	26 03	8 37	14 58	15 51	13 08	1 34	22 11	3 14
11	W	23:19:22	18 05 49	12 ♏ 20	12 39	12 32	2 15	7 53	8 30	28 15	26 00	8 36	14 58	15 42	12 58	1 57	22 38	3 14
12	Th	23:23:18	19 04 11	26 38	12 37	12 51	3 01	8 31	8 41	28 18	25 58	8 35	14 59	15 32	12 48	2 19	23 05	3 14
13	F	23:27:15	20 02 34	10 ♐ 32	12 37	13 05	3 46	9 09	8 53	28 21	25 56	8 34	14 59	15 21	12 39	2 42	23 32	3 15
14	Sa	23:31:11	21 00 59	24 03	12 37	13 ℞ 13	4 30	9 48	9 04	28 24	25 54	8 33	15 00	15 11	12 30	3 04	23 58	3 15
15	Su	23:35:08	21 59 25	7 ♑ 12	12 36	13 15	5 12	10 26	9 16	28 27	25 52	8 32	15 00	15 00	12 21	3 27	24 25	3 16
16	M	23:39:04	22 57 53	20 03	12 33	13 10	5 54	11 04	9 27	28 29	25 50	8 31	15 01	14 49	12 13	3 49	24 52	3 16
17	T	23:43:01	23 56 23	2 ♒ 39	12 28	12 59	6 35	11 42	9 38	28 32	25 48	8 30	15 02	14 37	12 05	4 12	25 19	3 17
18	W	23:46:58	24 54 54	15 04	12 20	12 41	7 15	12 20	9 50	28 35	25 46	8 29	15 02	14 26	11 57	4 34	25 45	3 18
19	Th	23:50:54	25 53 27	27 19	12 10	12 17	7 53	12 58	10 01	28 37	25 44	8 28	15 03	14 14	11 50	4 57	26 12	3 19
20	F	23:54:51	26 52 02	9 ♓ 26	11 58	11 45	8 31	13 37	10 12	28 40	25 42	8 27	15 04	14 02	11 43	5 19	26 39	3 20
21	Sa	23:58:47	27 50 39	21 27	11 44	11 06	9 07	14 15	10 23	28 42	25 40	8 26	15 05	13 50	11 36	5 41	27 06	3 21
22	Su	0:02:44	28 49 17	3 ♈ 23	11 31	10 21	9 42	14 53	10 34	28 44	25 38	8 25	15 06	13 37	11 30	6 04	27 32	3 22
23	M	0:06:40	29 47 58	15 15	11 19	9 29	10 16	15 31	10 44	28 46	25 36	8 24	15 06	13 25	11 24	6 26	27 59	3 23
24	T	0:10:37	0 ♎ 46 40	27 05	11 09	8 32	10 48	16 09	10 55	28 48	25 35	8 23	15 07	13 12	11 19	6 49	28 26	3 25
25	W	0:14:33	1 45 25	8 ♉ 55	11 02	7 31	11 19	16 47	11 06	28 50	25 33	8 22	15 08	12 59	11 14	7 11	28 52	3 26
26	Th	0:18:30	2 44 11	20 48	10 57	6 26	11 49	17 26	11 16	28 52	25 31	8 21	15 09	12 46	11 09	7 33	29 19	3 28
27	F	0:22:27	3 43 00	2 ♊ 47	10 D 56	5 20	12 17	18 04	11 27	28 53	25 29	8 21	15 10	12 33	11 04	7 56	29 45	3 29
28	Sa	0:26:23	4 41 52	14 57	10 55	4 13	12 43	18 42	11 37	28 55	25 28	8 20	15 11	12 20	11 00	8 18	0 ♍ 12	3 31
29	Su	0:30:20	5 40 45	27 22	10 ℞ 56	3 08	13 08	19 20	11 47	28 56	25 26	8 19	15 12	12 06	10 56	8 40	0 38	3 33
30	M	0:34:16	6 39 41	10 ♋ 07	10 56	2 06	13 31	19 58	11 57	28 58	25 24	8 19	15 14	11 53	10 53	9 03	1 05	3 35

EPHEMERIS CALCULATED FOR 12 MIDNIGHT GREENWICH MEAN TIME. ALL OTHER DATA AND FACING ASPECTARIAN PAGE IN **EASTERN STANDARD TIME (BOLD)** AND PACIFIC STANDARD TIME (REGULAR).

OCTOBER 2002

1 TUESDAY

☽ ⚺ ♄	**5:11 am**	2:11 am
☽ ⚹ ☿	**8:08 am**	5:08 am
☽ ⚺ ⚶	**10:08 am**	7:08 am
☉ △ ♆	**10:50 am**	7:50 am
☽ ⚻ ⚷	**1:21 pm**	10:21 am
☽ ☍ ♆	**9:25 pm**	6:25 pm
☽ ⚹ ☉	**10:14 pm**	7:14 pm
☽ ⚹ ⚵		9:08 pm
☽ ☍ ⚴		10:41 pm
☽ △ ⚳		11:41 pm

2 WEDNESDAY

☽ ⚹ ⚵	**12:08 am**	
☽ ☍ ⚴	**1:41 am**	
☽ △ ⚳	**2:41 am**	
☽ ☌ ♃	**4:23 am**	1:23 am
☽ □ ♀	**7:47 am**	4:47 am
☽ △ ♇	**9:21 am**	6:21 am
☽ ⚺ ♂	**8:31 pm**	5:31 pm
☽ ☍ ♅		11:10 pm

3 THURSDAY

☽ ☍ ♅	**2:10 am**	
☽ ⚹ ♄	**8:16 am**	5:16 am
☽ ⚺ ☿	**8:37 am**	5:37 am
☽ ☌ ⚶	**2:22 pm**	11:22 am
☽ △ ⚷	**3:55 pm**	12:55 pm
☉ ☌ ⚵	**4:32 pm**	1:32 pm
☿ □ ♄	**6:08 pm**	3:08 pm
☉ △ ⚴	**9:47 pm**	6:47 pm
☽ ⚻ ♆	**11:19 pm**	8:19 pm
☉ ☍ ⚳		11:30 pm

4 FRIDAY

☉ ☍ ⚳	**2:30 am**	
☽ ⚺ ⚵	**3:09 am**	12:09 am
☽ ⚻ ⚴	**3:14 am**	12:14 am
☽ ⚻ ⚳	**3:32 am**	12:32 am
☽ ⚺ ☉	**3:37 am**	12:37 am
⚴ △ ⚵	**5:51 am**	2:51 am
☽ ⚺ ♃	**6:25 am**	3:25 am
☽ ⚹ ♀	**9:57 am**	6:57 am
☽ □ ♇	**10:37 am**	7:37 am
⚳ ☍ ⚵	**12:43 pm**	9:43 am
☽ ☌ ♂	**11:15 pm**	8:15 pm
⚳ ⚹ ⚴		11:12 pm
☽ ⚻ ♅		11:24 pm

Eastern Standard Time in bold type
Pacific Standard Time in medium type

5 SATURDAY

⚳ ⚹ ⚴	**2:12 am**	
☽ ⚻ ♅	**2:24 am**	
☽ ☌ ☿	**7:27 am**	4:27 am
☽ □ ♄	**8:22 am**	5:22 am
☽ ⚺ ⚶	**3:36 pm**	12:36 pm
☽ □ ⚷	**3:48 pm**	12:48 pm
☽ △ ♆	**10:48 pm**	7:48 pm
⚷ △ ⚶	**11:28 pm**	8:28 pm
☽ ☍ ⚳		11:15 pm
☽ △ ⚴		11:35 pm

6 SUNDAY

☽ ☍ ⚳	**2:15 am**	
☽ △ ⚴	**2:35 am**	
☽ ☌ ⚵	**3:45 am**	12:45 am
☉ ⚹ ♃	**5:38 am**	2:38 am
☽ ⚹ ♃	**6:15 am**	3:15 am
☽ ☌ ☉	**6:18 am**	3:18 am
☽ ⚺ ♀	**9:49 am**	6:49 am
☽ ⚹ ♇	**9:56 am**	6:56 am
☽ ⚺ ♂		9:24 pm
♀ ⚺ ♇		9:51 pm
☽ △ ♅		10:26 pm

7 MONDAY

☽ ⚺ ♂	**12:24 am**	
♀ ⚺ ♇	**12:51 am**	
☽ △ ♅	**1:26 am**	
☽ ⚺ ☿	**6:22 am**	3:22 am
☽ △ ♄	**7:29 am**	4:29 am
☽ ⚹ ⚷	**3:05 pm**	12:05 pm
☽ ⚹ ⚶	**4:09 pm**	1:09 pm
☽ □ ♆	**10:02 pm**	7:02 pm
♂ ⚻ ♅		9:10 pm
☽ ⚻ ⚳		9:52 pm
☽ □ ⚴		10:52 pm

8 TUESDAY

♂ ⚻ ♅	**12:10 am**	
☽ ⚻ ⚳	**12:52 am**	
☽ □ ⚴	**1:52 am**	
☽ ⚺ ⚵	**4:18 am**	1:18 am
☽ □ ♃	**6:10 am**	3:10 am
☽ ⚺ ☉	**9:04 am**	6:04 am
☽ ⚺ ♇	**9:31 am**	6:31 am
☽ ☌ ♀	**9:42 am**	6:42 am
☉ ⚹ ♇	**4:05 pm**	1:05 pm
☉ ⚺ ♀	**7:31 pm**	4:31 pm

☽ □ ♅		10:25 pm
☽ ⚹ ♂		11:36 pm

9 WEDNESDAY

☽ □ ♅	**1:25 am**	
☽ ⚹ ♂	**2:36 am**	
☽ ⚹ ☿	**7:38 am**	4:38 am
☽ ⚻ ♄	**7:50 am**	4:50 am
☿ □ ♄	**1:27 pm**	10:27 am
☽ ⚺ ⚷	**3:55 pm**	12:55 pm
☽ □ ⚶	**6:26 pm**	3:26 pm
☽ ⚹ ♆	**11:05 pm**	8:05 pm
☽ △ ⚳		10:21 pm

10 THURSDAY

☽ △ ⚳	**1:21 am**	
☽ ⚹ ⚴	**3:10 am**	12:10 am
☽ ⚹ ⚵	**7:05 am**	4:05 am
☽ △ ♃	**8:16 am**	5:16 am
☽ ☌ ♇	**11:22 am**	8:22 am
☽ ⚺ ♀	**11:39 am**	8:39 am
☽ ⚹ ☉	**2:35 pm**	11:35 am

11 FRIDAY

☽ ⚹ ♅	**4:11 am**	1:11 am
☽ □ ♂	**8:01 am**	5:01 am
☽ ☍ ♄	**11:08 am**	8:08 am
☽ □ ☿	**1:28 pm**	10:28 am
☽ ☌ ⚷	**7:58 pm**	4:58 pm
☽ △ ⚶		9:14 pm

12 SATURDAY

☽ △ ⚶	**12:14 am**	
☽ ⚺ ♆	**3:28 am**	12:28 am
☽ □ ⚳	**5:03 am**	2:03 am
☽ ⚺ ⚴	**7:55 am**	4:55 am
☽ □ ⚵	**1:36 pm**	10:36 am
☽ ⚻ ♃	**1:57 pm**	10:57 am
☽ ⚺ ♇	**4:46 pm**	1:46 pm
☽ ⚹ ♀	**4:48 pm**	1:48 pm
♀ ⚺ ♇	**8:04 pm**	5:04 pm
☽ □ ☉		9:33 pm

13 SUNDAY

☽ □ ☉	**12:33 am**	
♃ ⚹ ⚵	**9:31 am**	6:31 am
☽ ⚺ ♅	**10:37 am**	7:37 am
☽ △ ♂	**5:42 pm**	2:42 pm
☽ ⚻ ♄	**6:07 pm**	3:07 pm
☽ △ ☿		10:10 pm
♂ □ ♄		10:56 pm

14 MONDAY

☽ △ ☿	**1:10 am**	
♂ □ ♄	**1:56 am**	
☽ ⚺ ⚷	**3:47 am**	12:47 am
☽ ⚻ ⚶	**10:06 am**	7:06 am
☽ ☌ ♆	**11:31 am**	8:31 am
☽ ⚹ ⚳	**12:15 pm**	9:15 am
☽ ☌ ⚴	**4:23 pm**	1:23 pm
☽ ☍ ♃	**11:19 pm**	8:19 pm
☽ △ ⚵		9:01 pm
☽ □ ♀		10:04 pm
☽ ⚹ ♇		10:46 pm

15 TUESDAY

☽ △ ⚵	**12:01 am**	
☽ □ ♀	**1:04 am**	
☽ ⚹ ♇	**1:46 am**	
☿ □ ⚷	**6:34 am**	3:34 am
☽ △ ☉	**2:54 pm**	11:54 am
☽ ☌ ♅	**8:21 pm**	5:21 pm
♀ ⚺ ⚵	**11:14 pm**	8:14 pm
♆ ⚻ ⚶		11:49 pm

16 WEDNESDAY

♆ ⚻ ⚶	**2:49 am**	
☽ △ ♄	**4:15 am**	1:15 am
⚳ ⚻ ⚶	**4:31 am**	1:31 am
☽ ⚻ ♂	**7:05 am**	4:05 am
♆ ⚹ ⚳	**8:04 am**	5:04 am
☽ ⚹ ⚷	**2:38 pm**	11:38 am
☽ ⚻ ☿	**6:18 pm**	3:18 pm
☽ ⚺ ⚳	**10:10 pm**	7:10 pm
☽ ⚺ ♆	**10:25 pm**	7:25 pm
☽ ☍ ⚶	**11:09 pm**	8:09 pm

17 THURSDAY

☽ ⚺ ⚴	**3:39 am**	12:39 am
☽ ⚻ ♃	**11:19 am**	8:19 am
☽ △ ♀	**11:20 am**	8:20 am
♀ □ ♃	**11:34 am**	8:34 am
☽ ⚻ ⚵	**1:14 pm**	10:14 am
☽ □ ♇	**1:17 pm**	10:17 am
♇ ⚹ ⚵	**2:53 pm**	11:53 am
☿ ☍ ⚳		9:03 pm

18 FRIDAY

☿ ☍ ⚳	**12:03 am**	
☿ △ ♆	**5:46 am**	2:46 am
☽ ⚻ ☉	**8:06 am**	5:06 am
☽ ⚺ ♅	**8:11 am**	5:11 am
☉ △ ♅	**9:08 am**	6:08 am

☽ □ ♄	**4:17 pm**	1:17 pm
☽ ☍ ♂	**10:38 pm**	7:38 pm

19 SATURDAY

☿ ⚺ ⚶	**3:01 am**	12:01 am
☽ □ ⚷	**3:11 am**	12:11 am
☽ ☌ ⚳	**9:32 am**	6:32 am
☽ ⚹ ♆	**10:48 am**	7:48 am
☽ ⚻ ⚶	**1:48 pm**	10:48 am
☽ ☍ ☿	**2:55 pm**	11:55 am
☽ ⚹ ⚴	**4:22 pm**	1:22 pm
☽ ⚻ ♀	**10:15 pm**	7:15 pm
☽ △ ♃		9:33 pm
☽ △ ♇		10:59 pm
☿ △ ⚴		11:35 pm

20 SUNDAY

☽ △ ♃	**12:33 am**	
☽ △ ♇	**1:59 am**	
☿ △ ⚴	**2:35 am**	
☽ ☍ ⚵	**3:43 am**	12:43 am
☽ ⚹ ♅	**8:48 pm**	5:48 pm
☽ ☍ ☉		11:20 pm

21 MONDAY

☽ ☍ ☉	**2:20 am**	
☽ ⚹ ♄	**4:55 am**	1:55 am
☿ ⚺ ♀	**1:10 pm**	10:10 am
☽ ⚻ ♂	**2:48 pm**	11:48 am
☽ △ ⚷	**4:12 pm**	1:12 pm
☽ ⚺ ⚳	**9:17 pm**	6:17 pm
☽ □ ♆	**11:30 pm**	8:30 pm

22 TUESDAY

☽ △ ⚶	**4:46 am**	1:46 am
☽ □ ⚴	**5:23 am**	2:23 am
☉ △ ♄	**8:31 am**	5:31 am
☽ ☍ ♀	**8:53 am**	5:53 am
☽ ⚻ ☿	**12:46 pm**	9:46 am
☽ □ ♃	**1:51 pm**	10:51 am
☽ ⚻ ♇	**2:46 pm**	11:46 am
☽ ⚻ ⚵	**6:15 pm**	3:15 pm
♂ □ ⚷	**7:18 pm**	4:18 pm
☿ ⚹ ♃	**9:20 pm**	6:20 pm
⚴ ⚻ ⚶		10:29 pm

23 WEDNESDAY

⚴ ⚻ ⚶	**1:29 am**	
☿ ⚹ ♇	**3:50 am**	12:50 am
☽ □ ♅	**9:14 am**	6:14 am
☽ ⚺ ♄	**5:11 pm**	2:11 pm
☽ ⚻ ☉	**8:11 pm**	5:11 pm

24 THURSDAY

☽ ⚻ ⚷	**4:42 am**	1:42 am
☽ △ ♂	**6:23 am**	3:23 am
☽ ⚹ ⚳	**8:29 am**	5:29 am
☽ △ ♆	**11:35 am**	8:35 am
♀ ⚹ ⚶	**12:52 pm**	9:52 am
☿ ☌ ⚵	**3:05 pm**	12:05 pm
☽ △ ⚴	**5:42 pm**	2:42 pm
☽ ⚻ ♀	**6:26 pm**	3:26 pm
☽ □ ⚶	**6:53 pm**	3:53 pm
☽ ⚹ ♃		11:11 pm
☽ ☍ ♇		11:38 pm

25 FRIDAY

☽ ⚹ ♃	**2:11 am**	
☽ ☍ ♇	**2:38 am**	
☽ △ ⚵	**7:43 am**	4:43 am
♀ □ ⚴	**8:55 am**	5:55 am
☽ △ ☿	**9:43 am**	6:43 am
♂ ☍ ⚳	**2:08 pm**	11:08 am
☽ △ ♅	**8:24 pm**	5:24 pm

26 SATURDAY

☽ ☌ ♄	**4:01 am**	1:01 am
☽ △ ☉	**12:08 pm**	9:08 am
☽ ☍ ⚷	**3:31 pm**	12:31 pm
☽ □ ⚳	**6:05 pm**	3:05 pm
☽ □ ♂	**7:58 pm**	4:58 pm
☽ ⚻ ♆	**9:51 pm**	6:51 pm
☽ △ ♀		11:00 pm

27 SUNDAY

☽ △ ♀	**2:00 am**	
☽ ⚻ ⚴	**4:06 am**	1:06 am
☽ ⚹ ⚶	**6:49 am**	3:49 am
☽ ⚺ ♃	**12:19 pm**	9:19 am
☽ ⚻ ♇	**12:22 pm**	9:22 am
☽ □ ⚵	**6:42 pm**	3:42 pm
♃ △ ♇	**6:42 pm**	3:42 pm

28 MONDAY

☽ □ ☿	**3:22 am**	12:22 am
☽ ⚻ ♅	**5:04 am**	2:04 am
♂ △ ♆	**9:27 am**	6:27 am
☉ ⚹ ⚷	**9:37 am**	6:37 am
☽ ⚺ ♄	**12:11 pm**	9:11 am
☿ △ ♅	**4:43 pm**	1:43 pm
☽ ⚻ ⚷	**11:25 pm**	8:25 pm
☽ □ ☉		9:28 pm
☽ △ ⚳		9:53 pm

29 TUESDAY

☽ □ ☉	**12:28 am**	
☽ △ ⚳	**12:53 am**	
☽ ☍ ♆	**5:07 am**	2:07 am
☉ ⚻ ⚳	**5:28 am**	2:28 am
☽ ⚹ ♂	**6:05 am**	3:05 am
☽ □ ♀	**6:42 am**	3:42 am
☽ ☍ ⚴	**11:22 am**	8:22 am
♀ ⚺ ♂	**1:09 pm**	10:09 am
☽ ⚺ ⚶	**3:14 pm**	12:14 pm
☽ △ ♇	**6:50 pm**	3:50 pm
☽ ☌ ♃	**7:06 pm**	4:06 pm
☽ ⚹ ⚵		11:05 pm

30 WEDNESDAY

☽ ⚹ ⚵	**2:05 am**	
☽ ☍ ♅	**10:19 am**	7:19 am
☽ ⚹ ☿	**3:57 pm**	12:57 pm
☽ ⚹ ♄	**4:51 pm**	1:51 pm
♀ □ ♆	**5:53 pm**	2:53 pm
☿ △ ♄	**11:28 pm**	8:28 pm

31 THURSDAY

☽ △ ⚷	**3:44 am**	12:44 am
☽ ⚻ ⚳	**4:19 am**	1:19 am
☉ ☌ ♀	**7:06 am**	4:06 am
☽ ⚹ ♀	**8:13 am**	5:13 am
☽ ⚹ ☉	**8:21 am**	5:21 am
☽ ⚻ ♆	**8:50 am**	5:50 am
☽ ⚺ ♂	**12:07 pm**	9:07 am
☽ ⚻ ⚴	**3:04 pm**	12:04 pm
☉ □ ♆	**3:16 pm**	12:16 pm
☽ ☌ ⚶	**7:49 pm**	4:49 pm
☽ □ ♇	**9:47 pm**	6:47 pm
☽ ⚺ ♃	**10:18 pm**	7:18 pm

OCTOBER 2002

☽ Last Aspect day	EST	hr:mn / PST	asp	☽ Ingress sign	day	EST	hr:mn / PST
9/30	**1:59 pm**	10:59 am	⚹♂	♌	1	**6:58 am**	3:58 am
3	**8:16 am**	5:16 am	⚹♄	♍	3	**9:52 am**	6:52 am
5	**8:22 am**	5:22 am	□♄	♎	5	**9:51 am**	6:51 am
7	**7:29 am**	4:29 am	△♄	♏	7	**8:57 am**	5:57 am
9	**7:38 am**	4:38 am	⚹☿	♐	9	**9:21 am**	6:21 am
11	**11:08 am**	8:08 am	☍♄	♑	11	**12:45 pm**	9:45 am
13	**5:42 pm**	2:42 pm	△♂	♒	13	**7:51 pm**	4:51 pm
16	**4:15 am**	1:15 am	△♄	♓	16	**6:07 am**	3:07 am
18	**4:17 pm**	1:17 pm	□♄	♈	18	**6:13 pm**	3:13 pm
21	**4:55 am**	1:55 am	⚹♄	♉	21	**6:57 am**	3:57 am
23	**9:14 am**	6:14 am	□♅	♊	23	**7:17 pm**	4:17 pm
26	**4:01 am**	1:01 am	☌♄	♋	26	**6:10 am**	3:10 am
28	**3:22 am**	12:22 am	□☿	♌	28	**2:20 pm**	11:20 am
30	**4:51 pm**	1:51 pm	⚹♄	♍	30	**6:59 pm**	3:59 pm

☽ Phases & Eclipses phase	day	EST	hr:mn / PST
New Moon	6	**6:18 am**	3:18 am
2nd Quarter	12		9:33 pm
2nd Quarter	13	**12:33 am**	
Full Moon	20		11:20 pm
Full Moon	21	**2:20 am**	
4th Quarter	28		9:28 pm
4th Quarter	29	**12:28 am**	

Planet Ingress	day	EST	hr:mn / PST
☿ ♍	2	**4:26 am**	1:26 am
☿ ♎	10		9:56 pm
☿ ♎	11	**12:56 am**	
♂ ♎	15	**12:38 pm**	9:38 am
⊙ ♏	23	**9:18 am**	6:18 am
☿ ♏	31	**5:43 pm**	2:43 pm

Planetary Motion	day	EST	hr:mn / PST
☿ D	6	**2:28 pm**	11:28 am
♀ D	8		9:56 pm
♀ D	9	**12:56 am**	
♀ R	10	**1:35 pm**	10:35 am
♄ R	11	**8:01 am**	5:01 am
♆ D	20	**8:53 am**	5:53 am

DATE		SID. TIME	SUN	MOON	NODE	MERCURY	VENUS	MARS	JUPITER	SATURN	URANUS	NEPTUNE	PLUTO	CERES	PALLAS	JUNO	VESTA	CHIRON
1	T	0:38:13	7 ♎ 38 39	23 ♋ 16	10 ♊ R 55	1 ♎ R 09	13 ♏ 52	20 ♍ 37	12 ♌ 07	28 ♊ 59	25 ♒ R 23	8 ♒ R 18	15 ♐ 15	11 ♈ R 39	10 ♒ R 50	9 ♎ 25	1 ♍ 31	3 ♑ 37
2	W	0:42:09	8 37 40	6 ♌ 53	10 52	0 18	14 12	21 15	12 17	29 00	25 21	8 17	15 16	11 26	10 47	9 47	1 58	3 39
3	Th	0:46:06	9 36 42	21 01	10 46	29 ♍ 35	14 29	21 53	12 27	29 01	25 20	8 17	15 17	11 12	10 45	10 10	2 24	3 41
4	F	0:50:02	10 35 47	5 ♍ 36	10 38	29 01	14 45	22 31	12 37	29 02	25 18	8 16	15 18	10 59	10 43	10 32	2 50	3 43
5	Sa	0:53:59	11 34 54	20 35	10 30	28 37	14 59	23 09	12 47	29 03	25 17	8 16	15 19	10 45	10 41	10 54	3 17	3 45
6	Su	0:57:56	12 34 03	5 ♎ 49	10 21	28 D 23	15 11	23 48	12 56	29 03	25 15	8 15	15 21	10 31	10 40	11 17	3 43	3 47
7	M	1:01:52	13 33 15	21 08	10 13	28 19	15 20	24 26	13 06	29 04	25 14	8 15	15 22	10 18	10 39	11 39	4 09	3 50
8	T	1:05:49	14 32 28	6 ♏ 20	10 06	28 27	15 28	25 04	13 15	29 04	25 13	8 14	15 23	10 04	10 38	12 01	4 35	3 52
9	W	1:09:45	15 31 43	21 16	10 03	28 44	15 33	25 42	13 24	29 05	25 11	8 14	15 25	9 51	10 D 38	12 23	5 02	3 55
10	Th	1:13:42	16 31 00	5 ♐ 48	10 D 01	29 12	15 R 36	26 21	13 33	29 05	25 10	8 14	15 26	9 37	10 38	12 45	5 28	3 58
11	F	1:17:38	17 30 19	19 53	10 02	29 49	15 37	26 59	13 42	29 R 05	25 09	8 13	15 27	9 24	10 39	13 07	5 54	4 00
12	Sa	1:21:35	18 29 40	3 ♑ 30	10 03	0 ♎ 35	15 35	27 37	13 51	29 05	25 08	8 13	15 29	9 11	10 39	13 29	6 20	4 03
13	Su	1:25:31	19 29 03	16 43	10 R 03	1 29	15 31	28 15	14 00	29 05	25 07	8 13	15 30	8 57	10 40	13 52	6 46	4 06
14	M	1:29:28	20 28 27	29 33	10 03	2 31	15 24	28 54	14 08	29 05	25 06	8 12	15 32	8 44	10 42	14 14	7 12	4 09
15	T	1:33:25	21 27 53	12 ♒ 05	10 01	3 39	15 15	29 32	14 17	29 04	25 05	8 12	15 33	8 32	10 44	14 36	7 38	4 12
16	W	1:37:21	22 27 20	24 22	9 56	4 52	15 04	0 ♎ 10	14 25	29 04	25 04	8 12	15 35	8 19	10 46	14 58	8 04	4 15
17	Th	1:41:18	23 26 50	6 ♓ 29	9 50	6 11	14 50	0 48	14 33	29 03	25 03	8 12	15 36	8 06	10 48	15 20	8 29	4 18
18	F	1:45:14	24 26 21	18 29	9 42	7 33	14 34	1 27	14 42	29 03	25 02	8 12	15 38	7 54	10 51	15 42	8 55	4 21
19	Sa	1:49:11	25 25 54	0 ♈ 23	9 33	9 00	14 15	2 05	14 50	29 02	25 01	8 12	15 40	7 42	10 54	16 03	9 21	4 25
20	Su	1:53:07	26 25 29	12 15	9 25	10 29	13 54	2 43	14 57	29 01	25 00	8 D 12	15 41	7 30	10 57	16 25	9 47	4 28
21	M	1:57:04	27 25 06	24 06	9 17	12 01	13 31	3 22	15 05	29 00	25 00	8 12	15 43	7 18	11 01	16 47	10 12	4 31
22	T	2:01:00	28 24 45	5 ♉ 58	9 11	13 36	13 06	4 00	15 13	28 59	24 59	8 12	15 45	7 07	11 05	17 09	10 38	4 35
23	W	2:04:57	29 24 26	17 52	9 07	15 11	12 39	4 38	15 20	28 58	24 58	8 12	15 46	6 55	11 09	17 31	11 03	4 39
24	Th	2:08:53	0 ♏ 24 09	29 51	9 D 04	16 49	12 10	5 16	15 27	28 57	24 58	8 12	15 48	6 44	11 13	17 52	11 29	4 42
25	F	2:12:50	1 23 54	11 ♊ 57	9 04	18 27	11 40	5 55	15 35	28 55	24 57	8 12	15 50	6 34	11 18	18 14	11 54	4 46
26	Sa	2:16:47	2 23 42	24 13	9 05	20 06	11 08	6 33	15 42	28 54	24 57	8 12	15 52	6 23	11 23	18 36	12 19	4 50
27	Su	2:20:43	3 23 31	6 ♋ 42	9 06	21 45	10 34	7 11	15 49	28 52	24 56	8 12	15 53	6 13	11 29	18 58	12 45	4 54
28	M	2:24:40	4 23 23	19 28	9 08	23 25	10 00	7 50	15 55	28 50	24 56	8 13	15 55	6 03	11 34	19 19	13 10	4 57
29	T	2:28:36	5 23 17	2 ♌ 35	9 R 09	25 05	9 24	8 28	16 02	28 48	24 55	8 13	15 57	5 54	11 40	19 41	13 35	5 01
30	W	2:32:33	6 23 13	16 05	9 09	26 45	8 48	9 06	16 08	28 46	24 55	8 13	15 59	5 44	11 47	20 02	14 00	5 05
31	Th	2:36:29	7 23 11	0 ♍ 00	9 07	28 25	8 12	9 45	16 15	28 44	24 55	8 14	16 01	5 35	11 53	20 24	14 25	5 10

EPHEMERIS CALCULATED FOR 12 MIDNIGHT GREENWICH MEAN TIME. ALL OTHER DATA AND FACING ASPECTARIAN PAGE IN **EASTERN STANDARD TIME (BOLD)** AND PACIFIC STANDARD TIME (REGULAR).

NOVEMBER 2002

1 FRIDAY

Aspect	EST	PST
☽ ⚺ ⚵	**5:45 am**	2:45 am
☽ ⚻ ♅	**12:15 pm**	9:15 am
☽ □ ♄	**6:19 pm**	3:19 pm
⚷ □ ⚳	**7:48 pm**	4:48 pm
☽ ⚺ ☿	**11:49 pm**	8:49 pm

2 SATURDAY

Aspect	EST	PST
☽ ☍ ⚳	**4:54 am**	1:54 am
☽ □ ⚷	**5:01 am**	2:01 am
☽ ⚺ ♀	**7:10 am**	4:10 am
☽ △ ♆	**9:41 am**	6:41 am
☽ ⚺ ☉	**12:41 pm**	9:41 am
☽ ☌ ♂	**2:57 pm**	11:57 am
☽ △ ♀	**4:01 pm**	1:01 pm
☽ ⚺ ⚶	**9:33 pm**	6:33 pm
☽ ⚹ ♇	**10:12 pm**	7:12 pm
☽ ⚹ ♃	**10:54 pm**	7:54 pm

3 SUNDAY

Aspect	EST	PST
☽ ☌ ⚵	**6:57 am**	3:57 am
☽ △ ♅	**12:07 pm**	9:07 am
☽ △ ♄	**5:56 pm**	2:56 pm
☿ ⚻ ⚳	**6:41 pm**	3:41 pm
♂ △ ♀	**9:36 pm**	6:36 pm
♇ □ ⚶	**11:16 pm**	8:16 pm
☿ ⚹ ⚷		9:40 pm
☿ ☌ ♀		11:43 pm

4 MONDAY

Aspect	EST	PST
☿ ⚹ ⚷	**12:40 am**	
☿ ☌ ♀	**2:43 am**	
☽ ⚻ ⚳	**4:05 am**	1:05 am
☽ ⚹ ⚷	**4:50 am**	1:50 am
☽ ☌ ♀	**4:57 am**	1:57 am
☽ ☌ ☿	**5:19 am**	2:19 am
♀ ⚹ ⚷	**7:41 am**	4:41 am
☽ □ ♆	**9:14 am**	6:14 am
☽ ☌ ☉	**3:34 pm**	12:34 pm
☽ □ ♀	**3:56 pm**	12:56 pm
☽ ⚺ ♂	**4:35 pm**	1:35 pm
☉ □ ♀	**9:41 pm**	6:41 pm
☽ ⚺ ♇	**9:50 pm**	6:50 pm
☽ ⚹ ⚶	**10:25 pm**	7:25 pm
☽ □ ♃	**10:44 pm**	7:44 pm

5 TUESDAY

Aspect	EST	PST
☽ ⚺ ⚵	**7:43 am**	4:43 am
♀ ⚻ ⚳	**10:18 am**	7:18 am
☽ □ ♅	**11:48 am**	8:48 am
♃ ⚺ ⚶	**1:06 pm**	10:06 am
☽ ⚻ ♄	**5:36 pm**	2:36 pm
☿ □ ♆	**5:37 pm**	2:37 pm

6 WEDNESDAY

Aspect	EST	PST
☽ ⚺ ♀	**3:16 am**	12:16 am
☽ △ ⚳	**3:47 am**	12:47 am
☽ ⚺ ⚷	**5:10 am**	2:10 am
☉ ⚺ ♂	**7:27 am**	4:27 am
☽ ⚹ ♆	**9:31 am**	6:31 am
☽ ⚺ ☿	**11:31 am**	8:31 am
☽ ⚹ ♀	**4:54 pm**	1:54 pm
☽ ⚹ ♂	**7:21 pm**	4:21 pm
☽ ⚺ ☉	**7:41 pm**	4:41 pm
☽ ☌ ♇	**10:42 pm**	7:42 pm
☽ △ ♃	**11:50 pm**	8:50 pm
☽ □ ⚶		9:38 pm

7 THURSDAY

Aspect	EST	PST
☽ □ ⚶	**12:38 am**	
☽ ⚹ ⚵	**10:13 am**	7:13 am
☽ ⚹ ♅	**1:17 pm**	10:17 am
☽ ☍ ♄	**7:14 pm**	4:14 pm

8 FRIDAY

Aspect	EST	PST
☽ ⚹ ♀	**3:52 am**	12:52 am
☽ □ ⚳	**5:51 am**	2:51 am
☽ ☌ ⚷	**7:59 am**	4:59 am
☽ ⚺ ♆	**12:23 pm**	9:23 am
☿ □ ♀	**3:29 pm**	12:29 pm
☉ ⚺ ♇	**4:36 pm**	1:36 pm
☽ ⚺ ♀	**8:47 pm**	5:47 pm
☽ ⚹ ☿	**9:26 pm**	6:26 pm
☽ □ ♂		10:26 pm
☽ ⚺ ♇		11:35 pm

9 SATURDAY

Aspect	EST	PST
☽ □ ♂	**1:26 am**	
☽ ⚺ ♇	**2:35 am**	
☽ ⚹ ☉	**3:22 am**	12:22 am
☽ ⚻ ♃	**3:58 am**	12:58 am
☽ △ ⚶	**6:08 am**	3:08 am
☉ □ ♃	**12:06 pm**	9:06 am
☽ □ ⚵	**4:14 pm**	1:14 pm
☽ ⚺ ♅	**6:07 pm**	3:07 pm
☽ ⚻ ♄		9:18 pm
♂ ⚹ ♇		11:54 pm

10 SUNDAY

Aspect	EST	PST
☽ ⚻ ♄	**12:18 am**	
♂ ⚹ ♇	**2:54 am**	
☽ □ ♀	**7:55 am**	4:55 am
☽ ⚹ ⚳	**11:31 am**	8:31 am
☽ ⚺ ⚷	**2:32 pm**	11:32 am
☿ ⚺ ♇	**5:05 pm**	2:05 pm
☽ ☌ ♆	**6:59 pm**	3:59 pm
☿ ⚺ ♂		10:55 pm

11 MONDAY

Aspect	EST	PST
☿ ⚺ ♂	**1:55 am**	
☽ ☌ ♀	**4:37 am**	1:37 am
☿ □ ♃	**6:09 am**	3:09 am
☽ ⚹ ♇	**10:19 am**	7:19 am
☽ △ ♂	**11:55 am**	8:55 am
☽ ☍ ♃	**11:59 am**	8:59 am
☽ □ ☿	**12:49 pm**	9:49 am
♂ ⚹ ♃	**1:22 pm**	10:22 am
☉ ⚹ ⚶	**3:05 pm**	12:05 pm
☽ ⚻ ⚶	**3:50 pm**	12:50 pm
☽ □ ☉	**3:52 pm**	12:52 pm
☽ △ ⚵		11:25 pm
☽ ☌ ♅		11:48 pm

12 TUESDAY

Aspect	EST	PST
☽ △ ⚵	**2:25 am**	
☽ ☌ ♅	**2:48 am**	
☽ △ ♄	**9:06 am**	6:06 am
☽ △ ♀	**3:41 pm**	12:41 pm
♅ △ ⚵	**4:34 pm**	1:34 pm
☿ ⚹ ⚶	**7:03 pm**	4:03 pm
☽ ⚺ ⚳	**8:54 pm**	5:54 pm
☽ ⚹ ⚷		9:50 pm

13 WEDNESDAY

Aspect	EST	PST
☽ ⚹ ⚷	**12:50 am**	
☽ ⚺ ♆	**5:12 am**	2:12 am
☽ ⚺ ♀	**4:05 pm**	1:05 pm
☽ □ ♇	**9:25 pm**	6:25 pm
☽ ⚻ ♃	**11:19 pm**	8:19 pm
☉ ☌ ☿	**11:40 pm**	8:40 pm
☽ ⚻ ♂		11:15 pm

14 THURSDAY

Aspect	EST	PST
☽ ⚻ ♂	**2:15 am**	
☽ ☍ ⚶	**5:02 am**	2:02 am
☽ △ ☉	**8:29 am**	5:29 am
☽ △ ☿	**8:59 am**	5:59 am

Aspect	EST	PST
☽ ⚺ ♅	**2:26 pm**	11:26 am
☽ ⚻ ⚵	**3:47 pm**	12:47 pm
☽ □ ♄	**8:38 pm**	5:38 pm
☽ ⚻ ♀		11:14 pm

15 FRIDAY

Aspect	EST	PST
☽ ⚻ ♀	**2:14 am**	
☽ ☌ ⚳	**8:46 am**	5:46 am
☽ □ ⚷	**1:30 pm**	10:30 am
☽ ⚹ ♆	**5:37 pm**	2:37 pm
☿ □ ♅		11:03 pm

16 SATURDAY

Aspect	EST	PST
☿ □ ♅	**2:03 am**	
☽ ⚹ ♀	**5:31 am**	2:31 am
☽ △ ♇	**10:13 am**	7:13 am
☽ △ ♃	**12:16 pm**	9:16 am
☽ ☍ ♂	**6:24 pm**	3:24 pm
☽ ⚻ ⚶	**7:50 pm**	4:50 pm
☿ ⚺ ⚵		9:07 pm
☽ ⚻ ☉		11:51 pm

17 SUNDAY

Aspect	EST	PST
☿ ⚺ ⚵	**12:07 am**	
☽ ⚻ ☉	**2:51 am**	
☽ ⚹ ♅	**3:15 am**	12:15 am
☽ ☍ ⚵	**6:21 am**	3:21 am
☽ ⚻ ☿	**7:06 am**	4:06 am
☉ □ ♅	**7:34 am**	4:34 am
☽ ⚹ ♄	**9:06 am**	6:06 am
☽ ☍ ♀	**2:01 pm**	11:01 am
☽ ⚺ ⚳	**9:17 pm**	6:17 pm
☿ ⚻ ♄	**9:36 pm**	6:36 pm
☽ △ ⚷		11:39 pm

18 MONDAY

Aspect	EST	PST
☽ △ ⚷	**2:39 am**	
☽ □ ♆	**6:23 am**	3:23 am
☽ □ ♀	**7:00 pm**	4:00 pm
☽ ⚻ ♇	**10:54 pm**	7:54 pm
☽ □ ♃		10:01 pm

19 TUESDAY

Aspect	EST	PST
☽ □ ♃	**1:01 am**	
☿ ⚺ ♀	**8:16 am**	5:16 am
☽ ⚻ ♂	**10:10 am**	7:10 am
☽ △ ⚶	**10:12 am**	7:12 am
♂ ⚺ ⚶	**11:35 am**	8:35 am
☉ ⚺ ⚵	**3:15 pm**	12:15 pm
☽ □ ♅	**3:32 pm**	12:32 pm
☽ ⚻ ⚵	**8:16 pm**	5:16 pm
☽ ☍ ☉	**8:34 pm**	5:34 pm

Aspect	EST	PST
☽ ⚺ ♄	**8:54 pm**	5:54 pm
☉ ⚻ ♄		9:21 pm
☽ ⚻ ♀		10:34 pm

20 WEDNESDAY

Aspect	EST	PST
☉ ⚻ ♄	**12:21 am**	
☽ ⚻ ♀	**1:34 am**	
☽ ☍ ☿	**4:14 am**	1:14 am
☽ ⚹ ⚳	**9:00 am**	6:00 am
☽ ⚻ ⚷	**2:48 pm**	11:48 am
♄ △ ⚵	**3:27 pm**	12:27 pm
☽ △ ♆	**6:06 pm**	3:06 pm

21 THURSDAY

Aspect	EST	PST
☽ △ ♀	**7:13 am**	4:13 am
☽ ☍ ♇	**10:16 am**	7:16 am
☽ ⚹ ♃	**12:22 pm**	9:22 am
☿ △ ⚳	**4:55 pm**	1:55 pm
☽ □ ⚶	**10:56 pm**	7:56 pm
☽ △ ♂		9:14 pm
☽ △ ♅		11:18 pm

22 FRIDAY

Aspect	EST	PST
☽ △ ♂	**12:14 am**	
☽ △ ♅	**2:18 am**	
☽ ☌ ♄	**7:07 am**	4:07 am
☽ △ ⚵	**8:26 am**	5:26 am
☉ ⚺ ♀	**8:58 am**	5:58 am
☽ △ ♀	**11:58 am**	8:58 am
☽ ⚻ ☉	**12:13 pm**	9:13 am
☽ □ ⚳	**7:04 pm**	4:04 pm
☽ ⚻ ☿	**10:46 pm**	7:46 pm
☽ ☍ ⚷		10:07 pm

23 SATURDAY

Aspect	EST	PST
☽ ☍ ⚷	**1:07 am**	
☽ ⚻ ♆	**3:59 am**	12:59 am
♂ △ ♅	**5:20 pm**	2:20 pm
☽ ⚻ ♀	**5:27 pm**	2:27 pm
☿ ⚺ ⚷	**6:52 pm**	3:52 pm
☽ ⚻ ♇	**7:39 pm**	4:39 pm
☽ ⚺ ♃	**9:40 pm**	6:40 pm

24 SUNDAY

Aspect	EST	PST
☽ ⚹ ⚶	**9:23 am**	6:23 am
☽ ⚻ ♅	**10:57 am**	7:57 am
☽ □ ♂	**11:51 am**	8:51 am
☽ ⚺ ♄	**3:12 pm**	12:12 pm
☿ ⚹ ♆	**5:38 pm**	2:38 pm
☽ □ ⚵	**6:15 pm**	3:15 pm
☽ □ ♀	**8:37 pm**	5:37 pm
☽ △ ☉		10:06 pm
☽ △ ⚳		11:58 pm

25 MONDAY

Aspect	EST	PST
☽ △ ☉	**1:06 am**	
☽ △ ⚳	**2:58 am**	
☽ ⚻ ⚷	**9:08 am**	6:08 am
☽ ☍ ♆	**11:35 am**	8:35 am
☽ △ ☿	**1:56 pm**	10:56 am
☽ ☍ ♀		10:13 pm
☉ △ ⚳		10:48 pm
☽ △ ♇		11:37 pm

26 TUESDAY

Aspect	EST	PST
☽ ☍ ♀	**1:13 am**	
☉ △ ⚳	**1:48 am**	
☽ △ ♇	**2:37 am**	
☽ ☌ ♃	**4:31 am**	1:31 am
☽ ⚺ ⚶	**5:07 pm**	2:07 pm
☽ ☍ ♅	**5:09 pm**	2:09 pm
♅ ⚻ ⚶	**6:33 pm**	3:33 pm
☽ ⚹ ♂	**8:35 pm**	5:35 pm
☽ ⚹ ♄	**8:51 pm**	5:51 pm
☽ ⚹ ⚵		10:22 pm
♂ △ ♄		10:33 pm

27 WEDNESDAY

Aspect	EST	PST
☽ ⚹ ⚵	**1:22 am**	
♂ △ ♄	**1:33 am**	
☽ ⚹ ♀	**3:02 am**	12:02 am
☽ ⚻ ⚳	**8:24 am**	5:24 am
☽ □ ☉	**10:46 am**	7:46 am
☽ △ ⚷	**2:34 pm**	11:34 am
☽ ⚻ ♆	**4:37 pm**	1:37 pm
☽ □ ☿		10:23 pm

28 THURSDAY

Aspect	EST	PST
☽ □ ☿	**1:23 am**	
☽ ⚻ ♀	**6:20 am**	3:20 am
☽ □ ♇	**7:01 am**	4:01 am
☽ ⚺ ♃	**8:46 am**	5:46 am
☽ ⚻ ♅	**8:49 pm**	5:49 pm
☽ ☌ ⚶	**10:05 pm**	7:05 pm
☽ □ ♄		9:01 pm
☽ ⚺ ♂		11:27 pm

29 FRIDAY

Aspect	EST	PST
☽ □ ♄	**12:01 am**	
☽ ⚺ ♂	**2:27 am**	
☽ ⚺ ⚵	**5:47 am**	2:47 am
☽ ⚺ ♀	**7:10 am**	4:10 am
☽ ☍ ⚳	**11:26 am**	8:26 am

Aspect	EST	PST
☽ ⚹ ☉	**5:25 pm**	2:25 pm
☽ □ ⚷	**5:33 pm**	2:33 pm
☽ △ ♆	**7:17 pm**	4:17 pm
☉ ⚺ ⚷	**7:33 pm**	4:33 pm

30 SATURDAY

Aspect	EST	PST
☿ ⚹ ♀	**4:57 am**	1:57 am
☿ ☌ ♇	**5:51 am**	2:51 am
☽ △ ♀	**9:09 am**	6:09 am
☽ ⚹ ♇	**9:11 am**	6:11 am
☽ ⚹ ☿	**9:34 am**	6:34 am
☽ ⚹ ♃	**10:48 am**	7:48 am
♇ ⚹ ♀	**12:26 pm**	9:26 am
☉ ⚹ ♆	**8:37 pm**	5:37 pm
☿ △ ♃	**9:19 pm**	6:19 pm
☽ △ ♅	**10:28 pm**	7:28 pm
☽ ⚺ ⚶		9:53 pm
☽ △ ♄		10:15 pm

Eastern Standard Time in bold type
Pacific Standard Time in medium type

NOVEMBER 2002

☽ Last Aspect day	EST / hr:mn / PST	asp	☽ Ingress sign day	EST / hr:mn / PST
1	**6:19 pm** 3:19 pm	□ ♄	♎ 1	**8:28 pm** 5:28 pm
3	**5:56 pm** 2:56 pm	△ ♄	♏ 3	**8:10 pm** 5:10 pm
5	**11:48 am** 8:48 am	□ ♅	♐ 5	**8:01 pm** 5:01 pm
7	**7:14 pm** 4:14 pm	☍ ♄	♑ 7	**9:59 pm** 6:59 pm
9	**3:22 am** 12:22 am	⚹ ☉	♒ 10	**3:27 am** 12:27 am
12	**9:06 am** 6:06 am	△ ♄	♓ 12	**12:42 pm** 9:42 am
14	**8:38 pm** 5:38 pm	□ ♄	♈ 14	9:38 pm
14	**8:38 pm** 5:38 pm	□ ♄	♈ 15	**12:38 am**
17	**9:06 am** 6:06 am	⚹ ♄	♉ 17	**1:23 pm** 10:23 am
19	**8:34 pm** 5:34 pm	☍ ☉	♊ 19	10:25 pm
19	**8:34 pm** 5:34 pm	☍ ☉	♊ 20	**1:25 am**
22	**7:07 am** 4:07 am	☌ ♄	♋ 22	**11:48 am** 8:48 am
24	**11:51 am** 8:51 am	□ ♂	♌ 24	**8:00 pm** 5:00 pm
26	**8:51 pm** 5:51 pm	⚹ ♄	♍ 26	10:42 pm
26	**8:51 pm** 5:51 pm	⚹ ♄	♍ 27	**1:42 am**
28	9:01 pm	□ ♄	♎ 29	**4:54 am** 1:54 am
29	**12:01 am**	□ ♄	♎ 29	**4:54 am** 1:54 am

☽ Phases & Eclipses phase	day	EST / hr:mn / PST
New Moon	4	**3:34 pm** 12:34 pm
2nd Quarter	11	**3:52 pm** 12:52 pm
Full Moon	19	**8:34 pm** 5:34 pm
●	19	27° ♉ 33'
4th Quarter	27	**10:46 am** 7:46 am

Planet Ingress	day	EST / hr:mn / PST
☿ ♐	19	**6:29 am** 3:29 am
☉ ♐	22	**6:54 am** 3:54 am
⚵ ♏	27	**3:09 pm** 12:09 pm

Planetary Motion	day	EST / hr:mn / PST
♅ D	3	10:27 pm
♅ D	4	**1:27 am**
♀ D	20	11:12 pm
♀ D	21	**2:12 am**
⚷ D	23	**12:25 pm** 9:25 am

DATE		SID.TIME	SUN	MOON	NODE	MERCURY	VENUS	MARS	JUPITER	SATURN	URANUS	NEPTUNE	PLUTO	CERES	PALLAS	JUNO	VESTA	CHIRON
1	F	2:40:26	8 ♏ 23 12	14 ♍ 21	9 ♊ R 04	0 ♏ 05	7 ♏ R 35	10 ♎ 23	16 ♌ 21	28 ♊ R 42	24 ♒ R 55	8 ♒ 14	16 ♐ 03	5 ♈ R 27	12 ♒ 00	20 ♎ 45	14 ♍ 50	5 ♑ 14
2	Sa	2:44:22	9 23 15	29 05	9 00	1 45	6 59	11 02	16 27	28 40	24 55	8 14	16 05	5 18	12 07	21 06	15 15	5 18
3	Su	2:48:19	10 23 19	14 ♎ 06	8 55	3 25	6 23	11 40	16 33	28 38	24 55	8 15	16 07	5 10	12 14	21 28	15 40	5 22
4	M	2:52:16	11 23 26	29 16	8 51	5 04	5 47	12 18	16 38	28 35	24 D 54	8 15	16 09	5 03	12 22	21 49	16 05	5 27
5	T	2:56:12	12 23 35	14 ♏ 24	8 49	6 43	5 13	12 57	16 44	28 33	24 55	8 16	16 11	4 55	12 29	22 10	16 29	5 31
6	W	3:00:09	13 23 45	29 22	8 D 47	8 22	4 39	13 35	16 49	28 30	24 55	8 16	16 13	4 49	12 37	22 32	16 54	5 35
7	Th	3:04:05	14 23 57	14 ♐ 01	8 47	10 00	4 07	14 13	16 54	28 27	24 55	8 17	16 15	4 42	12 46	22 53	17 18	5 40
8	F	3:08:02	15 24 11	28 16	8 48	11 38	3 36	14 52	16 59	28 24	24 55	8 17	16 17	4 36	12 54	23 14	17 43	5 44
9	Sa	3:11:58	16 24 27	12 ♑ 03	8 49	13 16	3 06	15 30	17 04	28 21	24 55	8 18	16 19	4 30	13 03	23 35	18 07	5 49
10	Su	3:15:55	17 24 44	25 24	8 51	14 53	2 39	16 09	17 09	28 18	24 55	8 19	16 21	4 25	13 12	23 56	18 31	5 54
11	M	3:19:52	18 25 02	8 ♒ 20	8 R 52	16 30	2 13	16 47	17 13	28 15	24 56	8 20	16 23	4 19	13 21	24 17	18 55	5 58
12	T	3:23:48	19 25 22	20 55	8 52	18 07	1 50	17 26	17 18	28 12	24 56	8 20	16 25	4 15	13 31	24 38	19 19	6 03
13	W	3:27:45	20 25 43	3 ♓ 12	8 52	19 43	1 28	18 04	17 22	28 09	24 56	8 21	16 27	4 10	13 40	24 59	19 43	6 08
14	Th	3:31:41	21 26 06	15 17	8 50	21 19	1 09	18 42	17 26	28 05	24 57	8 22	16 29	4 07	13 50	25 19	20 07	6 13
15	F	3:35:38	22 26 30	27 13	8 48	22 55	0 52	19 21	17 29	28 02	24 57	8 23	16 31	4 03	14 01	25 40	20 31	6 18
16	Sa	3:39:34	23 26 55	9 ♈ 04	8 46	24 30	0 38	19 59	17 33	27 58	24 58	8 24	16 33	4 00	14 11	26 01	20 55	6 23
17	Su	3:43:31	24 27 22	20 55	8 43	26 05	0 26	20 38	17 36	27 55	24 59	8 24	16 35	3 57	14 21	26 21	21 18	6 28
18	M	3:47:27	25 27 50	2 ♉ 47	8 41	27 40	0 17	21 16	17 40	27 51	24 59	8 25	16 38	3 55	14 32	26 42	21 42	6 33
19	T	3:51:24	26 28 20	14 43	8 40	29 15	0 10	21 55	17 43	27 47	25 00	8 26	16 40	3 53	14 43	27 02	22 05	6 38
20	W	3:55:20	27 28 51	26 46	8 D 39	0 ♐ 49	0 05	22 33	17 46	27 43	25 01	8 27	16 42	3 51	14 54	27 23	22 28	6 43
21	Th	3:59:17	28 29 24	8 ♊ 56	8 38	2 23	0 D 03	23 12	17 48	27 39	25 02	8 28	16 44	3 50	15 06	27 43	22 52	6 48
22	F	4:03:14	29 29 58	21 16	8 39	3 57	0 04	23 50	17 51	27 35	25 03	8 29	16 46	3 49	15 17	28 03	23 15	6 54
23	Sa	4:07:10	0 ♐ 30 34	3 ♋ 47	8 39	5 31	0 07	24 29	17 53	27 31	25 04	8 31	16 49	3 D 49	15 29	28 23	23 38	6 59
24	Su	4:11:07	1 31 12	16 30	8 40	7 05	0 12	25 07	17 55	27 27	25 04	8 32	16 51	3 49	15 41	28 43	24 00	7 04
25	M	4:15:03	2 31 51	29 27	8 41	8 38	0 20	25 46	17 57	27 23	25 06	8 33	16 53	3 49	15 53	29 03	24 23	7 09
26	T	4:19:00	3 32 31	12 ♌ 41	8 41	10 11	0 30	26 24	17 59	27 19	25 07	8 34	16 55	3 49	16 05	29 23	24 46	7 15
27	W	4:22:56	4 33 14	26 11	8 R 41	11 45	0 42	27 03	18 01	27 14	25 08	8 35	16 58	3 51	16 18	29 43	25 08	7 20
28	Th	4:26:53	5 33 58	9 ♍ 59	8 41	13 18	0 56	27 41	18 02	27 10	25 09	8 36	17 00	3 52	16 31	0 ♏ 03	25 30	7 26
29	F	4:30:50	6 34 43	24 06	8 41	14 51	1 12	28 20	18 03	27 06	25 10	8 38	17 02	3 54	16 43	0 23	25 53	7 31
30	Sa	4:34:46	7 35 30	8 ♎ 29	8 41	16 23	1 31	28 58	18 04	27 01	25 11	8 39	17 04	3 56	16 56	0 43	26 15	7 37

EPHEMERIS CALCULATED FOR 12 MIDNIGHT GREENWICH MEAN TIME. ALL OTHER DATA AND FACING ASPECTARIAN PAGE IN **EASTERN STANDARD TIME (BOLD)** AND PACIFIC STANDARD TIME (REGULAR).

DECEMBER 2002

1 SUNDAY
- ☽ ⚺ ⚶ **12:53 am**
- ☽ △ ♄ **1:15 am**
- ☽ ☌ ♂ **6:06 am** 3:06 am
- ☽ ☌ ⚵ **8:14 am** 5:14 am
- ☽ ☌ ♀ **9:38 am** 6:38 am
- ☽ ⚻ ⚳ **12:46 pm** 9:46 am
- ♄ □ ⚶ **1:05 pm** 10:05 am
- ☽ ⚹ ⚷ **6:55 pm** 3:55 pm
- ☽ □ ♆ **8:22 pm** 5:22 pm
- ☽ ⚺ ☉ **10:05 pm** 7:05 pm

2 MONDAY
- ☽ ⚺ ♇ **10:07 am** 7:07 am
- ☽ □ ♀ **10:42 am** 7:42 am
- ☽ □ ♃ **11:37 am** 8:37 am
- ☽ ⚺ ☿ **4:03 pm** 1:03 pm
- ☽ □ ♅ **11:15 pm** 8:15 pm
- ☽ ⚻ ♄ 10:42 pm
- ☽ ⚹ ⚶ 11:49 pm

3 TUESDAY
- ☽ ⚻ ♄ **1:42 am**
- ☽ ⚹ ⚶ **2:49 am**
- ☽ ⚺ ♂ **9:03 am** 6:03 am
- ☽ ⚺ ⚵ **10:03 am** 7:03 am
- ☽ ⚺ ♀ **11:45 am** 8:45 am
- ☽ △ ⚳ **1:42 pm** 10:42 am
- ☽ ⚺ ⚷ **8:02 pm** 5:02 pm
- ☽ ⚹ ♆ **9:16 pm** 6:16 pm
- ☽ ☌ ☉ 11:34 pm

4 WEDNESDAY
- ☽ ☌ ☉ **2:34 am**
- ☽ ☌ ♇ **11:18 am** 8:18 am
- ☽ ⚹ ♀ **12:33 pm** 9:33 am
- ☽ △ ♃ **12:43 pm** 9:43 am
- ♃ ☍ ♀ **10:47 pm** 7:47 pm
- ☽ ☌ ☿ **11:10 pm** 8:10 pm
- ☽ ⚹ ♅ 9:45 pm
- ☽ ☍ ♄ 11:55 pm

5 THURSDAY
- ☽ ⚹ ♅ **12:45 am**
- ☽ ☍ ♄ **2:55 am**
- ♂ ☌ ⚵ **5:34 am** 2:34 am
- ☽ □ ⚶ **5:37 am** 2:37 am
- ☽ ⚹ ⚵ **1:00 pm** 10:00 am
- ☽ ⚹ ♂ **1:10 pm** 10:10 am
- ☿ ⚹ ♅ **2:09 pm** 11:09 am
- ☽ ⚹ ♀ **3:20 pm** 12:20 pm
- ☽ □ ⚳ **3:53 pm** 12:53 pm
- ☽ ☌ ⚷ **10:36 pm** 7:36 pm
- ☽ ⚺ ♆ **11:38 pm** 8:38 pm

6 FRIDAY
- ☿ ☍ ♄ **8:36 am** 5:36 am
- ☽ ⚺ ☉ **9:06 am** 6:06 am
- ♀ ⚻ ⚳ **9:19 am** 6:19 am
- ☽ ⚺ ♇ **2:26 pm** 11:26 am
- ☽ ⚻ ♃ **3:46 pm** 12:46 pm
- ☽ ⚺ ♀ **4:30 pm** 1:30 pm

7 SATURDAY
- ☽ ⚺ ♅ **4:37 am** 1:37 am
- ☽ ⚻ ♄ **6:31 am** 3:31 am
- ☽ ⚺ ☿ **9:29 am** 6:29 am
- ☽ △ ⚶ **11:05 am** 8:05 am
- ☽ □ ⚵ **6:49 pm** 3:49 pm
- ☽ □ ♂ **8:24 pm** 5:24 pm
- ☽ ⚹ ⚳ **8:56 pm** 5:56 pm
- ☽ □ ♀ **10:13 pm** 7:13 pm

8 SUNDAY
- ☿ □ ⚶ **3:03 am** 12:03 am
- ☽ ⚺ ⚷ **4:10 am** 1:10 am
- ☽ ☌ ♆ **4:59 am** 1:59 am
- ♂ ⚻ ⚳ **8:57 am** 5:57 am
- ☽ ⚹ ☉ **7:38 pm** 4:38 pm
- ☽ ⚹ ♇ **8:53 pm** 5:53 pm
- ☽ ☍ ♃ **10:06 pm** 7:06 pm
- ☽ ☌ ♀ **11:58 pm** 8:58 pm

9 MONDAY
- ☉ ☌ ♇ **11:57 am** 8:57 am
- ☽ ☌ ♅ **12:02 pm** 9:02 am
- ☽ △ ♄ **1:35 pm** 10:35 am
- ☽ ⚻ ⚶ **8:24 pm** 5:24 pm
- ☽ ⚹ ☿ 9:52 pm
- ☉ △ ♃ 11:16 pm

10 TUESDAY
- ☽ ⚹ ☿ **12:52 am**
- ☉ △ ♃ **2:16 am**
- ☽ △ ⚵ **4:33 am** 1:33 am
- ☽ ⚺ ⚳ **5:47 am** 2:47 am
- ☽ △ ♂ **7:53 am** 4:53 am
- ☽ △ ♀ **9:32 am** 6:32 am
- ☽ ⚹ ⚷ **1:31 pm** 10:31 am
- ☽ ⚺ ♆ **2:04 pm** 11:04 am

11 WEDNESDAY
- ☽ □ ♇ **7:00 am** 4:00 am
- ☽ ⚻ ♃ **8:01 am** 5:01 am
- ☽ □ ☉ **10:49 am** 7:49 am
- ☽ ⚺ ♀ **11:18 am** 8:18 am
- ☿ ⚹ ⚵ **1:51 pm** 10:51 am
- ☉ ⚹ ♀ **6:19 pm** 3:19 pm
- ☿ □ ⚳ **7:45 pm** 4:45 pm
- ☽ ⚺ ♅ **10:57 pm** 7:57 pm
- ☽ □ ♄ 9:02 pm

12 THURSDAY
- ☽ □ ♄ **12:02 am**
- ☽ ☍ ⚶ **9:18 am** 6:18 am
- ☽ ⚻ ⚵ **5:41 pm** 2:41 pm
- ☽ ☌ ⚳ **5:55 pm** 2:55 pm
- ☽ □ ☿ **8:54 pm** 5:54 pm
- ☽ ⚻ ♂ **10:59 pm** 7:59 pm
- ☽ ⚻ ♀ 9:42 pm
- ☽ □ ⚷ 10:54 pm
- ☽ ⚹ ♆ 11:06 pm

13 FRIDAY
- ☽ ⚻ ♀ **12:42 am**
- ☽ □ ⚷ **1:54 am**
- ☽ ⚹ ♆ **2:06 am**
- ⚳ ⚻ ⚵ **8:15 am** 5:15 am
- ☽ △ ♇ **7:36 pm** 4:36 pm
- ☽ △ ♃ **8:18 pm** 5:18 pm
- ☿ ⚹ ♂ 9:25 pm
- ☽ ⚹ ♀ 10:06 pm
- ♀ ⚹ ⚷ 10:11 pm
- ♀ □ ♆ 11:18 pm

14 SATURDAY
- ☿ ⚹ ♂ **12:25 am**
- ☽ ⚹ ♀ **1:06 am**
- ♀ ⚹ ⚷ **1:11 am**
- ♀ □ ♆ **2:18 am**
- ☽ △ ☉ **4:58 am** 1:58 am
- ♆ ⚺ ⚷ **11:41 am** 8:41 am
- ☽ ⚹ ♅ **11:48 am** 8:48 am
- ☽ ⚹ ♄ **12:18 pm** 9:18 am
- ☿ ⚺ ♆ **3:05 pm** 12:05 pm
- ☿ ☌ ⚷ **3:15 pm** 12:15 pm
- ☽ ⚻ ⚶ **11:48 pm** 8:48 pm
- ☿ ⚹ ♀ 11:09 pm

15 SUNDAY
- ☿ ⚹ ♀ **2:09 am**
- ☽ ⚺ ⚳ **7:19 am** 4:19 am
- ☽ ☍ ⚵ **8:03 am** 5:03 am
- ♂ □ ♆ **11:07 am** 8:07 am
- ♂ ⚹ ⚷ **2:08 pm** 11:08 am
- ☽ □ ♆ **3:00 pm** 12:00 pm
- ☽ △ ⚷ **3:10 pm** 12:10 pm
- ☽ ☍ ♂ **3:13 pm** 12:13 pm
- ☽ ☍ ♀ **5:13 pm** 2:13 pm
- ☽ △ ☿ **6:18 pm** 3:18 pm

16 MONDAY
- ☽ ⚻ ♇ **8:20 am** 5:20 am
- ☽ □ ♃ **8:40 am** 5:40 am
- ☽ □ ♀ **2:52 pm** 11:52 am
- ♄ △ ♅ **4:35 pm** 1:35 pm
- ☽ ⚻ ☉ **10:54 pm** 7:54 pm
- ☽ ⚺ ♄ 9:07 pm
- ☽ □ ♅ 9:11 pm

17 TUESDAY
- ☽ ⚺ ♄ **12:07 am**
- ☽ □ ♅ **12:11 am**
- ☉ ☍ ♄ **12:28 pm** 9:28 am
- ☽ △ ⚶ **1:20 pm** 10:20 am
- ☉ ⚹ ♅ **2:50 pm** 11:50 am
- ☽ ⚹ ⚳ **7:39 pm** 4:39 pm
- ☽ ⚻ ⚵ **9:12 pm** 6:12 pm
- ☽ △ ♆ 11:34 pm

18 WEDNESDAY
- ☽ △ ♆ **2:34 am**
- ☽ ⚻ ⚷ **3:03 am** 12:03 am
- ☽ ⚻ ♂ **5:53 am** 2:53 am
- ♃ △ ♇ **8:41 am** 5:41 am
- ☽ ⚻ ♀ **8:21 am** 5:21 am
- ☽ ⚻ ☿ **1:22 pm** 10:22 am
- ☽ ⚹ ♃ **7:14 pm** 4:14 pm
- ☽ ☍ ♇ **7:18 pm** 4:18 pm
- ☽ △ ♀ 11:38 pm

19 THURSDAY
- ☽ △ ♀ **2:38 am**
- ☽ ☌ ♄ **9:53 am** 6:53 am
- ☽ △ ♅ **10:30 am** 7:30 am
- ☽ ☍ ☉ **2:10 pm** 11:10 am
- ☽ □ ⚶ 9:21 pm

20 FRIDAY
- ☽ □ ⚶ **12:21 am**
- ☽ □ ⚳ **5:38 am** 2:38 am
- ☽ △ ⚵ **7:47 am** 4:47 am
- ☽ ⚻ ♆ **11:42 am** 8:42 am
- ☽ ☍ ⚷ **12:29 pm** 9:29 am
- ☿ ⚻ ♃ **4:58 pm** 1:58 pm
- ☽ △ ♂ **5:43 pm** 2:43 pm
- ☽ △ ♀ **8:46 pm** 5:46 pm
- ☿ ⚺ ♇ **8:47 pm** 5:47 pm

21 SATURDAY
- ☽ ⚺ ♃ **3:18 am** 12:18 am
- ☽ ⚻ ♇ **3:45 am** 12:45 am
- ☽ ☍ ☿ **4:31 am** 1:31 am
- ☽ ⚻ ♀ **11:46 am** 8:46 am
- ☽ ⚺ ♄ **5:12 pm** 2:12 pm
- ☽ ⚻ ♅ **6:18 pm** 3:18 pm
- ☽ ⚻ ☉ 11:16 pm

22 SUNDAY
- ☽ ⚻ ☉ **2:16 am**
- ☽ ⚹ ⚶ **8:43 am** 5:43 am
- ☽ △ ⚳ **1:09 pm** 10:09 am
- ☽ □ ⚵ **3:47 pm** 12:47 pm
- ☽ ☍ ♆ **6:27 pm** 3:27 pm
- ☽ ⚻ ⚷ **7:30 pm** 4:30 pm
- ☽ □ ♂ 11:51 pm

23 MONDAY
- ☽ □ ♂ **2:51 am**
- ☽ □ ♀ **6:34 am** 3:34 am
- ☽ ☌ ♃ **9:07 am** 6:07 am
- ☽ △ ♇ **9:56 am** 6:56 am
- ☽ ⚻ ☿ **4:03 pm** 1:03 pm
- ☽ ☍ ♀ **6:37 pm** 3:37 pm
- ☽ ⚹ ♄ **10:27 pm** 7:27 pm
- ☽ ☍ ♅ **11:58 pm** 8:58 pm

24 TUESDAY
- ☽ △ ☉ **11:48 am** 8:48 am
- ☽ ⚺ ⚶ **2:57 pm** 11:57 am
- ☽ ⚻ ⚳ **6:44 pm** 3:44 pm
- ♀ □ ♃ **8:26 pm** 5:26 pm
- ☽ ⚹ ⚵ **9:44 pm** 6:44 pm
- ☽ ⚻ ♆ **11:21 pm** 8:21 pm
- ☽ △ ⚷ 9:37 pm

25 WEDNESDAY
- ☽ △ ⚷ **12:37 am**
- ☿ ⚺ ♀ **7:20 am** 4:20 am
- ☽ ⚹ ♂ **9:56 am** 6:56 am
- ☽ ⚺ ♃ **1:13 pm** 10:13 am
- ♀ ⚺ ♇ **2:04 pm** 11:04 am
- ☽ □ ♇ **2:24 pm** 11:24 am
- ☽ ⚹ ♀ **2:25 pm** 11:25 am
- ☽ ⚻ ♀ **11:46 pm** 8:46 pm
- ☽ △ ☿ 9:45 pm
- ☽ □ ♄ 11:10 pm

26 THURSDAY
- ☽ △ ☿ **12:45 am**
- ☽ □ ♄ **2:10 am**
- ☽ ⚻ ♅ **4:05 am** 1:05 am
- ☿ ⚻ ♄ **7:06 pm** 4:06 pm
- ☽ □ ☉ **7:31 pm** 4:31 pm
- ☽ ☌ ⚶ **7:39 pm** 4:39 pm
- ☉ □ ⚶ **10:04 pm** 7:04 pm
- ☽ ☍ ⚳ **10:56 pm** 7:56 pm
- ☽ ⚺ ⚵ 11:16 pm
- ☽ △ ♆ 11:54 pm

27 FRIDAY
- ☽ ⚺ ⚵ **2:16 am**
- ☽ △ ♆ **2:54 am**
- ☽ □ ⚷ **4:24 am** 1:24 am
- ☽ ⚺ ♂ **3:36 pm** 12:36 pm
- ☽ ⚹ ♃ **4:08 pm** 1:08 pm
- ☽ ⚹ ♇ **5:41 pm** 2:41 pm
- ☽ ⚺ ♀ **8:58 pm** 5:58 pm
- ♂ □ ♃ 11:22 pm

28 SATURDAY
- ♂ □ ♃ **2:22 am**
- ☽ △ ♀ **3:46 am** 12:46 am
- ☽ △ ♄ **4:49 am** 1:49 am
- ☿ ⚺ ♅ **5:19 am** 2:19 am
- ☽ △ ♅ **7:09 am** 4:09 am
- ☽ □ ☿ **7:15 am** 4:15 am
- ♆ □ ⚵ **3:21 pm** 12:21 pm
- ☽ ⚺ ⚶ **11:21 pm** 8:21 pm
- ☽ ⚹ ☉ 11:05 pm
- ☽ ⚻ ⚳ 11:15 pm

29 SUNDAY
- ☽ ⚹ ☉ **2:05 am**
- ☽ ⚻ ⚳ **2:15 am**
- ☉ □ ⚳ **4:46 am** 1:46 am
- ☽ □ ♆ **5:36 am** 2:36 am
- ☽ ☌ ⚵ **5:51 am** 2:51 am
- ☽ ⚹ ⚷ **7:20 am** 4:20 am
- ♂ ⚺ ♇ **4:11 pm** 1:11 pm
- ☽ □ ♃ **6:19 pm** 3:19 pm
- ☽ ⚺ ♇ **8:15 pm** 5:15 pm
- ☽ ☌ ♂ **8:26 pm** 5:26 pm
- ♄ △ ♀ **9:15 pm** 6:15 pm
- ☽ ☌ ♀ 11:48 pm

30 MONDAY
- ☽ ☌ ♀ **2:48 am**
- ☽ ⚻ ♄ **6:54 am** 3:54 am
- ☽ □ ♀ **7:09 am** 4:09 am
- ☽ □ ♅ **9:39 am** 6:39 am
- ☽ ⚹ ☿ **12:04 pm** 9:04 am
- ☽ ⚹ ⚶ 11:38 pm

31 TUESDAY
- ☽ ⚹ ⚶ **2:38 am**
- ☉ ⚺ ♆ **5:03 am** 2:03 am
- ☽ △ ⚳ **5:17 am** 2:17 am
- ☽ ⚹ ♆ **8:04 am** 5:04 am
- ☽ ⚺ ☉ **8:17 am** 5:17 am
- ☽ ⚺ ⚵ **9:10 am** 6:10 am
- ☽ ⚺ ⚷ **10:02 am** 7:02 am
- ☽ △ ♃ **8:26 pm** 5:26 pm
- ☽ ☌ ♇ **10:48 pm** 7:48 pm
- ☉ ⚹ ⚵ 9:40 pm
- ☽ ⚺ ♂ 10:15 pm

Eastern Standard Time in bold type
Pacific Standard Time in medium type

DECEMBER 2002

☽ Last Aspect day	EST / hr:mn / PST		asp	☽ Ingress sign day	EST / hr:mn / PST	
1	**6:06 am**	3:06 am	☌ ♂	♏ 1	**6:15 am**	3:15 am
2	**11:15 pm**	8:15 pm	□ ♅	♐ 3	**6:58 am**	3:58 am
4		11:55 pm	☍ ♄	♑ 5	**8:39 am**	5:39 am
5	**2:55 am**		☍ ♄	♑ 5	**8:39 am**	5:39 am
5	**3:20 pm**	12:20 pm	⚹ ♀	♒ 7	**12:54 pm**	9:54 am
9	**1:35 pm**	10:35 am	△ ♄	♓ 9	**8:46 pm**	5:46 pm
11		9:02 pm	□ ♄	♈ 12	**7:58 am**	4:58 am
12	**12:02 am**		□ ♄	♈ 12	**7:58 am**	4:58 am
14	**12:18 pm**	9:18 am	⚹ ♄	♉ 14	**8:43 pm**	5:43 pm
16		9:11 pm	□ ♅	♊ 17	**8:43 am**	5:43 am

☽ Last Aspect day	EST / hr:mn / PST		asp	☽ Ingress sign day	EST / hr:mn / PST	
17	**12:11 am**		□ ♅	♊ 17	**8:43 am**	5:43 am
19	**2:10 pm**	11:10 am	☍ ☉	♋ 19	**6:30 pm**	3:30 pm
21	**4:31 am**	1:31 am	☍ ☿	♌ 21		10:48 pm
21	**4:31 am**	1:31 am	☍ ☿	♌ 22	**1:48 am**	
23	**11:58 pm**	8:58 pm	☍ ♅	♍ 24	**7:05 am**	4:05 am
25		11:10 pm	□ ♄	♎ 26	**10:53 am**	7:53 am
26	**2:10 am**		□ ♄	♎ 26	**10:53 am**	7:53 am
28	**7:15 am**	4:15 am	□ ☿	♏ 28	**1:41 pm**	10:41 am
30	**12:04 pm**	9:04 am	⚹ ☿	♐ 30	**4:01 pm**	1:01 pm

☽ Phases & Eclipses phase	day	EST / hr:mn / PST	
New Moon	3		11:34 pm
New Moon	4	**2:34 am**	
●	4	11° ♐ 58'	
2nd Quarter	11	**10:49 am**	7:49 am
Full Moon	19	**2:10 pm**	11:10 am
4th Quarter	26	**7:31 pm**	4:31 pm

Planet Ingress	day	EST / hr:mn / PST	
♂ ♏	1	**9:26 am**	6:26 am
☿ ♑	8	**3:21 pm**	12:21 pm
⚶ ♎	10	**9:52 am**	6:52 am
☉ ♑	21	**8:14 pm**	5:14 pm

Planetary Motion	day	EST / hr:mn / PST	
♃ ℞	4	**7:22 am**	4:22 am

DATE		SID.TIME	SUN	MOON	NODE	MERCURY	VENUS	MARS	JUPITER	SATURN	URANUS	NEPTUNE	PLUTO	CERES	PALLAS	JUNO	VESTA	CHIRON
1	Su	4:38:43	8 ♐ 36 19	23 ♎ 06	8 ♊ D 41	17 ♐ 56	1 ♏ 51	29 ♎ 37	18 ♌ 05	26 ♊ ℞ 57	25 ♒ 13	8 ♒ 40	17 ♐ 07	3 ♈ 58	17 ♒ 10	1 ♏ 02	26 ♍ 37	7 ♑ 42
2	M	4:42:39	9 37 09	7 ♏ 51	8 41	19 29	2 14	0 ♏ 15	18 06	26 52	25 14	8 42	17 09	4 01	17 23	1 22	26 58	7 48
3	T	4:46:36	10 38 00	22 39	8 41	21 01	2 38	0 54	18 06	26 47	25 16	8 43	17 11	4 05	17 37	1 41	27 20	7 54
4	W	4:50:32	11 38 53	7 ♐ 22	8 ℞ 41	22 34	3 04	1 33	18 ℞ 06	26 43	25 17	8 44	17 13	4 08	17 50	2 00	27 42	7 59
5	Th	4:54:29	12 39 47	21 53	8 41	24 06	3 32	2 11	18 06	26 38	25 19	8 46	17 16	4 12	18 04	2 20	28 03	8 05
6	F	4:58:25	13 40 42	6 ♑ 06	8 41	25 38	4 01	2 50	18 06	26 33	25 20	8 47	17 18	4 16	18 18	2 39	28 24	8 11
7	Sa	5:02:22	14 41 37	19 56	8 40	27 10	4 32	3 28	18 06	26 28	25 22	8 49	17 20	4 21	18 32	2 58	28 45	8 16
8	Su	5:06:19	15 42 34	3 ♒ 23	8 40	28 42	5 04	4 07	18 05	26 24	25 23	8 50	17 23	4 26	18 46	3 17	29 06	8 22
9	M	5:10:15	16 43 32	16 25	8 39	0 ♑ 14	5 38	4 45	18 04	26 19	25 25	8 52	17 25	4 32	19 01	3 36	29 27	8 28
10	T	5:14:12	17 44 30	29 05	8 38	1 45	6 14	5 24	18 03	26 14	25 27	8 54	17 27	4 37	19 16	3 54	29 47	8 34
11	W	5:18:08	18 45 28	11 ♓ 26	8 D 37	3 16	6 50	6 03	18 02	26 09	25 29	8 55	17 30	4 43	19 30	4 13	0 ♎ 08	8 40
12	Th	5:22:05	19 46 27	23 32	8 37	4 47	7 28	6 41	18 01	26 04	25 30	8 57	17 32	4 50	19 45	4 32	0 28	8 45
13	F	5:26:01	20 47 27	5 ♈ 28	8 38	6 17	8 08	7 20	17 59	25 59	25 32	8 58	17 34	4 56	20 00	4 50	0 48	8 51
14	Sa	5:29:58	21 48 28	17 19	8 39	7 47	8 48	7 58	17 57	25 54	25 34	9 00	17 36	5 03	20 15	5 08	1 08	8 57
15	Su	5:33:54	22 49 29	29 09	8 40	9 16	9 30	8 37	17 55	25 49	25 36	9 02	17 39	5 11	20 31	5 27	1 28	9 03
16	M	5:37:51	23 50 30	11 ♉ 03	8 41	10 44	10 13	9 16	17 53	25 44	25 38	9 04	17 41	5 18	20 46	5 45	1 47	9 09
17	T	5:41:48	24 51 32	23 04	8 43	12 11	10 56	9 54	17 51	25 40	25 40	9 05	17 43	5 26	21 02	6 03	2 06	9 15
18	W	5:45:44	25 52 35	5 ♊ 15	8 ℞ 43	13 38	11 41	10 33	17 48	25 35	25 42	9 07	17 46	5 35	21 17	6 21	2 25	9 21
19	Th	5:49:41	26 53 38	17 38	8 43	15 02	12 27	11 11	17 46	25 30	25 44	9 09	17 48	5 43	21 33	6 39	2 44	9 27
20	F	5:53:37	27 54 42	0 ♋ 16	8 42	16 25	13 14	11 50	17 43	25 25	25 47	9 11	17 50	5 52	21 49	6 56	3 03	9 33
21	Sa	5:57:34	28 55 46	13 08	8 40	17 47	14 02	12 29	17 40	25 20	25 49	9 12	17 52	6 01	22 05	7 14	3 22	9 39
22	Su	6:01:30	29 56 51	26 14	8 36	19 06	14 51	13 07	17 36	25 15	25 51	9 14	17 55	6 11	22 21	7 31	3 40	9 45
23	M	6:05:27	0 ♑ 57 56	9 ♌ 34	8 33	20 22	15 40	13 46	17 33	25 10	25 53	9 16	17 57	6 21	22 37	7 49	3 58	9 51
24	T	6:09:23	1 59 02	23 07	8 30	21 35	16 31	14 25	17 29	25 05	25 56	9 18	17 59	6 31	22 54	8 06	4 16	9 57
25	W	6:13:20	3 00 09	6 ♍ 50	8 27	22 44	17 22	15 03	17 25	25 00	25 58	9 20	18 01	6 41	23 10	8 23	4 33	10 03
26	Th	6:17:17	4 01 16	20 44	8 25	23 50	18 14	15 42	17 21	24 55	26 01	9 22	18 04	6 51	23 27	8 40	4 51	10 09
27	F	6:21:13	5 02 24	4 ♎ 46	8 D 24	24 50	19 07	16 21	17 17	24 50	26 03	9 24	18 06	7 02	23 43	8 57	5 08	10 15
28	Sa	6:25:10	6 03 33	18 55	8 25	25 45	20 00	16 59	17 13	24 46	26 05	9 26	18 08	7 13	24 00	9 13	5 25	10 21
29	Su	6:29:06	7 04 42	3 ♏ 10	8 26	26 33	20 54	17 38	17 08	24 41	26 08	9 28	18 10	7 25	24 17	9 30	5 42	10 27
30	M	6:33:03	8 05 52	17 28	8 28	27 14	21 49	18 17	17 03	24 36	26 11	9 30	18 12	7 37	24 34	9 46	5 58	10 33
31	T	6:36:59	9 07 02	1 ♐ 47	8 ℞ 29	27 47	22 44	18 55	16 58	24 31	26 13	9 32	18 15	7 48	24 51	10 03	6 14	10 39

EPHEMERIS CALCULATED FOR 12 MIDNIGHT GREENWICH MEAN TIME. ALL OTHER DATA AND FACING ASPECTARIAN PAGE IN **EASTERN STANDARD TIME (BOLD)** AND PACIFIC STANDARD TIME (REGULAR).

JANUARY 2003

1 WEDNESDAY

☽ ⊻ ♂	**1:15 am**	
☽ ☍ ♄	**9:10 am**	6:10 am
☽ ⚹ ♀	**10:45 am**	7:45 am
☉ ☌ ⚷	**11:09 am**	8:09 am
☽ ⚹ ♅	**12:23 pm**	9:23 am
♀ ⊼ ♄	**1:14 pm**	10:14 am
☽ ⊻ ☿	**3:57 pm**	12:57 pm

2 THURSDAY

☽ □ ⚶	**6:31 am**	3:31 am
☽ □ ⚳	**9:01 am**	6:01 am
☽ ⊻ ♆	**11:14 am**	8:14 am
☽ ⚹ ⚵	**1:14 pm**	10:14 am
☽ ☌ ⚷	**1:30 pm**	10:30 am
☽ ☌ ☉	**3:23 pm**	12:23 pm
☽ ⊼ ♃	**11:30 pm**	8:30 pm
♀ □ ☿		9:28 pm
☽ ⊻ ♇		11:25 pm

3 FRIDAY

♀ □ ☿	**12:28 am**	
☽ ⊻ ♇	**2:25 am**	
☽ ⚹ ♂	**7:22 am**	4:22 am
⚷ ⚹ ⚵	**11:41 am**	8:41 am
☽ ⊼ ♄	**12:43 pm**	9:43 am
♀ □ ♅	**3:38 pm**	12:38 pm
☽ ⊻ ♀	**3:47 pm**	12:47 pm
☽ ⊻ ♅	**4:32 pm**	1:32 pm
☽ ⚹ ♀	**4:36 pm**	1:36 pm
☽ ☌ ☿	**7:56 pm**	4:56 pm

4 SATURDAY

☽ △ ⚶	**12:19 pm**	9:19 am
☽ ⚹ ⚳	**2:47 pm**	11:47 am
☽ ☌ ♆	**4:22 pm**	1:22 pm
☽ ⊻ ⚷	**7:01 pm**	4:01 pm
☽ □ ⚵	**7:25 pm**	4:25 pm
☽ ⊻ ☉		10:04 pm

5 SUNDAY

☽ ⊻ ☉	**1:04 am**	
☿ ⚹ ♀	**3:00 am**	12:00 am
☽ ☍ ♃	**4:46 am**	1:46 am
☽ ⚹ ♇	**8:22 am**	5:22 am
♅ ☌ ♀	**8:44 am**	5:44 am
☽ □ ♂	**4:18 pm**	1:18 pm
☽ △ ♄	**6:48 pm**	3:48 pm
☽ ☌ ♅	**11:21 pm**	8:21 pm
☽ ☌ ♀	**11:39 pm**	8:39 pm
☽ ⊻ ☿		9:50 pm

6 MONDAY

☽ ⊻ ☿	**12:50 am**	
☽ □ ♀	**3:44 am**	12:44 am
☿ ⊻ ♀	**3:09 pm**	12:09 pm
☉ ⊼ ♃	**8:34 pm**	5:34 pm
☽ ⊼ ⚶	**9:14 pm**	6:14 pm
☽ ⊻ ⚳	**11:47 pm**	8:47 pm
☿ ⊻ ♅	**11:50 pm**	8:50 pm
☽ ⊻ ♆		9:36 pm

7 TUESDAY

☽ ⊻ ♆	**12:36 am**	
☽ ⚹ ⚷	**3:43 am**	12:43 am
☽ △ ⚵	**4:51 am**	1:51 am
☽ ⊼ ♃	**1:08 pm**	10:08 am
♂ ⊼ ♄	**1:36 pm**	10:36 am
☽ ⚹ ☉	**2:47 pm**	11:47 am
☽ □ ♇	**5:35 pm**	2:35 pm

8 WEDNESDAY

☽ □ ♄	**4:08 am**	1:08 am
☽ △ ♂	**5:02 am**	2:02 am
☽ ⚹ ☿	**6:55 am**	3:55 am
☽ ⊻ ♅	**9:31 am**	6:31 am
☽ ⊻ ♀	**11:03 am**	8:03 am
☽ △ ♀	**7:09 pm**	4:09 pm
☿ ⚹ ♂	**7:18 pm**	4:18 pm
☉ ⊻ ♇		10:32 pm

9 THURSDAY

☉ ⊻ ♇	**1:32 am**	
♆ ⚹ ⚳	**3:05 am**	12:05 am
☽ ☍ ⚶	**9:28 am**	6:28 am
☽ ⚹ ♆	**12:01 pm**	9:01 am
☽ ☌ ⚳	**12:10 pm**	9:10 am
☿ ⊼ ♄	**2:30 pm**	11:30 am
☽ □ ⚷	**3:36 pm**	12:36 pm
☽ ⊼ ⚵	**5:32 pm**	2:32 pm
☽ △ ♃		9:23 pm

10 FRIDAY

☽ △ ♃	**12:23 am**	
☽ △ ♇	**5:41 am**	2:41 am
☽ □ ☉	**8:15 am**	5:15 am
☽ □ ☿	**1:43 pm**	10:43 am
☽ ⚹ ♄	**4:02 pm**	1:02 pm
☽ ⊼ ♂	**8:48 pm**	5:48 pm
☽ ⚹ ♅	**10:10 pm**	7:10 pm
☽ ⚹ ♀		10:04 pm

11 SATURDAY

☽ ⚹ ♀	**1:04 am**	
☽ ⊼ ♀	**1:26 pm**	10:26 am
☉ ☌ ☿	**3:02 pm**	12:02 pm
☽ ⊼ ⚶	**11:22 pm**	8:22 pm
♂ □ ♅	**11:47 pm**	8:47 pm
☽ □ ♆		9:59 pm
☽ ⊻ ⚳		11:14 pm

12 SUNDAY

☽ □ ♆	**12:59 am**	
☽ ⊻ ⚳	**2:14 am**	
☽ △ ⚷	**4:55 am**	1:55 am
☽ ☍ ⚵	**7:36 am**	4:36 am
☽ □ ♃	**12:36 pm**	9:36 am
☽ ⊼ ♇	**6:36 pm**	3:36 pm
☽ △ ☿	**8:20 pm**	5:20 pm
☽ △ ☉		11:36 pm

13 MONDAY

☽ △ ☉	**2:36 am**	
☽ ⊻ ♄	**4:18 am**	1:18 am
☽ □ ♅	**10:54 am**	7:54 am
☿ ⊻ ♇	**11:53 am**	8:53 am
☽ ☍ ♂	**12:44 pm**	9:44 am
☽ □ ♀	**3:03 pm**	12:03 pm
☉ ⊼ ♄	**9:39 pm**	6:39 pm

14 TUESDAY

☽ ☍ ♀	**7:02 am**	4:02 am
☽ △ ⚶	**12:06 pm**	9:06 am
☽ △ ♆	**12:51 pm**	9:51 am
☽ ⚹ ⚳	**3:06 pm**	12:06 pm
☽ ⊼ ⚷	**4:55 pm**	1:55 pm
☽ ⊼ ⚵	**8:09 pm**	5:09 pm
☽ ⚹ ♃	**11:16 pm**	8:16 pm
☽ ⊼ ☿		10:53 pm

15 WEDNESDAY

☽ ⊼ ☿	**1:53 am**	
☽ ☍ ♇	**5:41 am**	2:41 am
☽ ☌ ♄	**2:29 pm**	11:29 am
☽ ⊼ ☉	**6:16 pm**	3:16 pm
☽ △ ♅	**9:16 pm**	6:16 pm
☽ ⊼ ♂		10:51 pm
☽ △ ♀		11:23 pm

16 THURSDAY

☽ ⊼ ♂	**1:51 am**	
☽ △ ♀	**2:23 am**	
☿ ⊼ ♃	**1:20 pm**	10:20 am
☽ ⊼ ♀	**9:03 pm**	6:03 pm
♂ □ ♀	**9:38 pm**	6:38 pm
☽ □ ⚶	**9:41 pm**	6:41 pm
☽ ⊼ ♆	**9:43 pm**	6:43 pm
☽ □ ⚳		9:50 pm
♆ △ ⚶		9:53 pm
☽ ☍ ⚷		10:50 pm

17 FRIDAY

☽ □ ⚳	**12:50 am**	
♆ △ ⚶	**12:53 am**	
☽ ☍ ⚷	**1:50 am**	
☽ △ ⚵	**5:25 am**	2:25 am
♀ ⚹ ♆	**5:35 am**	2:35 am
☽ ☍ ☿	**5:54 am**	2:54 am
♀ ⚹ ⚶	**6:21 am**	3:21 am
☽ ⊻ ♃	**6:52 am**	3:52 am
☉ ⊻ ♅	**9:36 am**	6:36 am
☿ ⚹ ⚵	**11:49 am**	8:49 am
☽ ⊼ ♇	**1:34 pm**	10:34 am
☽ ⊻ ♄	**9:28 pm**	6:28 pm

18 SATURDAY

☽ ⊼ ♅	**4:21 am**	1:21 am
☽ ☍ ☉	**5:48 am**	2:48 am
☽ ⊼ ♀	**10:14 am**	7:14 am
☽ △ ♂	**11:11 am**	8:11 am

19 SUNDAY

☽ ☍ ♆	**3:26 am**	12:26 am
☽ ⚹ ⚶	**3:57 am**	12:57 am
☽ △ ♀	**7:08 am**	4:08 am
☽ △ ⚳	**7:19 am**	4:19 am
☽ ⊼ ⚷	**7:35 am**	4:35 am
☽ ⊼ ☿	**8:35 am**	5:35 am
♀ △ ⚳	**10:13 am**	7:13 am
☽ □ ⚵	**11:29 am**	8:29 am
☽ ☌ ♃	**11:33 am**	8:33 am
♀ ⊻ ⚷	**1:33 pm**	10:33 am
♃ □ ⚵	**1:56 pm**	10:56 am
☽ △ ♇	**6:31 pm**	3:31 pm
☿ ⊻ ♀	**8:29 pm**	5:29 pm
☽ ⚹ ♄		10:45 pm

20 MONDAY

☽ ⚹ ♄	**1:45 am**	
⚷ □ ⚳	**4:39 am**	1:39 am
☿ □ ⚳	**8:36 am**	5:36 am
☽ ☍ ♅	**8:46 am**	5:46 am
☿ ☌ ⚷	**10:09 am**	7:09 am
☽ ⊼ ☉	**2:03 pm**	11:03 am
☽ ☍ ♀	**3:26 pm**	12:26 pm
☽ □ ♂	**5:40 pm**	2:40 pm

21 TUESDAY

☽ ⊼ ♆	**7:04 am**	4:04 am
☽ ⊻ ⚶	**8:01 am**	5:01 am
♀ △ ♃	**10:35 am**	7:35 am
☽ △ ☿	**10:40 am**	7:40 am
☽ △ ⚷	**11:19 am**	8:19 am
☽ ⊼ ⚳	**11:43 am**	8:43 am
☽ ⊻ ♃	**2:23 pm**	11:23 am
☽ □ ♀	**2:44 pm**	11:44 am
☽ ⚹ ⚵	**3:33 pm**	12:33 pm
☉ ⊻ ♀	**5:09 pm**	2:09 pm
☽ □ ♇	**9:46 pm**	6:46 pm

22 WEDNESDAY

♀ ⊻ ⚵	**3:54 am**	12:54 am
☽ □ ♄	**4:34 am**	1:34 am
☽ ⊼ ♅	**11:52 am**	8:52 am
☽ ⊼ ♀	**7:25 pm**	4:25 pm
☽ △ ☉	**8:49 pm**	5:49 pm
☽ ⚹ ♂	**10:53 pm**	7:53 pm

23 THURSDAY

☽ △ ♆	**9:55 am**	6:55 am
☽ ☌ ⚶	**11:16 am**	8:16 am
☽ □ ☿	**1:12 pm**	10:12 am
☽ □ ⚷	**2:22 pm**	11:22 am
☽ ☍ ⚳	**3:26 pm**	12:26 pm
☽ ⚹ ♃	**4:38 pm**	1:38 pm
☽ ⊻ ⚵	**6:59 pm**	3:59 pm
☽ ⚹ ♀	**9:37 pm**	6:37 pm
☽ ⚹ ♇		9:34 pm

24 FRIDAY

☽ ⚹ ♇	**12:34 am**	
☽ △ ♄	**7:05 am**	4:05 am
☽ △ ♅	**2:48 pm**	11:48 am
☽ △ ♀	**11:22 pm**	8:22 pm

25 SATURDAY

☽ □ ☉	**3:33 am**	12:33 am
☽ ⊻ ♂	**4:08 am**	1:08 am
♃ △ ⚳	**8:19 am**	5:19 am
☽ □ ♆	**12:57 pm**	9:57 am
♀ ☌ ♇	**12:59 pm**	9:59 am
☽ ⊻ ⚶	**2:41 pm**	11:41 am
☽ ⚹ ☿	**4:58 pm**	1:58 pm
☽ ⚹ ⚷	**5:40 pm**	2:40 pm
☽ □ ♃	**7:08 pm**	4:08 pm
☽ ⊼ ⚳	**7:28 pm**	4:28 pm
☽ ☌ ⚵	**10:43 pm**	7:43 pm
☉ ⚹ ♂		9:26 pm

26 SUNDAY

☉ ⚹ ♂	**12:26 am**	
☽ ⊻ ♇	**3:44 am**	12:44 am
☽ ⊻ ♀	**4:57 am**	1:57 am
☽ ⊼ ♄	**10:02 am**	7:02 am
☽ □ ♅	**6:14 pm**	3:14 pm
☿ ☌ ⚷	**11:18 pm**	8:18 pm

27 MONDAY

☽ □ ♀	**3:54 am**	12:54 am
☽ ☌ ♂	**10:02 am**	7:02 am
☽ ⚹ ☉	**11:00 am**	8:00 am
☽ ⚹ ♆	**4:38 pm**	1:38 pm
☽ ⚹ ⚶	**6:41 pm**	3:41 pm
☿ ⊼ ♃	**8:51 pm**	5:51 pm
☽ ⊻ ⚷	**9:37 pm**	6:37 pm
☽ △ ♃	**10:16 pm**	7:16 pm
☽ ⊻ ☿	**10:20 pm**	7:20 pm
☽ △ ⚳		9:12 pm

28 TUESDAY

☽ △ ⚳	**12:12 am**	
☽ ⊻ ⚵	**3:06 am**	12:06 am
☽ ☌ ♇	**7:36 am**	4:36 am
☽ ☌ ♀	**1:13 pm**	10:13 am
☽ ☍ ♄	**1:43 pm**	10:43 am
♀ ☍ ♄	**7:13 pm**	4:13 pm
☽ ⚹ ♅	**10:26 pm**	7:26 pm

29 WEDNESDAY

☽ ⚹ ♀	**9:19 am**	6:19 am
♃ ⊼ ⚷	**1:26 pm**	10:26 am
☽ ⊻ ♂	**4:55 pm**	1:55 pm
☽ ⊻ ☉	**7:32 pm**	4:32 pm
☽ ⊻ ♆	**9:12 pm**	6:12 pm
☽ □ ⚶	**11:33 pm**	8:33 pm
☽ ⊼ ♃		11:17 pm
☽ ☌ ⚷		11:30 pm

30 THURSDAY

☽ ⊼ ♃	**2:17 am**	
☽ ☌ ⚷	**2:30 am**	
☽ ☌ ☿	**5:34 am**	2:34 am
☽ □ ⚳	**5:58 am**	2:58 am
☽ ⚹ ⚵	**8:28 am**	5:28 am
☽ ⊻ ♇	**12:27 pm**	9:27 am
☽ ♀	**12:29 pm**	9:29 am
☿ □ ⚳	**4:55 pm**	1:55 pm
☽ ⊼ ♄	**6:27 pm**	3:27 pm
☉ ☌ ♆	**6:32 pm**	3:32 pm
☽ ⊻ ♀	**10:53 pm**	7:53 pm

31 FRIDAY

☽ ⊻ ♅	**3:47 am**	12:47 am
☽ ⊻ ♀	**4:06 pm**	1:06 pm
☽ ⚹ ♂		10:21 pm

Eastern Standard Time in bold type
Pacific Standard Time in medium type

JANUARY 2003

☽ Last Aspect day	EST / hr:mn / PST	asp	☽ Ingress sign day	EST / hr:mn / PST
1	**12:23 pm** 9:23 am	✶♅	♑ 1	**6:42 pm** 3:42 pm
3	**7:56 pm** 4:56 pm	☌☿	♒ 3	**10:56 pm** 7:56 pm
6	**3:44 am** 12:44 am	□♀	♓ 6	**5:57 am** 2:57 am
8	**6:55 am** 3:55 am	✶☿	♈ 8	**4:15 pm** 1:15 pm
10	**10:10 pm** 7:10 pm	✶♅	♉ 11	**4:48 am** 1:48 am
13	**12:44 pm** 9:44 am	☍♂	♊ 13	**5:09 pm** 2:09 pm
15	**9:16 pm** 6:16 pm	△♅	♋ 15	11:56 pm
15	**9:16 pm** 6:16 pm	△♅	♋ 16	**2:56 am**
18	**5:48 am** 2:48 am	☍☉	♌ 18	**9:29 am** 6:29 am
20	**8:46 am** 5:46 am	☍♅	♍ 20	**1:32 pm** 10:32 am
22	**4:34 am** 1:34 am	□♄	♎ 22	**4:23 pm** 1:23 pm
24	**2:48 pm** 11:48 am	△♅	♏ 24	**7:09 pm** 4:09 pm
26	**6:14 pm** 3:14 am	□♅	♐ 26	**10:26 pm** 7:26 pm
28	**10:26 pm** 7:26 pm	✶♅	♑ 28	11:30 pm
28	**10:26 pm** 7:26 pm	✶♅	♑ 29	**2:30 am**
30	**5:34 am** 2:34 am	☌☿	♒ 31	**7:44 am** 4:44 am

☽ Phases & Eclipses phase	day	EST / hr:mn / PST
New Moon	2	**3:23 pm** 12:23 pm
2nd Quarter	10	**8:15 am** 5:15 am
Full Moon	18	**5:48 am** 2:48 am
4th Quarter	25	**3:33 am** 12:33 am

Planet Ingress	day	EST / hr:mn / PST
♀ ♐	7	**8:07 am** 5:07 am
♂ ♐	16	**11:22 pm** 8:22 pm
♀ ♓	16	10:15 pm
♀ ♓	17	**1:15 am**
☉ ♒	20	**6:53 am** 3:53 am

Planetary Motion	day	EST / hr:mn / PST
☿ ℞	2	**1:21 pm** 10:21 am
☿ D	22	**8:08 pm** 5:08 pm

DATE		SID.TIME	SUN	MOON	NODE	MERCURY	VENUS	MARS	JUPITER	SATURN	URANUS	NEPTUNE	PLUTO	CERES	PALLAS	JUNO	VESTA	CHIRON
1	W	6:40:56	10 ♑ 08 13	16 ♐ 02	8 ♊℞ 29	28 ♑ 11	23 ♏ 40	19 ♏ 34	16 ♌℞ 53	24 ♊℞ 27	26 ♒ 16	9 ♒ 34	18 ♐ 17	8 ♈ 01	25 ♒ 08	10 ♏ 19	6 ♎ 30	10 ♑ 45
2	Th	6:44:52	11 09 23	0 ♑ 10	8 27	28 ℞ 25	24 37	20 13	16 48	24 22	26 18	9 36	18 19	8 13	25 26	10 35	6 46	10 51
3	F	6:48:49	12 10 34	14 07	8 23	28 27	25 34	20 51	16 43	24 17	26 21	9 38	18 21	8 26	25 43	10 51	7 01	10 57
4	Sa	6:52:46	13 11 45	27 47	8 18	28 19	26 32	21 30	16 37	24 13	26 24	9 40	18 23	8 39	26 01	11 06	7 17	11 03
5	Su	6:56:42	14 12 56	11 ♒ 09	8 12	27 59	27 30	22 09	16 31	24 08	26 27	9 42	18 25	8 52	26 18	11 22	7 31	11 10
6	M	7:00:39	15 14 07	24 10	8 06	27 27	28 28	22 48	16 26	24 04	26 29	9 44	18 27	9 05	26 36	11 37	7 46	11 16
7	T	7:04:35	16 15 17	6 ♓ 52	7 59	26 43	29 27	23 26	16 20	24 00	26 32	9 46	18 30	9 19	26 53	11 53	8 00	11 22
8	W	7:08:32	17 16 27	19 15	7 54	25 49	0 ♐ 27	24 05	16 14	23 55	26 35	9 48	18 32	9 33	27 11	12 08	8 14	11 28
9	Th	7:12:28	18 17 37	1 ♈ 23	7 51	24 45	1 27	24 44	16 07	23 51	26 38	9 51	18 34	9 47	27 29	12 23	8 28	11 34
10	F	7:16:25	19 18 46	13 20	7 D 49	23 34	2 27	25 22	16 01	23 47	26 41	9 53	18 36	10 01	27 47	12 37	8 41	11 40
11	Sa	7:20:22	20 19 55	25 11	7 49	22 17	3 28	26 01	15 54	23 43	26 44	9 55	18 38	10 15	28 05	12 52	8 54	11 46
12	Su	7:24:18	21 21 03	7 ♉ 00	7 50	20 58	4 30	26 40	15 48	23 38	26 47	9 57	18 40	10 30	28 23	13 06	9 07	11 52
13	M	7:28:15	22 22 10	18 54	7 52	19 38	5 31	27 18	15 41	23 34	26 50	9 59	18 42	10 45	28 42	13 21	9 20	11 58
14	T	7:32:11	23 23 17	0 ♊ 57	7 ℞ 53	18 21	6 33	27 57	15 34	23 30	26 53	10 02	18 44	11 00	29 00	13 35	9 32	12 04
15	W	7:36:08	24 24 24	13 13	7 53	17 07	7 36	28 36	15 27	23 27	26 56	10 04	18 46	11 15	29 18	13 49	9 43	12 10
16	Th	7:40:04	25 25 30	25 47	7 51	16 01	8 38	29 14	15 20	23 23	26 59	10 06	18 48	11 31	29 37	14 02	9 55	12 15
17	F	7:44:01	26 26 35	8 ♋ 40	7 47	15 01	9 41	29 53	15 13	23 19	27 02	10 08	18 50	11 47	29 55	14 16	10 06	12 21
18	Sa	7:47:57	27 27 40	21 52	7 41	14 11	10 45	0 ♐ 32	15 06	23 15	27 05	10 10	18 51	12 02	0 ♓ 14	14 29	10 17	12 27
19	Su	7:51:54	28 28 44	5 ♌ 24	7 33	13 30	11 48	1 10	14 58	23 12	27 08	10 13	18 53	12 19	0 32	14 42	10 27	12 33
20	M	7:55:51	29 29 47	19 12	7 24	12 58	12 52	1 49	14 51	23 08	27 11	10 15	18 55	12 35	0 51	14 55	10 37	12 39
21	T	7:59:47	0 ♒ 30 50	3 ♍ 12	7 15	12 36	13 57	2 28	14 43	23 05	27 14	10 17	18 57	12 51	1 10	15 08	10 47	12 45
22	W	8:03:44	1 31 53	17 21	7 07	12 22	15 01	3 06	14 36	23 02	27 18	10 19	18 59	13 08	1 29	15 20	10 56	12 51
23	Th	8:07:40	2 32 55	1 ♎ 33	7 01	12 D 18	16 06	3 45	14 28	22 58	27 21	10 22	19 01	13 25	1 47	15 33	11 05	12 56
24	F	8:11:37	3 33 56	15 45	6 57	12 21	17 11	4 24	14 20	22 55	27 24	10 24	19 02	13 42	2 06	15 45	11 14	13 02
25	Sa	8:15:33	4 34 57	29 55	6 D 55	12 33	18 16	5 02	14 13	22 52	27 27	10 26	19 04	13 59	2 25	15 57	11 22	13 08
26	Su	8:19:30	5 35 58	14 ♏ 00	6 55	12 51	19 22	5 41	14 05	22 49	27 31	10 28	19 06	14 16	2 44	16 09	11 30	13 14
27	M	8:23:26	6 36 58	28 00	6 ℞ 56	13 15	20 28	6 20	13 57	22 46	27 34	10 31	19 08	14 33	3 04	16 20	11 37	13 19
28	T	8:27:23	7 37 58	11 ♐ 55	6 56	13 46	21 34	6 58	13 49	22 44	27 37	10 33	19 09	14 51	3 23	16 32	11 44	13 25
29	W	8:31:20	8 38 57	25 43	6 55	14 22	22 40	7 37	13 41	22 41	27 40	10 35	19 11	15 09	3 42	16 43	11 50	13 31
30	Th	8:35:16	9 39 56	9 ♑ 23	6 51	15 02	23 47	8 16	13 33	22 38	27 44	10 38	19 13	15 27	4 01	16 54	11 57	13 36
31	F	8:39:13	10 40 53	22 54	6 44	15 47	24 53	8 54	13 25	22 36	27 47	10 40	19 14	15 45	4 21	17 04	12 02	13 42

EPHEMERIS CALCULATED FOR 12 MIDNIGHT GREENWICH MEAN TIME. ALL OTHER DATA AND FACING ASPECTARIAN PAGE IN **EASTERN STANDARD TIME (BOLD)** AND PACIFIC STANDARD TIME (REGULAR).

FEBRUARY 2003

1 SATURDAY

☽ ✶ ♂	**1:21 am**	
☽ ☌ ♆	**3:10 am**	12:10 am
☽ ☌ ☉	**5:48 am**	2:48 am
☽ △ ⚶	**5:49 am**	2:49 am
☉ △ ⚶	**6:00 am**	3:00 am
☽ ☍ ♃	**7:45 am**	4:45 am
☽ ⚺ ⚷	**8:54 am**	5:54 am
☽ ✶ ⚳	**1:24 pm**	10:24 am
☽ ⚺ ☿	**3:21 pm**	12:21 pm
☽ □ ⚵	**3:25 pm**	12:25 pm
☿ ✶ ⚵	**4:34 pm**	1:34 pm
☽ ✶ ♇	**6:56 pm**	3:56 pm
☽ △ ♄		9:54 pm

2 SUNDAY

☽ △ ♄	**12:54 am**	
☉ ☍ ♃	**4:12 am**	1:12 am
☽ ✶ ♀	**10:54 am**	7:54 am
☽ ☌ ♅	**11:02 am**	8:02 am
♀ ✶ ♅	**12:27 pm**	9:27 am
♂ ✶ ♆	**4:39 pm**	1:39 pm
☽ ☌ ☿		10:06 pm
☉ ⚺ ⚷		10:22 pm

3 MONDAY

☽ ☌ ☿	**1:06 am**	
☉ ⚺ ⚷	**1:22 am**	
☽ ⚺ ♆	**11:25 am**	8:25 am
☽ □ ♂	**12:22 pm**	9:22 am
☽ ⚻ ⚶	**2:20 pm**	11:20 am
☽ ⚻ ♃	**3:26 pm**	12:26 pm
☿ ⚺ ♇	**5:27 pm**	2:27 pm
☽ ✶ ⚷	**5:39 pm**	2:39 pm
☽ ⚺ ☉	**6:58 pm**	3:58 pm
☽ ⚺ ⚳	**11:24 pm**	8:24 pm
☽ △ ⚵		9:50 pm

4 TUESDAY

☽ △ ⚵	**12:50 am**	
☽ □ ♇	**3:53 am**	12:53 am
☽ ✶ ☿	**4:48 am**	1:48 am
☽ □ ♄	**9:53 am**	6:53 am
☽ ⚺ ♅	**8:56 pm**	5:56 pm
☽ □ ♀		11:24 pm

5 WEDNESDAY

☽ □ ♀	**2:24 am**	
♂ ✶ ⚶	**6:12 am**	3:12 am
☽ ⚺ ☿	**1:03 pm**	10:03 am
♂ △ ♃	**2:25 pm**	11:25 am
☽ ✶ ♆	**10:24 pm**	7:24 pm
☽ ☍ ⚶		10:33 pm
☽ △ ♃		10:47 pm
☽ △ ♂		11:34 pm

6 THURSDAY

☽ ☍ ⚶	**1:33 am**	
☽ △ ♃	**1:47 am**	
☽ △ ♂	**2:34 am**	
☽ □ ⚷	**5:12 am**	2:12 am
☽ ✶ ☉	**11:37 am**	8:37 am
☽ ☌ ⚳	**12:22 pm**	9:22 am
☽ ⚻ ⚵	**1:01 pm**	10:01 am
☿ ⚻ ♄	**1:31 pm**	10:31 am
☽ △ ♇	**3:32 pm**	12:32 pm
♃ ✶ ⚶	**6:12 pm**	3:12 pm
☽ ✶ ♄	**9:28 pm**	6:28 pm
☽ □ ☿	**10:20 pm**	7:20 pm
☉ ✶ ⚳	**11:57 pm**	8:57 pm

7 FRIDAY

☉ □ ⚵	**6:29 am**	3:29 am
☽ ✶ ♅	**9:22 am**	6:22 am
☽ △ ♀	**9:06 pm**	6:06 pm

8 SATURDAY

☽ ✶ ☿	**3:20 am**	12:20 am
⚳ ⚻ ⚵	**7:49 am**	4:49 am
☉ ✶ ♇	**10:31 am**	7:31 am
♂ ⚺ ⚷	**10:48 am**	7:48 am
☽ □ ♆	**11:20 am**	8:20 am
☽ □ ♃	**1:54 pm**	10:54 am
☽ ⚻ ⚶	**2:30 pm**	11:30 am
☽ △ ⚷	**6:28 pm**	3:28 pm
☽ ⚻ ♂	**6:51 pm**	3:51 pm
☽ ☍ ⚵		11:38 pm
☽ ⚺ ⚳		11:56 pm

9 SUNDAY

☽ ☍ ⚵	**2:38 am**	
☽ ⚺ ⚳	**2:56 am**	
☽ ⚻ ♇	**4:32 am**	1:32 am
☽ □ ☉	**6:11 am**	3:11 am
☽ ⚺ ♄	**10:14 am**	7:14 am
☽ △ ☿	**5:55 pm**	2:55 pm
☽ □ ♅	**10:28 pm**	7:28 pm

10 MONDAY

☽ ⚻ ♀	**4:03 pm**	1:03 pm
☽ □ ☿	**5:31 pm**	2:31 pm
☽ △ ♆	**11:47 pm**	8:47 pm
☽ ✶ ♃		10:26 pm
☽ △ ⚶		11:44 pm

11 TUESDAY

☽ ✶ ♃	**1:26 am**	
☽ △ ⚶	**2:44 am**	
☉ △ ♄	**4:45 am**	1:45 am
☽ ⚻ ⚷	**6:55 am**	3:55 am
☽ ☍ ♂	**10:10 am**	7:10 am
♀ ✶ ☿	**1:17 pm**	10:17 am
☽ ⚻ ⚵	**2:58 pm**	11:58 am
☿ ⚺ ♅	**3:18 pm**	12:18 pm
☽ ✶ ⚳	**4:14 pm**	1:14 pm
☽ ☍ ♇	**4:15 pm**	1:15 pm
♇ △ ⚳	**5:04 pm**	2:04 pm
☽ ☌ ♄	**9:29 pm**	6:29 pm
☽ △ ☉	**11:00 pm**	8:00 pm

12 WEDNESDAY

☽ △ ♅	**9:29 am**	6:29 am
☽ ⚻ ☿	**11:26 am**	8:26 am

13 THURSDAY

☽ △ ☿	**4:39 am**	1:39 am
☽ ☍ ♀	**7:22 am**	4:22 am
☽ ⚻ ♆	**9:11 am**	6:11 am
☽ ⚺ ♃	**10:00 am**	7:00 am
☽ □ ⚶	**11:45 am**	8:45 am
☽ ☍ ⚷	**4:03 pm**	1:03 pm
☽ ⚻ ♂	**9:36 pm**	6:36 pm
☽ △ ⚵	**11:43 pm**	8:43 pm
☽ ⚻ ♇		9:29 pm
☽ □ ⚳		10:49 pm

14 FRIDAY

☽ ⚻ ♇	**12:29 am**	
☽ □ ⚳	**1:49 am**	
♀ ⚺ ♆	**4:31 am**	1:31 am
☽ ⚺ ♄	**5:12 am**	2:12 am
♀ ⚻ ♃	**10:34 am**	7:34 am
☽ ⚻ ☉	**11:12 am**	8:12 am
☽ ⚻ ♅	**4:40 pm**	1:40 pm
☽ ☍ ☿		9:08 pm

15 SATURDAY

☽ ☍ ☿	**12:08 am**	
♀ □ ⚶	**8:11 am**	5:11 am
☽ ⚻ ☿	**11:36 am**	8:36 am
☽ ☍ ♆	**2:40 pm**	11:40 am
☽ ☌ ♃	**2:49 pm**	11:49 am
☽ ✶ ⚶	**4:50 pm**	1:50 pm
☽ ⚻ ♀	**5:38 pm**	2:38 pm
☽ ⚻ ⚷	**9:15 pm**	6:15 pm
♂ ⚺ ⚵		10:55 pm

16 SUNDAY

♂ ⚺ ⚵	**1:55 am**	
♃ ☍ ♆	**4:12 am**	1:12 am
☽ □ ⚵	**4:32 am**	1:32 am
☽ △ ♂	**4:38 am**	1:38 am
☽ △ ♇	**4:55 am**	1:55 am
☽ △ ⚳	**7:22 am**	4:22 am
☽ ✶ ♄	**9:14 am**	6:14 am
♂ ☌ ♇	**11:00 am**	8:00 am
☽ ☍ ☉	**6:51 pm**	3:51 pm
☽ ☍ ♅	**8:18 pm**	5:18 pm

17 MONDAY

☽ ⚻ ☿	**8:33 am**	5:33 am
☽ ☍ ☿	**3:18 pm**	12:18 pm
☉ ☌ ♅	**4:38 pm**	1:38 pm
♀ ☌ ⚷	**4:39 pm**	1:39 pm
☽ ⚺ ♃	**4:46 pm**	1:46 pm
☽ ⚻ ♆	**5:10 pm**	2:10 pm
☽ ⚺ ⚶	**6:59 pm**	3:59 pm
☽ △ ⚷	**11:39 pm**	8:39 pm
☽ △ ♀		9:13 pm

18 TUESDAY

☽ △ ♀	**12:13 am**	
☽ ✶ ⚵	**6:45 am**	3:45 am
☽ □ ♇	**6:51 am**	3:51 am
☽ □ ♂	**8:48 am**	5:48 am
☽ ⚻ ⚳	**10:20 am**	7:20 am
☽ □ ♄	**10:56 am**	7:56 am
☽ ⚻ ♅	**9:58 pm**	6:58 pm
☽ ⚻ ☉		9:00 pm
♇ ⚺ ⚵		9:21 pm

19 WEDNESDAY

☽ ⚻ ☉	**12:00 am**	
♇ ⚺ ⚵	**12:21 am**	
♄ ✶ ⚳	**11:26 am**	8:26 am
♃ ⚻ ☿	**2:56 pm**	11:56 am
☽ △ ☿	**3:07 pm**	12:07 pm
☽ ✶ ♃	**5:34 pm**	2:34 pm
☽ ⚻ ☿	**5:39 pm**	2:39 pm
☽ △ ♆	**6:30 pm**	3:30 pm
☽ ☌ ⚶	**7:59 pm**	4:59 pm
☽ □ ⚷		10:06 pm

20 THURSDAY

☽ □ ⚷	**1:06 am**	
☽ □ ♀	**5:39 am**	2:39 am
☽ ✶ ♇	**8:06 am**	5:06 am
☽ ⚺ ⚵	**8:16 am**	5:16 am
♂ ☍ ♄	**9:14 am**	6:14 am
☽ △ ♄	**12:08 pm**	9:08 am
☽ ✶ ♂	**12:16 pm**	9:16 am
☽ ☍ ⚳	**12:45 pm**	9:45 am
☿ ☍ ♃	**2:12 pm**	11:12 am
☽ △ ♅	**11:29 pm**	8:29 pm
☿ ⚺ ♀	**11:31 pm**	8:31 pm
☿ ☌ ♆		10:50 pm

21 FRIDAY

☿ ☌ ♆	**1:50 am**	
☽ △ ☉	**5:04 am**	2:04 am
♆ ⚺ ☿	**10:41 am**	7:41 am
♂ △ ⚳	**11:02 am**	8:02 am
♀ ⚺ ♇	**12:47 pm**	9:47 am
☿ △ ⚶	**1:49 pm**	10:49 am
♀ ✶ ⚵	**4:36 pm**	1:36 pm
☽ □ ♃	**6:52 pm**	3:52 pm
☽ □ ♆	**8:20 pm**	5:20 pm
☽ △ ☿	**8:33 pm**	5:33 pm
☽ ⚺ ⚶	**9:29 pm**	6:29 pm
☽ □ ☿	**10:25 pm**	7:25 pm

22 SATURDAY

☽ ✶ ⚷	**3:16 am**	12:16 am
☽ ⚺ ♇	**10:14 am**	7:14 am
☽ ☌ ⚵	**10:37 am**	7:37 am
☽ ✶ ♀	**12:08 pm**	9:08 am
☽ ⚻ ♄	**2:20 pm**	11:20 am
☽ ⚻ ⚳	**4:14 pm**	1:14 pm
☽ ⚺ ♂	**4:52 pm**	1:52 pm
☽ □ ♅		11:15 pm

23 SUNDAY

☽ □ ♅	**2:15 am**	
☿ ⚻ ⚶	**4:25 am**	1:25 am
☽ □ ☉	**11:46 am**	8:46 am
♀ ⚻ ♄	**2:45 pm**	11:45 am
☽ △ ♃	**9:40 pm**	6:40 pm
☿ ⚺ ⚷	**10:33 pm**	7:33 pm
☽ ✶ ♆	**11:45 pm**	8:45 pm
☽ ✶ ⚶		9:28 pm
☽ □ ☿		10:06 pm

24 MONDAY

☽ ✶ ⚶	**12:28 am**	
☽ □ ☿	**1:06 am**	
☽ ⚺ ⚷	**7:04 am**	4:04 am
☽ ✶ ☿	**8:05 am**	5:05 am
☽ ☌ ♇	**2:05 pm**	11:05 am
☽ ⚺ ⚵	**2:41 pm**	11:41 am
☽ ☍ ♄	**6:16 pm**	3:16 pm
☽ ⚺ ♀	**8:51 pm**	5:51 pm
☽ △ ⚳	**9:36 pm**	6:36 pm
☽ ☌ ♂	**11:28 pm**	8:28 pm

25 TUESDAY

☽ ✶ ♅	**6:50 am**	3:50 am
♀ □ ⚳	**9:08 am**	6:08 am
☽ ✶ ☉	**8:45 pm**	5:45 pm
☽ ⚻ ♃		11:18 pm

26 WEDNESDAY

☽ ⚻ ♃	**2:18 am**	
☽ ⚺ ♆	**5:01 am**	2:01 am
☽ □ ⚶	**5:11 am**	2:11 am
☽ ✶ ☿	**7:40 am**	4:40 am
☽ ☌ ⚷	**12:45 pm**	9:45 am
☿ ✶ ♇	**1:34 pm**	10:34 am
☽ ⚺ ♇	**7:45 pm**	4:45 pm
♆ △ ⚶	**7:49 pm**	4:49 pm
☿ □ ⚵	**8:25 pm**	5:25 pm
☽ ✶ ⚵	**8:34 pm**	5:34 pm
☽ ⚺ ☿	**8:35 pm**	5:35 pm
☽ ⚻ ♄		9:04 pm

27 THURSDAY

☽ ⚻ ♄	**12:04 am**	
☽ □ ⚳	**4:59 am**	1:59 am
☽ ☌ ♀	**7:58 am**	4:58 am
☽ ⚺ ♂	**8:09 am**	5:09 am
♀ ⚺ ♂	**12:20 pm**	9:20 am
☽ ⚺ ♅	**1:16 pm**	10:16 am
☿ △ ♄		10:51 pm

28 FRIDAY

☿ △ ♄	**1:51 am**	
☽ ⚺ ☉	**7:59 am**	4:59 am
☽ ☍ ♃	**8:41 am**	5:41 am
☽ △ ⚶	**11:34 am**	8:34 am
☽ ☌ ♆	**12:04 pm**	9:04 am
☽ ⚺ ☿	**4:08 pm**	1:08 pm
☉ ⚻ ♃	**4:16 pm**	1:16 pm
☽ ⚺ ⚷	**8:13 pm**	5:13 pm

Eastern Standard Time in bold type
Pacific Standard Time in medium type

FEBRUARY 2003

☽ Last Aspect day	EST / hr:mn	PST	asp	☽ Ingress sign	day	EST / hr:mn	PST
2	**11:02 am**	8:02 am	☌ ♅	♓	2	**2:55 pm**	11:55 am
4	**9:53 am**	6:53 am	□ ♄	♈	4		9:44 pm
4	**9:53 am**	6:53 am	□ ♄	♈	5	**12:44 am**	
7	**9:22 am**	6:22 am	⚹ ♅	♉	7	**12:59 pm**	9:59 pm
9	**10:28 pm**	7:28 pm	□ ♅	♊	9		10:45 pm
9	**10:28 pm**	7:28 pm	□ ♅	♊	10	**1:45 am**	
12	**9:29 am**	6:29 am	△ ♅	♋	12	**12:19 pm**	9:19 am
13	**7:22 am**	4:22 am	☍ ♀	♌	14	**7:04 pm**	4:04 pm
16	**8:18 pm**	5:18 pm	☍ ♅	♍	16	**10:22 pm**	7:22 pm
18	**10:56 am**	7:56 am	□ ♄	♎	18	**11:48 pm**	8:48 pm
20	**11:29 pm**	8:29 pm	△ ♅	♏	20		10:09 pm
20	**11:29 pm**	8:29 pm	△ ♅	♏	21	**1:09 am**	
22		11:15 pm	□ ♅	♐	23	**3:46 am**	12:46 am
23	**2:15 am**		□ ♅	♐	23	**3:46 am**	12:46 am
25	**6:50 am**	3:50 am	⚹ ♅	♑	25	**8:11 am**	5:11 am
27	**7:58 am**	4:58 am	☌ ♀	♒	27	**2:24 pm**	11:24 am

☽ Phases & Eclipses phase	day	EST / hr:mn	PST
New Moon	1	**5:48 am**	2:48 am
2nd Quarter	9	**6:11 am**	3:11 am
Full Moon	16	**6:51 pm**	3:51 pm
4th Quarter	23	**11:46 am**	8:46 am

Planet Ingress		day	EST / hr:mn	PST
♀	♑	4	**8:27 am**	5:27 am
☿	♒	13	**8:00 pm**	5:00 pm
☉	♓	18	**9:00 pm**	6:00 pm

Planetary Motion		day	EST / hr:mn	PST
♇	℞	11	**4:36 pm**	1:36 pm
♄	D	21		11:41 pm
♄	D	22	**2:41 am**	

DATE		SID.TIME	SUN	MOON	NODE	MERCURY	VENUS	MARS	JUPITER	SATURN	URANUS	NEPTUNE	PLUTO	CERES	PALLAS	JUNO	VESTA	CHIRON
1	Sa	8:43:09	11 ♒ 41 50	6 ♒ 14	6 ♊℞ 34	16 ♑ 37	26 ♐ 00	9 ♐ 33	13 ♌℞ 17	22 ♊℞ 33	27 ♒ 50	10 ♒ 42	19 ♐ 16	16 ♈ 03	4 ♓ 40	17 ♏ 15	12 ♎ 08	13 ♑ 47
2	Su	8:47:06	12 42 46	19 20	6 22	17 29	27 07	10 12	13 09	22 31	27 54	10 44	19 17	16 22	4 59	17 25	12 12	13 53
3	M	8:51:02	13 43 40	2 ♓ 10	6 10	18 25	28 15	10 50	13 01	22 29	27 57	10 47	19 19	16 40	5 19	17 35	12 17	13 58
4	T	8:54:59	14 44 33	14 45	5 57	19 24	29 22	11 29	12 53	22 27	28 01	10 49	19 21	16 59	5 38	17 44	12 21	14 04
5	W	8:58:55	15 45 25	27 05	5 46	20 26	0 ♑ 30	12 07	12 45	22 25	28 04	10 51	19 22	17 18	5 58	17 54	12 24	14 09
6	Th	9:02:52	16 46 16	9 ♈ 12	5 38	21 30	1 38	12 46	12 37	22 23	28 07	10 54	19 23	17 37	6 17	18 03	12 27	14 15
7	F	9:06:49	17 47 05	21 08	5 32	22 37	2 45	13 25	12 29	22 21	28 11	10 56	19 25	17 56	6 37	18 12	12 30	14 20
8	Sa	9:10:45	18 47 53	2 ♉ 57	5 29	23 46	3 54	14 03	12 21	22 20	28 14	10 58	19 26	18 15	6 57	18 21	12 32	14 25
9	Su	9:14:42	19 48 39	14 46	5 D 27	24 57	5 02	14 42	12 13	22 18	28 18	11 00	19 28	18 34	7 16	18 29	12 33	14 30
10	M	9:18:38	20 49 24	26 38	5 ℞ 27	26 09	6 10	15 20	12 06	22 17	28 21	11 03	19 29	18 54	7 36	18 37	12 34	14 36
11	T	9:22:35	21 50 08	8 ♊ 40	5 27	27 23	7 19	15 59	11 58	22 15	28 25	11 05	19 30	19 13	7 56	18 45	12 ℞ 35	14 41
12	W	9:26:31	22 50 49	20 57	5 26	28 39	8 27	16 37	11 50	22 14	28 28	11 07	19 32	19 33	8 16	18 53	12 35	14 46
13	Th	9:30:28	23 51 30	3 ♋ 33	5 24	29 57	9 36	17 16	11 42	22 13	28 31	11 09	19 33	19 53	8 36	19 00	12 35	14 51
14	F	9:34:24	24 52 08	16 33	5 18	1 ♒ 16	10 45	17 55	11 35	22 12	28 35	11 12	19 34	20 13	8 55	19 07	12 34	14 56
15	Sa	9:38:21	25 52 45	29 58	5 10	2 36	11 54	18 33	11 27	22 11	28 38	11 14	19 35	20 33	9 15	19 14	12 33	15 01
16	Su	9:42:18	26 53 20	13 ♌ 47	4 59	3 57	13 03	19 12	11 20	22 10	28 42	11 16	19 36	20 53	9 35	19 21	12 31	15 06
17	M	9:46:14	27 53 54	27 59	4 47	5 20	14 13	19 50	11 12	22 10	28 45	11 18	19 38	21 13	9 55	19 27	12 29	15 11
18	T	9:50:11	28 54 26	12 ♍ 27	4 35	6 44	15 22	20 29	11 05	22 09	28 49	11 20	19 39	21 34	10 15	19 33	12 26	15 16
19	W	9:54:07	29 54 57	27 04	4 24	8 09	16 31	21 07	10 58	22 09	28 52	11 23	19 40	21 54	10 35	19 39	12 23	15 20
20	Th	9:58:04	0 ♓ 55 26	11 ♎ 43	4 15	9 35	17 41	21 45	10 51	22 08	28 56	11 25	19 41	22 15	10 55	19 44	12 19	15 25
21	F	10:02:00	1 55 54	26 17	4 09	11 02	18 51	22 24	10 44	22 08	28 59	11 27	19 42	22 36	11 15	19 49	12 15	15 30
22	Sa	10:05:57	2 56 21	10 ♏ 41	4 06	12 31	20 01	23 02	10 37	22 D 08	29 03	11 29	19 43	22 57	11 35	19 54	12 11	15 34
23	Su	10:09:53	3 56 46	24 53	4 05	14 00	21 11	23 41	10 30	22 08	29 06	11 31	19 44	23 17	11 55	19 59	12 05	15 39
24	M	10:13:50	4 57 11	8 ♐ 50	4 05	15 31	22 21	24 19	10 23	22 08	29 10	11 33	19 45	23 39	12 16	20 03	12 00	15 44
25	T	10:17:47	5 57 33	22 33	4 04	17 02	23 31	24 58	10 16	22 09	29 13	11 35	19 46	24 00	12 36	20 07	11 54	15 48
26	W	10:21:43	6 57 55	6 ♑ 04	4 02	18 35	24 41	25 36	10 10	22 09	29 16	11 38	19 46	24 21	12 56	20 10	11 47	15 52
27	Th	10:25:40	7 58 15	19 22	3 57	20 08	25 51	26 14	10 04	22 09	29 20	11 40	19 47	24 42	13 16	20 14	11 40	15 57
28	F	10:29:36	8 58 33	2 ♒ 30	3 49	21 43	27 02	26 53	9 57	22 10	29 23	11 42	19 48	25 04	13 36	20 17	11 32	16 01

EPHEMERIS CALCULATED FOR 12 MIDNIGHT GREENWICH MEAN TIME. ALL OTHER DATA AND FACING ASPECTARIAN PAGE IN **EASTERN STANDARD TIME (BOLD)** AND PACIFIC STANDARD TIME (REGULAR).

MARCH 2003

1 SATURDAY
☽ ⚹ ♇	**3:12 am**	12:12 am
☽ □ ⚵	**4:11 am**	1:11 am
☽ △ ♄	**7:39 am**	4:39 am
☽ ☌ ☿	**11:54 am**	8:54 am
☽ ⚹ ⚳	**2:18 pm**	11:18 am
☽ ⚹ ♂	**6:56 pm**	3:56 pm
☽ ⚺ ♀	**9:29 pm**	6:29 pm
☽ ☌ ♅	**9:30 pm**	6:30 pm
♀ ⚺ ♅	**9:39 pm**	6:39 pm
☉ ⚻ ⚴		9:54 pm

2 SUNDAY
☉ ⚻ ⚴	**12:54 am**	
☿ ⚹ ⚳	**11:16 am**	8:16 am
☉ ⚺ ♆	**2:19 pm**	11:19 am
☽ ⚻ ♃	**4:54 pm**	1:54 pm
☽ ⚻ ⚴	**7:41 pm**	4:41 pm
☽ ⚺ ♆	**9:01 pm**	6:01 pm
☽ ☌ ☉	**9:35 pm**	6:35 pm
☽ ☌ ♀		11:39 pm

3 MONDAY
☽ ☌ ♀	**2:39 am**	
☽ ⚹ ⚷	**5:38 am**	2:38 am
☽ □ ♇	**12:36 pm**	9:36 am
☽ △ ⚵	**1:43 pm**	10:43 am
☽ □ ♄	**5:14 pm**	2:14 pm
☽ ⚺ ⚳		10:49 pm
♂ ⚹ ♅		11:30 pm

4 TUESDAY
☽ ⚺ ⚳	**1:49 am**	
♂ ⚹ ♅	**2:30 am**	
☽ ⚺ ☿	**6:30 am**	3:30 am
☽ ⚺ ♅	**7:48 am**	4:48 am
☽ □ ♂	**8:04 am**	5:04 am
☽ ⚹ ♀	**1:44 pm**	10:44 am
☿ ☌ ♅	**4:16 pm**	1:16 pm
☿ ⚹ ♂		9:01 pm

5 WEDNESDAY
☿ ⚹ ♂	**12:01 am**	
☽ △ ♃	**3:13 am**	12:13 am
☽ ☍ ⚴	**5:46 am**	2:46 am
☽ ⚹ ♆	**8:06 am**	5:06 am
☽ ⚺ ☉	**1:54 pm**	10:54 am
☽ ⚺ ♀	**3:29 pm**	12:29 pm
☽ □ ⚷	**5:11 pm**	2:11 pm
☽ △ ♇		9:07 pm
☽ ⚻ ⚵		10:19 pm

6 THURSDAY
☽ △ ♇	**12:07 am**	
☽ ⚻ ⚵	**1:19 am**	
☽ ⚹ ♄	**4:58 am**	1:58 am
☽ ☌ ⚳	**3:37 pm**	12:37 pm
☉ ☌ ♀	**5:52 pm**	2:52 pm
☽ ⚹ ♅	**8:10 pm**	5:10 pm
☽ △ ♂	**11:35 pm**	8:35 pm

7 FRIDAY
☽ ⚹ ☿	**4:34 am**	1:34 am
☉ ⚹ ⚷	**7:38 am**	4:38 am
☽ □ ♀	**8:42 am**	5:42 am
☽ □ ♃	**3:22 pm**	12:22 pm
☽ ⚻ ⚴	**5:31 pm**	2:31 pm
☽ □ ♆	**8:57 pm**	5:57 pm

8 SATURDAY
☽ ⚹ ♀	**6:06 am**	3:06 am
☽ △ ⚷	**6:21 am**	3:21 am
☽ ⚹ ☉	**8:20 am**	5:20 am
☽ ⚻ ♇	**1:06 pm**	10:06 am
☽ ☍ ⚵	**2:17 pm**	11:17 am
⚷ ⚹ ♀	**4:42 pm**	1:42 pm
☽ ⚺ ♄	**6:04 pm**	3:04 pm

9 SUNDAY
☽ ⚺ ⚳	**6:37 am**	3:37 am
☽ □ ♅	**9:29 am**	6:29 am
☽ ⚻ ♂	**4:03 pm**	1:03 pm
♀ ☍ ♃	**11:18 pm**	8:18 pm
☿ ⚻ ♃		11:57 pm

10 MONDAY
☿ ⚻ ♃	**2:57 am**	
☽ ⚹ ♃	**3:49 am**	12:49 am
☽ □ ☿	**3:58 am**	12:58 am
☽ △ ♀	**4:21 am**	1:21 am
☽ △ ⚴	**5:22 am**	2:22 am
☽ △ ♆	**9:53 am**	6:53 am
☿ ⚺ ♀	**10:50 am**	7:50 am
☿ ⚻ ⚴	**12:34 pm**	9:34 am
♀ △ ⚴	**1:18 pm**	10:18 am
☉ □ ♇	**4:51 pm**	1:51 pm
☽ ⚻ ⚷	**7:13 pm**	4:13 pm
☽ □ ♀	**8:24 pm**	5:24 pm
☽ ☍ ♇		10:29 pm
☽ □ ☉		11:15 pm
☽ ⚻ ⚵		11:34 pm

11 TUESDAY
☽ ☍ ♇	**1:29 am**	
☽ □ ☉	**2:15 am**	
☽ ⚻ ⚵	**2:34 am**	
☉ △ ⚵	**5:55 am**	2:55 am
☽ ☌ ♄	**6:24 am**	3:24 am
☽ ⚹ ⚳	**8:10 pm**	5:10 pm
☿ ⚺ ♆	**8:11 pm**	5:11 pm
☽ △ ♅	**9:19 pm**	6:19 pm

12 WEDNESDAY
☽ ☍ ♂	**6:28 am**	3:28 am
♀ ☌ ♆	**1:35 pm**	10:35 am
☽ ⚺ ♃	**2:07 pm**	11:07 am
☽ □ ⚴	**2:58 pm**	11:58 am
☽ ⚻ ♆	**8:18 pm**	5:18 pm
☽ ⚻ ♀	**8:59 pm**	5:59 pm
☽ △ ☿		9:13 pm

13 THURSDAY
☽ △ ☿	**12:13 am**	
☽ ☍ ⚷	**5:11 am**	2:11 am
☉ □ ♄	**6:38 am**	3:38 am
☽ △ ♀	**7:35 am**	4:35 am
☽ ⚻ ♇	**10:49 am**	7:49 am
☽ △ ⚵	**11:41 am**	8:41 am
☽ ⚺ ♄	**3:31 pm**	12:31 pm
☽ △ ☉	**4:13 pm**	1:13 pm
♅ ⚹ ⚳	**5:07 pm**	2:07 pm

14 FRIDAY
☽ ⚻ ♅	**5:27 am**	2:27 am
☽ □ ⚳	**5:45 am**	2:45 am
☿ ⚹ ⚷	**11:58 am**	8:58 am
☽ ⚻ ♂	**4:24 pm**	1:24 pm
☽ ☌ ♃	**8:31 pm**	5:31 pm
☽ ⚹ ⚴	**8:42 pm**	5:42 pm
☽ ☍ ♆		11:36 pm

15 SATURDAY
☽ ☍ ♆	**2:36 am**	
☽ ☍ ♀	**8:10 am**	5:10 am
☽ ⚻ ⚷	**10:54 am**	7:54 am
♃ ⚹ ⚴	**12:07 pm**	9:07 am
☿ ☌ ♀	**1:32 pm**	10:32 am
☽ ⚻ ♀	**2:14 pm**	11:14 am
☽ ⚻ ☿	**2:19 pm**	11:19 am
☽ △ ♇	**3:55 pm**	12:55 pm
☽ □ ⚵	**4:35 pm**	1:35 pm
☽ ⚹ ♄	**8:24 pm**	5:24 pm
☽ ⚻ ☉		9:53 pm
☿ □ ♇		11:19 pm

16 SUNDAY
☽ ⚻ ☉	**12:53 am**	
☿ □ ♇	**2:19 am**	
☿ △ ⚵	**6:53 am**	3:53 am
☽ ☍ ♅	**9:23 am**	6:23 am
☽ △ ⚳	**10:52 am**	7:52 am
♀ ⚺ ⚷	**5:36 pm**	2:36 pm
☽ △ ♂	**9:43 pm**	6:43 pm
☽ ⚺ ⚴	**10:38 pm**	7:38 pm
☽ ⚺ ♃	**11:03 pm**	8:03 pm

17 MONDAY
☽ ⚻ ♆	**5:04 am**	2:04 am
☿ □ ♄	**12:34 pm**	9:34 am
☽ △ ⚷	**12:58 pm**	9:58 am
♂ □ ⚴	**1:28 pm**	10:28 am
☽ ⚻ ♀	**2:36 pm**	11:36 am
☽ ☍ ♀	**5:06 pm**	2:06 pm
☽ □ ♇	**5:33 pm**	2:33 pm
☽ ⚹ ⚵	**6:00 pm**	3:00 pm
☽ □ ♄	**9:56 pm**	6:56 pm
☽ ☍ ☿	**11:17 pm**	8:17 pm
♂ ⚻ ♃		11:05 pm

18 TUESDAY
♂ ⚻ ♃	**2:05 am**	
☽ ☍ ☉	**5:35 am**	2:35 am
☽ ⚻ ♅	**10:23 am**	7:23 am
☽ ⚻ ⚳	**12:54 pm**	9:54 am
♇ □ ♀	**12:58 pm**	9:58 am
☽ ☌ ⚴	**10:16 pm**	7:16 pm
☽ ⚹ ♃	**11:14 pm**	8:14 pm
☽ □ ♂		9:15 pm

19 WEDNESDAY
☽ □ ♂	**12:15 am**	
♀ △ ⚵	**3:07 am**	12:07 am
♀ ⚹ ♇	**3:29 am**	12:29 am
☽ △ ♆	**5:23 am**	2:23 am
♀ □ ⚵	**7:16 am**	4:16 am
♀ ⚺ ♀	**9:12 am**	6:12 am
☽ □ ⚷	**1:12 pm**	10:12 am
☽ ⚹ ♇	**5:33 pm**	2:33 pm
☽ ⚺ ⚵	**5:48 pm**	2:48 pm
☽ ⚻ ♀	**6:12 pm**	3:12 pm
☽ △ ♀	**6:46 pm**	3:46 pm
☽ △ ♄	**10:02 pm**	7:02 pm

20 THURSDAY
☽ ⚻ ☿	**6:21 am**	3:21 am
☽ ⚻ ☉	**8:54 am**	5:54 am
☽ △ ♅	**10:28 am**	7:28 am
☽ ☍ ⚳	**2:05 pm**	11:05 am
☽ ⚺ ⚴	**9:29 pm**	6:29 pm
☽ □ ♃	**11:07 pm**	8:07 pm
☽ ⚹ ♂		11:25 pm

21 FRIDAY
☽ ⚹ ♂	**2:25 am**	
☽ □ ♆	**5:35 am**	2:35 am
☉ ⚺ ♅	**9:55 am**	6:55 am
♀ △ ♄	**1:31 pm**	10:31 am
☽ ⚹ ⚷	**1:38 pm**	10:38 am
☿ ⚺ ♅	**2:21 pm**	11:21 am
☽ ⚺ ♇	**5:57 pm**	2:57 pm
☽ ☌ ⚵	**5:58 pm**	2:58 pm
☉ ☌ ☿	**6:34 pm**	3:34 pm
☽ △ ♀	**7:46 pm**	4:46 pm
♇ ⚺ ⚵	**10:18 pm**	7:18 pm
☽ ⚻ ♄	**10:43 pm**	7:43 pm
☽ □ ♀	**11:30 pm**	8:30 pm

22 SATURDAY
☽ □ ♅	**11:36 am**	8:36 am
☽ △ ☉	**1:24 pm**	10:24 am
☽ △ ☿	**2:55 pm**	11:55 am
☽ ⚻ ⚳	**4:31 pm**	1:31 pm
☽ ⚹ ⚴	**10:02 pm**	7:02 pm
☽ △ ♃		9:26 pm

23 SUNDAY
☽ △ ♃	**12:26 am**	
☿ ⚺ ⚳	**4:43 am**	1:43 am
☽ ⚺ ♂	**6:21 am**	3:21 am
☽ ⚹ ♆	**7:27 am**	4:27 am
☽ ⚺ ⚷	**3:57 pm**	12:57 pm
☽ ⚺ ⚵	**8:03 pm**	5:03 pm
☽ ☌ ♇	**8:20 pm**	5:20 pm
☽ □ ♀	**11:30 pm**	8:30 pm
☽ ☍ ♄		10:32 pm

24 MONDAY
☽ ☍ ♄	**1:32 am**	
☽ ⚹ ♀	**6:58 am**	3:58 am
♂ ⚺ ♆	**8:20 am**	5:20 am
☿ ☍ ⚴	**12:40 pm**	9:40 am
☽ ⚹ ♅	**3:06 pm**	12:06 pm
☽ □ ☉	**8:51 pm**	5:51 pm
☽ △ ⚳	**9:36 pm**	6:36 pm
☽ □ ⚴		9:58 pm

25 TUESDAY
☽ □ ⚴	**12:58 am**	
☽ □ ☿	**3:24 am**	12:24 am
☽ ⚻ ♃	**4:19 am**	1:19 am
☿ △ ♃	**9:27 am**	6:27 am
☽ ⚺ ♆	**11:58 am**	8:58 am
☉ ⚺ ⚳	**1:16 pm**	10:16 am
☽ ☌ ♂	**1:16 pm**	10:16 am
☽ ☌ ⚷	**9:00 pm**	6:00 pm
☽ ⚹ ⚵		9:46 pm
☽ ⚺ ♇		10:26 pm

26 WEDNESDAY
☽ ⚹ ⚵	**12:46 am**	
☽ ⚺ ♇	**1:26 am**	
☽ ⚹ ♀	**6:11 am**	3:11 am
☽ ⚻ ♄	**7:09 am**	4:09 am
☽ ⚺ ♀	**6:05 pm**	3:05 pm
☉ ☍ ⚴	**6:18 pm**	3:18 pm
☽ ⚺ ♅	**9:25 pm**	6:25 pm

27 THURSDAY
☽ □ ⚳	**5:44 am**	2:44 am
☽ △ ⚴	**6:30 am**	3:30 am
☽ ⚹ ☉	**7:47 am**	4:47 am
☽ ☍ ♃	**10:59 am**	7:59 am
☿ ⚹ ♆	**12:36 pm**	9:36 am
☽ ☌ ♆	**7:14 pm**	4:14 pm
☽ ⚹ ☿	**8:28 pm**	5:28 pm
⚳ ⚻ ⚴	**9:23 pm**	6:23 pm
☽ ⚺ ♂	**11:21 pm**	8:21 pm

28 FRIDAY
♄ □ ♀	**3:37 am**	12:37 am
☽ ⚺ ⚷	**4:45 am**	1:45 am
♀ ☌ ♅	**7:44 am**	4:44 am
☽ □ ⚵	**8:04 am**	5:04 am
☽ ⚹ ♇	**9:12 am**	6:12 am
☽ △ ♄	**3:27 pm**	12:27 pm
☽ ⚺ ♀	**3:43 pm**	12:43 pm
☿ □ ♂	**9:12 pm**	6:12 pm
☉ △ ♃		9:31 pm

29 SATURDAY
☉ △ ♃	**12:31 am**	
☽ ☌ ♅	**6:18 am**	3:18 am
☽ ☌ ♀	**8:36 am**	5:36 am
☽ ⚻ ⚴	**2:21 pm**	11:21 am
☽ ⚹ ⚳	**4:34 pm**	1:34 pm
☽ ⚻ ♃	**8:05 pm**	5:05 pm
☽ ⚺ ☉	**9:49 pm**	6:49 pm
☿ □ ⚷		10:11 pm

30 SUNDAY
☿ □ ⚷	**1:11 am**	
☽ ⚺ ♆	**4:51 am**	1:51 am
☽ ⚹ ♂	**12:06 pm**	9:06 am
☽ ⚹ ⚷	**2:47 pm**	11:47 am
☽ ⚺ ☿	**5:25 pm**	2:25 pm
☽ △ ⚵	**5:28 pm**	2:28 pm
☿ ⚻ ⚵	**5:42 pm**	2:42 pm
☽ □ ♇	**7:12 pm**	4:12 pm
☽ □ ♄		10:59 pm

31 MONDAY
☽ □ ♄	**1:59 am**	
☽ ☌ ♀	**3:37 am**	12:37 am
☿ △ ♇	**4:13 am**	1:13 am
♀ ⚻ ⚴	**10:44 am**	7:44 am
☽ ⚺ ♅	**5:14 pm**	2:14 pm
☽ ☍ ⚴		9:05 pm
☽ ⚺ ♀		10:53 pm

Eastern Standard Time in bold type
Pacific Standard Time in medium type

MARCH 2003

☽ Last Aspect day	EST / hr:mn / PST		asp	☽ Ingress sign day	EST / hr:mn / PST	
1	**9:30 pm**	6:30 pm	☌ ♅	♓ 1	**10:26 pm**	7:26 pm
4	**8:04 am**	5:04 am	□ ♀	♈ 4	**8:30 am**	5:30 am
6	**8:10 pm**	5:10 pm	⚹ ♅	♉ 6	**8:36 pm**	5:36 pm
9	**9:29 am**	6:29 am	□ ♅	♊ 9	**9:38 am**	6:38 am
11	**6:24 am**	3:24 am	☌ ♄	♋ 11	**9:12 pm**	6:12 pm
13	**4:13 pm**	1:13 pm	△ ☉	♌ 14	**5:06 am**	2:06 am
15	**8:24 pm**	5:24 pm	⚹ ♄	♍ 16	**8:52 am**	5:52 am
18	**5:35 am**	2:35 am	☍ ☉	♎ 18	**9:43 am**	6:43 am
19	**10:02 pm**	7:02 am	△ ♄	♏ 20	**9:38 am**	6:38 am
21	**11:30 pm**	8:30 pm	□ ♀	♐ 22	**10:33 am**	7:33 am
24	**6:58 am**	3:58 am	⚹ ♀	♑ 24	**1:48 pm**	10:48 am
25	**1:16 pm**	10:16 am	☌ ♂	♒ 26	**7:51 pm**	4:51 pm
28	**3:27 pm**	12:27 pm	△ ♄	♓ 29	**4:26 am**	1:26 am
30		10:59 pm	□ ♄	♈ 31	**3:04 pm**	12:04 pm
31	**1:59 am**		□ ♄	♈ 31	**3:04 pm**	12:04 pm

☽ Phases & Eclipses phase	day	EST / hr:mn / PST	
New Moon	2	**9:35 pm**	6:35 pm
2nd Quarter	10		11:15 pm
2nd Quarter	11	**2:15 am**	
Full Moon	18	**5:35 am**	2:35 am
4th Quarter	24	**8:51 pm**	5:51 pm

Planet Ingress	day	EST / hr:mn / PST	
♀ ♒	2	**7:40 am**	4:40 am
♂ ♑	4	**4:17 pm**	1:17 pm
☿ ♓	4	**9:04 pm**	6:04 pm
♅ ♓	10	**3:53 pm**	12:53 pm
⚳ ♉	13	**6:26 am**	3:26 am
☉ ♈	20	**8:00 pm**	5:00 am
☿ ♈	21	**7:16 am**	4:16 am
♀ ♓	27	**1:14 pm**	10:14 am

Planetary Motion	day	EST / hr:mn / PST	
⚵ ℞	8	**7:01 am**	4:01 am
♇ ℞	22		9:13 pm
♇ ℞	23	**12:13 am**	

DATE		SID.TIME	SUN	MOON	NODE	MERCURY	VENUS	MARS	JUPITER	SATURN	URANUS	NEPTUNE	PLUTO	CERES	PALLAS	JUNO	VESTA	CHIRON
1	Sa	10:33:33	9 ♓ 58 50	15 ♒ 26	3 ♊ ℞ 38	23 ♒ 19	28 ♑ 12	27 ♐ 31	9 ♌ ℞ 51	22 ♊ 11	29 ♒ 27	11 ♒ 44	19 ♐ 49	25 ♈ 25	13 ♓ 56	20 ♏ 19	11 ♎ ℞ 24	16 ♑ 05
2	Su	10:37:29	10 59 05	28 12	3 25	24 55	29 23	28 09	9 45	22 11	29 30	11 46	19 50	25 47	14 17	20 22	11 16	16 10
3	M	10:41:26	11 59 19	10 ♓ 45	3 11	26 33	0 ♒ 33	28 48	9 40	22 12	29 34	11 48	19 50	26 08	14 37	20 24	11 07	16 14
4	T	10:45:22	12 59 30	23 08	2 57	28 12	1 44	29 26	9 34	22 13	29 37	11 50	19 51	26 30	14 57	20 25	10 58	16 18
5	W	10:49:19	13 59 40	5 ♈ 19	2 45	29 51	2 55	0 ♑ 04	9 28	22 15	29 40	11 52	19 52	26 52	15 17	20 27	10 48	16 22
6	Th	10:53:16	14 59 48	17 20	2 35	1 ♓ 32	4 06	0 43	9 23	22 16	29 44	11 54	19 52	27 14	15 38	20 28	10 38	16 26
7	F	10:57:12	15 59 54	29 13	2 27	3 14	5 17	1 21	9 18	22 17	29 47	11 56	19 53	27 36	15 58	20 28	10 27	16 29
8	Sa	11:01:09	16 59 57	11 ♉ 01	2 23	4 57	6 27	1 59	9 13	22 19	29 50	11 58	19 53	27 58	16 18	20 ℞ 29	10 16	16 33
9	Su	11:05:05	17 59 59	22 48	2 D 21	6 41	7 39	2 37	9 08	22 20	29 54	12 00	19 54	28 20	16 39	20 29	10 05	16 37
10	M	11:09:02	18 59 59	4 ♊ 38	2 20	8 26	8 50	3 15	9 03	22 22	29 57	12 02	19 54	28 42	16 59	20 28	9 53	16 41
11	T	11:12:58	19 59 56	16 38	2 ℞ 21	10 13	10 01	3 53	8 59	22 24	0 ♓ 00	12 04	19 55	29 05	17 19	20 28	9 41	16 44
12	W	11:16:55	20 59 52	28 52	2 20	12 00	11 12	4 31	8 54	22 26	0 04	12 06	19 55	29 27	17 40	20 27	9 28	16 48
13	Th	11:20:51	21 59 45	11 ♋ 26	2 19	13 49	12 23	5 10	8 50	22 28	0 07	12 07	19 55	29 49	18 00	20 25	9 16	16 51
14	F	11:24:48	22 59 36	24 24	2 15	15 39	13 34	5 48	8 46	22 30	0 10	12 09	19 56	0 ♉ 12	18 20	20 24	9 03	16 55
15	Sa	11:28:45	23 59 24	7 ♌ 50	2 08	17 30	14 46	6 26	8 42	22 32	0 14	12 11	19 56	0 34	18 41	20 22	8 49	16 58
16	Su	11:32:41	24 59 11	21 45	2 00	19 22	15 57	7 04	8 38	22 34	0 17	12 13	19 56	0 57	19 01	20 19	8 36	17 01
17	M	11:36:38	25 58 55	6 ♍ 07	1 50	21 15	17 09	7 42	8 35	22 37	0 20	12 15	19 56	1 20	19 21	20 16	8 22	17 05
18	T	11:40:34	26 58 37	20 50	1 39	23 10	18 20	8 19	8 32	22 39	0 23	12 16	19 57	1 42	19 42	20 13	8 07	17 08
19	W	11:44:31	27 58 17	5 ♎ 48	1 30	25 05	19 32	8 57	8 28	22 42	0 26	12 18	19 57	2 05	20 02	20 10	7 53	17 11
20	Th	11:48:27	28 57 55	20 51	1 22	27 02	20 43	9 35	8 25	22 45	0 29	12 20	19 57	2 28	20 22	20 06	7 38	17 14
21	F	11:52:24	29 57 32	5 ♏ 50	1 17	28 59	21 55	10 13	8 23	22 48	0 33	12 22	19 57	2 51	20 42	20 02	7 24	17 17
22	Sa	11:56:20	0 ♈ 57 06	20 35	1 D 15	0 ♈ 58	23 06	10 51	8 20	22 51	0 36	12 23	19 57	3 14	21 03	19 58	7 09	17 19
23	Su	12:00:17	1 56 39	5 ♐ 03	1 15	2 58	24 18	11 29	8 18	22 54	0 39	12 25	19 ℞ 57	3 37	21 23	19 53	6 54	17 22
24	M	12:04:13	2 56 10	19 11	1 15	4 58	25 30	12 06	8 15	22 57	0 42	12 27	19 57	4 00	21 43	19 48	6 38	17 25
25	T	12:08:10	3 55 40	2 ♑ 57	1 ℞ 16	6 59	26 42	12 44	8 13	23 00	0 45	12 28	19 57	4 23	22 04	19 42	6 23	17 27
26	W	12:12:07	4 55 07	16 24	1 15	9 01	27 54	13 22	8 12	23 04	0 48	12 30	19 57	4 46	22 24	19 37	6 08	17 30
27	Th	12:16:03	5 54 33	29 33	1 12	11 03	29 05	14 00	8 10	23 07	0 51	12 31	19 57	5 10	22 44	19 30	5 52	17 32
28	F	12:20:00	6 53 57	12 ♒ 26	1 08	13 05	0 ♓ 17	14 37	8 09	23 11	0 54	12 33	19 57	5 33	23 05	19 24	5 37	17 35
29	Sa	12:23:56	7 53 19	25 05	1 00	15 07	1 29	15 15	8 07	23 14	0 57	12 34	19 57	5 56	23 25	19 17	5 21	17 37
30	Su	12:27:53	8 52 40	7 ♓ 33	0 51	17 09	2 41	15 52	8 06	23 18	1 00	12 36	19 56	6 20	23 45	19 10	5 06	17 39
31	M	12:31:49	9 51 58	19 50	0 42	19 10	3 53	16 30	8 05	23 22	1 03	12 37	19 56	6 43	24 05	19 03	4 51	17 42

EPHEMERIS CALCULATED FOR 12 MIDNIGHT GREENWICH MEAN TIME. ALL OTHER DATA AND FACING ASPECTARIAN PAGE IN **EASTERN STANDARD TIME (BOLD)** AND PACIFIC STANDARD TIME (REGULAR).

APRIL 2003

1 TUESDAY

☽ ☍ ⚶	**12:05 am**	
☽ ⚺ ♀	**1:53 am**	
☽ ⚺ ⚳	**5:35 am**	2:35 am
☽ △ ♃	**7:09 am**	4:09 am
☽ ☌ ☉	**2:19 pm**	11:19 am
☽ ⚹ ♆	**4:21 pm**	1:21 pm
♂ ☌ ⚷	**7:44 pm**	4:44 pm
☿ ⚹ ♄	**11:29 pm**	8:29 pm
☽ □ ⚷		11:37 pm
☽ □ ♂		11:58 pm

2 WEDNESDAY

☽ □ ⚷	**2:37 am**	
☽ □ ♂	**2:58 am**	
☽ ⚻ ⚵	**4:32 am**	1:32 am
☽ △ ♇	**6:57 am**	3:57 am
☽ ⚹ ♄	**2:16 pm**	11:16 am
☉ ⚹ ♆	**3:32 pm**	12:32 pm
☽ ☌ ☿	**5:05 pm**	2:05 pm
☽ ⚺ ♀	**5:22 pm**	2:22 pm
☿ ⚺ ♀	**7:07 pm**	4:07 pm

3 THURSDAY

♂ ⚹ ⚵	**3:44 am**	12:44 am
♃ □ ⚳	**4:57 am**	1:57 am
☽ ⚹ ♅	**5:47 am**	2:47 am
♀ ⚻ ♃	**6:24 am**	3:24 am
♀ ⚹ ⚳	**7:07 am**	4:07 am
☽ ⚻ ⚶	**11:16 am**	8:16 am
☽ □ ♃	**7:43 pm**	4:43 pm
☽ ☌ ⚳	**8:14 pm**	5:14 pm
☽ ⚹ ♀	**9:14 pm**	6:14 pm

4 FRIDAY

☽ □ ♆	**5:12 am**	2:12 am
☽ ⚺ ☉	**8:34 am**	5:34 am
☽ △ ⚷	**3:39 pm**	12:39 pm
☽ ☍ ⚵	**4:42 pm**	1:42 pm
☽ △ ♂	**7:15 pm**	4:15 pm
☽ ⚻ ♇	**7:51 pm**	4:51 pm

5 SATURDAY

☽ ⚺ ♄	**3:38 am**	12:38 am
♂ ⚺ ♇	**6:29 am**	3:29 am
☽ ⚹ ♀	**8:10 am**	5:10 am
☽ ⚺ ☿	**5:38 pm**	2:38 pm
☽ □ ♅	**7:05 pm**	4:05 pm
☽ △ ⚶	**11:05 pm**	8:05 pm

6 SUNDAY

☿ ⚹ ♅	**3:27 am**	12:27 am
☽ ⚹ ♃	**8:46 am**	5:46 am
☽ ⚺ ⚳	**11:21 am**	8:21 am
☽ □ ♀	**5:07 pm**	2:07 pm
☽ △ ♆	**6:16 pm**	3:16 pm
☿ ⚻ ⚶		11:25 pm
☽ ⚹ ☉		11:57 pm

7 MONDAY

☿ ⚻ ⚶	**2:25 am**	
☽ ⚹ ☉	**2:57 am**	
☽ ⚻ ⚷	**4:35 am**	1:35 am
♀ ⚺ ♆	**4:38 am**	1:38 am
☽ ⚻ ⚵	**4:42 am**	1:42 am
☽ ☍ ♇	**8:32 am**	5:32 am
☽ ⚻ ♂	**11:17 am**	8:17 am
⚷ ⚹ ⚵	**11:36 am**	8:36 am
☽ ☌ ♄	**4:34 pm**	1:34 pm
☉ ⚻ ⚵	**9:29 pm**	6:29 pm
☽ □ ♀	**10:20 pm**	7:20 pm
☉ □ ⚷	**11:26 pm**	8:26 pm

8 TUESDAY

☽ △ ♅	**7:25 am**	4:25 am
☽ □ ⚶	**9:55 am**	6:55 am
☽ ⚹ ☿	**3:36 pm**	12:36 pm
☽ ⚺ ♃	**8:26 pm**	5:26 pm
☽ ⚹ ⚳		9:49 pm

9 WEDNESDAY

☽ ⚹ ⚳	**12:49 am**	
☽ ⚻ ♆	**5:33 am**	2:33 am
☽ △ ♀	**10:40 am**	7:40 am
☽ △ ⚵	**2:37 pm**	11:37 am
☽ ☍ ⚷	**3:23 pm**	12:23 pm
☽ □ ☉	**6:40 pm**	3:40 pm
☽ ⚻ ♇	**6:58 pm**	3:58 pm
☉ △ ♇	**10:32 pm**	7:32 pm
☽ ☍ ♂		9:34 pm
☽ ⚺ ♄		11:57 pm

10 THURSDAY

☽ ☍ ♂	**12:34 am**	
☽ ⚺ ♄	**2:57 am**	
☿ □ ♃	**6:08 am**	3:08 am
☽ △ ♀	**9:33 am**	6:33 am
☽ ⚻ ♅	**4:44 pm**	1:44 pm
☽ ⚹ ⚶	**5:53 pm**	2:53 pm
♀ △ ⚵	**11:08 pm**	8:08 pm

11 FRIDAY

☽ ☌ ♃	**4:45 am**	1:45 am
☽ □ ☿	**7:31 am**	4:31 am
☽ □ ⚳	**10:28 am**	7:28 am
♀ ⚹ ⚷	**12:50 pm**	9:50 am
☽ ☍ ♆	**1:14 pm**	10:14 am
☽ □ ⚵	**8:51 pm**	5:51 pm
☽ ⚻ ⚷	**10:21 pm**	7:21 pm
☽ ⚻ ♀	**11:16 pm**	8:16 pm
☽ △ ♇		10:33 pm

12 SATURDAY

☽ △ ♇	**1:33 am**	
☽ △ ☉	**5:31 am**	2:31 am
☽ ⚻ ♂	**9:18 am**	6:18 am
☽ ⚹ ♄	**9:18 am**	6:18 am
♂ ⚻ ♄	**9:30 am**	6:30 am
☽ ⚻ ♀	**4:24 pm**	1:24 pm
☽ ☍ ♅	**9:53 pm**	6:53 pm
☽ ⚺ ⚶	**10:00 pm**	7:00 pm
☿ ☌ ⚳	**11:58 pm**	8:58 pm
♀ □ ♇		10:03 pm

13 SUNDAY

♀ □ ♇	**1:03 am**	
♅ ⚻ ⚶	**4:36 am**	1:36 am
☽ ⚺ ♃	**8:58 am**	5:58 am
☽ △ ⚳	**3:39 pm**	12:39 pm
☽ △ ☿	**4:40 pm**	1:40 pm
☽ ⚻ ♆	**4:49 pm**	1:49 pm
☿ □ ♆	**6:27 pm**	3:27 pm
☽ ⚹ ⚵	**11:11 pm**	8:11 pm
☽ △ ⚷		10:18 pm

14 MONDAY

☽ △ ⚷	**1:18 am**	
☽ □ ♇	**4:11 am**	1:11 am
☽ ☍ ♀	**6:38 am**	3:38 am
☽ ⚻ ☉	**11:31 am**	8:31 am
☽ □ ♄	**11:46 am**	8:46 am
☽ △ ♂	**1:38 pm**	10:38 am
☉ ⚹ ♄	**3:38 pm**	12:38 pm
☽ ☍ ☿	**7:16 pm**	4:16 pm
☽ ☌ ⚶	**10:45 pm**	7:45 pm
☽ ⚻ ♅	**11:27 pm**	8:27 pm

15 TUESDAY

☽ ⚹ ♃	**9:55 am**	6:55 am
♆ □ ⚳	**11:09 am**	8:09 am
☽ △ ♆	**5:21 pm**	2:21 pm
☽ ⚻ ⚳	**5:30 pm**	2:30 pm
☽ ⚻ ☿	**9:01 pm**	6:01 pm
☽ ⚺ ⚵	**10:48 pm**	7:48 pm
☽ □ ⚷		10:29 pm

16 WEDNESDAY

☽ □ ⚷	**1:29 am**	
☽ ⚹ ♇	**4:11 am**	1:11 am
☽ ⚻ ♀	**10:43 am**	7:43 am
☽ △ ♄	**11:50 am**	8:50 am
☽ ☍ ☉	**2:36 pm**	11:36 am
☽ □ ♂	**3:22 pm**	12:22 pm
☽ ⚻ ☿	**7:56 pm**	4:56 pm
☿ ☍ ⚵	**8:25 pm**	5:25 pm
☽ ⚺ ⚶	**9:41 pm**	6:41 pm
☽ △ ♅	**11:05 pm**	8:05 pm
♀ □ ♄		10:52 pm

17 THURSDAY

♀ □ ♄	**1:52 am**	
☽ □ ♃	**9:25 am**	6:25 am
☽ □ ♆	**4:43 pm**	1:43 pm
☽ ☍ ⚳	**6:07 pm**	3:07 pm
☉ □ ♂	**8:55 pm**	5:55 pm
☽ ☌ ⚵	**9:30 pm**	6:30 pm
☽ ☍ ☿	**11:24 pm**	8:24 pm
☽ ⚹ ⚷		9:52 pm

18 FRIDAY

☽ ⚹ ⚷	**12:52 am**	
☽ ⚺ ♇	**3:30 am**	12:30 am
☽ ⚻ ♄	**11:33 am**	8:33 am
☽ △ ♀	**2:17 pm**	11:17 am
☽ ⚹ ♂	**4:52 pm**	1:52 pm
☽ ⚻ ☉	**5:24 pm**	2:24 pm
☽ △ ☿	**8:36 pm**	5:36 pm
☽ ⚹ ⚶	**8:44 pm**	5:44 pm
☽ □ ♅	**10:52 pm**	7:52 pm
♀ ☍ ⚶		9:36 pm

19 SATURDAY

♀ ☍ ⚶	**12:36 am**	
☿ △ ⚷	**5:10 am**	2:10 am
☽ △ ♃	**9:31 am**	6:31 am
☽ ⚹ ♆	**4:59 pm**	1:59 pm
☽ ⚻ ⚳	**7:45 pm**	4:45 pm
☽ ⚺ ⚵	**9:13 pm**	6:13 pm
☽ ⚺ ⚷		10:26 pm
☽ ⚻ ☿		11:22 pm

20 SUNDAY

☽ ⚺ ⚷	**1:26 am**	
☽ ⚻ ☿	**2:22 am**	
☽ ☌ ♇	**4:06 am**	1:06 am
☽ ☍ ♄	**12:55 pm**	9:55 am
☉ ⚻ ⚶	**1:15 pm**	10:15 am
☽ □ ♀	**8:02 pm**	5:02 pm
☽ ⚺ ♂	**8:23 pm**	5:23 pm
☽ □ ⚶	**9:40 pm**	6:40 pm
☽ △ ☉	**10:24 pm**	7:24 pm
☽ □ ☿	**11:18 pm**	8:18 pm
☽ ⚹ ♅		9:38 pm

21 MONDAY

☽ ⚹ ♅	**12:38 am**	
♀ ⚹ ♂	**3:50 am**	12:50 am
⚳ ☍ ⚵	**7:07 am**	4:07 am
☽ ⚻ ♃	**11:58 am**	8:58 am
♀ ☍ ⚶	**1:08 pm**	10:08 am
☉ ⚺ ☿	**5:30 pm**	2:30 pm
☽ ⚺ ♆	**7:46 pm**	4:46 pm
♂ △ ⚶	**8:33 pm**	5:33 pm
☽ ⚹ ⚵	**11:27 pm**	8:27 pm
☽ △ ⚳		9:13 pm
☿ ⚻ ♇		11:28 pm

22 TUESDAY

☽ △ ⚳	**12:13 am**	
☿ ⚻ ♇	**2:28 am**	
☽ ☌ ⚷	**4:44 am**	1:44 am
☽ ⚺ ♇	**7:31 am**	4:31 am
☽ △ ☿	**7:40 am**	4:40 am
☉ ⚹ ♅	**7:57 am**	4:57 am
☽ ⚻ ♄	**5:20 pm**	2:20 pm
♀ ☌ ☿	**11:11 pm**	8:11 pm
☽ △ ⚶		10:43 pm

23 WEDNESDAY

☽ △ ⚶	**1:43 am**	
♀ ⚺ ♅	**3:21 am**	12:21 am
☽ ☌ ♂	**3:27 am**	12:27 am
☽ ⚹ ☿	**5:24 am**	2:24 am
☽ ⚺ ♅	**5:38 am**	2:38 am
☽ ⚹ ♀	**5:52 am**	2:52 am
☽ □ ☉	**7:18 am**	4:18 am
♅ ⚺ ☿	**3:52 pm**	12:52 pm
☽ ☍ ♃	**5:50 pm**	2:50 pm
☽ ☌ ♆		10:58 pm

24 THURSDAY

☽ ☌ ♆	**1:58 am**	
☽ □ ⚵	**4:57 am**	1:57 am
☽ □ ⚳	**8:26 am**	5:26 am
☽ ⚺ ⚷	**11:30 am**	8:30 am
☽ ⚹ ♇	**2:22 pm**	11:22 am
☽ □ ☿	**3:48 pm**	12:48 pm
☽ △ ♄		10:19 pm

25 FRIDAY

☽ △ ♄	**1:19 am**	
♂ ⚺ ♅	**6:21 am**	3:21 am
☽ ⚻ ⚶	**9:10 am**	6:10 am
☽ ☌ ♅	**2:05 pm**	11:05 am
☽ ⚺ ♂	**2:27 pm**	11:27 am
☽ ⚺ ☿	**3:12 pm**	12:12 pm
☽ ⚺ ♀	**8:14 pm**	5:14 pm
☽ ⚹ ☉	**8:30 pm**	5:30 pm

26 SATURDAY

☽ ⚻ ♃	**3:06 am**	12:06 am
☉ ⚺ ♀	**8:58 am**	5:58 am
☽ ⚺ ♆	**11:26 am**	8:26 am
☽ △ ⚵	**1:29 pm**	10:29 am
☽ ⚹ ⚳	**8:09 pm**	5:09 pm
☽ ⚹ ⚷	**9:23 pm**	6:23 pm
♂ ⚹ ☿		9:01 pm
☽ □ ♇		9:18 pm
☽ ⚹ ☿		11:04 pm

27 SUNDAY

♂ ⚹ ☿	**12:01 am**	
☽ □ ♇	**12:18 am**	
☽ ⚹ ☿	**2:04 am**	
☽ □ ♄	**12:18 pm**	9:18 am
☽ ☍ ⚶	**7:25 pm**	4:25 pm
☽ ⚺ ♅		10:16 pm

28 MONDAY

☽ ⚺ ♅	**1:16 am**	
☽ ☌ ☿	**3:54 am**	12:54 am
☽ ⚹ ♂	**4:34 am**	1:34 am
⚷ △ ⚳	**8:30 am**	5:30 am
☽ ⚺ ☉	**1:01 pm**	10:01 am
☽ ☌ ♀	**2:09 pm**	11:09 am
☽ △ ♃	**2:56 pm**	11:56 am
♀ △ ♃	**10:19 pm**	7:19 pm
☽ ⚹ ♆	**11:13 pm**	8:13 pm
☽ ⚻ ⚵		9:11 pm

29 TUESDAY

☽ ⚻ ⚵	**12:11 am**	
☽ □ ⚷	**9:23 am**	6:23 am
☽ ⚺ ⚳	**10:16 am**	7:16 am
☽ △ ♇	**12:19 pm**	9:19 am
☽ ⚺ ☿	**1:19 pm**	10:19 am
☉ □ ♃	**2:32 pm**	11:32 am
☽ ⚹ ♄		10:12 pm

30 WEDNESDAY

☽ ⚹ ♄	**1:12 am**	
☽ ⚻ ⚶	**7:25 am**	4:25 am
☽ ⚹ ♅	**2:01 pm**	11:01 am
☽ ⚺ ☿	**6:16 pm**	3:16 pm
☽ □ ♂	**8:25 pm**	5:25 pm
♆ □ ⚵		9:21 pm
☿ ⚻ ♇		11:38 pm

Eastern Standard Time in bold type
Pacific Standard Time in medium type

APRIL 2003

☽ Last Aspect day	EST / hr:mn / PST		asp	☽ Ingress sign	day	EST / hr:mn / PST	
2	**5:05 pm**	2:05 pm	☌ ☿	♉	3	**3:20 am**	12:20 am
4	**7:15 pm**	4:15 pm	△ ♂	♊	5	**4:24 pm**	1:24 pm
7	**4:34 pm**	1:34 pm	☌ ♄	♋	8	**4:36 am**	1:36 am
9		9:34 pm	☍ ♂	♌	10	**1:54 pm**	10:54 am
10	**12:34 am**		☍ ♂	♌	10	**1:54 pm**	10:54 am
12	**9:18 am**	6:18 am	⚹ ♄	♍	12	**7:07 pm**	4:07 pm
14	**1:38 pm**	10:38 am	△ ♂	♎	14	**8:42 pm**	5:42 pm
16	**3:22 pm**	12:22 pm	□ ♂	♏	16	**2:36 pm**	11:36 am
18	**4:52 pm**	1:52 pm	⚹ ♂	♐	18	**7:51 pm**	4:51 pm
20	**8:02 pm**	5:02 pm	□ ♀	♑	20	**9:20 pm**	6:20 pm
22	**7:40 am**	4:40 am	△ ☿	♒	22		10:58 pm
22	**7:40 am**	4:40 am	△ ☿	♒	23	**1:58 am**	
24		10:19 pm	△ ♄	♓	25	**10:02 am**	7:02 am
25	**1:19 am**		△ ♄	♓	25	**10:02 am**	7:02 am
27	**12:18 pm**	9:18 am	□ ♄	♈	27	**8:54 pm**	5:54 pm
29		10:12 pm	⚹ ♄	♉	30	**9:26 am**	6:26 am
30	**1:12 am**		⚹ ♄	♉	30	**9:26 am**	6:26 am

☽ Phases & Eclipses phase	day	EST / hr:mn / PST	
New Moon	1	**2:19 pm**	11:19 am
2nd Quarter	9	**6:40 pm**	3:40 pm
Full Moon	16	**2:36 pm**	11:36 am
4th Quarter	23	**7:18 am**	4:18 am

Planet Ingress		day	EST / hr:mn / PST	
☿	♉	5	**9:37 am**	6:37 am
♀	♈	17	**11:26 am**	8:26 am
☉	♉	20	**7:03 am**	4:03 am
♀	♈	21	**11:18 am**	8:18 am
♂	♒	21	**6:48 pm**	3:48 pm
⚶	♍	22	**3:23 am**	12:23 am

Planetary Motion		day	EST / hr:mn / PST	
♃	D	3	**10:04 pm**	7:04 pm
⚷	℞	25	**12:12 pm**	9:12 am
☿	℞	26	**6:59 am**	3:59 am

DATE		SID.TIME	SUN	MOON	NODE	MERCURY	VENUS	MARS	JUPITER	SATURN	URANUS	NEPTUNE	PLUTO	CERES	PALLAS	JUNO	VESTA	CHIRON
1	T	12:35:46	10 ♈ 51 15	1 ♈ 59	0 ♊ ℞ 32	21 ♈ 10	5 ♓ 05	17 ♑ 07	8 ♌ ℞ 05	23 ♊ 26	1 ♓ 06	12 ♒ 39	19 ♐ ℞ 56	7 ♉ 07	24 ♓ 26	18 ♏ ℞ 55	4 ♎ ℞ 35	17 ♑ 44
2	W	12:39:42	11 50 29	13 59	0 23	23 08	6 17	17 45	8 04	23 30	1 08	12 40	19 55	7 30	24 46	18 47	4 20	17 46
3	Th	12:43:39	12 48 41	25 53	0 16	25 05	7 29	18 22	8 04	23 34	1 11	12 41	19 55	7 54	25 06	18 39	4 05	17 47
4	F	12:47:36	13 48 51	7 ♉ 42	0 11	27 00	8 42	18 59	8 D 04	23 38	1 14	12 43	19 55	8 18	25 26	18 30	3 50	17 49
5	Sa	12:51:32	14 48 00	19 29	0 D 08	28 53	9 54	19 36	8 04	23 42	1 17	12 44	19 54	8 41	25 46	18 21	3 35	17 51
6	Su	12:55:29	15 47 06	1 ♊ 17	0 08	0 ♉ 42	11 06	20 14	8 04	23 47	1 19	12 45	19 54	9 05	26 06	18 12	3 20	17 53
7	M	12:59:25	16 46 09	13 08	0 09	2 29	12 18	20 51	8 04	23 51	1 22	12 47	19 53	9 29	26 27	18 02	3 05	17 54
8	T	13:03:22	17 45 11	25 08	0 10	4 12	13 30	21 28	8 05	23 56	1 25	12 48	19 53	9 52	26 47	17 52	2 51	17 56
9	W	13:07:18	18 44 10	7 ♋ 22	0 ℞ 11	5 50	14 42	22 05	8 06	24 00	1 27	12 49	19 52	10 16	27 07	17 42	2 37	17 57
10	Th	13:11:15	19 43 07	19 53	0 12	7 25	15 55	22 42	8 07	24 05	1 30	12 50	19 52	10 40	27 27	17 32	2 23	17 59
11	F	13:15:11	20 42 02	2 ♌ 47	0 11	8 55	17 07	23 19	8 08	24 10	1 32	12 51	19 51	11 04	27 47	17 21	2 10	18 00
12	Sa	13:19:08	21 40 55	16 07	0 09	10 21	18 19	23 55	8 10	24 15	1 35	12 52	19 51	11 28	28 07	17 10	1 56	18 01
13	Su	13:23:05	22 39 45	29 56	0 05	11 41	19 32	24 32	8 11	24 20	1 37	12 53	19 50	11 52	28 27	16 59	1 44	18 02
14	M	13:27:01	23 38 32	14 ♍ 14	0 00	12 56	20 44	25 09	8 13	24 25	1 40	12 54	19 49	12 16	28 47	16 48	1 31	18 03
15	T	13:30:58	24 37 18	28 57	29 ♉ 55	14 06	21 56	25 46	8 15	24 30	1 42	12 55	19 49	12 40	29 07	16 37	1 19	18 04
16	W	13:34:54	25 36 01	13 ♎ 59	29 50	15 10	23 09	26 22	8 17	24 35	1 45	12 56	19 48	13 04	29 27	16 25	1 07	18 05
17	Th	13:38:51	26 34 43	29 12	29 46	16 09	24 21	26 59	8 19	24 40	1 47	12 57	19 47	13 28	29 46	16 13	0 55	18 06
18	F	13:42:47	27 33 22	14 ♏ 25	29 43	17 02	25 33	27 35	8 22	24 46	1 49	12 58	19 46	13 52	0 ♈ 06	16 01	0 44	18 06
19	Sa	13:46:44	28 32 00	29 28	29 D 43	17 49	26 46	28 12	8 24	24 51	1 52	12 59	19 46	14 16	0 26	15 48	0 33	18 07
20	Su	13:50:40	29 30 36	14 ♐ 14	29 43	18 30	27 58	28 48	8 27	24 56	1 54	13 00	19 45	14 41	0 46	15 36	0 23	18 07
21	M	13:54:37	0 ♉ 29 10	28 37	29 45	19 05	29 11	29 24	8 30	25 02	1 56	13 01	19 44	15 05	1 06	15 23	0 13	18 08
22	T	13:58:34	1 27 43	12 ♑ 35	29 46	19 35	0 ♈ 23	0 ♒ 00	8 33	25 08	1 58	13 02	19 43	15 29	1 25	15 11	0 03	18 08
23	W	14:02:30	2 26 14	26 09	29 ℞ 47	19 58	1 36	0 36	8 37	25 13	2 00	13 03	19 42	15 53	1 45	14 58	29 ♍ 54	18 09
24	Th	14:06:27	3 24 43	9 ♒ 18	29 47	20 15	2 48	1 12	8 40	25 19	2 02	13 03	19 41	16 17	2 05	14 45	29 45	18 09
25	F	14:10:23	4 23 11	22 07	29 46	20 27	4 01	1 48	8 44	25 25	2 04	13 04	19 40	16 42	2 24	14 31	29 37	18 ℞ 09
26	Sa	14:14:20	5 21 37	4 ♓ 39	29 44	20 ℞ 33	5 13	2 24	8 48	25 31	2 06	13 05	19 39	17 06	2 44	14 18	29 29	18 09
27	Su	14:18:16	6 20 02	16 56	29 40	20 33	6 26	3 00	8 52	25 37	2 08	13 05	19 38	17 30	3 03	14 05	29 22	18 09
28	M	14:22:13	7 18 25	29 03	29 37	20 27	7 39	3 36	8 56	25 43	2 10	13 06	19 37	17 55	3 23	13 51	29 15	18 09
29	T	14:26:09	8 16 46	11 ♈ 01	29 33	20 16	8 51	4 11	9 01	25 49	2 12	13 06	19 36	18 19	3 42	13 38	29 09	18 08
30	W	14:30:06	9 15 05	22 53	29 30	20 01	10 04	4 47	9 05	25 55	2 14	13 07	19 35	18 44	4 02	13 24	29 03	18 08

EPHEMERIS CALCULATED FOR 12 MIDNIGHT GREENWICH MEAN TIME. ALL OTHER DATA AND FACING ASPECTARIAN PAGE IN **EASTERN STANDARD TIME (BOLD)** AND PACIFIC STANDARD TIME (REGULAR).

MAY 2003

1 THURSDAY
♆ □ ⚵ **12:21 am**
☿ ⚻ ♇ **2:38 am**
☽ □ ♃ **4:09 am** 1:09 am
☽ ☌ ☉ **7:15 am** 4:15 am
☽ ⚺ ♀ **9:54 am** 6:54 am
☿ ☌ ⚳ **11:18 am** 8:18 am
☽ ☍ ⚵ **11:55 am** 8:55 am
☽ □ ♆ **12:09 pm** 9:09 am
♇ ⚻ ⚳ **7:07 pm** 4:07 pm
☽ △ ⚷ **10:19 pm** 7:19 pm
☽ ☌ ☿ 9:27 pm
☽ ⚻ ♇ 10:12 pm
☽ ☌ ⚳ 10:25 pm
♀ ⚻ ⚵ 11:47 pm

2 FRIDAY
☽ ☌ ☿ **12:27 am**
☽ ⚻ ♇ **1:12 am**
☽ ☌ ⚳ **1:25 am**
♀ ⚻ ⚵ **2:47 am**
♀ ⚹ ♆ **7:57 am** 4:57 am
☽ ⚺ ♄ **2:46 pm** 11:46 am
☽ △ ⚶ **8:02 pm** 5:02 pm

3 SATURDAY
☽ □ ♅ **3:11 am** 12:11 am
☉ ☍ ⚵ **6:10 am** 3:10 am
☽ ⚹ ♀ **8:57 am** 5:57 am
☽ △ ♂ **12:34 pm** 9:34 am
☽ ⚹ ♃ **5:30 pm** 2:30 pm
☉ □ ♆ **7:18 pm** 4:18 pm
☽ ⚻ ⚵ **11:38 pm** 8:38 pm
☽ △ ♆ 10:02 pm
☽ ⚺ ☉ 10:33 pm

4 SUNDAY
☽ △ ♆ **1:02 am**
☽ ⚺ ☉ **1:33 am**
☿ △ ⚷ **3:31 am** 12:31 am
☽ ⚹ ♀ **5:39 am** 2:39 am
☽ ⚺ ☿ **10:39 am** 7:39 am
☽ ⚻ ⚷ **10:58 am** 7:58 am
☽ ☍ ♇ **1:46 pm** 10:46 am
☽ ⚺ ⚳ **4:14 pm** 1:14 pm

5 MONDAY
☽ ☌ ♄ **3:43 am** 12:43 am
☽ □ ⚶ **8:03 am** 5:03 am
☽ △ ♅ **3:26 pm** 12:26 pm
☿ ⚺ ♀ **4:31 pm** 1:31 pm
☽ □ ♀ **10:32 pm** 7:32 pm

6 TUESDAY
☽ ⚻ ♂ **3:25 am** 12:25 am
☽ ⚺ ♃ **5:40 am** 2:40 am
♀ □ ⚷ **9:39 am** 6:39 am
☽ △ ⚵ **10:04 am** 7:04 am
☽ ⚻ ♆ **12:32 pm** 9:32 am
☽ ⚹ ☉ **6:02 pm** 3:02 pm
☽ ⚹ ☿ **7:03 pm** 4:03 pm
☽ ☍ ⚷ **10:00 pm** 7:00 pm
☽ □ ♀ **11:21 pm** 8:21 pm
☽ ⚻ ♇ 9:40 pm
☉ ☌ ☿ 11:21 pm

7 WEDNESDAY
☽ ⚻ ♇ **12:40 am**
☉ ☌ ☿ **2:21 am**
☽ ⚹ ⚳ **5:06 am** 2:06 am
♀ △ ♇ **12:36 pm** 9:36 am
☽ ⚺ ♄ **2:37 pm** 11:37 am
☽ ⚹ ⚶ **6:05 pm** 3:05 pm
☽ ⚻ ♅ 10:23 pm

8 THURSDAY
☽ ⚻ ♅ **1:23 am**
☽ △ ♀ **9:27 am** 6:27 am
♂ ☍ ♃ **12:36 pm** 9:36 am
☽ ☌ ♃ **3:11 pm** 12:11 pm
☽ ☍ ♂ **3:17 pm** 12:17 pm
☽ □ ⚵ **5:57 pm** 2:57 pm
☉ △ ⚷ **8:12 pm** 5:12 pm
☽ ☍ ♆ **9:16 pm** 6:16 pm
☽ □ ☿ 9:51 pm

9 FRIDAY
☽ □ ☿ **12:51 am**
☽ ⚻ ⚷ **6:05 am** 3:05 am
☽ □ ☉ **6:53 am** 3:53 am
☽ △ ♇ **8:34 am** 5:34 am
☽ △ ♀ **1:03 pm** 10:03 am
☽ □ ⚳ **2:35 pm** 11:35 am
☽ ⚹ ♄ **10:13 pm** 7:13 pm
☽ ⚺ ⚶ 9:55 pm

10 SATURDAY
☽ ⚺ ⚶ **12:55 am**
☉ ⚻ ♇ **5:30 am** 2:30 am
☽ ☍ ♅ **7:55 am** 4:55 am
♂ □ ⚵ **11:55 am** 8:55 am
♀ ⚺ ⚳ **1:59 pm** 10:59 am
☽ ⚻ ♀ **4:38 pm** 1:38 pm
☽ ⚺ ♃ **9:07 pm** 6:07 pm
☽ ⚹ ⚵ **10:29 pm** 7:29 pm
☽ ⚻ ♂ **11:06 pm** 8:06 pm
☽ ⚻ ♆ 11:25 pm

11 SUNDAY
☽ ⚻ ♆ **2:25 am**
☽ △ ☿ **3:38 am** 12:38 am
☽ △ ⚷ **10:35 am** 7:35 am
☽ □ ♇ **12:53 pm** 9:53 am
☽ △ ☉ **3:13 pm** 12:13 pm
☽ △ ⚳ **8:08 pm** 5:08 pm
☽ ⚻ ♀ **9:58 pm** 6:58 pm
☽ □ ♄ 11:09 pm

12 MONDAY
☽ □ ♄ **2:09 am**
☽ ☌ ⚶ **4:16 am** 1:16 am
☽ ⚻ ♅ **10:55 am** 7:55 am
☿ □ ♆ **11:30 am** 8:30 am
☽ ☍ ♀ **8:08 pm** 5:08 pm
☽ ⚹ ♃ **11:38 pm** 8:38 pm
☽ ⚺ ⚵ **11:49 pm** 8:49 pm

13 TUESDAY
☽ △ ♂ **3:07 am** 12:07 am
☽ ⚻ ☿ **3:44 am** 12:44 am
☽ △ ♆ **4:16 am** 1:16 am
♃ □ ⚵ **7:48 am** 4:48 am
☽ □ ⚷ **11:56 am** 8:56 am
☿ □ ♂ **12:19 pm** 9:19 am
☽ ⚹ ♇ **2:07 pm** 11:07 am
☽ ⚻ ☉ **7:49 pm** 4:49 pm
☽ ⚻ ⚳ **10:28 pm** 7:28 pm

14 WEDNESDAY
☽ ☍ ♀ **3:08 am** 12:08 am
☽ △ ♄ **3:13 am** 12:13 am
♀ ⚹ ♄ **4:15 am** 1:15 am
☽ ⚺ ⚶ **4:57 am** 1:57 am
♂ ☌ ♆ **9:35 am** 6:35 am
☽ △ ♅ **11:21 am** 8:21 am
☽ ⚻ ♀ **9:12 pm** 6:12 pm
☽ ☌ ⚵ **11:06 pm** 8:06 pm
☽ □ ♃ **11:57 pm** 8:57 pm
♀ ⚻ ⚶ 11:08 pm
☽ ☍ ☿ 11:19 pm

15 THURSDAY
♀ ⚻ ⚶ **2:08 am**
☽ ☍ ☿ **2:19 am**
☽ □ ♆ **4:07 am** 1:07 am
☽ □ ♂ **4:49 am** 1:49 am
☽ ⚹ ⚷ **11:32 am** 8:32 am
☽ ⚺ ♇ **1:41 pm** 10:41 am
☽ ☍ ☉ **10:36 pm** 7:36 pm
☽ ☍ ⚳ **11:20 pm** 8:20 pm

16 FRIDAY
☽ ⚻ ♄ **3:05 am** 12:05 am
☽ ⚹ ⚶ **4:33 am** 1:33 am
☽ ⚻ ♀ **6:47 am** 3:47 am
☽ □ ♅ **10:53 am** 7:53 am
☉ ☌ ⚳ **5:57 pm** 2:57 pm
☽ △ ♀ **9:44 pm** 6:44 pm
☽ ⚺ ⚵ **10:00 pm** 7:00 pm
☽ △ ♃ **11:54 pm** 8:54 pm
☽ ⚻ ☿ 10:00 pm

17 SATURDAY
☽ ⚻ ☿ **1:00 am**
☽ ⚹ ♆ **3:45 am** 12:45 am
♀ ⚻ ⚵ **5:43 am** 2:43 am
☽ ⚹ ♂ **6:18 am** 3:18 am
☽ ⚺ ⚷ **11:13 am** 8:13 am
☽ ☌ ♇ **1:26 pm** 10:26 am
☽ ⚻ ⚳ 9:48 pm
☽ ⚻ ☉ 11:02 pm

18 SUNDAY
☽ ⚻ ⚳ **12:48 am**
☽ ⚻ ☉ **2:02 am**
☽ ☍ ♄ **3:41 am** 12:41 am
☽ □ ⚶ **4:59 am** 1:59 am
♀ ⚹ ♅ **10:39 am** 7:39 am
☽ ⚹ ♅ **11:27 am** 8:27 am
☽ △ ♀ **11:31 am** 8:31 am
☽ ⚹ ⚵ **10:19 pm** 7:19 pm
☽ □ ♀ **11:48 pm** 8:48 pm
☽ ⚻ ♃ 10:25 pm
☽ △ ☿ 10:38 pm

19 MONDAY
☽ ⚻ ♃ **1:25 am**
☽ △ ☿ **1:38 am**
☽ ⚺ ♆ **5:03 am** 2:03 am
☉ ⚺ ♄ **6:25 am** 3:25 am
☽ ⚺ ♂ **9:45 am** 6:45 am
☽ ☌ ⚷ **12:49 pm** 9:49 am
☽ ⚺ ♇ **3:11 pm** 12:11 pm
☿ □ ♃ **6:47 pm** 3:47 pm
☉ △ ⚶ 10:39 pm

20 TUESDAY
☉ △ ⚶ **1:39 am**
☽ △ ⚳ **4:54 am** 1:54 am
☽ ⚻ ♄ **6:52 am** 3:52 am
☽ △ ⚶ **8:02 am** 5:02 am
☽ △ ☉ **8:29 am** 5:29 am
☽ ⚺ ♅ **2:46 pm** 11:46 am
☽ □ ♀ **7:50 pm** 4:50 pm
☽ □ ⚵ 10:35 pm

21 WEDNESDAY
☽ □ ⚵ **1:35 am**
☽ ⚹ ♀ **5:09 am** 2:09 am
☽ □ ☿ **5:55 am** 2:55 am
☽ ☍ ♃ **6:10 am** 3:10 am
☽ ☌ ♆ **9:33 am** 6:33 am
☽ ☌ ♂ **4:53 pm** 1:53 pm
☽ ⚺ ⚷ **5:47 pm** 2:47 pm
☽ ⚹ ♇ **8:21 pm** 5:21 pm

22 THURSDAY
☽ □ ⚳ **12:59 pm** 9:59 am
♂ ⚺ ⚷ **1:16 pm** 10:16 am
☽ △ ♄ **1:49 pm** 10:49 am
☽ ⚻ ⚶ **2:55 pm** 11:55 am
☽ □ ☉ **7:31 pm** 4:31 pm
☽ ☌ ♅ **9:51 pm** 6:51 pm

23 FRIDAY
♀ ☍ ⚵ **3:28 am** 12:28 am
☽ △ ⚵ **8:33 am** 5:33 am
☽ ⚹ ♀ **9:10 am** 6:10 am
☽ ⚺ ♀ **2:36 pm** 11:36 am
☽ ⚹ ☿ **2:50 pm** 11:50 am
☽ ⚻ ♃ **2:54 pm** 11:54 am
☽ ⚺ ♆ **5:53 pm** 2:53 pm
☿ □ ♃ **8:25 pm** 5:25 pm
♄ ⚺ ⚳ 10:29 pm
☽ ⚹ ⚷ 11:31 pm
☉ □ ♅ 11:37 pm

24 SATURDAY
♄ ⚺ ⚳ **1:29 am**
☽ ⚹ ⚷ **2:31 am**
☉ □ ♅ **2:37 am**
☽ ⚺ ♂ **4:20 am** 1:20 am
☽ □ ♇ **5:19 am** 2:19 am
♃ △ ♀ **12:45 pm** 9:45 am
☽ □ ♄ 9:33 pm
☽ ⚹ ⚳ 10:07 pm
☽ ☍ ⚶ 10:36 pm
♂ ⚹ ♇ 10:58 pm

25 SUNDAY
☽ □ ♄ **12:33 am**
☽ ⚹ ⚳ **1:07 am**
☽ ☍ ⚶ **1:36 am**
♂ ⚹ ♇ **1:58 am**
☽ ⚺ ♅ **8:28 am** 5:28 am
☽ ⚹ ☉ **11:02 am** 8:02 am
☽ ⚻ ⚵ **6:45 pm** 3:45 pm
⚳ △ ⚶ **8:31 pm** 5:31 pm
♀ □ ♃ 11:29 pm
☽ △ ♃ 11:58 pm

26 MONDAY
♀ □ ♃ **2:29 am**
☽ △ ♃ **2:58 am**
☽ ⚺ ♀ **3:01 am** 12:01 am
☽ ☌ ♀ **3:29 am** 12:29 am
☽ ⚺ ☿ **4:03 am** 1:03 am
☽ ⚹ ♆ **5:22 am** 2:22 am
♀ ⚺ ♀ **9:06 am** 6:06 am
☽ □ ⚷ **2:11 pm** 11:11 am
☽ △ ♇ **5:08 pm** 2:08 pm
☽ ⚹ ♂ **7:02 pm** 4:02 pm
☿ ☌ ♀ **7:04 pm** 4:04 pm
♀ □ ♆ 11:01 pm

27 TUESDAY
♀ □ ♆ **2:01 am**
☿ □ ♆ **11:16 am** 8:16 am
☽ ⚹ ♄ **1:41 pm** 10:41 am
☽ ⚻ ⚶ **2:45 pm** 11:45 am
☽ ⚺ ⚳ **3:49 pm** 12:49 pm
☽ ⚹ ♅ **9:12 pm** 6:12 pm

28 WEDNESDAY
☽ ⚺ ☉ **5:09 am** 2:09 am
☽ ☍ ⚵ **6:43 am** 3:43 am
☽ □ ♃ **4:39 pm** 1:39 pm
☽ ⚺ ♀ **6:00 pm** 3:00 pm
☽ □ ♆ **6:18 pm** 3:18 pm
☽ ☌ ☿ **7:57 pm** 4:57 pm
☉ ⚻ ⚵ **9:49 pm** 6:49 pm
☽ ☌ ♀ **10:57 pm** 7:57 pm
☽ △ ⚷ 12:00 pm

29 THURSDAY
☽ △ ⚷ **3:00 am**
♆ ⚹ ♀ **5:40 am** 2:40 am
☽ ⚻ ♇ **6:02 am** 3:02 am
☽ □ ♂ **10:53 am** 7:53 am

30 FRIDAY
☽ ⚺ ♄ **3:20 am** 12:20 am
☽ △ ⚶ **4:27 am** 1:27 am
☽ ☌ ⚳ **6:59 am** 3:59 am
☽ □ ♅ **10:10 am** 7:10 am
♀ △ ⚷ **12:58 pm** 9:58 am
☽ ⚻ ⚵ **6:45 pm** 3:45 pm
☽ ☌ ☉ **11:20 pm** 8:20 pm

31 SATURDAY
☽ ⚹ ♃ **6:05 am** 3:05 am
☽ △ ♆ **6:56 am** 3:56 am
☽ ⚹ ♀ **8:12 am** 5:12 am
☽ ⚺ ☿ **12:27 pm** 9:27 am
☽ ⚻ ⚷ **3:18 pm** 12:18 pm
♀ ⚻ ♇ **6:20 pm** 3:20 pm
☽ ⚺ ♀ **6:21 pm** 3:21 pm
☽ ☍ ♇ **6:21 pm** 3:21 pm
☽ △ ♂ 10:53 pm

Eastern Standard Time in bold type
Pacific Standard Time in medium type

MAY 2003

☽ Last Aspect			☽ Ingress		
day	EST / hr:mn / PST	asp	sign day	EST / hr:mn / PST	
1	9:27 pm	☌ ☿	♊ 2	**10:27 pm**	7:27 pm
2 **12:27 am**		☌ ☿	♊ 2	**10:27 pm**	7:27 pm
5 **3:43 am**	12:43 am	☌ ♄	♋ 5	**10:42 am**	7:42 am
6 **11:21 pm**	8:21 pm	□ ♀	♌ 7	**8:46 pm**	5:46 pm
9 **10:13 pm**	7:13 pm	⚹ ♄	♍ 10	**3:31 am**	12:31 am
11	11:09 pm	□ ♄	♎ 12	**6:42 am**	3:42 am
12 **2:09 am**		□ ♄	♎ 12	**6:42 am**	3:42 am
14 **3:13 am**	12:13 am	△ ♄	♏ 14	**7:14 am**	4:14 am
15 **10:36 pm**	7:36 pm	☍ ☉	♐ 26	**6:43 am**	3:43 am
18 **3:41 am**	12:41 am	☍ ♄	♑ 18	**7:03 am**	4:03 am
20 **8:29 am**	5:29 am	△ ☉	♒ 20	**10:01 am**	7:01 am
22 **1:49 pm**	10:49 am	△ ♄	♓ 22	**4:41 pm**	1:41 pm
24	9:33 pm	□ ♄	♈ 24		11:59 pm
25 **12:33 am**		□ ♄	♈ 25	**2:59 am**	
27 **1:41 pm**	10:41 am	⚹ ♄	♉ 27	**3:32 pm**	12:32 pm
29 **10:53 am**	7:53 am	□ ♂	♊ 30	**4:32 am**	1:32 am

☽ Phases & Eclipses			
phase	day	EST / hr:mn / PST	
New Moon	1	**7:15 am**	4:15 am
2nd Quarter	9	**6:53 am**	3:53 am
Full Moon	15	**10:36 pm**	7:36 pm
●	15	24° ♏ 53'	
4th Quarter	22	**7:31 pm**	4:31 pm
New Moon	30	**11:20 pm**	8:20 pm
●	30	9° ♊ 20'	

Planet Ingress			
	day	EST / hr:mn / PST	
♀ ♉	16	**5:58 am**	2:58 am
☉ ♊	21	**6:12 am**	3:12 am
⚳ ♊	27	**7:48 am**	4:48 am
⚶ ♎	30	**11:06 am**	8:06 am

Planetary Motion			
	day	EST / hr:mn / PST	
⚶ D	10		9:43 pm
⚶ D	11	**12:43 am**	
♆ ℞	15	**7:48 pm**	4:48 pm
☿ D	19		11:32 pm
☿ D	20	**2:32 am**	

DATE		SID.TIME	SUN	MOON	NODE	MERCURY	VENUS	MARS	JUPITER	SATURN	URANUS	NEPTUNE	PLUTO	CERES	PALLAS	JUNO	VESTA	CHIRON
1	Th	14:34:03	10 ♉ 13 23	4 ♉ 42	29 ♉℞ 28	19 ♉℞ 41	11 ♈ 16	5 ♒ 22	9 ♌ 10	26 ♊ 01	2 ♓ 16	13 ♒ 07	19 ♐℞ 34	19 ♉ 08	4 ♈ 21	13 ♏℞ 11	28 ♍℞ 58	18 ♑℞ 08
2	F	14:37:59	11 11 39	16 30	29 26	19 16	12 29	5 57	9 15	26 07	2 17	13 08	19 33	19 32	4 40	12 57	28 53	18 07
3	Sa	14:41:56	12 09 53	28 18	29 D 25	18 48	13 42	6 32	9 20	26 14	2 19	13 08	19 31	19 57	5 00	12 43	28 49	18 07
4	Su	14:45:52	13 08 06	10 ♊ 09	29 26	18 17	14 54	7 07	9 25	26 20	2 21	13 09	19 30	20 21	5 19	12 30	28 45	18 06
5	M	14:49:49	14 06 16	22 06	29 27	17 44	16 07	7 42	9 30	26 26	2 22	13 09	19 29	20 46	5 38	12 16	28 41	18 05
6	T	14:53:45	15 04 25	4 ♋ 12	29 28	17 08	17 20	8 17	9 36	26 33	2 24	13 10	19 28	21 10	5 57	12 02	28 38	18 04
7	W	14:57:42	16 02 32	16 30	29 29	16 32	18 32	8 52	9 41	26 40	2 25	13 10	19 27	21 35	6 16	11 49	28 36	18 04
8	Th	15:01:38	17 00 37	29 04	29 30	15 54	19 45	9 26	9 47	26 46	2 27	13 10	19 25	21 59	6 35	11 35	28 34	18 03
9	F	15:05:35	17 58 41	11 ♌ 56	29 ℞ 31	15 17	20 58	10 01	9 53	26 53	2 28	13 10	19 24	22 24	6 54	11 22	28 33	18 02
10	Sa	15:09:32	18 56 42	25 12	29 31	14 41	22 10	10 35	9 59	26 59	2 30	13 11	19 23	22 48	7 13	11 08	28 32	18 01
11	Su	15:13:28	19 54 41	8 ♍ 52	29 30	14 06	23 23	11 09	10 05	27 06	2 31	13 11	19 21	23 13	7 32	10 55	28 D 32	17 59
12	M	15:17:25	20 52 38	22 58	29 29	13 32	24 36	11 43	10 12	27 13	2 32	13 11	19 20	23 38	7 51	10 42	28 32	17 58
13	T	15:21:21	21 50 34	7 ♎ 29	29 29	13 02	25 49	12 17	10 18	27 20	2 34	13 11	19 19	24 02	8 10	10 29	28 32	17 57
14	W	15:25:18	22 48 27	22 20	29 28	12 34	27 01	12 51	10 25	27 27	2 35	13 11	19 17	24 27	8 28	10 16	28 33	17 55
15	Th	15:29:14	23 46 19	7 ♏ 25	29 27	12 09	28 14	13 24	10 32	27 34	2 36	13 11	19 16	24 51	8 47	10 03	28 35	17 54
16	F	15:33:11	24 44 10	22 36	29 D 27	11 49	29 27	13 58	10 39	27 41	2 37	13 ℞ 11	19 14	25 16	9 05	9 50	28 37	17 52
17	Sa	15:37:07	25 41 59	7 ♐ 43	29 27	11 32	0 ♉ 40	14 31	10 46	27 48	2 38	13 11	19 13	25 41	9 24	9 38	28 40	17 51
18	Su	15:41:04	26 39 47	22 38	29 27	11 19	1 52	15 04	10 53	27 55	2 39	13 11	19 12	26 05	9 42	9 25	28 43	17 49
19	M	15:45:01	27 37 33	7 ♑ 12	29 27	11 11	3 05	15 37	11 00	28 02	2 40	13 11	19 10	26 30	10 01	9 13	28 46	17 47
20	T	15:48:57	28 35 19	21 22	29 ℞ 28	11 D 08	4 18	16 10	11 08	28 09	2 41	13 11	19 09	26 54	10 19	9 01	28 50	17 45
21	W	15:52:54	29 33 03	5 ♒ 05	29 28	11 08	5 31	16 43	11 15	28 16	2 42	13 11	19 07	27 19	10 37	8 49	28 55	17 43
22	Th	15:56:50	0 ♊ 30 46	18 21	29 28	11 14	6 44	17 15	11 23	28 23	2 43	13 11	19 06	27 44	10 55	8 37	28 59	17 41
23	F	16:00:47	1 28 28	1 ♓ 13	29 D 28	11 24	7 56	17 48	11 31	28 30	2 43	13 10	19 04	28 08	11 13	8 26	29 05	17 39
24	Sa	16:04:43	2 26 09	13 45	29 28	11 38	9 09	18 20	11 39	28 38	2 44	13 10	19 03	28 33	11 31	8 15	29 10	17 37
25	Su	16:08:40	3 23 48	25 59	29 28	11 57	10 22	18 52	11 47	28 45	2 45	13 10	19 01	28 58	11 49	8 04	29 17	17 35
26	M	16:12:36	4 21 27	8 ♈ 01	29 28	12 20	11 35	19 23	11 55	28 52	2 46	13 10	19 00	29 22	12 07	7 53	29 23	17 33
27	T	16:16:33	5 19 05	19 54	29 29	12 48	12 48	19 55	12 03	29 00	2 46	13 09	18 58	29 47	12 25	7 43	29 30	17 30
28	W	16:20:30	6 16 42	1 ♉ 42	29 29	13 20	14 01	20 26	12 12	29 07	2 47	13 09	18 57	0 ♊ 12	12 43	7 32	29 38	17 28
29	Th	16:24:26	7 14 18	13 29	29 30	13 55	15 14	20 57	12 20	29 14	2 47	13 08	18 55	0 36	13 00	7 22	29 46	17 26
30	F	16:28:23	8 11 52	25 18	29 ℞ 30	14 35	16 27	21 28	12 29	29 22	2 48	13 08	18 53	1 01	13 18	7 12	29 54	17 23
31	Sa	16:32:19	9 09 26	7 ♊ 11	29 30	15 19	17 39	21 59	12 38	29 29	2 48	13 08	18 52	1 25	13 35	7 03	0 ♎ 03	17 21

EPHEMERIS CALCULATED FOR 12 MIDNIGHT GREENWICH MEAN TIME. ALL OTHER DATA AND FACING ASPECTARIAN PAGE IN **EASTERN STANDARD TIME (BOLD)** AND PACIFIC STANDARD TIME (REGULAR).

JUNE 2003

1 SUNDAY
☽ △ ♂ **1:53 am**
☽ ☌ ♄ **3:55 pm** 12:55 pm
☽ □ ⚶ **5:09 pm** 2:09 pm
☽ ⚺ ⚳ **8:56 pm** 5:56 pm
☽ △ ♅ **9:59 pm** 6:59 pm
☿ △ ⚷ 11:54 pm

2 MONDAY
☿ △ ⚷ **2:54 am**
☽ △ ⚵ **5:34 am** 2:34 am
☽ ⚺ ☉ **3:44 pm** 12:44 pm
☽ ⚺ ♃ **6:00 pm** 3:00 pm
☽ ⚻ ♆ **6:03 pm** 3:03 pm
☽ □ ⚴ **8:43 pm** 5:43 pm
♃ ☍ ♆ **9:55 pm** 6:55 pm
☽ ☍ ⚷ 10:58 pm

3 TUESDAY
☽ ☍ ⚷ **1:58 am**
☽ ⚹ ☿ **3:54 am** 12:54 am
♅ □ ⚳ **4:17 am** 1:17 am
☽ ⚻ ♇ **5:00 am** 2:00 am
☽ ⚹ ♀ **11:27 am** 8:27 am
☽ ⚻ ♂ **2:48 pm** 11:48 am
☿ ⚻ ♇ **5:37 pm** 2:37 pm
☉ △ ♆ **9:27 pm** 6:27 pm
☉ ⚹ ♃ 11:14 pm
☽ ⚺ ♄ 11:29 pm

4 WEDNESDAY
☉ ⚹ ♃ **2:14 am**
☽ ⚺ ♄ **2:29 am**
☽ ⚹ ⚶ **3:52 am** 12:52 am
☽ ⚻ ♅ **7:44 am** 4:44 am
☽ ⚹ ⚳ **8:39 am** 5:39 am
☽ □ ⚵ **2:23 pm** 11:23 am
☽ ☍ ♆ 11:55 pm

5 THURSDAY
☽ ☍ ♆ **2:55 am**
☽ ☌ ♃ **3:36 am** 12:36 am
☽ ⚹ ☉ **5:17 am** 2:17 am
☽ △ ⚴ **6:46 am** 3:46 am
☽ ⚻ ⚷ **10:19 am** 7:19 am
☽ △ ♇ **1:19 pm** 10:19 am
☽ □ ☿ **5:12 pm** 2:12 pm
♀ □ ♂ **6:53 pm** 3:53 pm
☽ ☍ ♂ 9:55 pm
☽ □ ♀ 10:18 pm

6 FRIDAY
☽ ☍ ♂ **12:55 am**
☽ □ ♀ **1:18 am**
☉ ⚹ ⚴ **9:11 am** 6:11 am
☽ ⚹ ♄ **10:26 am** 7:26 am
☽ ⚺ ⚶ **12:00 pm** 9:00 am
☽ ☍ ♅ **2:55 pm** 11:55 am
☽ □ ⚳ **5:31 pm** 2:31 pm
☽ ⚹ ⚵ **8:43 pm** 5:43 pm

7 SATURDAY
☽ ⚻ ♆ **9:05 am** 6:05 am
☽ ⚺ ♃ **10:25 am** 7:25 am
☽ ⚻ ⚴ **1:56 pm** 10:56 am
☽ □ ☉ **3:28 pm** 12:28 pm
☽ △ ⚷ **3:58 pm** 12:58 pm
☽ □ ♇ **6:54 pm** 3:54 pm
☉ ⚻ ⚷ **10:27 pm** 7:27 pm

8 SUNDAY
☽ △ ☿ **3:36 am** 12:36 am
☽ ⚻ ♂ **7:55 am** 4:55 am
☽ △ ♀ **11:27 am** 8:27 am
☽ □ ♄ **3:32 pm** 12:32 pm
☽ ☌ ⚶ **5:18 pm** 2:18 pm
☽ ⚻ ♅ **7:19 pm** 4:19 pm
☽ △ ⚳ **11:20 pm** 8:20 pm
☽ ⚺ ⚵ 9:25 pm

9 MONDAY
☽ ⚺ ⚵ **12:25 am**
☽ △ ♆ **12:32 pm** 9:32 am
☽ ⚹ ♃ **2:26 pm** 11:26 am
☉ ☍ ♇ **3:44 pm** 12:44 pm
☽ ☍ ⚴ **6:12 pm** 3:12 pm
☽ □ ⚷ **6:57 pm** 3:57 pm
☽ ⚹ ♇ **9:50 pm** 6:50 pm
☽ △ ☉ **10:17 pm** 7:17 pm

10 TUESDAY
⚳ ⚻ ⚵ **5:03 am** 2:03 am
☽ ⚻ ☿ **11:08 am** 8:08 am
☽ △ ♂ **12:00 pm** 9:00 am
♀ ⚺ ♄ **3:38 pm** 12:38 pm
☽ △ ♄ **6:05 pm** 3:05 pm
☽ ⚻ ♀ **6:17 pm** 3:17 pm
☽ ⚺ ⚶ **8:04 pm** 5:04 pm
☽ △ ♅ **9:15 pm** 6:15 pm
☿ □ ♂ 9:48 pm
☽ ☌ ⚵ 10:49 pm
☽ ⚻ ⚳ 11:33 pm

11 WEDNESDAY
☿ □ ♂ **12:48 am**
☽ ☌ ⚵ **1:49 am**
☽ ⚻ ⚳ **2:33 am**
⚷ □ ⚴ **3:48 am** 12:48 am
☽ □ ♆ **1:48 pm** 10:48 am
☽ □ ♃ **4:14 pm** 1:14 pm
☽ ⚹ ⚷ **7:53 pm** 4:53 pm
♀ △ ⚶ **8:08 pm** 5:08 pm
☽ ⚻ ⚴ **8:14 pm** 5:14 pm
☽ ⚺ ♇ **10:46 pm** 7:46 pm
☽ ⚻ ☉ 11:39 pm

12 THURSDAY
☽ ⚻ ☉ **2:39 am**
♀ □ ♅ **5:56 am** 2:56 am
☽ □ ♂ **2:11 pm** 11:11 am
☽ ☍ ☿ **4:51 pm** 1:51 pm
☽ ⚻ ♄ **7:03 pm** 4:03 pm
☽ ⚹ ⚶ **9:18 pm** 6:18 pm
☽ □ ♅ **9:43 pm** 6:43 pm
☽ ☍ ♀ **11:07 pm** 8:07 pm
☽ ⚺ ⚵ 10:55 pm

13 FRIDAY
☽ ⚺ ⚵ **1:55 am**
☽ ☍ ⚳ **4:19 am** 1:19 am
☽ ⚹ ♆ **2:04 pm** 11:04 am
☿ ⚺ ♄ **4:57 pm** 1:57 pm
☽ △ ♃ **5:05 pm** 2:05 pm
☽ ⚺ ⚷ **7:59 pm** 4:59 pm
☽ △ ⚴ **9:25 pm** 6:25 pm
☽ ☌ ♇ **10:58 pm** 7:58 pm
♅ ⚻ ⚶ **11:09 pm** 8:09 pm

14 SATURDAY
☽ ☍ ☉ **6:16 am** 3:16 am
♀ ⚻ ⚵ **7:23 am** 4:23 am
☽ ⚹ ♂ **4:05 pm** 1:05 pm
☿ □ ♅ **5:04 pm** 2:04 pm
☽ ☍ ♄ **7:56 pm** 4:56 pm
☿ △ ⚶ **8:23 pm** 5:23 pm
☽ ⚹ ♅ **10:12 pm** 7:12 pm
☽ □ ⚶ **10:36 pm** 7:36 pm
☽ ⚻ ☿ **10:49 pm** 7:49 pm
☽ ⚹ ⚵ 11:15 pm

15 SUNDAY
☽ ⚹ ⚵ **2:15 am**
☽ ⚻ ♀ **4:04 am** 1:04 am
☽ ⚻ ⚳ **6:22 am** 3:22 am
☽ ⚺ ♆ **2:56 pm** 11:56 am
☽ ⚻ ♃ **6:41 pm** 3:41 pm
☽ ☌ ⚷ **8:55 pm** 5:55 pm
☽ □ ⚴ **11:30 pm** 8:30 pm
☽ ⚺ ♇ 9:06 pm

16 MONDAY
☽ ⚺ ♇ **12:06 am**
☿ ⚻ ⚵ **4:58 am** 1:58 am
☽ ⚻ ☉ **11:22 am** 8:22 am
☽ ⚺ ♂ **7:38 pm** 4:38 pm
♀ ☌ ⚳ **8:13 pm** 5:13 pm
☽ ⚻ ♄ **10:34 pm** 7:34 pm
☽ ⚺ ♅ 9:28 pm
☽ △ ⚶ 10:49 pm

17 TUESDAY
☽ ⚺ ♅ **12:28 am**
☽ △ ⚶ **1:49 am**
☽ □ ⚵ **4:30 am** 1:30 am
♇ △ ⚴ **4:55 am** 1:55 am
☽ △ ☿ **7:50 am** 4:50 am
☽ △ ⚳ **10:40 am** 7:40 am
☽ △ ♀ **11:36 am** 8:36 am
☽ ☌ ♆ **6:08 pm** 3:08 pm
☽ ☍ ♃ **10:52 pm** 7:52 pm
☽ ⚺ ⚷ 9:21 pm

18 WEDNESDAY
☽ ⚺ ⚷ **12:21 am**
☽ ⚹ ♇ **3:52 am** 12:52 am
☽ ⚹ ⚴ **4:22 am** 1:22 am
☿ ☌ ⚳ **1:01 pm** 10:01 am
☽ △ ☉ **8:08 pm** 5:08 pm
☽ ☌ ♂ 11:39 pm

19 THURSDAY
☽ ☌ ♂ **2:39 am**
☽ △ ♄ **4:35 am** 1:35 am
☽ ☌ ♅ **6:03 am** 3:03 am
☽ ⚻ ⚶ **8:37 am** 5:37 am
☽ △ ⚵ **10:09 am** 7:09 am
☽ □ ⚳ **6:50 pm** 3:50 pm
☽ □ ☿ **10:32 pm** 7:32 pm
☽ □ ♀ **11:49 pm** 8:49 pm
☽ ⚺ ♆ 9:59 pm

20 FRIDAY
☽ ⚺ ♆ **12:59 am**
☽ ⚻ ♃ **6:57 am** 3:57 am
☽ ⚹ ⚷ **7:30 am** 4:30 am
☽ □ ♇ **11:24 am** 8:24 am
♀ △ ♆ **11:52 am** 8:52 am
☽ ⚺ ⚴ **1:13 pm** 10:13 am
☿ △ ♆ **3:32 pm** 12:32 pm
☿ ☌ ♀ **10:53 pm** 7:53 pm

21 SATURDAY
☽ □ ☉ **9:45 am** 6:45 am
♃ ⚻ ⚷ **12:02 pm** 9:02 am
☽ ⚺ ♂ **1:52 pm** 10:52 am
☽ □ ♄ **2:36 pm** 11:36 am
☽ ⚺ ♅ **3:29 pm** 12:29 pm
☽ ☍ ⚶ **7:35 pm** 4:35 pm
☽ ⚻ ⚵ **7:41 pm** 4:41 pm
⚵ ⚺ ⚶ **11:29 pm** 8:29 pm

22 SUNDAY
☽ ⚹ ⚳ **7:10 am** 4:10 am
☿ ⚻ ⚷ **9:53 am** 6:53 am
☽ ⚹ ♆ **11:33 am** 8:33 am
☿ ⚹ ♃ **12:55 pm** 9:55 am
☽ ⚹ ♀ **5:03 pm** 2:03 pm
☽ □ ⚷ **6:12 pm** 3:12 pm
☽ △ ♃ **6:49 pm** 3:49 pm
☽ ⚹ ☿ **7:51 pm** 4:51 pm
☽ △ ♇ **10:28 pm** 7:28 pm
♂ △ ♄ **11:21 pm** 8:21 pm
☽ ☌ ⚴ 10:47 pm

23 MONDAY
☽ ☌ ⚴ **1:47 am**
♀ ⚻ ⚷ **3:52 am** 12:52 am
☿ ☍ ♇ **11:46 am** 8:46 am
♀ ⚹ ♃ **1:07 pm** 10:07 am
♂ ☌ ♅ **3:02 pm** 12:02 pm

24 TUESDAY
☽ ⚹ ☉ **3:11 am** 12:11 am
☽ ⚹ ♄ **3:34 am** 12:34 am
☽ ⚹ ♅ **3:45 am** 12:45 am
☽ ⚹ ♂ **4:11 am** 1:11 am
☽ ☍ ⚵ **7:58 am** 4:58 am
☉ ☌ ♄ **8:39 am** 5:39 am
☽ ⚻ ⚶ **9:31 am** 6:31 am
☉ △ ♅ **10:08 am** 7:08 am
☿ ⚹ ⚴ **12:15 pm** 9:15 am
♄ △ ♅ **6:34 pm** 3:34 pm
♀ ☍ ♇ **9:00 pm** 6:00 pm
☽ ⚺ ⚳ **10:03 pm** 7:03 pm
☉ △ ♂ **10:54 pm** 7:54 pm
☽ □ ♆ 9:15 pm

25 WEDNESDAY
☽ □ ♆ **12:15 am**
☽ △ ⚷ **6:47 am** 3:47 am
☽ □ ♃ **8:41 am** 5:41 am
☽ ⚻ ♇ **11:16 am** 8:16 am
☽ ⚺ ♀ **12:57 pm** 9:57 am
☽ ⚺ ⚴ **4:02 pm** 1:02 pm
☽ ⚺ ☿ **9:04 pm** 6:04 pm

26 THURSDAY
☉ △ ⚵ **1:10 pm** 10:10 am
☽ □ ♅ **4:36 pm** 1:36 pm
☽ ⚺ ♄ **5:10 pm** 2:10 pm
☽ □ ♂ **7:02 pm** 4:02 pm
☽ ⚻ ⚵ **8:44 pm** 5:44 pm
☽ ⚺ ☉ **9:24 pm** 6:24 pm
☽ △ ⚶ **11:54 pm** 8:54 pm
♀ ⚹ ⚴ 10:23 pm

27 FRIDAY
♀ ⚹ ⚴ **1:23 am**
♆ △ ⚳ **11:19 am** 8:19 am
☽ △ ♆ **12:46 pm** 9:46 am
☽ ☌ ⚳ **12:49 pm** 9:49 am
☽ ⚻ ⚷ **6:57 pm** 3:57 pm
☽ ⚹ ♃ **10:03 pm** 7:03 pm
☽ ☍ ♇ **11:30 pm** 8:30 pm

28 SATURDAY
☽ ⚹ ⚴ **5:29 am** 2:29 am
☽ ☌ ♀ **8:00 am** 5:00 am
☉ □ ⚶ **5:59 pm** 2:59 pm
☽ ☌ ☿ **9:31 pm** 6:31 pm

29 SUNDAY
☽ △ ♅ **3:59 am** 12:59 am
♂ △ ⚵ **4:58 am** 1:58 am
☽ ☌ ♄ **5:14 am** 2:14 am
☽ △ ⚵ **8:02 am** 5:02 am
☽ △ ♂ **8:07 am** 5:07 am
☽ □ ⚶ **12:36 pm** 9:36 am
☽ ☌ ☉ **1:39 pm** 10:39 am
☽ ⚻ ♆ **11:24 pm** 8:24 pm
☽ ⚺ ⚳ 10:30 pm

30 MONDAY
☽ ⚺ ⚳ **1:30 am**
☽ ☍ ⚷ **5:09 am** 2:09 am
☽ ⚺ ♃ **9:18 am** 6:18 am
☽ ⚻ ♇ **9:41 am** 6:41 am
☿ △ ♅ **10:27 am** 7:27 am
☽ □ ⚴ **4:38 pm** 1:38 pm
☿ ☌ ♄ **8:14 pm** 5:14 pm
☽ ⚺ ♀ 9:08 pm

Eastern Standard Time in bold type
Pacific Standard Time in medium type

JUNE 2003

☽ Last Aspect day	EST / hr:mn / PST	asp	☽ Ingress sign day	EST / hr:mn / PST
1	**3:55 pm** 12:55 pm	☌ ♄	♋ 1	**4:27 pm** 1:27 pm
3	**11:27 am** 8:27 am	⚹ ♀	♌ 3	11:25 pm
3	**11:27 am** 8:27 am	⚹ ♀	♌ 4	**2:25 am**
5	10:18 pm	□ ♀	♍ 6	**9:51 am** 6:51 am
6	**1:18 am**	□ ♀	♍ 6	**9:51 am** 6:51 am
8	**11:27 am** 8:27 am	△ ♀	♎ 8	**2:30 pm** 11:30 am
10	**12:00 pm** 9:00 am	△ ♂	♏ 10	**4:39 pm** 1:39 pm
12	**4:51 pm** 1:51 pm	☍ ☿	♐ 12	**5:12 pm** 2:12 pm
14	**4:05 pm** 1:05 pm	⚹ ♂	♑ 14	**5:38 pm** 2:38 pm
14	**10:12 pm** 7:12 pm	⚹ ♅	♒ 16	**7:41 pm** 4:41 pm
18	**8:08 pm** 5:08 pm	△ ☉	♓ 18	9:57 pm
18	**8:08 pm** 5:08 pm	△ ☉	♓ 19	**12:57 am**
21	**9:45 am** 6:45 am	□ ☉	♈ 21	**10:06 am** 7:06 am
22	**10:28 pm** 7:28 pm	△ ♇	♉ 23	**10:15 pm** 7:15 pm
25	**8:41 am** 5:41 am	□ ♃	♊ 26	**11:13 am** 8:13 am
28	**9:31 pm** 6:31 pm	☌ ☿	♋ 28	**10:52 pm** 7:52 pm
29	**1:39 pm** 10:39 am	☌ ☉	♌ 7/1	**8:13 am** 5:13 am

☽ Phases & Eclipses phase	day	EST / hr:mn / PST
2nd Quarter	7	**3:28 pm** 12:28 pm
Full Moon	14	**6:16 am** 3:16 am
4th Quarter	21	**9:45 am** 6:45 am
New Moon	29	**1:39 pm** 10:39 am

Planet Ingress	day	EST / hr:mn / PST
♄ ♋	3	**8:28 pm** 5:28 pm
♀ ♊	9	**10:32 pm** 7:32 pm
☿ ♊	12	**8:34 pm** 5:34 pm
☉ ♋	21	**2:10 pm** 11:10 am
☿ ♋	29	**5:17 am** 2:17 am

Planetary Motion	day	EST / hr:mn / PST
♅ R	6	10:58 pm
♅ R	7	**1:58 am**
⚵ D	29	**8:46 am** 5:46 am

DATE		SID.TIME	SUN	MOON	NODE	MERCURY	VENUS	MARS	JUPITER	SATURN	URANUS	NEPTUNE	PLUTO	CERES	PALLAS	JUNO	VESTA	CHIRON
1	Su	16:36:16	10 ♊ 06 59	19 ♊ 10	29 ♉ R 30	16 ♉ 06	18 ♉ 52	22 ♒ 29	12 ♌ 47	29 ♊ 37	2 ♓ 48	13 ♒ R 07	18 ♐ R 50	1 ♊ 50	13 ♈ 53	6 ♏ R 54	0 ♎ 12	17 ♑ R 18
2	M	16:40:12	11 04 31	1 ♋ 18	29 29	16 57	20 05	22 59	12 56	29 44	2 49	13 07	18 49	2 15	14 10	6 45	0 22	17 15
3	T	16:44:09	12 02 01	13 36	29 27	17 51	21 18	23 29	13 05	29 52	2 49	13 06	18 47	2 39	14 27	6 36	0 32	17 12
4	W	16:48:05	12 59 31	26 06	29 25	18 49	22 31	23 59	13 14	0 ♋ 00	2 49	13 05	18 46	3 04	14 44	6 28	0 42	17 10
5	Th	16:52:02	13 56 59	8 ♌ 49	29 23	19 50	23 44	24 28	13 23	0 07	2 49	13 05	18 44	3 29	15 02	6 20	0 53	17 07
6	F	16:55:59	14 54 26	21 49	29 22	20 55	24 57	24 57	13 33	0 15	2 49	13 04	18 42	3 53	15 18	6 12	1 04	17 04
7	Sa	16:59:55	15 51 51	5 ♍ 06	29 D 21	22 03	26 10	25 26	13 42	0 22	2 R 49	13 03	18 41	4 18	15 35	6 05	1 15	17 01
8	Su	17:03:52	16 49 16	18 42	29 21	23 14	27 23	25 54	13 52	0 30	2 49	13 03	18 39	4 42	15 52	5 58	1 27	16 58
9	M	17:07:48	17 46 39	2 ♎ 38	29 21	24 28	28 36	26 23	14 02	0 38	2 49	13 02	18 38	5 07	16 09	5 51	1 39	16 55
10	T	17:11:45	18 44 01	16 54	29 22	25 45	29 49	26 51	14 11	0 45	2 49	13 01	18 36	5 32	16 25	5 44	1 52	16 52
11	W	17:15:41	19 41 23	1 ♏ 26	29 23	27 05	1 ♊ 02	27 18	14 21	0 53	2 49	13 01	18 34	5 56	16 42	5 38	2 05	16 49
12	Th	17:19:38	20 38 43	16 13	29 R 24	28 28	2 15	27 46	14 31	1 01	2 49	13 00	18 33	6 21	16 58	5 32	2 18	16 45
13	F	17:23:34	21 36 02	1 ♐ 07	29 25	29 54	3 28	28 13	14 41	1 09	2 48	12 59	18 31	6 45	17 14	5 27	2 32	16 42
14	Sa	17:27:31	22 33 21	16 02	29 24	1 ♊ 23	4 41	28 39	14 51	1 16	2 48	12 58	18 30	7 10	17 30	5 22	2 46	16 39
15	Su	17:31:28	23 30 39	0 ♑ 50	29 22	2 55	5 55	29 06	15 02	1 24	2 48	12 57	18 28	7 34	17 46	5 17	3 00	16 36
16	M	17:35:24	24 27 56	15 23	29 19	4 30	7 08	29 32	15 12	1 32	2 47	12 56	18 26	7 59	18 02	5 12	3 14	16 32
17	T	17:39:21	25 25 13	29 36	29 16	6 08	8 21	29 57	15 23	1 40	2 47	12 55	18 25	8 23	18 18	5 08	3 29	16 29
18	W	17:43:17	26 22 29	13 ♒ 24	29 12	7 49	9 34	0 ♓ 23	15 33	1 47	2 46	12 54	18 23	8 48	18 33	5 04	3 45	16 26
19	Th	17:47:14	27 19 45	26 45	29 09	9 32	10 47	0 48	15 44	1 55	2 46	12 53	18 22	9 12	18 49	5 01	4 00	16 22
20	F	17:51:10	28 17 00	9 ♓ 42	29 06	11 18	12 00	1 12	15 54	2 03	2 45	12 52	18 20	9 37	19 04	4 57	4 16	16 19
21	Sa	17:55:07	29 14 16	22 16	29 D 05	13 07	13 13	1 36	16 05	2 11	2 45	12 51	18 19	10 01	19 20	4 54	4 32	16 15
22	Su	17:59:04	0 ♋ 11 31	4 ♈ 31	29 05	14 59	14 26	2 00	16 16	2 19	2 44	12 50	18 17	10 25	19 35	4 52	4 48	16 12
23	M	18:03:00	1 08 46	16 32	29 05	16 53	15 40	2 24	16 27	2 26	2 43	12 49	18 15	10 50	19 50	4 50	5 05	16 08
24	T	18:06:57	2 06 00	28 24	29 07	18 50	16 53	2 46	16 38	2 34	2 43	12 48	18 14	11 14	20 05	4 48	5 22	16 04
25	W	18:10:53	3 03 15	10 ♉ 12	29 09	20 49	18 06	3 09	16 49	2 42	2 42	12 47	18 12	11 38	20 19	4 46	5 39	16 01
26	Th	18:14:50	4 00 30	22 00	29 R 10	22 50	19 19	3 31	17 00	2 50	2 41	12 46	18 11	12 03	20 34	4 45	5 57	15 57
27	F	18:18:46	4 57 44	3 ♊ 52	29 10	24 53	20 33	3 53	17 11	2 58	2 40	12 44	18 09	12 27	20 48	4 44	6 14	15 54
28	Sa	18:22:43	5 54 59	15 51	29 09	26 59	21 46	4 14	17 22	3 05	2 39	12 43	18 08	12 51	21 03	4 43	6 32	15 50
29	Su	18:26:39	6 52 13	28 01	29 06	29 05	22 59	4 34	17 34	3 13	2 38	12 42	18 06	13 16	21 17	4 D 43	6 51	15 46
30	M	18:30:36	7 49 27	10 ♋ 23	29 01	1 ♋ 13	24 13	4 54	17 45	3 21	2 37	12 41	18 05	13 40	21 31	4 43	7 09	15 43

EPHEMERIS CALCULATED FOR 12 MIDNIGHT GREENWICH MEAN TIME. ALL OTHER DATA AND FACING ASPECTARIAN PAGE IN **EASTERN STANDARD TIME (BOLD)** AND PACIFIC STANDARD TIME (REGULAR).

JULY 2003

1 TUESDAY

☽⊻♀	12:08 am	
♃△♇	7:47 am	4:47 am
☿△⚵	9:56 am	6:56 am
☽⊼♅	1:03 pm	10:03 am
☽⊻♄	2:55 pm	11:55 am
☽□⚵	5:02 pm	2:02 pm
☽⊻☿	6:27 pm	3:27 pm
☽⊼♂	6:33 pm	3:33 pm
☿△♂	7:06 pm	4:06 pm
☽✶⚶	10:48 pm	7:48 pm
☽⊻☉		11:53 pm

2 WEDNESDAY

☽⊻☉	2:53 am	
☽☍♆	7:39 am	4:39 am
☽✶⚳	11:33 am	8:33 am
☽⊼⚷	1:00 pm	10:00 am
☽△♇	5:31 pm	2:31 pm
☽☌♃	6:05 pm	3:05 pm
☿□⚶		9:03 pm
☽△⚴		10:16 pm

3 THURSDAY

☿□⚶	12:03 am	
☽△⚴	1:16 am	
☽✶♀	1:06 pm	10:06 am
☽☍♅	7:50 pm	4:50 pm
☽✶♄	10:15 pm	7:15 pm
☽✶⚵	11:49 pm	8:49 pm
☽☍♂		11:28 pm

4 FRIDAY

☽☍♂	2:28 am	
⚷⊼⚳	4:27 am	1:27 am
☽⊻⚶	6:39 am	3:39 am
☽✶☿	11:39 am	8:39 am
☽✶☉	1:22 pm	10:22 am
☽⊼♆	1:44 pm	10:44 am
☉⊼♆	6:28 pm	3:28 pm
☽△⚷	6:44 pm	3:44 pm
☽□⚳	7:14 pm	4:14 pm
☽□♇	11:15 pm	8:15 pm
☿⊼♆		9:30 pm
☽⊻♃		9:40 pm

Eastern Standard Time in bold type
Pacific Standard Time in medium type

5 SATURDAY

☿⊼♆	12:30 am	
☽⊻♃	12:40 am	
☉☌☿	5:20 am	2:20 am
☽⊼⚴	7:41 am	4:41 am
☽□♀	11:25 pm	8:25 pm
☽⊼♅		9:40 pm

6 SUNDAY

☽⊼♅	12:40 am	
☽□♄	3:35 am	12:35 am
☽⊻⚵	4:43 am	1:43 am
☿☍⚷	6:50 am	3:50 am
☽⊼♂	8:15 am	5:15 am
☽☌⚶	12:30 pm	9:30 am
♀△♅	1:21 pm	10:21 am
☽△♆	5:59 pm	2:59 pm
☿⊻⚳	8:08 pm	5:08 pm
☽□☉	9:32 pm	6:32 pm
☽□⚷	10:40 pm	7:40 pm
☽△⚳		9:56 pm
☽□☿		10:38 pm

7 MONDAY

☽△⚳	12:56 am	
☽□☿	1:38 am	
☽✶♇	3:11 am	12:11 am
☽✶♃	5:23 am	2:23 am
☿⊼♇	11:44 am	8:44 am
☽☍⚴	12:15 pm	9:15 am
☉☍⚷	1:17 pm	10:17 am

8 TUESDAY

♀☌♄	3:30 am	12:30 am
☽△♅	3:51 am	12:51 am
☿⊻♃	4:24 am	1:24 am
☽△♄	7:13 am	4:13 am
☽△♀	7:32 am	4:32 am
☽☌⚵	8:00 am	5:00 am
☽△♂	12:15 pm	9:15 am
♀△⚵	1:17 pm	10:17 am
☽⊻⚶	4:40 pm	1:40 pm
☽□♆	8:41 pm	5:41 pm
☽✶⚷		10:07 pm

9 WEDNESDAY

☽✶⚷	1:07 am	
☽△☉	3:49 am	12:49 am
☽⊼⚳	4:58 am	1:58 am
☽⊻♇	5:39 am	2:39 am
☽□♃	8:35 am	5:35 am
☽△☿	12:58 pm	9:58 am
☽⊼⚴	3:19 pm	12:19 pm

10 THURSDAY

♇☍⚳	4:19 am	1:19 am
☽□♅	5:46 am	2:46 am
☿□⚴	6:34 am	3:34 am
☉⊼♇	6:57 am	3:57 am
☉⊻⚳	8:57 am	5:57 am
☽⊼♄	9:36 am	6:36 am
☽⊻⚵	10:07 am	7:07 am
☽⊼♀	2:04 pm	11:04 am
☽□♂	2:56 pm	11:56 am
☽✶⚶	7:41 pm	4:41 pm
☽✶♆	10:20 pm	7:20 pm
♀△♂		11:28 pm
☽⊻⚷		11:35 pm

11 FRIDAY

♀△♂	2:28 am	
☽⊻⚷	2:35 am	
☽☌♇	7:13 am	4:13 am
☽☍⚳	8:01 am	5:01 am
☽⊼☉	8:57 am	5:57 am
☽△♃	10:53 am	7:53 am
☽△⚴	5:34 pm	2:34 pm
☽⊼☿	10:49 pm	7:49 pm

12 SATURDAY

☽✶♅	7:14 am	4:14 am
☽☍♄	11:37 am	8:37 am
☽✶⚵	11:53 am	8:53 am
☽✶♂	5:17 pm	2:17 pm
☽☍♀	8:15 pm	5:15 pm
☉⊻♃	9:49 pm	6:49 pm
☽□⚶	10:35 pm	7:35 pm
☽⊻♆	11:55 pm	8:55 pm

13 SUNDAY

☽☌⚷	4:06 am	1:06 am
☽⊻♇	8:56 am	5:56 am
☽⊼⚳	11:15 am	8:15 am
☽⊼♃	1:28 pm	10:28 am
☽☍☉	2:21 pm	11:21 am
☽□⚴	8:17 pm	5:17 pm

14 MONDAY

☽☍☿	9:21 am	6:21 am
☽⊻♅	9:33 am	6:33 am
♀□⚶	9:58 am	6:58 am
☿⊼♅	10:42 am	7:42 am
♀⊼♆	2:25 pm	11:25 am
☽⊼♄	2:38 pm	11:38 am
☽□⚵	2:43 pm	11:43 am
☽⊻♂	8:46 pm	5:46 pm
♆△⚶		9:14 pm
☽☌♆		11:52 pm
☽△⚶		11:57 pm

15 TUESDAY

♆△⚶	12:14 am	
☽☌♆	2:52 am	
☽△⚶	2:57 am	
☽⊼♀	4:07 am	1:07 am
☽⊻⚷	7:06 am	4:06 am
☽✶♇	12:20 pm	9:20 am
♄△⚵	2:01 pm	11:01 am
☽△⚳	4:23 pm	1:23 pm
☽☍♃	5:57 pm	2:57 pm
☽⊼☉	10:02 pm	7:02 pm
☽✶⚴		10:05 pm
☿□⚵		10:05 pm
☿⊻♄		10:21 pm

16 WEDNESDAY

☽✶⚴	1:05 am	
☿□⚵	1:05 am	
☿⊻♄	1:21 am	
♀☍⚷	12:05 pm	9:05 am
☽☌♅	2:16 pm	11:16 am
☽△⚵	8:12 pm	5:12 pm
☽△♄	8:18 pm	5:18 pm
☽⊼☿	11:20 pm	8:20 pm

17 THURSDAY

☽☌♂	3:01 am	12:01 am
☽⊻♆	8:43 am	5:43 am
☽⊼⚶	10:30 am	7:30 am
☽✶⚷	1:04 pm	10:04 am
☽△♀	3:51 pm	12:51 pm
☽□♇	6:50 pm	3:50 pm
☽□⚳		10:01 pm
☽⊼♃		10:50 pm
☉□⚴		11:24 pm
☿⊼♂		11:36 pm

18 FRIDAY

☽□⚳	1:01 am	
☽⊼♃	1:50 am	
☉□⚴	2:24 am	
☿⊼♂	2:36 am	
☽⊻⚴	9:21 am	6:21 am
☽△☉	9:49 am	6:49 am
♀⊼♇	10:26 pm	7:26 pm
☽⊻♅	10:31 pm	7:31 pm

19 SATURDAY

☽⊼⚵	5:24 am	2:24 am
☽□♄	5:40 am	2:40 am
☽⊻♂	12:54 pm	9:54 am
☿☍♆	3:58 pm	12:58 pm
☽✶♆	6:11 pm	3:11 pm
☽△☿	6:35 pm	3:35 pm
☽☍⚶	10:04 pm	7:04 pm
☽□⚷	10:40 pm	7:40 pm

20 SUNDAY

☽△♇	4:58 am	1:58 am
♃✶⚳	7:52 am	4:52 am
☽□♀	8:29 am	5:29 am
☽△♃	1:30 pm	10:30 am
☽✶⚳	1:35 pm	10:35 am
⚷□⚶	2:25 pm	11:25 am
☿⊼⚷	9:14 pm	6:14 pm
☽☌⚴	9:15 pm	6:15 pm
☿✶⚶	11:23 pm	8:23 pm
☽□☉		11:01 pm

21 MONDAY

☽□☉	2:01 am	
☽✶♅	10:01 am	7:01 am
☽☍⚵	5:52 pm	2:52 pm
☽✶♄	6:15 pm	3:15 pm
☽✶♂		10:41 pm

22 TUESDAY

☽✶♂	1:41 am	
☽□♆	6:26 am	3:26 am
☽△⚷	10:51 am	7:51 am
☽⊼⚶	12:35 pm	9:35 am
☿△♇	4:38 pm	1:38 pm
☽⊼♇	5:30 pm	2:30 pm
☽□☿	5:39 pm	2:39 pm
♀⊻♃	6:25 pm	3:25 pm

23 WEDNESDAY

☽□♃	3:22 am	12:22 am
☽✶♀	4:14 am	1:14 am
☽⊻⚳	4:27 am	1:27 am
♀⊻⚳	7:12 am	4:12 am
☽⊻⚴	10:57 am	7:57 am
☽✶☉	8:15 pm	5:15 pm
☽□♅	10:45 pm	7:45 pm

24 THURSDAY

☽⊼⚵	7:18 am	4:18 am
☽⊻♄	7:45 am	4:45 am
☽□♂	2:51 pm	11:51 am
☽△♆	7:00 pm	4:00 pm
☽⊼⚷	11:10 pm	8:10 pm
☉⊼♅		11:31 pm

25 FRIDAY

☉⊼♅	2:31 am	
☽△⚶	3:12 am	12:12 am
☽☍♇	5:53 am	2:53 am
☽✶☿	3:52 pm	12:52 pm
☽✶♃	4:38 pm	1:38 pm
☽☌⚳	6:37 pm	3:37 pm
☿☌♃	10:17 pm	7:17 pm
☽⊻♀	11:09 pm	8:09 pm
☽✶⚴	11:39 pm	8:39 pm

26 SATURDAY

♀□⚴	4:51 am	1:51 am
☽△♅	10:07 am	7:07 am
☽⊻☉	12:51 pm	9:51 am
☿✶⚳	6:02 pm	3:02 pm
☽△⚵	7:04 pm	4:04 pm
☽☌♄	7:29 pm	4:29 pm
☽△♂		10:53 pm

27 SUNDAY

☽△♂	1:53 am	
☽⊼♆	5:31 am	2:31 am
☽☍⚷	9:22 am	6:22 am
☽□⚶	3:21 pm	12:21 pm
☽⊼♇	3:56 pm	12:56 pm

28 MONDAY

☽⊻♃	3:11 am	12:11 am
☽⊻⚳	5:53 am	2:53 am
☿△⚴	8:17 am	5:17 am
♇✶⚶	9:05 am	6:05 am
☽□⚴	9:31 am	6:31 am
☽⊻☿	9:41 am	6:41 am
☽☌♀	2:25 pm	11:25 am
☽⊼♅	6:41 pm	3:41 pm
☽☌☉		10:53 pm

29 TUESDAY

☽☌☉	1:53 am	
☽□⚵	3:53 am	12:53 am
☽⊻♄	4:14 am	1:14 am
☽⊼♂	9:50 am	6:50 am
☽☍♆	1:08 pm	10:08 am
☽⊼⚷	4:40 pm	1:40 pm
☽△♇	11:06 pm	8:06 pm
☽✶⚶		9:20 pm

30 WEDNESDAY

☽✶⚶	12:20 am	
☉□⚵	9:49 am	6:49 am
♀⊼♅	10:16 am	7:16 am
☽☌♃	10:46 am	7:46 am
☽✶⚳	2:04 pm	11:04 am
☉⊻♄	2:23 pm	11:23 am
☽△⚴	4:28 pm	1:28 pm
☽☌☿	10:58 pm	7:58 pm
☽☍♅		9:34 pm
☽⊻♀		11:02 pm

31 THURSDAY

☽☍♅	12:34 am	
☽⊻♀	2:02 am	
☽✶⚵	10:07 am	7:07 am
☽✶♄	10:21 am	7:21 am
☽⊻☉	11:40 am	8:40 am
☿☍♅	1:24 pm	10:24 am
☽☍♂	3:13 pm	12:13 pm
☽⊼♆	6:21 pm	3:21 pm
☽△⚷	9:40 pm	6:40 pm

JULY 2003

☽ Last Aspect day	EST / hr:mn / PST	asp	☽ Ingress sign day	EST / hr:mn / PST
6/29	**1:39 pm** 10:39 am	☌☉	♌ 1	**8:13 am** 5:13 am
3	**12:39 pm** 9:39 pm	✶♀	♍ 3	**3:16 pm** 12:16 pm
4	**11:15 pm** 8:15 pm	□♇	♎ 5	**8:20 pm** 5:20 pm
7	**5:23 am** 2:23 am	✶♃	♏ 7	**11:43 pm** 8:43 pm
9	**12:58 pm** 9:58 am	△☿	♐ 9	10:48 pm
9	**12:58 pm** 9:58 am	△☿	♐ 10	**1:48 am**
11	**10:53 am** 7:53 am	△♃	♑ 12	**3:21 am** 12:21 am
13	**2:21 pm** 11:21 am	☍☉	♒ 14	**5:38 am** 2:38 am
15	**5:57 pm** 3:57 pm	☍♃	♓ 16	**10:14 am** 7:14 am
18	**9:49 am** 6:49 am	△☉	♈ 18	**6:20 pm** 3:20 pm

☽ Last Aspect day	EST / hr:mn / PST	asp	☽ Ingress sign day	EST / hr:mn / PST
20	11:01 pm	□☉	♉ 21	**5:48 am** 2:48 am
21	**2:01 am**	□☉	♉ 21	**5:48 am** 2:48 am
23	**4:14 am** 1:14 am	✶♀	♊ 23	**6:42 pm** 3:42 pm
25	**4:38 pm** 1:38 pm	✶♃	♋ 26	**6:23 am** 3:23 am
28	**2:25 pm** 11:25 am	☌♀	♌ 28	**3:17 pm** 12:17 pm
30	**10:46 am** 7:46 am	☌♃	♍ 30	**9:27 pm** 6:27 pm

☽ Phases & Eclipses

phase	day	EST / hr:mn / PST
2nd Quarter	6	**9:32 pm** 6:32 pm
Full Moon	13	**2:21 pm** 11:21 am
4th Quarter	20	11:01 pm
4th Quarter	21	**2:01 am**
New Moon	29	10:53 pm
New Moon	30	**1:53 am**

Planet Ingress

	day	EST / hr:mn / PST
♀ ♋	4	**12:39 pm** 9:39 am
☿ ♌	13	**7:10 am** 4:10 am
☉ ♌	22	10:04 pm
☉ ♌	23	**1:04 am**
♀ ♌	28	**11:25 pm** 8:25 pm
☿ ♍	30	**9:05 am** 6:05 am

Planetary Motion

	day	EST / hr:mn / PST
♂ ℞	28	10:53 pm
♂ ℞	29	**2:36 am**

DATE		SID.TIME	SUN	MOON	NODE	MERCURY	VENUS	MARS	JUPITER	SATURN	URANUS	NEPTUNE	PLUTO	CERES	PALLAS	JUNO	VESTA	CHIRON
1	T	18:34:33	8 ♋ 46 41	22 ♋ 58	28 ♉ ℞ 55	3 ♋ 22	25 ♊ 26	5 ♓ 14	17 ♌ 56	3 ♋ 29	2 ♓ ℞ 36	12 ♒ ℞ 40	18 ♐ ℞ 03	14 ♊ 04	21 ♈ 45	4 ♏ 43	7 ♎ 28	15 ♑ ℞ 39
2	W	18:38:29	9 43 55	5 ♌ 47	28 48	5 32	26 39	5 33	18 08	3 37	2 35	12 38	18 02	14 28	21 58	4 43	7 47	15 35
3	Th	18:42:26	10 41 08	18 49	28 41	7 43	27 53	5 51	18 20	3 44	2 34	12 37	18 00	14 53	22 12	4 44	8 06	15 31
4	F	18:46:22	11 38 21	2 ♍ 05	28 35	9 53	29 06	6 09	18 31	3 52	2 33	12 36	17 59	15 17	22 25	4 46	8 26	15 28
5	Sa	18:50:19	12 35 34	15 33	28 30	12 04	0 ♋ 19	6 27	18 43	4 00	2 31	12 34	17 58	15 41	22 38	4 47	8 45	15 24
6	Su	18:54:15	13 32 47	29 14	28 27	14 14	1 33	6 44	18 55	4 08	2 30	12 33	17 56	16 05	22 52	4 49	9 05	15 20
7	M	18:58:12	14 29 59	13 ♎ 07	28 D 27	16 24	2 46	7 00	19 06	4 15	2 29	12 32	17 55	16 29	23 04	4 51	9 26	15 16
8	T	19:02:08	15 27 11	27 12	28 27	18 33	4 00	7 15	19 18	4 23	2 27	12 30	17 53	16 53	23 17	4 54	9 46	15 13
9	W	19:06:05	16 24 23	11 ♏ 28	28 28	20 41	5 13	7 31	19 30	4 31	2 26	12 29	17 52	17 17	23 30	4 56	10 07	15 09
10	Th	19:10:02	17 21 35	25 53	28 ℞ 29	22 47	6 27	7 45	19 42	4 38	2 24	12 27	17 51	17 41	23 42	4 59	10 28	15 05
11	F	19:13:58	18 18 46	10 ♐ 25	28 28	24 53	7 40	7 59	19 54	4 46	2 23	12 26	17 49	18 05	23 54	5 03	10 49	15 01
12	Sa	19:17:55	19 15 58	24 57	28 26	26 56	8 54	8 12	20 06	4 54	2 21	12 24	17 48	18 29	24 06	5 06	11 10	14 58
13	Su	19:21:51	20 13 10	9 ♑ 26	28 21	28 59	10 07	8 25	20 18	5 01	2 20	12 23	17 47	18 53	24 18	5 10	11 31	14 54
14	M	19:25:48	21 10 22	23 44	28 14	0 ♌ 59	11 21	8 37	20 31	5 09	2 18	12 21	17 46	19 16	24 29	5 14	11 53	14 50
15	T	19:29:44	22 07 34	7 ♒ 47	28 06	2 58	12 34	8 48	20 43	5 17	2 17	12 20	17 44	19 40	24 41	5 19	12 15	14 47
16	W	19:33:41	23 04 47	21 30	27 57	4 55	13 48	8 58	20 55	5 24	2 15	12 18	17 43	20 04	24 52	5 24	12 37	14 43
17	Th	19:37:37	24 02 00	4 ♓ 50	27 49	6 51	15 01	9 08	21 07	5 32	2 13	12 17	17 42	20 28	25 03	5 29	12 59	14 39
18	F	19:41:34	24 59 13	17 46	27 42	8 44	16 15	9 17	21 20	5 39	2 12	12 15	17 41	20 51	25 14	5 34	13 22	14 36
19	Sa	19:45:31	25 56 27	0 ♈ 21	27 36	10 36	17 29	9 26	21 32	5 47	2 10	12 14	17 39	21 15	25 24	5 39	13 44	14 32
20	Su	19:49:27	26 53 42	12 37	27 33	12 26	18 42	9 34	21 45	5 54	2 08	12 12	17 38	21 39	25 34	5 45	14 07	14 28
21	M	19:53:24	27 50 57	24 39	27 D 32	14 14	19 56	9 40	21 57	6 02	2 06	12 11	17 37	22 02	25 45	5 51	14 30	14 25
22	T	19:57:20	28 48 14	6 ♉ 31	27 32	16 01	21 10	9 47	22 10	6 09	2 04	12 09	17 36	22 26	25 54	5 58	14 53	14 21
23	W	20:01:17	29 45 31	18 19	27 ℞ 33	17 45	22 24	9 52	22 22	6 17	2 03	12 08	17 35	22 49	26 04	6 04	15 16	14 18
24	Th	20:05:13	0 ♌ 42 49	0 ♊ 09	27 33	19 28	23 37	9 57	22 35	6 24	2 01	12 06	17 34	23 13	26 13	6 11	15 40	14 14
25	F	20:09:10	1 40 08	12 05	27 32	21 09	24 51	10 01	22 47	6 31	1 59	12 04	17 33	23 36	26 23	6 18	16 03	14 11
26	Sa	20:13:06	2 37 27	24 11	27 29	22 48	26 05	10 04	23 00	6 39	1 57	12 03	17 32	23 59	26 32	6 25	16 27	14 07
27	Su	20:17:03	3 34 48	6 ♋ 31	27 23	24 26	27 19	10 06	23 13	6 46	1 55	12 01	17 31	24 23	26 40	6 33	16 51	14 04
28	M	20:21:00	4 32 09	19 08	27 15	26 01	28 33	10 07	23 25	6 53	1 53	12 00	17 30	24 46	26 49	6 41	17 15	14 00
29	T	20:24:56	5 29 31	2 ♌ 01	27 05	27 35	29 46	10 ℞ 08	23 38	7 00	1 51	11 58	17 29	25 09	26 57	6 49	17 39	13 57
30	W	20:28:53	6 26 54	15 11	26 54	29 07	1 ♌ 00	10 08	23 51	7 07	1 49	11 56	17 28	25 32	27 05	6 57	18 04	13 54
31	Th	20:32:49	7 24 18	28 37	26 43	0 ♍ 37	2 14	10 07	24 04	7 15	1 46	11 55	17 27	25 55	27 12	7 06	18 28	13 50

EPHEMERIS CALCULATED FOR 12 MIDNIGHT GREENWICH MEAN TIME. ALL OTHER DATA AND FACING ASPECTARIAN PAGE IN **EASTERN STANDARD TIME (BOLD)** AND PACIFIC STANDARD TIME (REGULAR).

AUGUST 2003

1 FRIDAY
☽ □ ♇	**4:02 am**	1:02 am
☽ ⚺ ⚶	**6:55 am**	3:55 am
☽ ⚺ ♃	**4:14 pm**	1:14 pm
☽ □ ⚳	**8:06 pm**	5:06 pm
☽ ⚻ ⚴	**9:24 pm**	6:24 pm

2 SATURDAY
☽ ⚻ ♅	**4:43 am**	1:43 am
☽ ⚺ ☿	**9:20 am**	6:20 am
☽ ✶ ♀	**11:20 am**	8:20 am
☉ ⚻ ♂	**12:13 pm**	9:13 am
☽ ⚺ ⚵	**2:44 pm**	11:44 am
☽ □ ♄	**2:50 pm**	11:50 am
☽ ⚻ ♂	**6:59 pm**	3:59 pm
☽ ✶ ☉	**7:31 pm**	4:31 pm
☽ △ ♆	**10:08 pm**	7:08 pm
☽ □ ⚷		10:18 pm

3 SUNDAY
☽ □ ⚷	**1:18 am**	
☽ ✶ ♇	**7:42 am**	4:42 am
☽ ☌ ⚶	**12:10 pm**	9:10 am
☽ ✶ ♃	**8:33 pm**	5:33 pm
☽ △ ⚳		10:01 pm
☽ ☍ ⚴		10:17 pm
♄ △ ⚵		11:42 pm

4 MONDAY
☽ △ ⚳	**1:01 am**	
☽ ☍ ⚴	**1:17 am**	
♄ △ ⚵	**2:42 am**	
♀ ⚺ ♄	**6:45 am**	3:45 am
♀ □ ⚵	**6:55 am**	3:55 am
☽ △ ♅	**7:57 am**	4:57 am
☉ ☍ ♆	**8:54 am**	5:54 am
⚳ ✶ ⚴	**1:49 pm**	10:49 am
☽ ✶ ☿	**6:11 pm**	3:11 pm
☽ △ ♄	**6:32 pm**	3:32 pm
☽ ☌ ⚵	**6:35 pm**	3:35 pm
☽ □ ♀	**7:33 pm**	4:33 pm
☽ △ ♂	**9:56 pm**	6:56 pm
☿ ✶ ♄	**10:12 pm**	7:12 pm
☿ ✶ ⚵	**10:58 pm**	7:58 pm
☽ □ ♆		10:14 pm
☽ □ ☉		11:28 pm

Eastern Standard Time in bold type
Pacific Standard Time in medium type

5 TUESDAY
☽ □ ♆	**1:14 am**	
☽ □ ☉	**2:28 am**	
☽ ✶ ⚷	**4:17 am**	1:17 am
☽ ⚺ ♇	**10:46 am**	7:46 am
☽ ⚺ ⚶	**4:49 pm**	1:49 pm
♀ ⚻ ♂	**9:02 pm**	6:02 pm
☽ □ ♃		9:22 pm

6 WEDNESDAY
☽ □ ♃	**12:22 am**	
☉ ⚻ ⚷	**4:03 am**	1:03 am
☽ ⚻ ⚴	**4:38 am**	1:38 am
☽ ⚻ ⚳	**5:25 am**	2:25 am
☿ ☍ ♂	**8:12 am**	5:12 am
☽ □ ♅	**10:47 am**	7:47 am
☽ ⚻ ♄	**9:51 pm**	6:51 pm
☽ ⚺ ⚵	**10:06 pm**	7:06 pm
☽ □ ♂		9:28 pm
☽ □ ☿		11:12 pm

7 THURSDAY
☽ □ ♂	**12:28 am**	
☽ □ ☿	**2:12 am**	
☽ △ ♀	**3:19 am**	12:19 am
☽ ✶ ♆	**4:01 am**	1:01 am
☽ ⚺ ⚷	**6:59 am**	3:59 am
☽ △ ☉	**9:02 am**	6:02 am
♀ ☍ ♆	**11:18 am**	8:18 am
☽ ☌ ♇	**1:35 pm**	10:35 am
☽ ✶ ⚶	**9:15 pm**	6:15 pm
☿ ⚻ ♆	**10:37 pm**	7:37 pm

8 FRIDAY
☽ △ ♃	**4:01 am**	1:01 am
☽ △ ⚴	**7:48 am**	4:48 am
☽ ☍ ⚳	**9:40 am**	6:40 am
☽ ✶ ♅	**1:31 pm**	10:31 am
♀ ⚻ ⚷	**7:55 pm**	4:55 pm
☽ ☍ ♄		10:11 pm
☽ ✶ ⚵		10:39 pm
☽ ✶ ♂		11:56 pm

9 SATURDAY
☽ ☍ ♄	**1:11 am**	
☽ ✶ ⚵	**1:39 am**	
☽ ✶ ♂	**2:56 am**	
☽ ⚺ ♆	**6:53 am**	3:53 am
☿ △ ⚷	**8:01 am**	5:01 am
☽ ☌ ⚷	**9:47 am**	6:47 am
☽ △ ☿	**9:57 am**	6:57 am
☽ ⚻ ♀	**11:10 am**	8:10 am
☽ ⚻ ☉	**3:46 pm**	12:46 pm
☽ ⚺ ♇	**4:35 pm**	1:35 pm
☽ □ ⚶		11:01 pm

10 SUNDAY
☽ □ ⚶	**2:01 am**	
☉ △ ♇	**3:42 am**	12:42 am
☽ ⚻ ♃	**8:03 am**	5:03 am
☽ □ ⚴	**11:23 am**	8:23 am
☽ ⚻ ⚳	**2:25 pm**	11:25 am
☽ ⚺ ♅	**4:46 pm**	1:46 pm

11 MONDAY
☽ ⚻ ♄	**5:16 am**	2:16 am
☽ □ ⚵	**6:00 am**	3:00 am
☽ ⚺ ♂	**6:05 am**	3:05 am
♂ △ ⚵	**9:11 am**	6:11 am
☽ ☌ ♆	**10:35 am**	7:35 am
☽ ⚺ ⚷	**1:30 pm**	10:30 am
☽ ⚻ ☿	**6:31 pm**	3:31 pm
☽ ☍ ♀	**8:17 pm**	5:17 pm
☽ ✶ ♇	**8:39 pm**	5:39 pm
☽ ☍ ☉	**11:48 pm**	8:48 pm
♀ △ ♇		9:19 pm

12 TUESDAY
♀ △ ♇	**12:19 am**	
☽ △ ⚶	**8:12 am**	5:12 am
☽ ☍ ♃	**1:35 pm**	10:35 am
☽ ✶ ⚴	**4:27 pm**	1:27 pm
☽ △ ⚳	**8:52 pm**	5:52 pm
☽ ☌ ♅	**9:38 pm**	6:38 pm
♂ △ ♄	**9:55 pm**	6:55 pm
☿ □ ♇	**10:01 pm**	7:01 pm

13 WEDNESDAY
☽ ☌ ♂	**11:01 am**	8:01 am
☽ △ ♄	**11:19 am**	8:19 am
☽ △ ⚵	**12:25 pm**	9:25 am
☽ ⚺ ♆	**4:21 pm**	1:21 pm
☽ ✶ ⚷	**7:20 pm**	4:20 pm
♅ △ ⚳	**9:51 pm**	6:51 pm

14 THURSDAY
☽ □ ♇	**3:01 am**	12:01 am
☽ ☍ ☿	**5:29 am**	2:29 am
☽ ⚻ ♀	**8:27 am**	5:27 am
☽ ⚻ ☉	**10:48 am**	7:48 am
☽ ⚻ ⚶	**5:13 pm**	2:13 pm
☽ ⚻ ♃	**9:54 pm**	6:54 pm
☽ ⚺ ⚴		9:12 pm

15 FRIDAY
☽ ⚺ ⚴	**12:12 am**	
☽ ⚺ ♅	**5:17 am**	2:17 am
☽ □ ⚳	**6:20 am**	3:20 am
☽ ⚺ ♂	**6:45 pm**	3:45 pm
☽ □ ♄	**8:27 pm**	5:27 pm
☽ ⚻ ⚵	**10:02 pm**	7:02 pm
☽ ✶ ♆		10:10 pm

16 SATURDAY
☽ ✶ ♆	**1:10 am**	
☽ □ ⚷	**4:16 am**	1:16 am
☽ △ ♇	**12:33 pm**	9:33 am
☽ ⚻ ☿	**7:51 pm**	4:51 pm
☽ △ ♀		9:55 pm
☽ △ ☉		10:49 pm

17 SUNDAY
☽ △ ♀	**12:55 am**	
☽ △ ☉	**1:49 am**	
☽ ☍ ⚶	**5:50 am**	2:50 am
☽ △ ♃	**9:36 am**	6:36 am
☽ ☌ ⚴	**11:08 am**	8:08 am
☽ ✶ ♅	**4:05 pm**	1:05 pm
☽ ✶ ⚳	**7:15 pm**	4:15 pm

18 MONDAY
☽ ✶ ♂	**5:17 am**	2:17 am
☽ ✶ ♄	**8:40 am**	5:40 am
☽ ☍ ⚵	**10:49 am**	7:49 am
☽ □ ♆	**12:54 pm**	9:54 am
☉ ☌ ♀	**1:05 pm**	10:05 am
☽ △ ⚷	**4:03 pm**	1:03 pm
☽ ⚻ ♇		9:47 pm

19 TUESDAY
☽ ⚻ ♇	**12:47 am**	
☽ △ ☿	**12:32 pm**	9:32 am
☽ □ ☉	**7:48 pm**	4:48 pm
☽ □ ♀	**8:36 pm**	5:36 pm
☽ ⚻ ⚶	**8:55 pm**	5:55 pm
☽ □ ♃	**11:29 pm**	8:29 pm
☽ ⚺ ⚴		9:01 pm
♀ ✶ ⚶		10:13 pm

20 WEDNESDAY
☽ ⚺ ⚴	**12:01 am**	
♀ ✶ ⚶	**1:13 am**	
☽ □ ♅	**4:43 am**	1:43 am
☽ ⚺ ⚳	**10:02 am**	7:02 am
☽ □ ♂	**4:59 pm**	1:59 pm
☉ ✶ ⚶	**8:45 pm**	5:45 pm
☽ ⚺ ♄	**10:04 pm**	7:04 pm
☽ ⚻ ⚵		9:47 pm
☽ △ ♆		10:37 pm

21 THURSDAY
☽ ⚻ ⚵	**12:47 am**	
☽ △ ♆	**1:37 am**	
☽ ⚻ ⚷	**4:42 am**	1:42 am
♀ ☌ ♃	**5:23 am**	2:23 am
♀ △ ⚴	**5:33 am**	2:33 am
♃ △ ⚴	**6:20 am**	3:20 am
☽ ☍ ♇	**1:29 pm**	10:29 am
☉ △ ⚴		9:05 pm

22 FRIDAY
☉ △ ⚴	**12:05 am**	
☽ □ ☿	**4:11 am**	1:11 am
☉ ☌ ♃	**5:08 am**	2:08 am
☽ △ ⚶	**11:30 am**	8:30 am
☽ ✶ ♀	**12:13 pm**	9:13 am
☽ ✶ ♃	**12:45 pm**	9:45 am
☽ ✶ ☉	**1:15 pm**	10:15 am
☽ ✶ ⚴	**3:39 pm**	12:39 pm
☽ △ ♅	**4:30 pm**	1:30 pm
♆ □ ⚵	**6:29 pm**	3:29 pm
☽ ☌ ⚳	**11:37 pm**	8:37 pm
♀ ☍ ♅	**11:49 pm**	8:49 pm

23 SATURDAY
☽ △ ♂	**3:18 am**	12:18 am
☿ ☍ ⚶	**6:27 am**	3:27 am
☽ ☌ ♄	**9:49 am**	6:49 am
☽ ⚻ ♆	**12:37 pm**	9:37 am
☽ △ ⚵	**12:58 pm**	9:58 am
☽ ☍ ⚷	**3:30 pm**	12:30 pm
☽ ⚻ ♇	**11:58 pm**	8:58 pm

24 SUNDAY
☉ ☍ ♅	**5:02 am**	2:02 am
☽ ✶ ☿	**3:51 pm**	12:51 pm
☽ □ ♀	**9:24 pm**	6:24 pm
☽ □ ⚶	**10:52 pm**	7:52 pm
☽ ⚺ ♃	**10:55 pm**	7:55 pm
☽ ⚻ ♅		10:17 pm
♃ ✶ ⚶		10:21 pm
☽ ⚺ ☉		11:58 pm

25 MONDAY
☽ ⚻ ♅	**1:17 am**	
♃ ✶ ⚶	**1:21 am**	
☽ ⚺ ☉	**2:58 am**	
☽ ⚺ ♀	**6:38 am**	3:38 am
☽ ⚺ ⚳	**9:43 am**	6:43 am
☽ ⚻ ♂	**10:31 am**	7:31 am
☽ ⚺ ♄	**6:08 pm**	3:08 pm
☽ ☍ ♆	**8:14 pm**	5:14 pm
☽ □ ⚵	**9:37 pm**	6:37 pm
☽ ⚻ ⚷	**10:55 pm**	7:55 pm
♂ △ ⚳		12:00 pm

26 TUESDAY
♂ △ ⚳	**3:00 am**	
☽ △ ♇	**7:00 am**	4:00 am
♀ ☍ ♂	**5:17 pm**	2:17 pm
☽ ⚺ ☿	**10:52 pm**	7:52 pm

27 WEDNESDAY
☽ △ ⚴	**3:05 am**	12:05 am
♀ ✶ ⚳	**3:15 am**	12:15 am
☽ ☌ ♃	**5:28 am**	2:28 am
☽ ✶ ⚶	**6:25 am**	3:25 am
☽ ☍ ♅	**6:41 am**	3:41 am
☽ ☌ ☉	**12:26 pm**	9:26 am
♅ △ ⚶	**1:54 pm**	10:54 am
☽ ☍ ♂	**2:35 pm**	11:35 am
☽ ✶ ⚳	**4:12 pm**	1:12 pm
☽ ☌ ♀	**5:06 pm**	2:06 pm
☽ ✶ ♄	**11:10 pm**	8:10 pm
☽ ⚻ ♆		9:43 pm

28 THURSDAY
☽ ⚻ ♆	**12:43 am**	
☽ ✶ ⚵	**3:00 am**	12:00 am
☽ △ ⚷	**3:16 am**	12:16 am
☉ ☍ ♂	**12:59 pm**	9:59 am
⚷ ✶ ⚵	**5:00 pm**	2:00 pm
☽ ☌ ☿		11:26 pm

29 FRIDAY
☽ ☌ ☿	**2:26 am**	
☽ ⚻ ♀	**6:17 am**	3:17 am
☽ ⚺ ♃	**9:30 am**	6:30 am
☽ ⚻ ♅	**9:45 am**	6:45 am
☽ ⚺ ⚶	**11:22 am**	8:22 am
☽ ⚻ ♂	**4:37 pm**	1:37 pm
☽ ⚺ ☉	**7:11 pm**	4:11 pm
☽ □ ⚳	**8:24 pm**	5:24 pm
♃ ☍ ♅	**11:37 pm**	8:37 pm
☽ ⚺ ♀		9:51 pm
☽ □ ♄		11:16 pm

30 SATURDAY
☽ ⚺ ♀	**12:51 am**	
☽ □ ♄	**2:16 am**	
☽ △ ♆	**3:22 am**	12:22 am
☽ □ ⚷	**5:51 am**	2:51 am
☽ ⚺ ⚵	**6:32 am**	3:32 am
☽ ✶ ♇	**1:37 pm**	10:37 am
♀ ✶ ♄	**6:23 pm**	3:23 pm
☉ ✶ ⚳	**10:49 pm**	7:49 pm

31 SUNDAY
☽ ⚺ ☿	**4:11 am**	1:11 am
♀ ⚻ ♆	**5:21 am**	2:21 am
☽ ☍ ♀	**8:26 am**	5:26 am
☽ △ ♅	**11:55 am**	8:55 am
☽ ✶ ♃	**12:35 pm**	9:35 am
☽ ☌ ⚶	**3:22 pm**	12:22 pm
☽ △ ♂	**5:59 pm**	2:59 pm
☽ △ ⚳	**11:56 pm**	8:56 pm
☽ ✶ ☉		10:06 pm

AUGUST 2003

☽ Last Aspect day	EST	hr:mn / PST	asp	☽ Ingress sign	day	EST	hr:mn / PST
1	**4:02 am**	1:02 am	□ ♇	♎	1		10:48 pm
1	**4:02 am**	1:02 am	□ ♇	♎	2	**1:48 am**	
3	**8:33 pm**	5:33 pm	⚹ ♃	♏	4	**5:12 am**	2:12 am
5		9:22 pm	□ ♃	♐	6	**8:11 am**	5:11 am
6	**12:22 am**		□ ♃	♐	6	**8:11 am**	5:11 am
8	**4:01 am**	1:01 am	△ ♃	♑	8	**11:02 am**	8:02 am
9	**9:57 am**	6:57 am	△ ☿	♒	10	**2:23 pm**	11:23 am
12	**1:35 pm**	10:35 am	☍ ♃	♓	12	**7:19 pm**	4:19 pm
14	**5:29 am**	2:29 am	☍ ☿	♈	15	**3:00 am**	12:00 am
17	**9:36 am**	6:36 am	△ ♃	♉	17	**1:52 pm**	10:52 am
19	**11:29 pm**	8:29 pm	□ ♃	♊	19		11:41 pm
19	**11:29 pm**	8:29 pm	□ ♃	♊	20	**2:41 am**	
22	**1:15 pm**	10:15 am	⚹ ☉	♋	22	**2:44 pm**	11:44 am
24	**3:51 pm**	12:51 am	⚹ ☿	♌	24	**11:48 pm**	8:48 pm
26	**7:00 am**	4:00 am	△ ♇	♍	27	**5:27 am**	2:27 am
28		11:26 pm	☌ ☿	♎	29	**8:41 am**	5:41 am
29	**2:26 am**		☌ ☿	♎	29	**8:41 am**	5:41 am
30	**1:37 pm**	10:37 am	⚹ ♇	♏	31	**11:00 am**	8:00 am

☽ Phases & Eclipses phase	day	EST	hr:mn / PST
2nd Quarter	4		11:28 pm
2nd Quarter	5	**2:28 am**	
Full Moon	11	**11:48 pm**	8:48 pm
4th Quarter	19	**7:48 pm**	4:48 pm
New Moon	27	**12:26 pm**	9:26 am

Planet Ingress	day	EST	hr:mn / PST
⚳ ♋	10	**1:15 pm**	10:15 am
♀ ♍	22	**6:35 am**	3:35 am
☉ ♍	23	**8:08 am**	5:08 am
⚵ ♏	25		10:27 pm
⚵ ♏	26	**1:27 am**	
♃ ♍	27	**4:26 am**	1:26 am

Planetary Motion	day	EST	hr:mn / PST
⚴ ℞	22	**3:56 pm**	12:56 pm
☿ ℞	28	**8:41 am**	5:41 am
♇ D	28	**10:34 pm**	7:34 pm

DATE		SID.TIME	SUN	MOON	NODE	MERCURY	VENUS	MARS	JUPITER	SATURN	URANUS	NEPTUNE	PLUTO	CERES	PALLAS	JUNO	VESTA	CHIRON
1	F	20:36:46	8 ♌ 21 42	12 ♍ 15	26 ♉ ℞ 33	2 ♍ 05	3 ♌ 28	10 ♓ ℞ 05	24 ♌ 16	7 ♋ 22	1 ♓ ℞ 44	11 ♒ ℞ 53	17 ♐ ℞ 26	26 ♊ 18	27 ♈ 20	7 ♏ 14	18 ♎ 53	13 ♑ ℞ 47
2	Sa	20:40:42	9 19 07	26 04	26 24	3 32	4 42	10 03	24 29	7 29	1 42	11 51	17 26	26 41	27 27	7 23	19 18	13 44
3	Su	20:44:39	10 16 32	10 ♎ 00	26 19	4 56	5 56	9 59	24 42	7 36	1 40	11 50	17 25	27 04	27 34	7 33	19 43	13 41
4	M	20:48:35	11 13 58	24 01	26 16	6 19	7 10	9 55	24 55	7 43	1 38	11 48	17 24	27 27	27 40	7 42	20 08	13 38
5	T	20:52:32	12 11 25	8 ♏ 06	26 D 15	7 40	8 24	9 50	25 08	7 50	1 36	11 47	17 23	27 50	27 46	7 52	20 34	13 35
6	W	20:56:29	13 08 52	22 14	26 ℞ 15	8 59	9 38	9 45	25 21	7 57	1 33	11 45	17 22	28 13	27 52	8 01	20 59	13 32
7	Th	21:00:25	14 06 20	6 ♐ 23	26 15	10 16	10 52	9 38	25 34	8 03	1 31	11 43	17 22	28 35	27 58	8 11	21 25	13 29
8	F	21:04:22	15 03 49	20 33	26 13	11 30	12 06	9 31	25 47	8 10	1 29	11 42	17 21	28 58	28 03	8 22	21 50	13 26
9	Sa	21:08:18	16 01 19	4 ♑ 41	26 09	12 43	13 20	9 23	26 00	8 17	1 27	11 40	17 20	29 20	28 08	8 32	22 16	13 23
10	Su	21:12:15	16 58 50	18 44	26 02	13 53	14 34	9 15	26 13	8 24	1 24	11 38	17 20	29 43	28 13	8 43	22 42	13 20
11	M	21:16:11	17 56 21	2 ♒ 40	25 53	15 01	15 48	9 06	26 26	8 30	1 22	11 37	17 19	0 ♋ 05	28 17	8 54	23 08	13 17
12	T	21:20:08	18 53 54	16 23	25 41	16 07	17 02	8 56	26 39	8 37	1 20	11 35	17 19	0 28	28 21	9 05	23 34	13 15
13	W	21:24:05	19 51 27	29 50	25 29	17 10	18 16	8 46	26 52	8 43	1 17	11 34	17 18	0 50	28 25	9 16	24 00	13 12
14	Th	21:28:01	20 49 02	12 ♓ 58	25 17	18 11	19 30	8 35	27 05	8 50	1 15	11 32	17 18	1 12	28 28	9 27	24 27	13 09
15	F	21:31:58	21 46 38	25 48	25 07	19 09	20 45	8 23	27 18	8 56	1 13	11 30	17 17	1 34	28 31	9 39	24 53	13 07
16	Sa	21:35:54	22 44 15	8 ♈ 18	24 58	20 04	21 59	8 11	27 31	9 03	1 10	11 29	17 17	1 56	28 34	9 51	25 20	13 04
17	Su	21:39:51	23 41 54	20 32	24 53	20 56	23 13	7 58	27 44	9 09	1 08	11 27	17 16	2 18	28 36	10 03	25 47	13 02
18	M	21:43:47	24 39 35	2 ♉ 33	24 50	21 45	24 27	7 45	27 57	9 15	1 06	11 26	17 16	2 40	28 38	10 15	26 14	13 00
19	T	21:47:44	25 37 17	14 25	24 49	22 31	25 41	7 31	28 10	9 22	1 03	11 24	17 16	3 02	28 40	10 27	26 41	12 57
20	W	21:51:40	26 35 00	26 13	24 D 48	23 13	26 56	7 17	28 23	9 28	1 01	11 22	17 15	3 24	28 41	10 40	27 08	12 55
21	Th	21:55:37	27 32 45	8 ♊ 03	24 ℞ 48	23 52	28 10	7 02	28 36	9 34	0 59	11 21	17 15	3 46	28 42	10 52	27 35	12 53
22	F	21:59:33	28 30 32	20 01	24 47	24 26	29 24	6 47	28 49	9 40	0 56	11 19	17 15	4 07	28 ℞ 43	11 05	28 02	12 51
23	Sa	22:03:30	29 28 21	2 ♋ 11	24 44	24 57	0 ♍ 38	6 32	29 03	9 46	0 54	11 18	17 15	4 29	28 43	11 18	28 30	12 49
24	Su	22:07:27	0 ♍ 26 11	14 37	24 38	25 23	1 53	6 17	29 16	9 52	0 51	11 16	17 15	4 50	28 43	11 31	28 57	12 47
25	M	22:11:23	1 24 03	27 24	24 29	25 44	3 07	6 01	29 29	9 58	0 49	11 15	17 14	5 12	28 42	11 45	29 25	12 45
26	T	22:15:20	2 21 57	10 ♌ 32	24 19	26 01	4 21	5 45	29 42	10 04	0 47	11 13	17 14	5 33	28 41	11 58	29 53	12 43
27	W	22:19:16	3 19 52	24 02	24 07	26 12	5 36	5 29	29 55	10 09	0 44	11 12	17 14	5 54	28 40	12 12	0 ♏ 20	12 41
28	Th	22:23:13	4 17 48	7 ♍ 50	23 55	26 ℞ 18	6 50	5 13	0 ♍ 08	10 15	0 42	11 10	17 14	6 15	28 38	12 26	0 48	12 40
29	F	22:27:09	5 15 46	21 54	23 44	26 19	8 04	4 57	0 21	10 21	0 39	11 09	17 D 14	6 36	28 35	12 40	1 16	12 38
30	Sa	22:31:06	6 13 46	6 ♎ 08	23 35	26 13	9 19	4 41	0 34	10 26	0 37	11 07	17 14	6 57	28 33	12 54	1 44	12 37
31	Su	22:35:02	7 11 47	20 27	23 29	26 02	10 33	4 25	0 47	10 32	0 35	11 06	17 14	7 18	28 30	13 08	2 13	12 35

EPHEMERIS CALCULATED FOR 12 MIDNIGHT GREENWICH MEAN TIME. ALL OTHER DATA AND FACING ASPECTARIAN PAGE IN **EASTERN STANDARD TIME (BOLD)** AND PACIFIC STANDARD TIME (REGULAR).

SEPTEMBER 2003

1 MONDAY
- ☽ ⚹ ☉ **1:06 am**
- ☽ △ ♄ **4:52 am** 1:52 am
- ☽ □ ♆ **5:34 am** 2:34 am
- ☽ ⚹ ♀ **7:55 am** 4:55 am
- ☽ ⚹ ⚷ **8:04 am** 5:04 am
- ♀ △ ⚷ **9:37 am** 6:37 am
- ☽ ☌ ⚵ **9:42 am** 6:42 am
- ☽ ⚺ ♇ **3:58 pm** 12:58 pm

2 TUESDAY
- ☽ ⚹ ☿ **5:18 am** 2:18 am
- ♀ ⚹ ⚵ **8:55 am** 5:55 am
- ☽ ⚻ ♀ **10:42 am** 7:42 am
- ☽ □ ♅ **2:19 pm** 11:19 am
- ☽ □ ♃ **3:55 pm** 12:55 pm
- ♂ △ ⚶ **7:28 pm** 4:28 pm
- ☽ □ ♂ **7:42 pm** 4:42 pm
- ☽ ⚺ ⚶ **7:43 pm** 4:43 pm

3 WEDNESDAY
- ☽ ⚻ ⚳ **3:53 am** 12:53 am
- ☽ □ ☉ **7:34 am** 4:34 am
- ☽ ⚻ ♄ **7:58 am** 4:58 am
- ☽ ⚹ ♆ **8:16 am** 5:16 am
- ☽ ⚺ ⚷ **10:49 am** 7:49 am
- ☽ ⚺ ⚵ **1:27 pm** 10:27 am
- ☉ ⚹ ♄ **1:48 pm** 10:48 am
- ☽ □ ♀ **3:40 pm** 12:40 pm
- ☉ ⚻ ♆ **5:31 pm** 2:31 pm
- ☽ ☌ ♇ **6:55 pm** 3:55 pm

4 THURSDAY
- ☽ □ ☿ **6:23 am** 3:23 am
- ☽ △ ♀ **1:40 pm** 10:40 am
- ☽ ⚹ ♅ **5:31 pm** 2:31 pm
- ☽ △ ♃ **8:06 pm** 5:06 pm
- ☽ ⚹ ♂ **10:14 pm** 7:14 pm
- ♄ ⚻ ♆ 9:09 pm
- ☽ ⚹ ⚶ 9:59 pm

5 FRIDAY
- ♄ ⚻ ♆ **12:09 am**
- ☽ ⚹ ⚶ **12:59 am**
- ♀ □ ♇ **4:31 am** 1:31 am
- ☉ △ ⚷ **5:53 am** 2:53 am
- ☽ ☍ ⚳ **8:47 am** 5:47 am
- ☽ ⚺ ♆ **11:52 am** 8:52 am
- ☽ ☍ ♄ **11:58 am** 8:58 am
- ☽ ☌ ⚷ **2:29 pm** 11:29 am
- ☽ △ ☉ **3:09 pm** 12:09 pm
- ☽ ⚹ ⚵ **6:12 pm** 3:12 pm
- ☽ ⚺ ♇ **10:50 pm** 7:50 pm
- ☽ △ ♀ 9:39 pm

6 SATURDAY
- ☽ △ ♀ **12:39 am**
- ☽ △ ☿ **7:43 am** 4:43 am
- ☽ □ ♀ **5:37 pm** 2:37 pm
- ☽ ⚺ ♅ **9:46 pm** 6:46 pm
- ☽ ⚻ ♃ 10:25 pm
- ☽ ⚺ ♂ 10:51 pm

7 SUNDAY
- ☽ ⚻ ♃ **1:25 am**
- ☽ ⚺ ♂ **1:51 am**
- ☽ □ ⚶ **7:30 am** 4:30 am
- ☽ ⚻ ⚳ **2:54 pm** 11:54 am
- ♂ ☍ ♃ **3:00 pm** 12:00 pm
- ☽ ☌ ♆ **4:39 pm** 1:39 pm
- ☽ ⚻ ♄ **5:09 pm** 2:09 pm
- ☽ ⚺ ⚷ **7:22 pm** 4:22 pm
- ☽ ⚻ ☉ 9:14 pm
- ☽ □ ⚵ 9:16 pm
- ☿ ☌ ♀ 9:35 pm
- ☉ ⚹ ⚵ 9:41 pm

8 MONDAY
- ☽ ⚻ ☉ **12:14 am**
- ☽ □ ⚵ **12:16 am**
- ☿ ☌ ♀ **12:35 am**
- ☉ ⚹ ⚵ **12:41 am**
- ☽ ⚹ ♇ **4:01 am** 1:01 am
- ☽ ⚻ ☿ **9:41 am** 6:41 am
- ☽ ⚻ ♀ **11:21 am** 8:21 am
- ☽ ⚹ ♀ **10:55 pm** 7:55 pm

9 TUESDAY
- ☽ ☌ ♅ **3:30 am** 12:30 am
- ☽ ☌ ♂ **7:00 am** 4:00 am
- ☽ ☍ ♃ **8:20 am** 5:20 am
- ☽ △ ⚶ **3:49 pm** 12:49 pm
- ☽ △ ⚳ **10:50 pm** 7:50 pm
- ☽ ⚺ ♆ **11:08 pm** 8:08 pm
- ☽ △ ♄ 9:05 pm
- ☽ ⚹ ⚷ 10:59 pm

10 WEDNESDAY
- ☽ △ ♄ **12:05 am**
- ☽ ⚹ ⚷ **1:59 am**
- ☉ □ ♇ **4:37 am** 1:37 am
- ☽ △ ⚵ **8:16 am** 5:16 am
- ♆ ⚻ ⚳ **10:13 am** 7:13 am
- ☽ □ ♇ **11:05 am** 8:05 am
- ☽ ☍ ☉ **11:36 am** 8:36 am
- ☽ ☍ ☿ **12:56 pm** 9:56 am
- ☉ ☌ ☿ **8:57 pm** 5:57 pm
- ☽ ☍ ♀ 9:41 pm

11 THURSDAY
- ☽ ☍ ♀ **12:41 am**
- ☽ ⚺ ♀ **6:12 am** 3:12 am
- ☽ ⚺ ♅ **11:24 am** 8:24 am
- ☿ □ ♇ **12:42 pm** 9:42 am
- ☽ ⚺ ♂ **2:20 pm** 11:20 am
- ☽ ⚻ ♃ **5:36 pm** 2:36 pm
- ☽ ⚻ ⚶ 11:45 pm

12 FRIDAY
- ☽ ⚻ ⚶ **2:45 am**
- ☽ ⚹ ♆ **8:01 am** 5:01 am
- ☽ □ ⚳ **9:20 am** 6:20 am
- ☽ □ ♄ **9:27 am** 6:27 am
- ☽ □ ⚷ **11:04 am** 8:04 am
- ☿ ⚹ ⚵ **12:03 pm** 9:03 am
- ♄ ☌ ⚳ **3:31 pm** 12:31 pm
- ☽ ⚻ ☿ **6:19 pm** 3:19 pm
- ☽ ⚻ ⚵ **6:57 pm** 3:57 pm
- ☽ △ ♇ **8:40 pm** 5:40 pm
- ☽ ⚻ ☉ 11:10 pm

13 SATURDAY
- ☽ ⚻ ☉ **2:10 am**
- ♀ ⚻ ♀ **3:41 am** 12:41 am
- ☽ ☌ ♀ **3:58 pm** 12:58 pm
- ☽ ⚻ ♀ **5:33 pm** 2:33 pm
- ☽ ⚹ ♅ **9:54 pm** 6:54 pm
- ☽ ⚹ ♂ 9:18 pm

14 SUNDAY
- ☽ ⚹ ♂ **12:18 am**
- ☽ △ ♃ **5:38 am** 2:38 am
- ☽ ☍ ⚶ **4:39 pm** 1:39 pm
- ☽ □ ♆ **7:29 pm** 4:29 pm
- ☽ ⚹ ♄ **9:26 pm** 6:26 pm
- ☽ ⚹ ⚳ **10:35 pm** 7:35 pm
- ☽ △ ⚷ **10:43 pm** 7:43 pm
- ☽ △ ☿ 11:19 pm

15 MONDAY
- ☽ △ ☿ **2:19 am**
- ⚷ ☍ ⚳ **3:24 am** 12:24 am
- ☽ ☍ ⚵ **8:19 am** 5:19 am
- ☽ ⚻ ♇ **8:44 am** 5:44 am
- ♀ ⚻ ♅ **10:37 am** 7:37 am
- ☽ △ ☉ **7:47 pm** 4:47 pm

16 TUESDAY
- ♇ ⚺ ⚵ **3:07 am** 12:07 am
- ☽ ⚺ ♀ **3:44 am** 12:44 am
- ♀ ⚻ ♂ **4:25 am** 1:25 am
- ☽ □ ♅ **10:25 am** 7:25 am
- ☽ □ ♂ **12:17 pm** 9:17 am
- ☽ △ ♀ **1:19 pm** 10:19 am
- ☽ □ ♃ **7:35 pm** 4:35 pm
- ☿ ⚹ ⚳ 10:05 pm

17 WEDNESDAY
- ☿ ⚹ ⚳ **1:05 am**
- ☽ ⚻ ⚶ **8:15 am** 5:15 am
- ☽ △ ♆ **8:22 am** 5:22 am
- ☽ ⚺ ♄ **10:46 am** 7:46 am
- ♆ □ ⚶ **10:50 am** 7:50 am
- ☽ ⚻ ⚷ **11:41 am** 8:41 am
- ☽ □ ☿ **12:28 pm** 9:28 am
- ☽ ⚺ ⚳ **1:13 pm** 10:13 am
- ☽ ☍ ♇ **9:45 pm** 6:45 pm
- ☽ ⚻ ⚵ **10:43 pm** 7:43 pm

18 THURSDAY
- ☽ □ ☉ **2:03 pm** 11:03 am
- ☽ ⚹ ♀ **3:35 pm** 12:35 pm
- ☿ △ ⚷ **5:32 pm** 2:32 pm
- ☽ △ ♅ **10:50 pm** 7:50 pm
- ☽ △ ♂ 9:14 pm

19 FRIDAY
- ☽ △ ♂ **12:14 am**
- ☉ ⚻ ♀ **6:02 am** 3:02 am
- ☽ □ ♀ **8:44 am** 5:44 am
- ☽ ⚹ ♃ **8:59 am** 5:59 am
- ♀ ⚺ ♃ **11:41 am** 8:41 am
- ☽ ⚻ ♆ **8:10 pm** 5:10 pm
- ☽ △ ⚶ **10:39 pm** 7:39 pm
- ☽ ☌ ♄ **10:53 pm** 7:53 pm
- ☽ ⚹ ☿ **11:08 pm** 8:08 pm
- ☽ ☍ ⚷ **11:27 pm** 8:27 pm
- ☽ ☌ ⚳ 11:25 pm

20 SATURDAY
- ☽ ☌ ⚳ **2:25 am**
- ♄ △ ⚶ **5:03 am** 2:03 am
- ☽ ⚻ ♇ **9:07 am** 6:07 am
- ☿ ⚹ ⚶ **10:37 am** 7:37 am
- ☽ △ ⚵ **11:20 am** 8:20 am
- ⚷ ⚹ ⚶ **6:29 pm** 3:29 pm
- ☽ □ ♀ 10:03 pm

21 SUNDAY
- ☽ □ ♀ **1:03 am**
- ☽ ⚹ ☉ **5:21 am** 2:21 am
- ☽ ⚻ ♅ **8:37 am** 5:37 am
- ☽ ⚻ ♂ **9:40 am** 6:40 am
- ☿ △ ⚷ **2:52 pm** 11:52 am
- ☽ ⚺ ♃ **7:14 pm** 4:14 pm
- ☽ ⚹ ♀ 9:05 pm

22 MONDAY
- ☽ ⚹ ♀ **12:05 am**
- ☽ ☍ ♆ **4:40 am** 1:40 am
- ☽ ⚺ ♄ **7:32 am** 4:32 am
- ☽ ⚻ ⚷ **7:49 am** 4:49 am
- ☽ ⚺ ☿ **8:11 am** 5:11 am
- ☽ □ ⚶ **9:15 am** 6:15 am
- ☽ ⚺ ⚳ **11:52 am** 8:52 am
- ☽ △ ♇ **4:51 pm** 1:51 pm
- ☽ □ ⚵ **8:04 pm** 5:04 pm
- ☉ ⚻ ♅ **11:00 pm** 8:00 pm

23 TUESDAY
- ☽ △ ♀ **6:49 am** 3:49 am
- ☉ ⚻ ♂ **10:54 am** 7:54 am
- ☽ ☍ ♅ **2:33 pm** 11:33 am
- ☽ ☍ ♂ **3:25 pm** 12:25 pm
- ☽ ⚺ ☉ **3:47 pm** 12:47 pm
- ♀ △ ♆ 9:03 pm
- ☽ ☌ ♃ 10:23 pm

24 WEDNESDAY
- ♀ △ ♆ **12:03 am**
- ☽ ☌ ♃ **1:23 am**
- ☽ ⚻ ♆ **9:20 am** 6:20 am
- ☽ ⚺ ♀ **10:15 am** 7:15 am
- ☽ ⚹ ♄ **12:17 pm** 9:17 am
- ☽ △ ⚷ **12:22 pm** 9:22 am
- ☽ ☌ ☿ **2:44 pm** 11:44 am
- ☽ ⚹ ⚶ **3:36 pm** 12:36 pm
- ☽ ⚹ ⚳ **5:14 pm** 2:14 pm
- ☽ □ ♇ **8:52 pm** 5:52 pm
- ☽ ⚹ ⚵ 9:54 pm

25 THURSDAY
- ☽ ⚹ ⚵ **12:54 am**
- ☽ ⚻ ♀ **9:12 am** 6:12 am
- ♀ □ ♄ **10:21 am** 7:21 am
- ♀ □ ⚷ **10:27 am** 7:27 am
- ♄ ☍ ⚷ **1:28 pm** 10:28 am
- ☽ ⚻ ♅ **5:13 pm** 2:13 pm
- ☽ ⚻ ♂ **6:02 pm** 3:02 pm
- ☽ ☌ ☉ **10:09 pm** 7:09 pm

26 FRIDAY
- ☽ ⚺ ♃ **4:22 am** 1:22 am
- ☿ ⚹ ⚶ **5:18 am** 2:18 am
- ☽ △ ♆ **11:13 am** 8:13 am
- ☽ □ ⚷ **2:13 pm** 11:13 am
- ☽ □ ♄ **2:17 pm** 11:17 am
- ☽ ☌ ♀ **4:46 pm** 1:46 pm
- ☽ ⚺ ⚶ **7:04 pm** 4:04 pm
- ☽ ⚺ ☿ **7:32 pm** 4:32 pm
- ☽ □ ⚳ **7:53 pm** 4:53 pm
- ☽ ⚹ ♇ **10:28 pm** 7:28 pm
- ☿ ⚹ ⚳ 11:35 pm

27 SATURDAY
- ☿ ⚹ ⚳ **2:35 am**
- ☽ ⚺ ⚵ **3:19 am** 12:19 am
- ☽ ☍ ♀ **9:38 am** 6:38 am
- ☽ △ ♅ **6:10 pm** 3:10 pm
- ☽ △ ♂ **7:04 pm** 4:04 pm
- ☽ ⚺ ☉ 11:38 pm

28 SUNDAY
- ☽ ⚺ ☉ **2:38 am**
- ☽ ⚹ ♃ **5:59 am** 2:59 am
- ☿ □ ♇ **11:31 am** 8:31 am
- ☽ □ ♆ **12:04 pm** 9:04 am
- ♀ ⚺ ⚶ **1:00 pm** 10:00 am
- ☽ ⚹ ⚷ **3:08 pm** 12:08 pm
- ☽ △ ♄ **3:20 pm** 12:20 pm
- ♀ □ ⚳ **3:31 pm** 12:31 pm
- ☽ ☌ ⚶ **9:41 pm** 6:41 pm
- ☽ △ ⚳ **9:43 pm** 6:43 pm
- ☽ ⚺ ♀ **10:10 pm** 7:10 pm
- ☽ ⚺ ♇ **11:24 pm** 8:24 pm
- ⚳ △ ⚶ **11:43 pm** 8:43 pm
- ☽ ⚹ ☿ 9:27 pm

29 MONDAY
- ☽ ⚹ ☿ **12:27 am**
- ☽ ☌ ⚵ **5:13 am** 2:13 am
- ☽ ⚻ ♀ **9:46 am** 6:46 am
- ♀ ⚹ ♇ **12:53 pm** 9:53 am
- ☽ □ ♅ **7:09 pm** 4:09 pm
- ☽ □ ♂ **8:14 pm** 5:14 pm

30 TUESDAY
- ☽ ⚹ ☉ **7:27 am** 4:27 am
- ☽ □ ♃ **7:58 am** 4:58 am
- ☽ ⚹ ♆ **1:27 pm** 10:27 am
- ☽ ⚺ ⚷ **4:42 pm** 1:42 pm
- ☉ ⚺ ♃ **4:57 pm** 1:57 pm
- ☽ ⚻ ♄ **5:01 pm** 2:01 pm
- ☽ ⚻ ⚳ 9:23 pm
- ♇ ⚺ ⚶ 9:54 pm
- ☽ ☌ ♇ 10:11 pm
- ☽ ⚺ ⚶ 10:12 pm

Eastern Standard Time in bold type
Pacific Standard Time in medium type

SEPTEMBER 2003

☽ Last Aspect day	EST / hr:mn / PST	asp	☽ Ingress sign day	EST / hr:mn / PST
2	**5:18 am** 2:18 am	⚹ ☿	♐ 2	**1:32 pm** 10:32 am
4	**6:23 am** 3:23 am	□ ☿	♑ 4	**4:51 pm** 1:51 pm
6	**7:43 am** 4:43 am	△ ☿	♒ 6	**9:15 pm** 6:15 pm
8	**4:01 am** 1:01 am	⚹ ♇	♓ 9	**3:07 am** 12:07 am
10	9:41 pm	☍ ♀	♈ 11	**11:09 am** 8:09 am
11	**12:41 am**	☍ ♀	♈ 11	**11:09 am** 8:09 am
12	**8:40 pm** 5:40 pm	△ ♇	♉ 13	**9:50 pm** 6:50 pm
16	**10:25 am** 7:25 am	□ ♅	♊ 16	**10:32 am** 7:32 am
18	**10:50 pm** 7:50 pm	△ ♅	♋ 18	**11:08 pm** 8:08 pm
21	**5:21 am** 2:21 am	⚹ ☉	♌ 21	**9:02 am** 6:02 am
23	**2:33 pm** 11:33 am	☍ ♅	♍ 23	**3:04 pm** 12:04 pm
24	**8:52 pm** 5:52 pm	□ ♇	♎ 25	**5:49 pm** 2:49 pm
27	**6:10 pm** 3:10 pm	△ ♅	♏ 27	**6:52 pm** 3:52 pm
29	**7:09 pm** 4:09 pm	□ ♅	♐ 29	**7:57 pm** 4:57 pm

☽ Phases & Eclipses phase	day	EST / hr:mn / PST
2nd Quarter	3	**7:34 am** 4:34 am
Full Moon	10	**11:36 am** 8:36 am
4th Quarter	18	**2:03 pm** 11:03 am
New Moon	25	**10:09 pm** 7:09 pm

Planet Ingress	day	EST / hr:mn / PST
♅ ♒	14	**10:47 pm** 7:47 pm
♀ ♎	15	**10:58 am** 7:58 am
☉ ♎	23	**5:47 am** 2:47 am

Planetary Motion	day	EST / hr:mn / PST
⚷ D	17	9:33 pm
⚷ D	18	**12:33 am**
☿ D	20	**3:51 am** 12:51 am
♂ D	26	11:52 pm
♂ D	27	**2:52 am**

DATE		SID.TIME	SUN	MOON	NODE	MERCURY	VENUS	MARS	JUPITER	SATURN	URANUS	NEPTUNE	PLUTO	CERES	PALLAS	JUNO	VESTA	CHIRON
1	M	22:38:59	8 ♍ 09 49	4 ♏ 46	23 ♉℞ 26	25 ♍℞ 44	11 ♍ 48	4 ♓℞ 09	1 ♍ 00	10 ♋ 37	0 ♓℞ 32	11 ♒℞ 05	17 ♐ 14	7 ♋ 38	28 ♈℞ 26	13 ♏ 22	2 ♏ 41	12 ♑℞ 34
2	T	22:42:56	9 07 53	19 03	23 D 25	25 21	13 02	3 54	1 13	10 42	0 30	11 03	17 14	7 59	28 22	13 37	3 09	12 33
3	W	22:46:52	10 05 58	3 ♐ 13	23 ℞ 25	24 51	14 17	3 38	1 26	10 47	0 28	11 02	17 15	8 19	28 18	13 51	3 38	12 31
4	Th	22:50:49	11 04 05	17 18	23 25	24 15	15 31	3 23	1 39	10 53	0 25	11 00	17 15	8 40	28 13	14 06	4 06	12 30
5	F	22:54:45	12 02 13	1 ♑ 15	23 24	23 33	16 45	3 09	1 52	10 58	0 23	10 59	17 15	9 00	28 08	14 21	4 35	12 29
6	Sa	22:58:42	13 00 22	15 04	23 20	22 46	18 00	2 54	2 05	11 03	0 21	10 58	17 15	9 20	28 03	14 36	5 04	12 28
7	Su	23:02:38	13 58 33	28 44	23 14	21 55	19 14	2 40	2 18	11 08	0 18	10 56	17 15	9 40	27 57	14 52	5 32	12 27
8	M	23:06:35	14 56 45	12 ♒ 14	23 05	20 59	20 29	2 27	2 31	11 12	0 16	10 55	17 16	10 00	27 50	15 07	6 01	12 26
9	T	23:10:31	15 54 59	25 33	22 55	20 01	21 43	2 14	2 44	11 17	0 14	10 54	17 16	10 20	27 43	15 22	6 30	12 26
10	W	23:14:28	16 53 15	8 ♓ 38	22 43	19 01	22 58	2 01	2 57	11 22	0 11	10 53	17 16	10 39	27 36	15 38	6 59	12 25
11	Th	23:18:25	17 51 32	21 30	22 32	18 01	24 12	1 49	3 10	11 27	0 09	10 51	17 17	10 59	27 28	15 54	7 28	12 24
12	F	23:22:21	18 49 51	4 ♈ 06	22 22	17 02	25 27	1 37	3 23	11 31	0 07	10 50	17 17	11 18	27 20	16 09	7 57	12 24
13	Sa	23:26:18	19 48 12	16 27	22 15	16 05	26 41	1 26	3 35	11 35	0 05	10 49	17 18	11 38	27 12	16 25	8 27	12 23
14	Su	23:30:14	20 46 35	28 35	22 10	15 11	27 56	1 16	3 48	11 40	0 03	10 48	17 18	11 57	27 03	16 42	8 56	12 23
15	M	23:34:11	21 45 00	10 ♉ 32	22 D 07	14 23	29 10	1 07	4 01	11 44	0 00	10 47	17 19	12 16	26 53	16 58	9 25	12 23
16	T	23:38:07	22 43 27	22 22	22 06	13 41	0 ♎ 25	0 58	4 14	11 48	29 ♒ 58	10 46	17 19	12 35	26 43	17 14	9 55	12 22
17	W	23:42:04	23 41 56	4 ♊ 10	22 07	13 06	1 40	0 49	4 26	11 52	29 56	10 44	17 20	12 53	26 33	17 30	10 24	12 22
18	Th	23:46:00	24 40 28	15 59	22 ℞ 07	12 39	2 54	0 42	4 39	11 56	29 54	10 43	17 21	13 12	26 22	17 47	10 54	12 D 22
19	F	23:49:57	25 39 01	27 56	22 08	12 21	4 09	0 35	4 52	12 00	29 52	10 42	17 21	13 30	26 11	18 04	11 24	12 22
20	Sa	23:53:54	26 37 37	10 ♋ 05	22 07	12 D 13	5 23	0 29	5 04	12 04	29 50	10 41	17 22	13 49	26 00	18 20	11 53	12 22
21	Su	23:57:50	27 36 15	22 33	22 04	12 14	6 38	0 23	5 17	12 08	29 48	10 40	17 23	14 07	25 48	18 37	12 23	12 22
22	M	0:01:47	28 34 55	5 ♌ 22	21 59	12 25	7 52	0 19	5 29	12 12	29 46	10 39	17 23	14 25	25 35	18 54	12 53	12 23
23	T	0:05:43	29 33 37	18 36	21 52	12 46	9 07	0 15	5 42	12 15	29 44	10 38	17 24	14 43	25 23	19 11	13 23	12 23
24	W	0:09:40	0 ♎ 32 22	2 ♍ 16	21 43	13 16	10 22	0 12	5 54	12 19	29 42	10 38	17 25	15 00	25 10	19 28	13 53	12 23
25	Th	0:13:36	1 31 08	16 19	21 35	13 55	11 36	0 09	6 07	12 22	29 40	10 37	17 26	15 18	24 56	19 46	14 23	12 24
26	F	0:17:33	2 29 57	0 ♎ 43	21 27	14 43	12 51	0 08	6 19	12 25	29 38	10 36	17 27	15 35	24 42	20 03	14 53	12 25
27	Sa	0:21:29	3 28 47	15 21	21 21	15 39	14 05	0 D 07	6 32	12 28	29 36	10 35	17 28	15 53	24 28	20 20	15 23	12 25
28	Su	0:25:26	4 27 40	0 ♏ 05	21 17	16 42	15 20	0 07	6 44	12 31	29 34	10 34	17 29	16 10	24 14	20 38	15 53	12 26
29	M	0:29:23	5 26 34	14 49	21 D 16	17 52	16 35	0 08	6 56	12 34	29 32	10 33	17 30	16 26	23 59	20 56	16 24	12 27
30	T	0:33:19	6 25 30	29 25	21 16	19 08	17 49	0 10	7 08	12 37	29 31	10 33	17 31	16 43	23 44	21 13	16 54	12 28

EPHEMERIS CALCULATED FOR 12 MIDNIGHT GREENWICH MEAN TIME. ALL OTHER DATA AND FACING ASPECTARIAN PAGE IN **EASTERN STANDARD TIME (BOLD)** AND PACIFIC STANDARD TIME (REGULAR).

OCTOBER 2003

1 WEDNESDAY

☽ ⚻ ⚳	**12:23 am**	
♇ ⚺ ⚶	**12:54 am**	
☽ ☌ ♇	**1:11 am**	
☽ ⚺ ⚶	**1:12 am**	
☽ ⚹ ♀	**4:37 am**	1:37 am
☽ □ ☿	**7:24 am**	4:24 am
☽ ⚺ ⚵	**8:12 am**	5:12 am
☽ △ ⚴	**10:56 am**	7:56 am
☿ ⚹ ⚵	**4:59 pm**	1:59 pm
☽ ⚹ ♅	**9:25 pm**	6:25 pm
☽ ⚹ ♂	**10:50 pm**	7:50 pm

2 THURSDAY

☽ △ ♃	**11:34 am**	8:34 am
☿ ⚻ ⚴	**12:36 pm**	9:36 am
☽ □ ☉	**2:09 pm**	11:09 am
☽ ⚺ ♆	**4:28 pm**	1:28 pm
☽ ☌ ⚷	**7:57 pm**	4:57 pm
☽ ☍ ♄	**8:22 pm**	5:22 pm
♇ ⚻ ⚳	**10:14 pm**	7:14 pm

3 FRIDAY

☽ ⚺ ♇	**4:47 am**	1:47 am
☽ ☍ ⚳	**4:54 am**	1:54 am
☽ ⚹ ⚶	**6:43 am**	3:43 am
♀ ⚺ ⚵	**9:19 am**	6:19 am
☽ ⚹ ⚵	**1:11 pm**	10:11 am
☽ □ ♀	**1:28 pm**	10:28 am
☽ □ ⚴	**1:51 pm**	10:51 am
♀ ☍ ⚴	**4:53 pm**	1:53 pm
☽ △ ☿	**5:40 pm**	2:40 pm
☉ △ ♆	**10:22 pm**	7:22 pm
☽ ⚺ ♅		10:40 pm

4 SATURDAY

☽ ⚺ ♅	**1:40 am**	
☽ ⚺ ♂	**3:33 am**	12:33 am
⚴ ⚻ ⚵	**5:14 am**	2:14 am
☽ ⚻ ♃	**5:20 pm**	2:20 pm
☽ ☌ ♆	**9:35 pm**	6:35 pm
☽ △ ☉	**11:28 pm**	8:28 pm
☽ ⚺ ⚷		10:21 pm
☽ ⚻ ♄		10:51 pm

5 SUNDAY

☽ ⚺ ⚷	**1:21 am**	
☽ ⚻ ♄	**1:51 am**	
☽ ⚹ ♇	**10:32 am**	7:32 am
☽ ⚻ ⚳	**11:40 am**	8:40 am
☽ □ ⚶	**2:39 pm**	11:39 am
☽ ⚹ ♀	**6:46 pm**	3:46 pm
☽ □ ⚵	**8:29 pm**	5:29 pm
☽ △ ♀		10:12 pm
☉ □ ⚷		10:17 pm

6 MONDAY

☽ △ ♀	**1:12 am**	
☉ □ ⚷	**1:17 am**	
☽ ⚻ ☿	**7:40 am**	4:40 am
☽ ☌ ♅	**8:06 am**	5:06 am
☉ □ ♄	**8:40 am**	5:40 am
☽ ☌ ♂	**10:38 am**	7:38 am
☿ ⚻ ♅	**10:55 am**	7:55 am
☽ ☍ ♃		10:22 pm

7 TUESDAY

☽ ☍ ♃	**1:22 am**	
☽ ⚺ ♆	**4:54 am**	1:54 am
☿ ⚻ ♂	**8:01 am**	5:01 am
☽ ⚹ ⚷	**8:57 am**	5:57 am
☽ △ ♄	**9:32 am**	6:32 am
☽ ⚻ ☉	**11:33 am**	8:33 am
☽ □ ♇	**6:30 pm**	3:30 pm
☽ △ ⚳	**8:44 pm**	5:44 pm
☽ △ ⚶		10:04 pm
☽ ⚺ ⚴		10:44 pm

8 WEDNESDAY

☽ △ ⚶	**1:04 am**	
☽ ⚺ ⚴	**1:44 am**	
☽ △ ⚵	**6:10 am**	3:10 am
⚴ ⚻ ⚶	**11:42 am**	8:42 am
☽ ⚻ ♀	**3:56 pm**	12:56 pm
☽ ⚺ ♅	**4:44 pm**	1:44 pm
☽ ⚺ ♂	**8:07 pm**	5:07 pm
♀ △ ♅	**11:48 pm**	8:48 pm
☽ ☍ ☿		10:26 pm

9 THURSDAY

☽ ☍ ☿	**1:26 am**	
☽ ⚻ ♃	**11:43 am**	8:43 am
☽ ⚹ ♆	**2:25 pm**	11:25 am
☽ □ ⚷	**6:48 pm**	3:48 pm
☽ □ ♄	**7:25 pm**	4:25 pm
☽ ☍ ☉		11:27 pm

10 FRIDAY

☽ ☍ ☉	**2:27 am**	
☽ △ ♇	**4:41 am**	1:41 am
☽ □ ⚳	**8:06 am**	5:06 am
☽ ☌ ⚴	**10:43 am**	7:43 am
☽ ⚻ ⚶	**1:59 pm**	10:59 am
♀ △ ♂	**3:32 pm**	12:32 pm
☽ ⚻ ⚵	**6:14 pm**	3:14 pm

11 SATURDAY

☽ ⚹ ♅	**3:31 am**	12:31 am
☉ ⚹ ♇	**6:33 am**	3:33 am
☽ ⚹ ♂	**7:59 am**	4:59 am
☽ ☍ ♀	**9:37 am**	6:37 am
☽ ⚻ ☿	**10:46 pm**	7:46 pm
☽ △ ♃		9:15 pm
☽ □ ♆		11:02 pm

12 SUNDAY

☽ △ ♃	**12:15 am**	
☽ □ ♆	**2:02 am**	
☽ △ ⚷	**6:44 am**	3:44 am
☽ ⚹ ♄	**7:22 am**	4:22 am
☿ ⚺ ♃	**9:55 am**	6:55 am
☽ ⚻ ♇	**4:53 pm**	1:53 pm
☽ ⚻ ☉	**7:56 pm**	4:56 pm
⚳ □ ⚴	**8:41 pm**	5:41 pm
☿ △ ♆	**8:53 pm**	5:53 pm
☽ ⚺ ⚴	**9:28 pm**	6:28 pm
☽ ⚹ ⚳	**9:30 pm**	6:30 pm

13 MONDAY

☽ ☍ ⚶	**5:04 am**	2:04 am
☽ ☍ ⚵	**8:18 am**	5:18 am
☉ ☍ ⚴	**10:16 am**	7:16 am
☽ □ ♅	**4:02 pm**	1:02 pm
☉ □ ⚳	**7:44 pm**	4:44 pm
☽ □ ♂	**9:44 pm**	6:44 pm

14 TUESDAY

☽ ⚻ ♀	**5:32 am**	2:32 am
☿ □ ⚷	**5:49 am**	2:49 am
☿ □ ♄	**9:49 am**	6:49 am
☽ □ ♃	**2:12 pm**	11:12 am
☽ △ ♆	**2:59 pm**	11:59 am
☽ ⚻ ⚷	**7:56 pm**	4:56 pm
☽ ⚺ ♄	**8:30 pm**	5:30 pm
☽ △ ☿	**10:20 pm**	7:20 pm

15 WEDNESDAY

☽ ☍ ♇	**6:04 am**	3:04 am
☽ ⚹ ⚴	**9:00 am**	6:00 am
☽ ⚺ ⚳	**11:45 am**	8:45 am
☽ △ ☉	**2:35 pm**	11:35 am
☽ ⚻ ⚶	**8:54 pm**	5:54 pm
☽ ⚻ ⚵	**11:00 pm**	8:00 pm

16 THURSDAY

☽ △ ♅	**4:54 am**	1:54 am
☽ △ ♂	**11:46 am**	8:46 am
♃ ⚻ ♆	**1:48 pm**	10:48 am
☽ △ ♀		10:16 pm

17 FRIDAY

☽ △ ♀	**1:16 am**	
☿ ⚹ ♇	**3:27 am**	12:27 am
☽ ⚻ ♆	**3:29 am**	12:29 am
☽ ⚹ ♃	**3:42 am**	12:42 am
☽ ☍ ⚷	**8:30 am**	5:30 am
☽ ☌ ♄	**8:58 am**	5:58 am
☿ ☍ ⚴	**1:38 pm**	10:38 am
☽ ⚻ ♇	**6:15 pm**	3:15 pm
☽ □ ♀	**7:31 pm**	4:31 pm
☽ □ ☿	**8:39 pm**	5:39 pm
♀ □ ♆	**10:42 pm**	7:42 pm
☽ ☌ ⚳		9:40 pm

18 SATURDAY

☽ ☌ ⚳	**12:40 am**	
♀ ⚹ ♃	**4:33 am**	1:33 am
☽ □ ☉	**7:31 am**	4:31 am
☽ △ ⚶	**10:57 am**	7:57 am
☽ △ ⚵	**11:56 am**	8:56 am
☽ ⚻ ♅	**3:55 pm**	12:55 pm
☽ ⚻ ♂	**11:43 pm**	8:43 pm

19 SUNDAY

☿ □ ⚳	**4:46 am**	1:46 am
☽ ☍ ♆	**1:20 pm**	10:20 am
☽ ⚺ ♃	**2:23 pm**	11:23 am
☽ □ ♀	**5:28 pm**	2:28 pm
☽ ⚻ ⚷	**6:14 pm**	3:14 pm
♇ △ ⚴	**6:17 pm**	3:17 pm
☽ ⚺ ♄	**6:33 pm**	3:33 pm
♀ ⚹ ⚷		10:43 pm

20 MONDAY

♀ ⚹ ⚷	**1:43 am**	
☽ △ ⚴	**3:05 am**	12:05 am
☽ △ ♇	**3:18 am**	12:18 am
♀ △ ♄	**4:48 am**	1:48 am
☽ ⚺ ⚳	**10:04 am**	7:04 am
☽ ⚹ ☿	**1:54 pm**	10:54 am
☽ ⚹ ☉	**8:04 pm**	5:04 pm
☽ □ ⚶	**9:01 pm**	6:01 pm
☽ □ ⚵	**9:02 pm**	6:02 pm
⚵ ☌ ⚶	**9:34 pm**	6:34 pm
☽ ☍ ♅	**11:18 pm**	8:18 pm

21 TUESDAY

☽ ☍ ♂	**7:45 am**	4:45 am
☉ ⚺ ⚵	**2:56 pm**	11:56 am
☽ ⚻ ♆	**7:15 pm**	4:15 pm
☽ ☌ ♃	**8:57 pm**	5:57 pm
☉ ⚺ ⚶	**10:19 pm**	7:19 pm
☽ △ ⚷	**11:58 pm**	8:58 pm
☽ ⚹ ♄		9:08 pm

22 WEDNESDAY

☽ ⚹ ♄	**12:08 am**	
☽ ⚹ ♀	**4:20 am**	1:20 am
☽ ⚻ ⚴	**6:54 am**	3:54 am
☽ □ ♇	**8:19 am**	5:19 am
☽ ⚹ ⚳	**3:14 pm**	12:14 pm
☉ △ ♅	**3:18 pm**	12:18 pm
☽ ⚺ ☿		10:03 pm
☽ ⚹ ⚵		10:55 pm
☽ ⚹ ⚶		11:40 pm
☽ ⚻ ♅		11:48 pm

23 THURSDAY

☽ ⚺ ☿	**1:03 am**	
☽ ⚹ ⚵	**1:55 am**	
☽ ⚹ ⚶	**2:40 am**	
☽ ⚻ ♅	**2:48 am**	
☽ ⚺ ☉	**3:39 am**	12:39 am
♀ ⚻ ⚴	**4:17 am**	1:17 am
♅ □ ⚶	**6:13 am**	3:13 am
☿ ⚺ ⚵	**10:00 am**	7:00 am
☽ ⚻ ♂	**11:48 am**	8:48 am
☿ △ ♅	**3:57 pm**	12:57 pm
☿ ⚺ ⚶	**8:29 pm**	5:29 pm
☽ △ ♆	**9:33 pm**	6:33 pm
☽ ⚺ ♃	**11:45 pm**	8:45 pm
☽ □ ⚷		11:09 pm
☽ □ ♄		11:10 pm
♀ ⚺ ♇		11:25 pm

24 FRIDAY

☽ □ ⚷	**2:09 am**	
☽ □ ♄	**2:10 am**	
♀ ⚺ ♇	**2:25 am**	
♄ ☍ ⚷	**7:03 am**	4:03 am
☽ ☍ ⚴	**7:35 am**	4:35 am
☽ ⚹ ♇	**10:00 am**	7:00 am
☽ ⚺ ♀	**10:40 am**	7:40 am
♅ □ ⚵	**3:42 pm**	12:42 pm
☽ □ ⚳	**5:06 pm**	2:06 pm

25 SATURDAY

☽ △ ♅	**3:31 am**	12:31 am
☽ ⚺ ⚵	**3:47 am**	12:47 am
☉ ☌ ☿	**4:58 am**	1:58 am
☽ ⚺ ⚶	**5:11 am**	2:11 am
☽ ☌ ☉	**7:50 am**	4:50 am
☽ ☌ ☿	**7:59 am**	4:59 am
☽ △ ♂	**1:17 pm**	10:17 am
☽ □ ♆	**9:43 pm**	6:43 pm
☽ ⚹ ♃		9:25 pm
☽ △ ♄		11:13 pm
☽ ⚹ ⚷		11:21 pm

26 SUNDAY

☽ ⚹ ♃	**12:25 am**	
☽ △ ♄	**2:13 am**	
☽ ⚹ ⚷	**2:21 am**	
☽ ⚻ ⚴	**6:37 am**	3:37 am
☽ ⚺ ♇	**10:00 am**	7:00 am
☽ ☌ ♀	**2:53 pm**	11:53 am
☽ △ ⚳	**5:29 pm**	2:29 pm

27 MONDAY

☽ □ ♅	**3:15 am**	12:15 am
☽ ☌ ⚵	**4:37 am**	1:37 am
☽ ☌ ⚶	**6:42 am**	3:42 am
☽ ⚺ ☉	**11:02 am**	8:02 am
☽ ⚺ ☿	**1:41 pm**	10:41 am
☽ □ ♂	**2:11 pm**	11:11 am
☿ △ ♂	**7:29 pm**	4:29 pm
☽ ⚹ ♆	**9:37 pm**	6:37 pm
☽ □ ♃		9:55 pm
☽ ⚻ ♄		11:11 pm
☽ ⚺ ⚷		11:30 pm
♀ △ ⚳		11:57 pm

28 TUESDAY

☽ □ ♃	**12:55 am**	
☽ ⚻ ♄	**2:11 am**	
☽ ⚺ ⚷	**2:30 am**	
♀ △ ⚳	**2:57 am**	
☽ △ ⚴	**5:45 am**	2:45 am
☽ ☌ ♇	**10:14 am**	7:14 am
☽ ⚻ ⚳	**6:22 pm**	3:22 pm
☽ ⚺ ♀	**7:37 pm**	4:37 pm

29 WEDNESDAY

☽ ⚹ ♅	**3:51 am**	12:51 am
☽ ⚺ ⚵	**6:26 am**	3:26 am
☽ ⚺ ⚶	**9:19 am**	6:19 am
☽ ⚹ ☉	**3:37 pm**	12:37 pm
☽ ⚹ ♂	**4:29 pm**	1:29 pm
☽ ⚹ ☿	**9:01 pm**	6:01 pm
☽ ⚺ ♆	**11:01 pm**	8:01 pm

30 THURSDAY

☽ △ ♃	**3:04 am**	12:04 am
☽ ☍ ♄	**3:46 am**	12:46 am
☽ ☌ ⚷	**4:18 am**	1:18 am
☽ □ ⚴	**6:34 am**	3:34 am
☉ △ ♂	**10:55 am**	7:55 am
☽ ⚺ ♇	**12:20 pm**	9:20 am
☿ □ ♆	**2:41 pm**	11:41 am
☽ ☍ ⚳	**9:22 pm**	6:22 pm

31 FRIDAY

☽ ⚹ ♀	**3:07 am**	12:07 am
☽ ⚺ ♅	**6:48 am**	3:48 am
☽ ⚹ ⚵	**10:50 am**	7:50 am
☽ ⚹ ⚶	**2:40 pm**	11:40 am
☽ ⚺ ♂	**9:40 pm**	6:40 pm
☽ □ ☉	**11:25 pm**	8:25 pm

Eastern Standard Time in bold type
Pacific Standard Time in medium type

OCTOBER 2003

☽ Last Aspect day	EST / hr:mn / PST	asp	☽ Ingress sign day	EST / hr:mn / PST
1	**9:25 pm** 6:25 pm	⚹ ♅	♑ 1	**10:21 pm** 7:21 pm
3	**5:40 pm** 2:40 pm	△ ☿	♒ 3	11:45 pm
3	**5:40 pm** 2:40 pm	△ ☿	♒ 4	2:45 am
6	**8:06 am** 5:06 am	☌ ♅	♓ 6	**9:21 am** 6:21 am
7	**6:30 pm** 3:30 pm	□ ♇	♈ 8	**6:07 pm** 3:07 pm
11	**3:31 am** 12:31 am	⚹ ♅	♉ 11	5:05 am 2:05 am
13	**4:02 pm** 1:02 pm	□ ♅	♊ 13	**5:45 pm** 2:45 pm
16	**4:54 am** 1:54 am	△ ♅	♋ 16	**6:41 am** 3:41 am
18	**7:31 am** 4:31 am	□ ☉	♌ 18	**5:41 pm** 2:41 pm
20	**11:18 pm** 8:18 pm	☍ ♅	♍ 20	10:01 pm
20	**11:18 pm** 8:18 pm	☍ ♅	♍ 21	1:01 am
22	**8:19 am** 5:19 am	□ ♇	♎ 23	**4:27 am** 1:27 am
25	**3:31 am** 12:31 am	△ ♅	♏ 25	**5:08 am** 2:08 am
27	**3:15 am** 12:15 am	□ ♅	♐ 27	**4:55 am** 1:55 am
29	**3:51 am** 12:51 am	⚹ ♅	♑ 29	**5:37 am** 2:37 am
31	**3:07 am** 12:07 am	⚹ ♀	♒ 31	**8:41 am** 5:41 am

☽ Phases & Eclipses phase	day	EST / hr:mn / PST
2nd Quarter	2	**2:09 pm** 11:09 am
Full Moon	9	11:27 pm
Full Moon	10	**2:27 am**
4th Quarter	18	**7:31 am** 4:31 am
New Moon	25	**7:50 am** 4:50 am
2nd Quarter	31	**11:25 pm** 8:25 pm

Planet Ingress	day	EST / hr:mn / PST
☿ ♎	6	**8:28 pm** 5:28 pm
♀ ♏	9	**1:56 pm** 10:56 am
☉ ♏	23	**3:08 pm** 12:08 pm
☿ ♏	24	**6:20 am** 3:20 am
⚶ ♐	25	**3:51 am** 12:51 am
⚵ ♐	27	**6:07 pm** 3:07 pm

Planetary Motion	day	EST / hr:mn / PST
♆ D	22	**8:54 pm** 5:54 pm
♄ ℞	25	**6:42 pm** 3:42 pm

DATE		SID.TIME	SUN	MOON	NODE	MERCURY	VENUS	MARS	JUPITER	SATURN	URANUS	NEPTUNE	PLUTO	CERES	PALLAS	JUNO	VESTA	CHIRON
1	W	0:37:16	7 ♎ 24 28	13 ♐ 51	21 ♉ 17	20 ♍ 29	19 ♎ 04	0 ♓ 13	7 ♍ 20	12 ♋ 40	29 ♒ ℞ 29	10 ♒ ℞ 32	17 ♐ 32	16 ♋ 59	23 ♈ ℞ 28	21 ♏ 31	17 ♏ 24	12 ♑ 29
2	Th	0:41:12	8 23 28	28 02	21 ℞ 18	21 55	20 19	0 16	7 33	12 43	29 27	10 31	17 33	17 16	23 12	21 49	17 55	12 30
3	F	0:45:09	9 22 29	11 ♑ 58	21 18	23 25	21 33	0 20	7 45	12 45	29 26	10 31	17 34	17 32	22 56	22 07	18 25	12 31
4	Sa	0:49:05	10 21 33	25 38	21 17	24 58	22 48	0 25	7 57	12 48	29 24	10 30	17 35	17 48	22 40	22 25	18 56	12 32
5	Su	0:53:02	11 20 38	9 ♒ 03	21 14	26 35	24 03	0 31	8 09	12 50	29 22	10 29	17 36	18 03	22 23	22 43	19 27	12 33
6	M	0:56:58	12 19 44	22 14	21 10	28 13	25 17	0 37	8 20	12 52	29 21	10 29	17 37	18 19	22 07	23 02	19 57	12 35
7	T	1:00:55	13 18 53	5 ♓ 11	21 04	29 54	26 32	0 45	8 32	12 54	29 19	10 28	17 39	18 34	21 50	23 20	20 28	12 36
8	W	1:04:52	14 18 03	17 55	20 57	1 ♎ 36	27 46	0 53	8 44	12 56	29 18	10 28	17 40	18 49	21 32	23 38	20 59	12 38
9	Th	1:08:48	15 17 15	0 ♈ 27	20 51	3 19	29 01	1 01	8 56	12 58	29 16	10 27	17 41	19 04	21 15	23 57	21 30	12 39
10	F	1:12:45	16 16 29	12 47	20 45	5 03	0 ♏ 16	1 11	9 07	13 00	29 15	10 27	17 42	19 19	20 57	24 15	22 00	12 41
11	Sa	1:16:41	17 15 45	24 56	20 41	6 47	1 30	1 21	9 19	13 02	29 14	10 26	17 44	19 33	20 40	24 34	22 31	12 43
12	Su	1:20:38	18 15 03	6 ♉ 56	20 38	8 32	2 45	1 32	9 30	13 03	29 12	10 26	17 45	19 47	20 22	24 53	23 02	12 45
13	M	1:24:34	19 14 24	18 49	20 D 37	10 17	4 00	1 44	9 42	13 05	29 11	10 26	17 46	20 01	20 04	25 11	23 33	12 47
14	T	1:28:31	20 13 46	0 ♊ 37	20 38	12 02	5 14	1 56	9 53	13 06	29 10	10 25	17 48	20 15	19 46	25 30	24 04	12 49
15	W	1:32:27	21 13 11	12 24	20 39	13 47	6 29	2 09	10 05	13 08	29 09	10 25	17 49	20 29	19 27	25 49	24 35	12 51
16	Th	1:36:24	22 12 38	24 13	20 41	15 32	7 44	2 22	10 16	13 09	29 07	10 25	17 51	20 42	19 09	26 08	25 06	12 53
17	F	1:40:20	23 12 08	6 ♋ 09	20 43	17 16	8 58	2 36	10 27	13 10	29 06	10 25	17 52	20 55	18 51	26 27	25 38	12 55
18	Sa	1:44:17	24 11 40	18 17	20 ℞ 44	19 00	10 13	2 51	10 38	13 11	29 05	10 24	17 54	21 08	18 33	26 46	26 09	12 58
19	Su	1:48:14	25 11 13	0 ♌ 41	20 44	20 43	11 27	3 07	10 49	13 12	29 04	10 24	17 55	21 20	18 14	27 05	26 40	13 00
20	M	1:52:10	26 10 50	13 27	20 43	22 26	12 42	3 23	11 00	13 12	29 03	10 24	17 57	21 33	17 56	27 25	27 11	13 02
21	T	1:56:07	27 10 28	26 37	20 40	24 09	13 57	3 39	11 11	13 13	29 02	10 24	17 58	21 45	17 38	27 44	27 43	13 05
22	W	2:00:03	28 10 09	10 ♍ 15	20 38	25 51	15 11	3 57	11 22	13 14	29 01	10 24	18 00	21 56	17 20	28 03	28 14	13 07
23	Th	2:04:00	29 09 52	24 20	20 34	27 32	16 26	4 14	11 32	13 14	29 01	10 D 24	18 02	22 08	17 02	28 23	28 45	13 10
24	F	2:07:56	0 ♏ 09 37	8 ♎ 50	20 32	29 13	17 41	4 33	11 43	13 14	29 00	10 24	18 03	22 19	16 44	28 42	29 17	13 13
25	Sa	2:11:53	1 09 24	23 40	20 29	0 ♏ 53	18 55	4 52	11 54	13 ℞ 14	28 59	10 24	18 05	22 30	16 26	29 02	29 48	13 16
26	Su	2:15:49	2 09 13	8 ♏ 42	20 D 28	2 32	20 10	5 11	12 04	13 14	28 58	10 24	18 07	22 40	16 09	29 21	0 ♐ 20	13 19
27	M	2:19:46	3 09 04	23 47	20 28	4 11	21 25	5 31	12 14	13 14	28 58	10 24	18 08	22 51	15 51	29 41	0 51	13 22
28	T	2:23:43	4 08 57	8 ♐ 47	20 28	5 50	22 39	5 52	12 25	13 14	28 57	10 24	18 10	23 01	15 34	0 ♐ 01	1 23	13 25
29	W	2:27:39	5 08 52	23 34	20 29	7 28	23 54	6 13	12 35	13 14	28 56	10 25	18 12	23 11	15 17	0 20	1 55	13 28
30	Th	2:31:36	6 08 49	8 ♑ 02	20 31	9 05	25 09	6 34	12 45	13 13	28 56	10 25	18 14	23 20	15 00	0 40	2 26	13 31
31	F	2:35:32	7 08 47	22 08	20 31	10 42	26 23	6 56	12 55	13 13	28 56	10 25	18 16	23 29	14 43	1 00	2 58	13 34

EPHEMERIS CALCULATED FOR 12 MIDNIGHT GREENWICH MEAN TIME. ALL OTHER DATA AND FACING ASPECTARIAN PAGE IN **EASTERN STANDARD TIME (BOLD)** AND PACIFIC STANDARD TIME (REGULAR).

NOVEMBER 2003

1 SATURDAY
☽ ☌ ♆ **3:09 am** 12:09 am
☿ ⚹ ♃ **7:48 am** 4:48 am
☽ ⚻ ♃ **8:05 am** 5:05 am
☽ □ ☿ **8:07 am** 5:07 am
☽ ⚻ ♄ **8:08 am** 5:08 am
☿ △ ♄ **8:17 am** 5:17 am
☽ ⚺ ⚷ **8:57 am** 5:57 am
☽ ⚹ ♀ **10:05 am** 7:05 am
♃ ⚹ ♄ **12:13 pm** 9:13 am
☿ ⚹ ⚷ **3:19 pm** 12:19 pm
☽ ⚹ ♇ **5:24 pm** 2:24 pm
♀ □ ♅ **7:43 pm** 4:43 pm
☿ ⚻ ♀ **10:31 pm** 7:31 pm

2 SUNDAY
☽ ⚻ ⚳ **3:27 am** 12:27 am
☽ ☌ ♅ **12:51 pm** 9:51 am
☽ □ ♀ **2:40 pm** 11:40 am
☽ □ ⚵ **6:35 pm** 3:35 pm
☽ □ ⚶ **11:33 pm** 8:33 pm
☉ □ ♆ 10:54 pm

3 MONDAY
☉ □ ♆ **1:54 am**
☽ ☌ ♂ **6:21 am** 3:21 am
⚷ □ ♀ **9:30 am** 6:30 am
☽ ⚺ ♆ **10:27 am** 7:27 am
☽ △ ☉ **11:11 am** 8:11 am
☽ △ ♄ **3:37 pm** 12:37 pm
☽ ☍ ♃ **4:21 pm** 1:21 pm
☽ ⚺ ♀ **4:38 pm** 1:38 pm
☽ ⚹ ⚷ **4:48 pm** 1:48 pm
☽ △ ☿ **11:42 pm** 8:42 pm
♃ ⚻ ♀ 10:04 pm
☽ □ ♇ 10:36 pm

4 TUESDAY
♃ ⚻ ♀ **1:04 am**
☽ □ ♇ **1:36 am**
☽ △ ⚳ **12:39 pm** 9:39 am
☿ ⚺ ♇ **3:05 pm** 12:05 pm
♀ ☌ ⚵ **8:39 pm** 5:39 pm
☽ ⚺ ♅ **9:54 pm** 6:54 pm

5 WEDNESDAY
☽ △ ⚵ **5:32 am** 2:32 am
☽ △ ♀ **6:16 am** 3:16 am
☽ △ ⚶ **11:45 am** 8:45 am
☽ ⚺ ♂ **6:13 pm** 3:13 pm
☉ △ ♄ **6:24 pm** 3:24 pm
☉ ⚻ ♀ **7:24 pm** 4:24 pm
☽ ⚹ ♆ **8:33 pm** 5:33 pm
♄ □ ♀ 9:03 pm
☽ ☌ ♀ 10:47 pm
☽ □ ♄ 10:49 pm
☽ ⚻ ☉ 11:30 pm

6 THURSDAY
♄ □ ♀ **12:03 am**
☽ ☌ ♀ **1:47 am**
☽ □ ♄ **1:49 am**
☽ ⚻ ☉ **2:30 am**
♃ △ ⚷ **3:19 am** 12:19 am
☽ ⚻ ♃ **3:25 am** 12:25 am
☽ □ ⚷ **3:25 am** 12:25 am
☽ △ ♇ **12:26 pm** 9:26 am
☉ ⚹ ⚷ **2:21 pm** 11:21 am
☉ ⚹ ♃ **3:33 pm** 12:33 pm
☽ ⚻ ☿ **7:05 pm** 4:05 pm
☽ □ ⚳ 9:18 pm

7 FRIDAY
☽ □ ⚳ **12:18 am**
☽ ⚹ ♅ **9:16 am** 6:16 am
☽ ⚻ ⚵ **6:53 pm** 3:53 pm
☽ ⚻ ♀ 9:51 pm
☽ ⚻ ⚶ 11:20 pm

8 SATURDAY
☽ ⚻ ♀ **12:51 am**
☽ ⚻ ⚶ **2:20 am**
☽ ⚹ ♂ **8:23 am** 5:23 am
☽ □ ♆ **8:36 am** 5:36 am
☽ ⚺ ♀ **12:46 pm** 9:46 am
☽ ⚹ ♄ **1:50 pm** 10:50 am
☿ △ ⚳ **1:51 pm** 10:51 am
♂ ⚺ ♆ **2:36 pm** 11:36 am
☽ △ ⚷ **3:55 pm** 12:55 pm
☽ △ ♃ **4:23 pm** 1:23 pm
☽ ☍ ☉ **8:13 pm** 5:13 pm
♀ ☌ ⚶ 9:26 pm
☽ ⚻ ♇ 9:58 pm

9 SUNDAY
♀ ☌ ⚶ **12:26 am**
☽ ⚻ ♇ **12:58 am**
☽ ⚹ ⚳ **1:24 pm** 10:24 am
☽ ☍ ☿ **4:44 pm** 1:44 pm
☽ □ ♅ **10:00 pm** 7:00 pm

10 MONDAY
☽ ☍ ⚵ **9:31 am** 6:31 am
☽ ☍ ⚶ **6:07 pm** 3:07 pm
☽ ☍ ♀ **8:56 pm** 5:56 pm
☽ △ ♆ **9:37 pm** 6:37 pm
☽ □ ♂ **11:42 pm** 8:42 pm
☽ ⚹ ♀ 9:39 pm
☽ ⚺ ♄ 11:41 pm

11 TUESDAY
☽ ⚹ ♀ **12:39 am**
☽ ⚺ ♄ **2:41 am**
♀ ⚹ ♆ **3:30 am** 12:30 am
☽ ⚻ ⚷ **5:15 am** 2:15 am
☉ ⚺ ♇ **5:58 am** 2:58 am
☽ □ ♃ **6:09 am** 3:09 am
☿ □ ♅ **9:05 am** 6:05 am
☽ ☍ ♇ **2:10 pm** 11:10 am
☽ ⚻ ☉ **2:54 pm** 11:54 am
♂ ⚺ ♀ **5:25 pm** 2:25 pm
☽ ⚺ ⚳ 11:51 pm

12 WEDNESDAY
☽ ⚺ ⚳ **2:51 am**
♀ △ ♀ **3:51 am** 12:51 am
☽ △ ♅ **10:57 am** 7:57 am
♀ □ ♂ **12:27 pm** 9:27 am
☽ ⚻ ☿ **2:46 pm** 11:46 am
☽ ⚻ ⚵ 9:08 pm
♀ ⚻ ♄ 11:20 pm

13 THURSDAY
☽ ⚻ ⚵ **12:08 am**
♀ ⚻ ♄ **2:20 am**
☽ ⚻ ⚶ **9:40 am** 6:40 am
☽ ⚻ ♆ **10:20 am** 7:20 am
☽ □ ♀ **12:17 pm** 9:17 am
☽ △ ♂ **2:41 pm** 11:41 am
☽ ☌ ♄ **3:05 pm** 12:05 pm
☽ ⚻ ♀ **4:36 pm** 1:36 pm
☽ ☍ ⚷ **6:06 pm** 3:06 pm
☽ ⚹ ♃ **7:22 pm** 4:22 pm
♂ △ ♄ 9:27 pm
♆ ⚹ ⚶ 9:59 pm
☽ ⚻ ♇ 11:39 pm

14 FRIDAY
♂ △ ♄ **12:27 am**
♆ ⚹ ⚶ **12:59 am**
☽ ⚻ ♇ **2:39 am**
♀ ⚺ ⚷ **7:58 am** 4:58 am
☽ △ ☉ **8:39 am** 5:39 am
☽ ☌ ⚳ **3:10 pm** 12:10 pm
♀ □ ♃ **10:34 pm** 7:34 pm
☽ ⚻ ♅ **10:41 pm** 7:41 pm

15 SATURDAY
♀ △ ⚶ **6:01 am** 3:01 am
☽ △ ☿ **10:41 am** 7:41 am
☽ △ ⚵ **1:01 pm** 10:01 am
☽ ☍ ♆ **9:12 pm** 6:12 pm
☽ △ ♀ **10:10 pm** 7:10 pm
☽ △ ⚶ **11:07 pm** 8:07 pm
☽ ⚺ ♄ 10:30 pm

16 SUNDAY
☽ ⚺ ♄ **1:30 am**
☽ ⚻ ♂ **3:32 am** 12:32 am
☽ ⚻ ⚷ **4:52 am** 1:52 am
☽ ⚺ ♃ **6:24 am** 3:24 am
☽ △ ♀ **9:28 am** 6:28 am
☿ ☌ ⚵ **10:53 am** 7:53 am
☽ △ ♇ **12:50 pm** 9:50 am
☽ □ ☉ **11:15 pm** 8:15 pm
☽ ⚺ ⚳ 9:46 pm

17 MONDAY
☽ ⚺ ⚳ **12:46 am**
☽ ☍ ♅ **7:38 am** 4:38 am
☉ △ ⚳ **7:30 pm** 4:30 pm
♂ ⚹ ⚷ **8:42 pm** 5:42 pm
♀ ☌ ♇ **8:51 pm** 5:51 pm
☽ □ ⚵ **10:34 pm** 7:34 pm
☽ □ ☿ 11:04 pm

18 TUESDAY
☽ □ ☿ **2:04 am**
♄ ⚻ ⚶ **3:41 am** 12:41 am
☽ ⚻ ♆ **4:47 am** 1:47 am
☽ ⚻ ♀ **4:59 am** 1:59 am
☽ ⚹ ♄ **8:36 am** 5:36 am
☽ □ ⚶ **8:49 am** 5:49 am
☽ △ ⚷ **12:12 pm** 9:12 am
☽ ☍ ♂ **12:41 pm** 9:41 am
☽ ☌ ♃ **1:52 pm** 10:52 am
☽ □ ♇ **7:29 pm** 4:29 pm
♆ ⚹ ♀ **8:06 pm** 5:06 pm
☽ □ ♀ **9:40 pm** 6:40 pm
☿ △ ♀ 11:04 pm
☿ ⚹ ♆ 11:43 pm

19 WEDNESDAY
☿ △ ♀ **2:04 am**
☿ ⚹ ♆ **2:43 am**
☽ ⚹ ⚳ **6:36 am** 3:36 am
☽ ⚹ ☉ **9:15 am** 6:15 am
☽ ⚻ ♅ **12:54 pm** 9:54 am

20 THURSDAY
☽ ⚹ ⚵ **4:03 am** 1:03 am
☽ ☍ ♀ **8:15 am** 5:15 am
☽ △ ♆ **8:38 am** 5:38 am
♂ ☍ ♃ **8:59 am** 5:59 am
☿ ⚻ ♄ **11:24 am** 8:24 am
☽ □ ♄ **11:59 am** 8:59 am
☽ ⚹ ☿ **12:03 pm** 9:03 am
☽ ⚹ ⚶ **2:20 pm** 11:20 am
☽ □ ⚷ **3:46 pm** 12:46 pm
☽ ⚺ ♃ **5:32 pm** 2:32 pm
☽ ⚻ ♂ **5:45 pm** 2:45 pm
☽ ⚹ ♇ **10:27 pm** 7:27 pm

21 FRIDAY
☽ ⚹ ♀ **5:03 am** 2:03 am
☽ □ ⚳ **8:51 am** 5:51 am
☉ □ ♅ **12:14 pm** 9:14 am
☽ △ ♅ **2:44 pm** 11:44 am
☽ ⚺ ☉ **2:55 pm** 11:55 am
☿ ☌ ⚶ **9:40 pm** 6:40 pm
☿ ⚺ ⚷ 11:08 pm

22 SATURDAY
☿ ⚺ ⚷ **2:08 am**
☽ ⚺ ⚵ **6:12 am** 3:12 am
☽ ⚻ ♀ **8:38 am** 5:38 am
☽ □ ♆ **9:28 am** 6:28 am
⚷ ⚺ ⚶ **11:12 am** 8:12 am
☽ △ ♄ **12:27 pm** 9:27 am
☽ ⚹ ⚷ **4:28 pm** 1:28 pm
☽ ⚺ ⚶ **4:38 pm** 1:38 pm
☽ ⚺ ☿ **5:56 pm** 2:56 pm
☽ ⚹ ♃ **6:19 pm** 3:19 pm
☽ △ ♂ **7:47 pm** 4:47 pm
☿ □ ♃ **10:09 pm** 7:09 pm
☽ ⚺ ♇ **10:46 pm** 7:46 pm
♀ ⚻ ⚳ 11:30 pm

23 SUNDAY
♀ ⚻ ⚳ **2:30 am**
☽ △ ⚳ **8:44 am** 5:44 am
☽ ⚺ ♀ **9:17 am** 6:17 am
☽ □ ♅ **2:28 pm** 11:28 am
☽ ☌ ☉ **5:59 pm** 2:59 pm
☿ □ ♂ **10:13 pm** 7:13 pm

24 MONDAY
☽ ☌ ⚵ **6:42 am** 3:42 am
☽ △ ♀ **7:40 am** 4:40 am
☽ ⚹ ♆ **8:53 am** 5:53 am
☽ ⚻ ♄ **11:38 am** 8:38 am
☽ ⚺ ⚷ **4:02 pm** 1:02 pm
☽ ☌ ⚶ **5:41 pm** 2:41 pm
☽ □ ♃ **6:00 pm** 3:00 pm
☽ □ ♂ **8:44 pm** 5:44 pm
☿ ☌ ♇ **9:13 pm** 6:13 pm
☽ ☌ ♇ **10:11 pm** 7:11 pm
☽ ☌ ☿ **10:17 pm** 7:17 pm

25 TUESDAY
♃ □ ⚶ **4:39 am** 1:39 am
☽ ⚻ ⚳ **8:06 am** 5:06 am
☽ ☌ ♀ **12:57 pm** 9:57 am
☽ ⚹ ♅ **1:57 pm** 10:57 am
♀ △ ⚵ **4:12 pm** 1:12 pm
☽ ⚺ ☉ **8:57 pm** 5:57 pm
♀ ⚹ ♅ 10:22 pm

26 WEDNESDAY
♀ ⚹ ♅ **1:22 am**
☽ □ ♀ **7:14 am** 4:14 am
☽ ⚺ ⚵ **7:41 am** 4:41 am
☽ ⚺ ♆ **8:51 am** 5:51 am
☽ ☍ ♄ **11:28 am** 8:28 am
☽ ☌ ⚷ **4:27 pm** 1:27 pm
♂ □ ♇ **6:24 pm** 3:24 pm
☽ △ ♃ **6:37 pm** 3:37 pm
☽ ⚺ ⚶ **7:46 pm** 4:46 pm
☽ ⚺ ♇ **10:43 pm** 7:43 pm
☽ ⚹ ♂ **10:52 pm** 7:52 pm

27 THURSDAY
☽ ⚺ ☿ **4:03 am** 1:03 am
☽ ☍ ⚳ **8:56 am** 5:56 am
☽ ⚺ ♅ **3:12 pm** 12:12 pm
☽ ⚺ ♀ **6:47 pm** 3:47 pm
☽ ⚹ ☉ 11:24 pm

28 FRIDAY
☽ ⚹ ☉ **2:24 am**
☽ ⚹ ♀ **9:11 am** 6:11 am
☽ ⚹ ⚵ **11:14 am** 8:14 am
☽ ☌ ♆ **11:16 am** 8:16 am
♆ ⚹ ⚵ **12:25 pm** 9:25 am
☽ ⚻ ♄ **1:46 pm** 10:46 am
☽ ⚺ ⚷ **7:35 pm** 4:35 pm
☽ ⚻ ♃ **10:01 pm** 7:01 pm
☽ ⚹ ⚶ 9:57 pm
☽ ⚹ ♇ 11:09 pm

29 SATURDAY
☽ ⚹ ⚶ **12:57 am**
☽ ⚹ ♇ **2:09 am**
☽ ⚺ ♂ **4:15 am** 1:15 am
☿ ⚻ ⚳ **4:54 am** 1:54 am
☽ ⚻ ⚳ **12:50 pm** 9:50 am
☽ ⚹ ☿ **1:47 pm** 10:47 am
☽ ☌ ♅ **7:46 pm** 4:46 pm

30 SUNDAY
☽ ⚹ ♀ **5:05 am** 2:05 am
♇ ☌ ⚶ **9:29 am** 6:29 am
☽ □ ☉ **12:16 pm** 9:16 am
☽ ⚺ ♀ **2:49 pm** 11:49 am
☽ ⚺ ♆ **5:22 pm** 2:22 pm
☽ □ ⚵ **6:45 pm** 3:45 pm
☽ △ ♄ **7:44 pm** 4:44 pm
☽ ⚹ ⚷ 11:36 pm

Eastern Standard Time in bold type
Pacific Standard Time in medium type

NOVEMBER 2003

☽ Last Aspect day	EST / hr:mn / PST	asp	☽ Ingress sign day	EST / hr:mn / PST
2	**2:40 pm** 11:40 am	□ ♀	♓ 2	**2:52 pm** 11:52 am
3	10:36 pm	□ ♇	♈ 4	9:02 pm
4	**1:36 am**	□ ♇	♈ 5	**12:02 am**
7	**9:16 am** 6:16 am	✶ ♅	♉ 7	**11:29 am** 8:29 am
9	**10:00 pm** 7:00 pm	□ ♅	♊ 9	9:14 pm
9	**10:00 pm** 7:00 pm	□ ♅	♊ 10	**12:14 am**
12	**10:57 am** 7:57 am	△ ♅	♋ 12	**1:10 pm** 10:10 am
14	**8:39 am** 5:39 am	△ ☉	♌ 14	9:48 pm
14	**8:39 am** 5:39 am	△ ☉	♌ 15	**12:48 am**
17	**7:38 am** 4:38 am	☍ ♅	♍ 17	**9:36 am** 6:36 am
19	**9:15 am** 6:15 am	✶ ☉	♎ 19	**2:42 pm** 11:42 am
21	**2:44 pm** 11:44 am	△ ♅	♏ 21	**4:24 pm** 1:24 pm
23	**2:28 pm** 11:28 am	□ ♅	♐ 23	**4:02 pm** 1:02 pm
25	**1:57 pm** 10:57 am	✶ ♅	♑ 25	**3:31 pm** 12:31 pm
26	**10:52 pm** 7:52 am	✶ ♂	♒ 27	**4:48 pm** 1:48 pm
29	**7:46 pm** 4:46 pm	☌ ♅	♓ 29	**9:25 pm** 6:25 pm

☽ Phases & Eclipses phase	day	EST / hr:mn / PST
Full Moon	8	**8:13 pm** 5:13 pm
●	8	16° ♉ 13'
4th Quarter	16	**11:15 pm** 8:15 pm
New Moon	23	**5:59 pm** 2:59 pm
●	23	1° ♐ 14'
2nd Quarter	30	**12:16 pm** 9:16 am

Planet Ingress		day	EST / hr:mn / PST
♀	♐	2	**4:42 pm** 1:42 pm
☿	♐	11	11:19 pm
☿	♐	12	**2:19 am**
☉	♐	22	**12:43 pm** 9:43 am
♀	♑	26	**8:07 pm** 5:07 pm

Planetary Motion		day	EST / hr:mn / PST
♅	D	8	**7:44 am** 4:44 am
⚳	℞	23	**9:32 pm** 6:32 pm

DATE		SID.TIME	SUN	MOON	NODE	MERCURY	VENUS	MARS	JUPITER	SATURN	URANUS	NEPTUNE	PLUTO	CERES	PALLAS	JUNO	VESTA	CHIRON
1	Sa	2:39:29	8 ♏ 08 47	5 ♒ 51	20 ♉℞ 32	12 ♏ 19	27 ♏ 38	7 ♓ 18	13 ♍ 05	13 ♋℞ 12	28 ♒℞ 55	10 ♒ 25	18 ♐ 17	23 ♋ 38	14 ♈℞ 27	1 ♐ 20	3 ♐ 30	13 ♑ 37
2	Su	2:43:25	9 08 48	19 12	20 32	13 55	28 53	7 41	13 15	13 12	28 55	10 26	18 19	23 46	14 11	1 40	4 01	13 41
3	M	2:47:22	10 08 51	2 ♓ 13	20 31	15 30	0 ♐ 07	8 05	13 24	13 11	28 54	10 26	18 21	23 54	13 55	2 00	4 33	13 44
4	T	2:51:18	11 08 55	14 56	20 30	17 05	1 22	8 29	13 34	13 10	28 54	10 26	18 23	24 02	13 40	2 20	5 05	13 48
5	W	2:55:15	12 09 01	27 25	20 29	18 40	2 36	8 53	13 43	13 09	28 54	10 27	18 25	24 10	13 25	2 40	5 37	13 51
6	Th	2:59:12	13 09 09	9 ♈ 40	20 28	20 14	3 51	9 17	13 53	13 08	28 54	10 27	18 27	24 17	13 10	3 00	6 09	13 55
7	F	3:03:08	14 09 18	21 46	20 27	21 48	5 06	9 42	14 02	13 06	28 54	10 28	18 29	24 24	12 56	3 20	6 41	13 58
8	Sa	3:07:05	15 09 29	3 ♉ 44	20 26	23 22	6 20	10 08	14 11	13 05	28 D 54	10 28	18 31	24 30	12 42	3 41	7 12	14 02
9	Su	3:11:01	16 09 42	15 37	20 D 26	24 55	7 35	10 34	14 20	13 03	28 54	10 29	18 33	24 36	12 29	4 01	7 44	14 06
10	M	3:14:58	17 09 56	27 25	20 26	26 27	8 49	11 00	14 29	13 02	28 54	10 29	18 35	24 42	12 15	4 21	8 16	14 10
11	T	3:18:54	18 10 13	9 ♊ 13	20 26	28 00	10 04	11 26	14 38	13 00	28 54	10 30	18 37	24 47	12 03	4 41	8 48	14 14
12	W	3:22:51	19 10 31	21 01	20 26	29 32	11 18	11 53	14 47	12 58	28 54	10 31	18 39	24 52	11 50	5 02	9 20	14 18
13	Th	3:26:47	20 10 51	2 ♋ 54	20 ℞ 26	1 ♐ 04	12 33	12 20	14 55	12 56	28 54	10 31	18 41	24 57	11 38	5 22	9 52	14 22
14	F	3:30:44	21 11 13	14 53	20 26	2 35	13 48	12 48	15 04	12 54	28 54	10 32	18 43	25 01	11 27	5 43	10 24	14 26
15	Sa	3:34:41	22 11 36	27 02	20 26	4 06	15 02	13 15	15 12	12 52	28 55	10 33	18 45	25 05	11 16	6 03	10 56	14 30
16	Su	3:38:37	23 12 02	9 ♌ 25	20 26	5 37	16 17	13 44	15 20	12 50	28 55	10 34	18 47	25 08	11 06	6 24	11 29	14 34
17	M	3:42:34	24 12 29	22 06	20 D 26	7 08	17 31	14 12	15 28	12 48	28 56	10 35	18 49	25 11	10 55	6 44	12 01	14 38
18	T	3:46:30	25 12 59	5 ♍ 09	20 26	8 38	18 46	14 41	15 36	12 45	28 56	10 35	18 51	25 14	10 46	7 05	12 33	14 42
19	W	3:50:27	26 13 30	18 37	20 26	10 08	20 00	15 10	15 44	12 43	28 57	10 36	18 54	25 16	10 37	7 25	13 05	14 47
20	Th	3:54:23	27 14 03	2 ♎ 32	20 27	11 37	21 15	15 39	15 52	12 40	28 57	10 37	18 56	25 18	10 28	7 46	13 37	14 51
21	F	3:58:20	28 14 37	16 52	20 28	13 06	22 29	16 09	15 59	12 37	28 58	10 38	18 58	25 20	10 20	8 06	14 09	14 56
22	Sa	4:02:16	29 15 14	1 ♏ 37	20 28	14 35	23 44	16 38	16 07	12 35	28 58	10 39	19 00	25 21	10 12	8 27	14 41	15 00
23	Su	4:06:13	0 ♐ 15 52	16 40	20 ℞ 29	16 03	24 58	17 09	16 14	12 32	28 59	10 40	19 02	25 22	10 05	8 48	15 14	15 05
24	M	4:10:10	1 16 32	1 ♐ 53	20 28	17 31	26 13	17 39	16 21	12 29	29 00	10 41	19 04	25 ℞ 22	9 59	9 08	15 46	15 09
25	T	4:14:06	2 17 13	17 06	20 28	18 59	27 28	18 10	16 28	12 25	29 01	10 42	19 07	25 22	9 52	9 29	16 18	15 14
26	W	4:18:03	3 17 55	2 ♑ 10	20 26	20 25	28 42	18 41	16 35	12 22	29 02	10 43	19 09	25 21	9 47	9 50	16 50	15 19
27	Th	4:21:59	4 18 39	16 56	20 25	21 52	29 57	19 12	16 42	12 19	29 02	10 45	19 11	25 20	9 42	10 11	17 23	15 23
28	F	4:25:56	5 19 24	1 ♒ 18	20 23	23 17	1 ♑ 11	19 43	16 48	12 16	29 03	10 46	19 13	25 19	9 37	10 31	17 55	15 28
29	Sa	4:29:52	6 20 09	15 13	20 21	24 41	2 25	20 15	16 55	12 12	29 04	10 47	19 15	25 17	9 33	10 52	18 27	15 33
30	Su	4:33:49	7 20 56	28 40	20 D 20	26 05	3 40	20 47	17 01	12 09	29 05	10 48	19 18	25 15	9 30	11 13	19 00	15 38

EPHEMERIS CALCULATED FOR 12 MIDNIGHT GREENWICH MEAN TIME. ALL OTHER DATA AND FACING ASPECTARIAN PAGE IN **EASTERN STANDARD TIME (BOLD)** AND PACIFIC STANDARD TIME (REGULAR).

DECEMBER 2003

1 MONDAY

☽ ⚹ ⚷	**2:36 am**	
☽ ☍ ♃	**5:18 am**	2:18 am
☽ □ ♇	**9:27 am**	6:27 am
☽ □ ⚶	**10:27 am**	7:27 am
☽ ☌ ♂	**2:00 pm**	11:00 am
☉ △ ⚴	**7:35 pm**	4:35 pm
☽ △ ⚳	**8:32 pm**	5:32 pm
☿ ⚹ ♅		9:53 pm
♄ ⚻ ⚵		10:23 pm

2 TUESDAY

☿ ⚹ ♅	**12:53 am**	
♄ ⚻ ⚵	**1:23 am**	
☽ ⚺ ♅	**4:15 am**	1:15 am
☽ □ ☿	**4:39 am**	1:39 am
☽ □ ♀	**8:32 pm**	5:32 pm
☽ ☌ ⚴		9:16 pm
☽ △ ☉		11:57 pm

3 WEDNESDAY

☽ ☌ ⚴	**12:16 am**	
☽ △ ☉	**2:57 am**	
☽ ⚹ ♆	**3:15 am**	12:15 am
☽ □ ♄	**5:20 am**	2:20 am
☽ △ ⚵	**6:19 am**	3:19 am
☉ ⚹ ♆	**6:34 am**	3:34 am
☽ □ ⚷	**1:18 pm**	10:18 am
☽ ⚻ ♃	**4:13 pm**	1:13 pm
☽ △ ♇	**8:18 pm**	5:18 pm
☽ △ ⚶	**11:55 pm**	8:55 pm

4 THURSDAY

☽ ⚺ ♂	**3:40 am**	12:40 am
☉ ⚻ ♄	**5:56 am**	2:56 am
☽ □ ⚳	**7:24 am**	4:24 am
♀ □ ⚴	**8:39 am**	5:39 am
☽ ⚹ ♅	**3:52 pm**	12:52 pm
☽ △ ☿	**11:25 pm**	8:25 pm

5 FRIDAY

☽ ⚺ ⚴	**12:22 pm**	9:22 am
☉ ☌ ⚵	**2:25 pm**	11:25 am
☽ △ ♀	**3:38 pm**	12:38 pm
☽ □ ♆	**3:38 pm**	12:38 pm
♀ ⚺ ♆	**3:38 pm**	12:38 pm
☽ ⚹ ♄	**5:20 pm**	2:20 pm
☽ ⚻ ⚵	**8:30 pm**	5:30 pm
☽ ⚻ ☉	**8:53 pm**	5:53 pm
☽ △ ⚷		11:15 pm

6 SATURDAY

☽ △ ⚷	**2:15 am**	
☽ △ ♃	**5:15 am**	2:15 am
♀ ☍ ♄	**7:04 am**	4:04 am
☽ ⚻ ♇	**9:09 am**	6:09 am
☽ ⚻ ⚶	**3:33 pm**	12:33 pm
☽ ⚹ ♂	**7:26 pm**	4:26 pm
☽ ⚹ ⚳	**7:48 pm**	4:48 pm
♂ △ ⚳		11:25 pm

7 SUNDAY

♂ △ ⚳	**2:25 am**	
☽ □ ♅	**4:54 am**	1:54 am
☽ ⚻ ☿	**7:09 pm**	4:09 pm
☽ ⚹ ⚴		10:24 pm

8 MONDAY

☽ ⚹ ⚴	**1:24 am**	
☽ △ ♆	**4:47 am**	1:47 am
☽ ⚺ ♄	**6:00 am**	3:00 am
♀ ⚺ ⚵	**6:14 am**	3:14 am
☽ ☍ ⚵	**11:22 am**	8:22 am
☽ ⚻ ♀	**11:48 am**	8:48 am
☽ ☍ ☉	**3:37 pm**	12:37 pm
☽ ⚻ ⚷	**3:41 pm**	12:41 pm
☉ ⚺ ⚷	**4:31 pm**	1:31 pm
☽ □ ♃	**6:40 pm**	3:40 pm
☽ ☍ ♇	**10:18 pm**	7:18 pm

9 TUESDAY

☽ ☍ ⚶	**7:21 am**	4:21 am
☽ ⚺ ⚳	**8:10 am**	5:10 am
☽ □ ♂	**11:17 am**	8:17 am
☽ △ ♅	**5:48 pm**	2:48 pm
⚳ ⚻ ⚶	**10:37 pm**	7:37 pm

10 WEDNESDAY

♀ ☌ ⚷	**3:28 am**	12:28 am
☉ □ ♃	**5:58 am**	2:58 am
☽ ☍ ☿	**1:17 pm**	10:17 am
☽ □ ⚴	**1:59 pm**	10:59 am
☽ ⚻ ♆	**5:18 pm**	2:18 pm
☽ ☌ ♄	**6:01 pm**	3:01 pm
☿ □ ⚴	**11:11 pm**	8:11 pm
☽ ⚻ ⚵		10:25 pm

11 THURSDAY

☽ ⚻ ⚵	**1:25 am**	
☽ ☍ ⚷	**4:17 am**	1:17 am
☽ ☍ ♀	**6:55 am**	3:55 am
☽ ⚹ ♃	**7:09 am**	4:09 am
☽ ⚻ ☉	**9:17 am**	6:17 am
♀ △ ♃	**9:22 am**	6:22 am
☽ ⚻ ♇	**10:30 am**	7:30 am
☽ ☌ ⚳	**7:23 pm**	4:23 pm
☽ ⚻ ⚶	**9:55 pm**	6:55 pm
☉ ☌ ♇		9:28 pm
☽ △ ♂		10:53 pm

12 FRIDAY

☉ ☌ ♇	**12:28 am**	
☽ △ ♂	**1:53 am**	
☽ ⚻ ♅	**5:28 am**	2:28 am
♀ ⚺ ♇	**7:12 pm**	4:12 pm
☽ △ ⚴		10:08 pm

13 SATURDAY

☽ △ ⚴	**1:08 am**	
☽ ⚻ ☿	**4:11 am**	1:11 am
☽ ☍ ♆	**4:15 am**	1:15 am
☽ ⚺ ♄	**4:28 am**	1:28 am
☿ ⚺ ♆	**5:22 am**	2:22 am
☿ ☍ ♄	**9:13 am**	6:13 am
☽ △ ⚵	**1:39 pm**	10:39 am
☽ ⚻ ⚷	**3:09 pm**	12:09 pm
☽ ⚺ ♃	**5:49 pm**	2:49 pm
☽ △ ♇	**8:55 pm**	5:55 pm
☽ ⚻ ♀	**11:37 pm**	8:37 pm
☽ △ ☉		9:39 pm

14 SUNDAY

☽ △ ☉	**12:39 am**	
☽ ⚺ ⚳	**4:41 am**	1:41 am
♄ ⚻ ♆	**7:48 am**	4:48 am
☽ △ ⚶	**10:16 am**	7:16 am
☽ ⚻ ♂	**2:13 pm**	11:13 am
☽ ☍ ♅	**3:05 pm**	12:05 pm

15 MONDAY

☽ ⚻ ⚴	**10:02 am**	7:02 am
♂ ⚺ ♅	**10:33 am**	7:33 am
☽ ⚹ ♄	**12:37 pm**	9:37 am
☽ ⚻ ♆	**12:51 pm**	9:51 am
☽ △ ☿	**2:50 pm**	11:50 am
☉ ⚻ ⚳	**9:10 pm**	6:10 pm
♀ ☍ ⚳	**10:40 pm**	7:40 pm
☽ □ ⚵	**11:12 pm**	8:12 pm
☽ △ ⚷	**11:29 pm**	8:29 pm
☽ ☌ ♃		10:55 pm

16 TUESDAY

☽ ☌ ♃	**1:55 am**	
☽ □ ♇	**4:45 am**	1:45 am
☉ ⚺ ♀	**6:35 am**	3:35 am
☽ ⚹ ⚳	**11:22 am**	8:22 am
☽ □ ☉	**12:42 pm**	9:42 am
☽ △ ♀	**12:49 pm**	9:49 am
⚷ ⚺ ⚵	**2:05 pm**	11:05 am
☽ □ ⚶	**7:32 pm**	4:32 pm
☽ ⚻ ♅	**9:55 pm**	6:55 pm
☽ ☍ ♂	**11:25 pm**	8:25 pm

17 WEDNESDAY

☽ ☍ ⚴	**4:01 pm**	1:01 pm
☽ □ ♄	**5:51 pm**	2:51 pm
☽ △ ♆	**6:28 pm**	3:28 pm
☽ □ ☿	**8:43 pm**	5:43 pm

18 THURSDAY

☽ □ ⚷	**4:44 am**	1:44 am
☽ ⚹ ⚵	**5:27 am**	2:27 am
☽ ⚺ ♃	**6:52 am**	3:52 am
☽ ⚹ ♇	**9:28 am**	6:28 am
☽ □ ⚳	**2:59 pm**	11:59 am
☽ ⚹ ☉	**8:50 pm**	5:50 pm
☽ □ ♀	**9:53 pm**	6:53 pm
☽ ⚹ ⚶		10:18 pm
☽ △ ♅		10:39 pm

19 FRIDAY

☽ ⚹ ⚶	**1:18 am**	
☽ △ ♅	**1:39 am**	
☽ ⚻ ♂	**5:06 am**	2:06 am
♅ ⚹ ⚶	**11:14 am**	8:14 am
☽ ⚻ ⚴	**6:58 pm**	3:58 pm
☽ △ ♄	**8:04 pm**	5:04 pm
☽ □ ♆	**9:02 pm**	6:02 pm
☽ ⚹ ☿	**10:09 pm**	7:09 pm

20 SATURDAY

☽ ⚹ ⚷	**6:58 am**	3:58 am
☽ ⚺ ⚵	**8:33 am**	5:33 am
☽ ⚹ ♃	**8:52 am**	5:52 am
☽ ⚺ ♇	**11:18 am**	8:18 am
☽ △ ⚳	**3:51 pm**	12:51 pm
♀ ⚺ ♅	**6:41 pm**	3:41 pm
♃ □ ⚵	**11:24 pm**	8:24 pm
☿ ⚺ ♆		10:07 pm
☽ ⚺ ☉		10:36 pm
☽ □ ♅		11:43 pm

21 SUNDAY

☿ ⚺ ♆	**1:07 am**	
☽ ⚺ ☉	**1:36 am**	
☽ □ ♅	**2:43 am**	
☽ ⚹ ♀	**3:25 am**	12:25 am
☽ ⚺ ⚶	**4:06 am**	1:06 am
☽ △ ♂	**7:54 am**	4:54 am
♀ ⚺ ⚶	**5:35 pm**	2:35 pm
☉ ⚹ ♅	**6:34 pm**	3:34 pm
☽ △ ⚴	**7:39 pm**	4:39 pm
☽ ⚻ ♄	**8:06 pm**	5:06 pm
☽ ⚺ ☿	**8:22 pm**	5:22 pm
☽ ⚹ ♆	**9:23 pm**	6:23 pm
☿ ☍ ♄		10:35 pm

22 MONDAY

☿ ☍ ♄	**1:35 am**	
☿ □ ⚴	**7:08 am**	4:08 am
☽ ⚺ ⚷	**7:15 am**	4:15 am
☽ □ ♃	**8:56 am**	5:56 am
☽ ☌ ⚵	**9:38 am**	6:38 am
☽ ☌ ♇	**11:18 am**	8:18 am
☽ ⚻ ⚳	**3:05 pm**	12:05 pm
☽ ⚹ ♅		11:29 pm

23 TUESDAY

☽ ⚹ ♅	**2:29 am**	
☽ ☌ ☉	**4:43 am**	1:43 am
♄ □ ⚴	**4:43 am**	1:43 am
☽ ☌ ⚶	**5:31 am**	2:31 am
☽ ⚺ ♀	**7:19 am**	4:19 am
☽ □ ♂	**9:29 am**	6:29 am
☽ ☌ ☿	**5:04 pm**	2:04 pm
☽ ☍ ♄	**7:30 pm**	4:30 pm
☽ □ ⚴	**7:43 pm**	4:43 pm
☽ ⚺ ♆	**9:08 pm**	6:08 pm

24 WEDNESDAY

☉ ☌ ⚶	**4:55 am**	1:55 am
☽ ☌ ⚷	**7:19 am**	4:19 am
☽ △ ♃	**8:52 am**	5:52 am
☽ ⚺ ⚵	**10:36 am**	7:36 am
☽ ⚺ ♇	**11:17 am**	8:17 am
☽ ☍ ⚳	**2:25 pm**	11:25 am
☽ ⚺ ♅		11:54 pm

25 THURSDAY

☽ ⚺ ♅	**2:54 am**	
☽ ⚺ ⚶	**7:46 am**	4:46 am
♀ ⚹ ♂	**8:29 am**	5:29 am
☽ ⚺ ☉	**8:43 am**	5:43 am
☽ ⚹ ♂	**12:06 pm**	9:06 am
☽ ☌ ♀	**12:17 pm**	9:17 am
☽ ⚺ ☿	**2:03 pm**	11:03 am
♇ ☌ ⚵	**6:57 pm**	3:57 pm
☽ ⚻ ♄	**8:13 pm**	5:13 pm
☽ ⚹ ⚴	**9:13 pm**	6:13 pm
☽ ☌ ♆	**10:20 pm**	7:20 pm
☿ ⚺ ♀	**11:07 pm**	8:07 pm

26 FRIDAY

☿ □ ♂	**3:53 am**	12:53 am
☽ ⚺ ⚷	**9:18 am**	6:18 am
☽ ⚻ ♃	**10:43 am**	7:43 am
☽ ⚹ ♇	**1:18 pm**	10:18 am
☽ ⚹ ⚵	**1:43 pm**	10:43 am
☽ ⚻ ⚳	**3:46 pm**	12:46 pm
☉ ☌ ☿	**8:11 pm**	5:11 pm

27 SATURDAY

☽ ☌ ♅	**5:58 am**	2:58 am
☿ ☌ ⚶	**12:04 pm**	9:04 am
☽ ⚹ ☿	**1:02 pm**	10:02 am
☽ ⚹ ⚶	**1:11 pm**	10:11 am
☽ ⚹ ☉	**4:16 pm**	1:16 pm
☽ ⚺ ♂	**6:07 pm**	3:07 pm
☽ ⚺ ♀	**9:08 pm**	6:08 pm
☽ △ ♄		9:07 pm
☽ ⚺ ⚴		11:09 pm
☽ ⚺ ♆		11:51 pm

28 SUNDAY

☽ △ ♄	**12:07 am**	
☽ ⚺ ⚴	**2:09 am**	
☽ ⚺ ♆	**2:51 am**	
☽ ⚹ ⚷	**2:57 pm**	11:57 am
☽ ☍ ♃	**4:11 pm**	1:11 pm
⚳ ⚻ ⚵	**5:44 pm**	2:44 pm
☽ □ ♇	**7:03 pm**	4:03 pm
☽ △ ⚳	**8:42 pm**	5:42 pm
☽ □ ⚵	**8:50 pm**	5:50 pm

29 MONDAY

♀ ⚻ ♄	**3:38 am**	12:38 am
☽ ⚺ ♅	**1:06 pm**	10:06 am
☽ □ ☿	**3:19 pm**	12:19 pm
☽ □ ⚶	**11:14 pm**	8:14 pm
☉ □ ♂		9:55 pm

30 TUESDAY

☉ □ ♂	**12:55 am**	
☽ ☌ ♂	**4:55 am**	1:55 am
☽ □ ☉	**5:03 am**	2:03 am
☽ □ ♄	**8:09 am**	5:09 am
♀ ⚹ ⚴	**11:27 am**	8:27 am
☽ ⚹ ♀	**11:31 am**	8:31 am
☽ ☌ ⚴	**11:31 am**	8:31 am
☽ ⚹ ♆	**11:36 am**	8:36 am
♀ ☌ ♆	**12:19 pm**	9:19 am
☿ ⚹ ♅	**2:30 pm**	11:30 am
♆ ⚹ ⚴	**6:21 pm**	3:21 pm
☽ □ ⚷		9:53 pm
☽ ⚻ ♃		10:50 pm

31 WEDNESDAY

☽ □ ⚷	**12:53 am**	
☽ ⚻ ♃	**1:50 am**	
☽ △ ♇	**5:00 am**	2:00 am
☽ □ ⚳	**5:33 am**	2:33 am
☽ △ ⚵	**8:26 am**	5:26 am
☉ ☍ ♄	**3:57 pm**	12:57 pm
☽ △ ☿	**9:27 pm**	6:27 pm
☽ ⚹ ♅		9:11 pm

Eastern Standard Time in bold type
Pacific Standard Time in medium type

DECEMBER 2003

☽ Last Aspect day	EST / hr:mn / PST	asp	☽ Ingress sign day	EST / hr:mn / PST
2	**4:39 am** 1:39 am	□ ☿	♈ 2	**5:56 am** 2:56 am
4	**3:52 pm** 12:52 pm	✶ ♅	♉ 4	**5:30 pm** 2:30 pm
7	**4:54 am** 1:54 am	□ ♅	♊ 7	**6:26 am** 3:26 am
9	**5:48 pm** 2:48 pm	△ ♅	♋ 9	**7:11 pm** 4:11 pm
11	10:53 pm	△ ♂	♌ 12	**6:40 am** 3:40 am
12	**1:53 am**	△ ♂	♌ 12	**6:40 am** 3:40 am
14	**3:05 pm** 12:05 pm	☍ ♅	♍ 14	**4:07 pm** 1:07 pm
16	**12:49 pm** 9:49 am	△ ♀	♎ 16	**10:46 pm** 7:46 pm
18	10:39 pm	△ ♅	♏ 18	11:20 pm
19	**1:39 am**	△ ♅	♏ 19	**2:20 am**

☽ Last Aspect day	EST / hr:mn / PST	asp	☽ Ingress sign day	EST / hr:mn / PST
20	11:43 pm	□ ♅	♐ 21	**3:16 am** 12:16 am
21	**2:43 am**	□ ♅	♐ 21	**3:16 am** 12:16 am
22	11:29 pm	✶ ♅	♑ 22	11:55 pm
23	**2:29 am**	✶ ♅	♑ 23	**2:55 am**
24	**8:52 am** 5:52 am	△ ♃	♒ 25	**3:13 am** 12:13 am
27	**5:58 am** 2:58 am	☌ ♅	♓ 27	**6:10 am** 3:10 am
28	**7:03 pm** 4:03 pm	□ ♇	♈ 29	**1:08 pm** 10:08 am
31	**9:27 pm** 6:27 pm	△ ☿	♉ 31	9:02 pm
31	**9:27 pm** 6:27 pm	△ ☿	♉ 1/1	**12:02 am**

☽ Phases & Eclipses phase	day	EST / hr:mn / PST
Full Moon	8	**3:37 pm** 12:37 pm
4th Quarter	16	**12:42 pm** 9:42 am
New Moon	23	**4:43 am** 1:43 am
2nd Quarter	30	**5:03 am** 2:03 am

Planet Ingress	day	EST / hr:mn / PST
☿ ♑	2	**4:34 pm** 1:34 pm
♂ ♈	16	**8:24 am** 5:24 am
⚶ ♑	20	**4:53 am** 1:53 am
♀ ♒	20	10:32 pm
♀ ♒	21	**1:32 am**
☉ ♑	21	11:04 pm
☉ ♑	22	**2:04 am**
♅ ♓	30	**4:14 am** 1:14 am
☿ ♐	30	**2:52 pm** 11:52 am

Planetary Motion	day	EST / hr:mn / PST
♀ D	6	**6:35 am** 3:35 am
☿ ℞	17	**11:02 am** 8:02 am

DATE		SID.TIME	SUN	MOON	NODE	MERCURY	VENUS	MARS	JUPITER	SATURN	URANUS	NEPTUNE	PLUTO	CERES	PALLAS	JUNO	VESTA	CHIRON
1	M	4:37:46	8 ♐ 21 44	11 ♓ 42	20 ♉ 20	27 ♐ 27	4 ♑ 54	21 ♓ 19	17 ♍ 07	12 ♋℞ 05	29 ♒ 07	10 ♒ 49	19 ♐ 20	25 ♋℞ 12	9 ♈℞ 27	11 ♐ 34	19 ♐ 32	15 ♑ 43
2	T	4:41:42	9 22 32	24 21	20 21	28 48	6 09	21 51	17 13	12 01	29 08	10 51	19 22	25 09	9 24	11 55	20 04	15 47
3	W	4:45:39	10 23 21	6 ♈ 41	20 22	0 ♑ 08	7 23	22 23	17 19	11 58	29 09	10 52	19 24	25 05	9 22	12 16	20 36	15 52
4	Th	4:49:35	11 24 12	18 48	20 24	1 26	8 38	22 56	17 25	11 54	29 10	10 53	19 27	25 01	9 21	12 37	21 09	15 57
5	F	4:53:32	12 25 03	0 ♉ 45	20 25	2 42	9 52	23 29	17 30	11 50	29 12	10 55	19 29	24 57	9 20	12 57	21 41	16 02
6	Sa	4:57:28	13 25 55	12 35	20 ℞ 26	3 56	11 06	24 02	17 36	11 46	29 13	10 56	19 31	24 52	9 D 19	13 18	22 13	16 07
7	Su	5:01:25	14 26 48	24 23	20 27	5 07	12 21	24 35	17 41	11 42	29 14	10 58	19 33	24 47	9 19	13 39	22 46	16 13
8	M	5:05:21	15 27 42	6 ♊ 11	20 26	6 14	13 35	25 08	17 46	11 38	29 16	10 59	19 36	24 41	9 20	14 00	23 18	16 18
9	T	5:09:18	16 28 37	18 00	20 23	7 19	14 49	25 42	17 51	11 33	29 17	11 01	19 38	24 35	9 21	14 21	23 51	16 23
10	W	5:13:15	17 29 33	29 55	20 19	8 19	16 04	26 15	17 55	11 29	29 19	11 02	19 40	24 29	9 22	14 42	24 23	16 28
11	Th	5:17:11	18 30 30	11 ♋ 55	20 15	9 15	17 18	26 49	18 00	11 25	29 20	11 04	19 43	24 22	9 24	15 03	24 55	16 33
12	F	5:21:08	19 31 28	24 03	20 09	10 06	18 32	27 23	18 04	11 21	29 22	11 05	19 45	24 15	9 27	15 24	25 28	16 39
13	Sa	5:25:04	20 32 27	6 ♌ 20	20 04	10 50	19 47	27 57	18 08	11 16	29 24	11 07	19 47	24 07	9 29	15 45	26 00	16 44
14	Su	5:29:01	21 33 27	18 49	19 59	11 28	21 01	28 32	18 12	11 12	29 26	11 08	19 49	23 59	9 33	16 06	26 32	16 49
15	M	5:32:57	22 34 28	1 ♍ 33	19 56	11 58	22 15	29 06	18 16	11 07	29 27	11 10	19 52	23 51	9 37	16 27	27 05	16 54
16	T	5:36:54	23 35 29	14 33	19 D 54	12 19	23 29	29 41	18 20	11 03	29 29	11 12	19 54	23 42	9 41	16 47	27 37	17 00
17	W	5:40:50	24 36 32	27 52	19 54	12 ℞ 31	24 43	0 ♈ 15	18 23	10 58	29 31	11 13	19 56	23 33	9 46	17 08	28 10	17 05
18	Th	5:44:47	25 37 36	11 ♎ 34	19 55	12 33	25 57	0 50	18 27	10 53	29 33	11 15	19 59	23 23	9 51	17 29	28 42	17 11
19	F	5:48:44	26 38 41	25 38	19 56	12 24	27 12	1 25	18 30	10 49	29 35	11 17	20 01	23 13	9 57	17 50	29 14	17 16
20	Sa	5:52:40	27 39 47	10 ♏ 04	19 ℞ 57	12 03	28 26	2 00	18 33	10 44	29 37	11 19	20 03	23 03	10 03	18 11	29 47	17 22
21	Su	5:56:37	28 40 53	24 51	19 58	11 31	29 40	2 35	18 35	10 39	29 39	11 20	20 05	22 52	10 10	18 32	0 ♑ 19	17 27
22	M	6:00:33	29 42 01	9 ♐ 52	19 56	10 47	0 ♒ 54	3 11	18 38	10 34	29 41	11 22	20 08	22 42	10 17	18 53	0 51	17 33
23	T	6:04:30	0 ♑ 43 09	25 00	19 52	9 52	2 08	3 46	18 40	10 29	29 43	11 24	20 10	22 30	10 24	19 14	1 24	17 38
24	W	6:08:26	1 44 17	10 ♑ 06	19 47	8 48	3 22	4 22	18 43	10 25	29 45	11 26	20 12	22 19	10 32	19 35	1 56	17 44
25	Th	6:12:23	2 45 26	24 59	19 40	7 35	4 36	4 57	18 45	10 20	29 47	11 28	20 14	22 07	10 41	19 56	2 29	17 49
26	F	6:16:20	3 46 35	9 ♒ 31	19 33	6 16	5 50	5 33	18 46	10 15	29 50	11 30	20 17	21 55	10 49	20 17	3 01	17 55
27	Sa	6:20:16	4 47 45	23 37	19 26	4 55	7 04	6 09	18 48	10 10	29 52	11 31	20 19	21 43	10 59	20 37	3 33	18 00
28	Su	6:24:13	5 48 54	7 ♓ 13	19 21	3 33	8 18	6 45	18 50	10 05	29 54	11 33	20 21	21 30	11 08	20 58	4 06	18 06
29	M	6:28:09	6 50 03	20 22	19 17	2 13	9 32	7 21	18 51	10 00	29 57	11 35	20 23	21 17	11 18	21 19	4 38	18 11
30	T	6:32:06	7 51 12	3 ♈ 04	19 D 16	0 57	10 45	7 57	18 52	9 55	29 59	11 37	20 25	21 04	11 29	21 40	5 10	18 17
31	W	6:36:02	8 52 21	15 25	19 16	29 ♐ 49	11 59	8 34	18 53	9 50	0 ♓ 02	11 39	20 28	20 51	11 39	22 01	5 43	18 23

EPHEMERIS CALCULATED FOR 12 MIDNIGHT GREENWICH MEAN TIME. ALL OTHER DATA AND FACING ASPECTARIAN PAGE IN **EASTERN STANDARD TIME (BOLD)** AND PACIFIC STANDARD TIME (REGULAR).

Notes

Notes

Notes